Essays on International & Comparative Law

T.M.C. ASSER INSTITUUT

ESSAYS ON

INTERNATIONAL & COMPARATIVE LAW

IN HONOUR OF

JUDGE ERADES

E RADICE ARBOR

PRESENTED BY THE BOARD OF THE

NETHERLANDS INTERNATIONAL LAW REVIEW

Springer-Science+Business Media, B.V.

ISBN 978-94-017-1470-9 ISBN 978-94-017-1468-6 (eBook)
DOI 10.1007/978-94-017-1468-6

Originally published by T.M.C. Asser Instituut, The Hague, in 1983.
Sofrcover reprint of the hardcover 1st edition 1983

The T.M.C. Asser Instituut was founded in 1965 by the Dutch universities offering courses in international law to promote education and research in the fields of law covered by the departments of the Institute: Private International Law, including International Commercial Arbitration, Public International Law and Law of the European Communities. The Institute discharges this task by the establishment and management of documentation and research projects, in some instances in co-operation with non-Dutch or international organisations, by the dissemination of information deriving therefrom and by publication of monographs and series. In addition, the Institute participates in the editing of the Yearbook Commercial Arbitration and in the editing and publishing of, *inter alia*, the Netherlands International Law Review and the Netherlands Yearbook of International Law.

CONTENTS

JUDGE ERADES

Lambertus ("Bob") Erades was born in The Hague on the eleventh day of the eleventh month of the year 1911. Astrologists no doubt will have their own word to say about the deeper significance of this remarkable date, and maybe inquire whether the future judge saw the light of day at 11.11 a.m. or p.m. Granting the fact that at 11.11 p.m. there will not have been too much light of day, I feel satisfied with the symbolism of the mere date admirably fitting a single-purposed man if ever there was one.

Young Erades went to school in the town of his birth – *le plus beau village de l'Europe,* as it was known in the eighteenth century – and finished his education there in 1929. The next year he successfully passed a supplementary examination, the so-called *Staatsexamen,* in order to qualify for the study of law. He then read law in Leyden from 1930 to 1934.

Erades' professional career started in 1935 when as un unpaid assistant he joined the Minors Protection Board *(Voogdijraad)* at The Hague and established himself as a Member of the Bar. Two years later, he switched to a stock-broker's firm in Amsterdam as a trainee, and in 1938 he took a job as a legal counsellor with the Royal Netherlands Blast Furnaces and Steel Manufacturers of IJmuiden, where he was to stay until 1945. Following an interval with the Military Government in Haarlem, he then served from 1946 to 1948 with the Special Tribunal for War Cases and as an *ad hoc* Member of the Court of First Instance in that city, a period which proved to be decisive in Erades' career, for in 1948 he was appointed a regular Judge of the Court of First Instance in Rotterdam where, as early as 1958, he was to rise to the rank of Vice-President. Judge Erades still held that position when he retired after having reached the age of seventy on 11 November 1981.

This being but the skeleton of Judge Erades' active life, there fortunately is very much to add before any degree of completeness in the description of his person and work can be reached. However, no such description would be adequate without mention being made of his marriage on 17 June 1942 to Miss Marie Elisabeth Hurenkamp. Two daughters sprang from their union, and it is in his family life that this devoted husband and father found the necessary counterweight to the many pressures in the professional field.

Judge Erades' professional life was bounded by his judicial and arbitral activities, his work on a number of Committees, his writings on international law, and – last but by no means least – his crucial contribution to the Netherlands International Law Review.

No one familiar with the bustling Port of Rotterdam will have any illusion about the demands made on the judicial authorities by those who are daily engaged in its vigorous struggle for life or otherwise partaking in its manifold activities. As a commercial and industrial centre, Rotterdam grew considerably after the Second World War: its area increased greatly, as did its population. It is only natural that the Rotterdam Court of First Instance had to keep abreast with developments reflected in a far greater number of cases than was ever submitted to it before in its history. Furthermore, in the Dutch judicial system, much weight is placed on the President and Vice-Presidents of the Courts of First Instance due to the possibility under existing law to approach them for a judgment laying down "measures of order" in legal disputes of an urgent character without there being given at once a verdict on the merits. In this sort of proceedings (the so-called *kort geding*), the President and Vice-Presidents have to show discernment and a keen sense of legal and social reality. It is not surprising that this form of judicial service is very much in demand in a centre like Rotterdam. In addition, problems of private and public international law inevitably abound at this cross-roads of international interests. Although it is rather for others to say so, Judge Erades seems to have been very much in place in a Court having to deal with the uncommonly variegated legal life of a metropolis where all imaginable interests from all over the world are accustomed to meet. But his judicial talents found recognition outside his home country as well. Twice he acted as Chairman of an international arbitral body, first in 1967 and 1968 in the Lake Ontario Claims Tribunal United States and Canada which sat in Ottawa and Washington, D.C., on the *Gut Dam Case,* then from 1968 to 1970 in *Turriff's Construction (Sudan) Ltd.* v. *Government of the Republic of Sudan,* a case argued in the Peace Palace at The Hague.[1]

Judge Erades' Committee work provides another clue to his personality. In 1959, he was chosen to represent the Netherlands in the Sixth Committee of the United Nations General Assembly. He served the *Union internationale des magistrats* from 1969 to 1971 as a Chairman of its Committee on Questions of International Law, and in 1975 was appointed Chairman of the Advisory Committee on such questions in the Ministry of Foreign Affairs of the Netherlands. I limit myself to these committees, others being omitted for reasons of space.

Judge Erades also proved to be a scholar of competence. Being a student of the late Professor B.M. Telders (1903-1945) of Leyden University, he submitted to him a doctoral thesis on *The Influence of War on the Validity of Treaties* (in Dutch) which in 1938 earned him the degree of Doctor of Laws.[2] In 1949, another book followed under the title *The Meeting-point of International Law and Dutch Constitutional Law* (in Dutch)[3], and in 1961 together with Professor Wesley L. Gould of Purdue University he published the volume *The Relation Between International Law and Municipal Law in the Netherlands and in the*

1. See Stuyt, *Survey of International Arbitrations 1794-1970* (1972) pp. 452, 490 respectively.

2. Original title: *De invloed van oorlog op de geldigheid van verdragen* (Amsterdam, 1938) XIII and 402 pages.

3. Original title: *Waar volkenrecht en Nederlands Staatsrecht elkaar raken* (Een historisch-juridische studie) (Haarlem, 1949) VIII and 157 pages.

United States.[4] The two latter subjects must have been suggested to him by his judicial practice, but even the former cannot fail to have been of considerable import in his subsequent life as a judge. Again for reasons of economy, further references here to Judge Erades' scientific output must be left aside.[5]

I now come to the field in which from 1952 until the present I have had the most elaborate contacts with him: in the founding, management, and direction of the Netherlands International Law Review. In my own doctoral thesis of 1951, or rather on the traditional loose page covered with the most diverse legal propositions which the candidate for the doctoral degree offers to entertain, I had inscribed the – not so "legal" – suggestion that "a Dutch journal of international law would supply a need". Little did I then imagine the success with which these few words were to be blessed! Judge Erades himself in "The Editor-in-Chief Looks Back Some Twenty-Five Years" [6] recounted some of the early and later history of the Review. With due respect, he hardly gave any true impression of the huge amount of work, especially on his part, behind the then twenty-five volumes produced. Dryly he noted: "The handling of the daily work for the editorial side of the Review was first done by myself alone and later with the assistance of some younger lawyers". But before there could be any question of editorial work, there was the founding of the Review. This summer, I happened to uncover a file of correspondence with Judge Erades over the years 1952 to 1964. We corresponded extensively, in particular during my own tenure at the United Nations Legal Department (later styled Legal Office) in New York from 1952 to 1958. The principal topic was always the Review, although we exchanged besides all possible news in the world of international law we could lay our hands upon. Reading over this voluminous mass of air mail stationery, I was amused at the thought that once we had been so young and optimistic as to start an enterprise the outcome of which could not possibly have been foreseen. Certainly, we immediately enlisted the help of Dr. (later Professor) Louis de Winter (1911-1972)[7], and together we convinced Professors Kollewijn (1892-1972) and Verzijl to join us in the Board of Editors. Also, we were in the midst of the tremendous upsurge of a country utterly devastated in the war. Yet, one of us at least had to bear the brunt of our correspondence with prospective sponsors, authors, and publisher; of reporting back to colleagues; of repeating time and again requests that went unanswered; of being patient, diplomatic, and nonetheless of pressing on. Judge Erades did it – and the others were fortunate, for it is difficult to see who of them might have done the groundwork in his stead and with equal result. As a matter of fact, Judge Erades liked the work. On 13 June 1953, at the first meeting of the Editorial Board, he was made Editor-Secretary, and he was to retain this function for more than ten years. In this capacity, he virtually managed the Review single-handedly,

4. (Leyden and New York, 1961) 510 pages.
5. See, Bibliography, *infra* p. 258.
6. *Netherlands International Law Review* XXVI (1979) pp 1-4.
7. On De Winter, see Erades, "M. de Winter, membre de la rédaction", NILR XIX (1972) pp. 99-101.

and in a letter to me of 20 January 1954 he joyfully exclaimed "ever more to feel like a manager". Meanwhile, the first issue had appeared: on 12 November 1953, at 11.45 p.m., a parcel containing ten copies was delivered to Judge Erades' home by a young mailman most energetically ringing the doorbell. We may take this to be the birth of the Review. Specimen copies were sent around the world, and the reception was invariably favourable: even in Parliament satisfaction was expressed!

This is not the place to go into the details of the problems the Board found itself faced with in the course of the Review's existence. I mention only a few. First, there was the general policy to be followed: the room to be allotted to public and private international law, respectively, and to documents; the size per issue; active planning of future issues or passive waiting for contributions to come in? acceptance of materials already published elsewhere? and occasional excursions in the field of comparative law and political science? Second, as with every other Board of Editors, we had to develop criteria for judging quality and tone of articles offered for publication, as well as for their editing; and for years we struggled with the problem of correct texts in foreign languages, a problem for which foreign legal periodicals published in the mother tongue of their Editors need not particularly envy us. Third, there were the long-term and day-to-day questions regarding the management: finances, the number of subscriptions, the promotion of the Review, and the like. With regard to two items only from this catalogue I wish to add a word. As to language and editing: the support ever since 1973, in all aspects of management, of the T.M.C. Asser Institute for International Law, The Hague, has relieved us of the translation and revision problems accompanying foreign language texts and has provided us with a house-style, the existence and implementation of which Judge Erades in 1960 still found "maddening". And in the matter of comparative law, we recently decided formally to expand into that field as from 1 January 1982, co-opting two new Editors for the purpose. Both facts testify to the Board's determination to make as good a journal as is possible under the circumstances. To quote from a last letter of Judge Erades dated 23 July 1953: "We will, indeed, work and fight for it that our Review takes an honourable place in society". Thanks to his unstinting dedication, we may not have fallen too far below our own expectations.

The present volume, offered as a token of friendship and gratitude, was planned so as to illustrate those particular fields of law – not only international law! – in which Judge Erades himself in the course of his active life took an interest. We started with national maritime law, thus evoking the Port of Rotterdam, and then modulated into public international law, arbitration, the relationship between national and international law, State immunity, private international law and comparative law. A wide spectrum of subjects, to be sure, but a faithful reflection of the scope of Judge Erades' mind. And since a tree has many branches, we found that – as an allusion to Judge Erades' name and his manifold activities – it might be appropriate to term this volume *E Radice Arbor* – from the root a tree came forth.

I am happy to know that, although on 11 November 1981 he reached the statutory age of retirement, his services to international law did not stop there and then. New publications are in preparation, and I am sure to reflect the feelings of all contributors to this volume when expressing the sincere hope that, surrounded by his wife and daughters and supported by his usual robust health, he will for a long time to come be allowed to continue his studies.

Zeist, March 1983 M.B.

PROLEGOMENA TO THE IDENTIFICATION OF CUSTOM IN INTERNATIONAL LAW

by Maarten Bos*

1. INTRODUCTION**

In previous studies, much attention was devoted to the interpretation of the written RMIL. Passing now to the question of the ascertainment of the content of custom, it may be useful in a few words to recall, and somewhat to elaborate on, what was said earlier on the relations between the different RMIL. They were seen as a sheaf, a conglomerate, of independent, yet coherent projections of the NCL for international relations. Each RMIL was said to have its own merits, differing from those of another one, and its character was submitted largely to depend on the measure of induction or deduction it represented.[1] The expressions "induction" and "deduction" were understood to refer to reliance on external *versus* internal factors, i.e., data "outside" or "inside" the lawyer. No contrast was meant between reasoning "from the specific to the general" as opposed to reasoning "from the general to the specific", being another sense in which the two terms may validly be taken. It is suggested that the "outside-inside" issue is of special relevance with regard to custom. Consequently, but also generally, there is no good reason to be prejudiced against deduction as Professor Schwarzenberger proved to be when he called his own inductive approach to international law "an empirical device (. . .) to safeguard international law against the subjectivism of deductive speculation and eclectic caprice".[2] For anybody believing, as the present writer does, in the specificness of legal thought and the assistance lent by legal method in discovering one's own *juridicité* [3], "deduction" represents a search into the depths of one's own legal personality. To re-state this with some degree of exaggeration: the more a lawyer is left to his own devices, the more he becomes a lawyer in his own right. And the more eminent a representative he is of his profession, the less his findings will be speculative and capricious.

Speaking in terms of induction and deduction, this writer envisaged the conglomerate of RMIL in the following manner – to quote – "The manifestations

* Professor of International Law in the University of Utrecht; Vice-President, International Law Association; *Membre de l'Institut de Droit International*; Member of the Board of Editors.

**Abbreviations used: NCL = Normative Concept of Law; RML = Recognized Manifestation(s) ("Sources") of Law; RMIL = Recognized Manifestation(s) of International Law.

1. See this writer's study on "The Recognized Manifestations of International Law: A New Theory of "Sources", G.Y.I.L., 1977, pp. 72-76.

2. Georg Schwarzenberger, as cited by Parry, *The Sources and Evidences of International Law* (Manchester, 1965), p. 6.

3. See this writer, "Theory and Practice of Treaty Interpretation", N.I.L.R., 1980, p. 33.

of international law most permitting of induction no doubt are treaties and certain decisions of international organizations. Some deduction, however, is inherent even in their handling. More deduction creeps in with custom, more still with the general principles of law, and finally, with complementary natural law it may be said that deduction reigns supreme".[4] Certain judicial decisions being another variety of RMIL, and their form being in writing, it is suggested that they too, with treaties and organizational decisions, are susceptible of a maximum degree of induction. For is not a written text, i.e., a thought "*ex*-pressed" and fixed on paper, the most "outward", and clearest, thing one can think of when it comes to manifestations of law and the ascertainment of their message? But no sooner does one leave the realm of the written than one is thrown back upon less inductive, more deductive, ways and means of determining the law between two (or any restricted number of) subjects of law: with custom, the element of "practice" can never rank with a written text in clarity, and the indispensable *opinio iuris* more often than not requires a measure of deduction greater than would be necessary in the interpretation of a written RMIL; with a general principle of law as meant by Article 38, paragraph 1, *c,* of the International Court's Statute, there is no practice to be taken into account – at least not in the sense attributed to the term in the context of custom – with the result that deduction increases; and in applying complementary natural law, the lawyer's "second sight" is his only compass.[5]

2. FACTUAL SUBSTANCE OF, AND FACTORS OF DIFFERENCE BETWEEN, THE RMIL

In addition to a difference in induction and deduction, there is another, no less fundamental, dichotomy to be seen between the RMIL. Treaties and conduct-decisions of international organizations, indeed, are the embodiment of a *voluntas,* whereas custom, general principles of law recognized by civilized nations, and complementary natural law reflect an *opinio.*[6] Judicial decisions as a RMIL, though often called "opinions", seem to strike a middle course by partaking of *voluntas* and *opinio* as well.[7]

4. "Recognized Manifestations", p. 28.
5. *Ibid.,* p. 43.
6. In the voluntarist conception of custom, rejected here, custom is based on an agreement, which is either an express or a tacit one *(pactum tacitum).* The use of custom so understood besides treaty as an independent RMIL has never been explained, and the voluntarist conception of custom as a result amounts to a virtual denial of custom as a RMIL. The voluntarist view is represented, *e.g.,* by Professor Grigory I. Tunkin, *Theory of International Law* (London, 1974), p. 123, and in this country by Professor Herman Meijers in his inaugural lecture *Fasen van volkenrechtsvorming en het nut van internationaal gewoonterecht* (Alphen aan den Rijn, 1979), pp. 6, 7 and 16, corresponding with pp. 5, 7 and 13 of the English language version of the lecture published under the title of "How is international law made? – The stages of growth of international law and the use of its customary rules", *Netherlands Yearbook of International Law,* 1978.
7. See Gorphe, *Les décisions de justice* (Paris 1952), pp. 31, 34, 35, 36, 72. Dutch readers may be referred to this writer's contribution to *Quod Iuris* (Deventer, 1977), under the title

As an introduction to paragraph 3 on *voluntas* and *opinio,* it is thought useful first to identify the facts pertaining to each of the six RMIL (paragraph 2.1), then to develop a scheme offering a survey of the different factors with respect to which the RMIL may differ *inter se* (paragraph 2.2).

2.1 Factual analysis of the RMIL

Treaty – In concluding a treaty, the States parties to it expressly bind each other, subject to ratification, either to something they thereby cause to become law (constitutive treaty), or something they recognize as already existing law (declaratory treaty). When "expressly" binding each other, they may do so either in written form (Article 2, paragraph 1(a), of the Vienna Convention on the Law of Treaties), or orally. In the latter case, the less solemn name of "agreement" seems to be preferable.

Conduct-decision of an international organization – The international organization expressly imposes a certain conduct upon its members. Only the written form is found.

Judicial decisions – Either in writing, or orally, the court produces a concrete rule of law applying to the parties before it. Under the conditions set forth elsewhere [8], the court's decision has an effect *vis-à-vis* the subjects of international law at large.

Custom – States which behave in a certain way for some time in the conduct of their international relations without any treaty or customary law obligation to do so, subsequently come to regard this behaviour as "obligatory" under international law. The same may apply to behaviour which formerly escaped regulation and, thus, was not contrary to international law, then is considered to be "permissible" under international law. States may express their "feelings" [9] in written form, orally, or by conduct, and in some cases these feelings may even be assumed. In the case of general custom, feelings, whatever the manner of their expression, do not necessarily need to be expressed with a view to one or more specific subjects of international law. With respect to local or regional custom this may be different.[10]

"De betekenis van het rechterlijk proces voor de rechtsvorming" (The Significance of Judicial Proceedings in the Process of Law), pp. 27 and 29-30.

8. "Recognized Manifestations", pp. 58-59.

9. A term suggested by the International Court of Justice in its judgment of 20 February 1969 *(North Sea Continental Shelf Cases), ICJ Reports* 1969, p. 44, para. 77: "The States concerned must therefore *feel* that they are conforming to what amounts to a legal obligation" (emphasis added).

10. It is submitted that the extension of the validity of a "fundamentally norm-creating" treaty rule to States non-parties to the treaty as exceptionally allowed by the International Court of Justice in case of "a very widespread and representative participation" in the treaty, including that of States whose interests are specially affected, basically has nothing to do with custom. See the judgment quoted in footnote 9 *supra,* p. 42 (para. 73). Speaking in terms of RMIL, the Court obviously had no other name than custom for a rule which in the said circumstances passes into "the general *corpus* of international law" (p. 41, para. 71), becomes "a general rule of international law" (p. 42, para. 73). In fact, the phenomenon,

General principles of law recognized by civilized nations – A principle of law of a general character occurs commonly in the legal order of nations conforming to a certain standard of civilization.

Complementary natural law – A structural principle of the international legal order is deemed to exist on the basis of insight into that order.

2.2 Factors of difference among the RMIL

Basic fact: (1) an act prompted by the will, (2) an intimate conviction, (3) insight.

Subject: (1) a specific subject of law (e.g., State A), (2) an abstraction (a State, viz., a civilized one).

Addressee: (1) a specific subject of law (a fellow-subject, members of an international organization), (2) subjects of law at large.

Manner: (1) explicit (written, oral), (2) tacit, (3) inferred, (4) assumed.

Purport: (1) constitutive, (2) declaratory.

As to the two yardsticks of "induction *versus* deduction" and "*voluntas* or *opinio*", they are implied by the key-words "Manner" and "Basic fact", respectively, *opinio* comprising both conviction and insight.

2.3 A comparison of the RMIL

On the basis of the foregoing analysis of facts and factors, it may be concluded that the RMIL together constitute a most heterogeneous spectrum, at the extremes of which one may imagine a voluntary, written, and constitutive instrument binding on specific subjects of law, i.e., a treaty, on the one hand; and on the other hand the existence, as a matter of insight and thus independent even of any declaratory expression, of a principle valid for all subjects of law. Somewhere in between those extremes, custom is to be found, and from an inquiry into the proof of custom it becomes apparent, first, that its exact location depends on one's definition of custom, and secondly, that a correct definition probably leaves room for a shifting location according to circumstances.

Although extremely heterogeneous as a collection, the RMIL nevertheless comprise two clearly identifiable groups, namely those characterised by *voluntas,* and those reflecting an *opinio.* In paragraph 2, the distribution of RMIL over the two groups has already been set forth. It is proposed now to examine what the expressions *voluntas* and *opinio* represent.

---

just like that of *ius cogens,* has everything to do with the struggle for a really "objective" international law. The opinion expressed here of course does not intend to deny the possibility of a fundamentally norm-creating treaty rule becoming a rule of customary international law according to the normal procedure as set forth in the text above. It is to this procedure that the Court addressed itself at pp. 43 and 44 (paras. 74 and 77) of its judgment.

3. VOLUNTAS AND OPINIO

3.1 The limited scope of voluntas

When speaking of *voluntas,* it is appropriate first to focus on the place of *voluntas* in legal thought generally.

From a phenomenological point of view, legal thought is something "existing beforehand", a complex collection of assumptions, methods, and procedures leading to a characteristic result called "law". Man as a *genus* is possessed of it; it is an element of human culture, an element of human life *tout court.* As such, though active within us, it is autonomous in the sense of being beyond the reach of man's will. In the final analysis, therefore, it is not man's will *(voluntas)* which determines what is law, and there is no room for voluntarism. Man's will can only be relevant *within* legal method, i.e., to the extent that legal method itself allows it a margin in which to exert itself. But the will thus *set* free may then fancy itself free *from the outset,* i.e., not through the intercession of legal method, but by nature. It may also imagine itself to be omnipotent, or at least at the origin of every single legal rule in existence. The result would, again, be voluntarism.

In this writer's opinion, the farthest one can go in the recognition of a possible "monopoly" of the will is to state that a particular legal order may be based on a NCL – part of legal method – restricting law to the deliberately contrived and expressly promulgated products of the will – whether this promulgation takes a written form or occurs orally. Wherever such a streamlined situation occurs, theories are likely to spring up according to which law is *always* "created" law. However, the NCL is perfectly free to widen the scope of law and to let in, in addition to the products of the will, rules based on an *opinio,* a conviction, rather than on a *voluntas.*

3.2 Opinio iuris

The *opinio* meant here is the *opinio iuris,* the conviction that some rule or other "makes good law" even though it may not boast of any *voluntas* behind it.[11] The *opinio iuris* may be a conviction about the way in which the subjects of law should or may behave in their relations with each other. It may also be derived from a completely intellectual sort of "insight" into the abstractions of the structure of a particular legal order. In the context of international law, in admitting other RML than those which are products of the will alone, all too often

11. Comp. the International Court's judgment of 6 April 1955 *(Nottebohm Case), I.C.J. Reports,* 1955, p. 22: "la *conviction* que, pour mériter d'être invoquée contre un autre Etat, la nationalité doit correspondre à la situation de fait" (English translation: "the view of these States that . . .") (emphasis added). Too strong is Judge Chagla's language: "there must be an overriding feeling of compulsion – not physical but legal" (dissenting opinion in the *Case Concerning Right of Passage over Indian Territory, I.C.J. Reports,* 1960, p. 120). But see also the International Court in the *North Sea Continental Shelf Cases:* "There is no evidence that they (the States concerned - B) so acted because they felt legally compelled to draw them in this way . . ." *(I.C.J. Reports,* 1969, pp. 44-45).

attempts are made to force them into the narrow confines of *voluntas.* It is clear that the ascertainment of their content suffers as a result.

RMIL embodying a *voluntas,* especially when expressed in writing, have a number of advantages over those RMIL, necessarily unwritten, which can muster no more than an *opinio* to sustain them. An agreed text, for instance, can eliminate much that is equivocal. To this extent, the products of the will are "superior" to the other RML. At the same time, however, they lack the flexibility of the latter, which should be highly valued in societies not sufficiently integrated to bring forth a legal order in which virtually nothing of interest is left unregulated by acts of the will. In such societies, a legal order recognizing no law beyond the "willed" would be unworkable, and in this respect, therefore, RML reflecting an *opinio*, not a *voluntas,* have some sort of "superiority" of their own.

In the international legal order in particular it would be fatal not to be aware of this, and to act as if *voluntas* should be a *conditio sine qua non* for a RMIL to exist. It is no less crippling for international law to fail to recognize any of the manifestations of it based on an *opinio* instead of *voluntas:* custom, general principles of law recognized by civilized nations, complementary natural law.

As to their flexibility, one should realize that an *opinio iuris,* instead of perpetuating itself, may come and go. A State the *opinio iuris* of which on a particular subject has been modified in the course of time sooner or later may contribute to a change in the relevant RMIL, and there is no reason to think that a State should be prohibited from doing so. The only question, here, is how many States should have changed their minds, and over which period of time, in order to affect the existence of an unwritten RMIL. Particularly with regard to rules of customary international law, it has been proposed that their abrogation or replacement with other customary rules under the traditional doctrine requiring *opinio iuris* as a pre-condition of custom is unthinkable either without an error about the content of the existing rule, or without an open violation of it.[12] For is not an *opinio iuris* a conviction about "existing" law, and how can a State act against the existing law otherwise than in error or by way of violation? Apart from the fact that a State, though no more believing in a rule of customary international law, still may behave in accordance with it, the mistake is above all that the "existence" of a rule of customary international law to a certain extent *depends* on the *opinio iuris* and, therefore, must come to an end when the number of States harbouring the conviction has fallen below an acceptable minimum. Consequently, it is not to be seen why the requirement of an *opinio iuris* should be an impediment to the formation of new rules of customary international law. It is rather the opposite which is true. The *opinio iuris* required for the existence of custom is the belief, not that A *is a rule of law* [13], but that a certain practice

12. See the authors quoted in Herbert Günther, *Zur Entstehung von Völkergewohnheitsrecht* (Berlin, 1970), pp. 134-137, and R. Fidelio Unger, *Völkergewohnheitsrecht – objektives Recht oder Geflecht bilateraler Beziehungen?* (Munich, 1978), p. 36, footnote 160.

13. As the International Court of Justice had it in an unfortunate phrase in its judgment of 20 February 1969 *(North Sea Continental Shelf Cases), I.C.J. Reports,* 1969, p. 44, para. 77 ("a belief that this practice is rendered obligatory by the existence of a rule of law

should or may be followed *by rights* because it satisfies a conception of legal propriety held by the States concerned and rooted in their NCL for international relations. At the same time, however, it is possible for any State participating in a rule of customary international law, though not without restrictions, to change its *opinio iuris* and, little by little, to loosen the customary bond binding it to other States, or to modify its content, in a way not to be compared with any form of withdrawal from, or modification of, treaty relations. And here, precisely, is the *raison d'être* of international custom. Any other reading of international custom fails to acknowledge its proper nature.

In the remaining part of the present observations, it is to custom in international law that the reader's attention will be directed.

4. CUSTOM AND EVIDENCE

4.1 Theories of custom and their impact on the question of ascertainment of the content of custom

In ascertaining the content of custom, it is self-evident that one's view of what custom is must be all-important. As this writer put it elsewhere [14], "for a custom to exist one merely has to ascertain the existence of the alleged factual aspects of it, i.e., its material and psychological components, and to put these to the test of the definition of custom". Custom was defined as "what one is in the habit of doing, convinced that such behaviour is legally obligatory *(opinio iuris)*, although not ordered by a written rule".[15] In paragraph 2 *supra,* the factual content of custom was examined in some detail. Paragraph 3 made it clear that the "psychological component" of custom, *opinio iuris,* was plainly distinguishable from the corresponding element in treaties and conduct-decisions of international organizations, viz., *voluntas.* Consequently, no proof of *voluntas* is required to establish the existence of custom. Finally, the question of induction and deduction was broached (paragraph 1), and it remains to be seen to what extent each of them has a *rôle* to play.

If all this may be called a "programme" for evidence, it is obvious that other views of custom may lead to other "programmes". One only has to remember Professor d'Amato's rejection of both the material and psychological elements traditionally found in custom – common behaviour stretching over some period of time, and a common *opinio iuris* – to be convinced of this.[16] But whatever may be proposed for inclusion in any such programme, it should be realized that no theory of custom can be sound which fails to appreciate the particular place

---

requiring it"). The phrase, however, was immediately corrected by the Court itself in the statement quoted footnote 9, *supra.*

14. "Theory and Practice of Treaty Interpretation", N.I.L.R.. 1980, p. 10.
15. "Recognized Manifestations", p. 25.
16. *Ibid.,* pp. 27-28.

taken by custom among the other RMIL. Custom should not be allowed to become confused either with treaty law or with the general principles of law recognized by civilized nations.

One more remark of a theoretical nature remains to be made. If where custom is concerned "content merges with existence", and if the existence of custom thus depends on one's definition of it [17], it is this definition which assumes paramount importance. Again, one may speak of the impact of theory on questions of ascertainment of content. This impact is very much in evidence in the context of "general" custom, the most important variety of custom in international law. It is a matter of life or death for general custom whether or not States not participating in a practice alleged to give rise to a general custom may be bound by it. If one's theoretical outlook is such that a general custom may also "exist" for non-participating States, then it should be crystal-clear not only that *voluntas* is foreign to custom, but also that the *opinio iuris* underlying custom is not necessarily a personal one. In the final analysis, this may be precisely so *because* the will has no part in custom.

4.2 Some observations on evidence in relation to custom

It is not only theories of custom which are relevant in the present context. Theories of evidence should also be borne in mind, because, as explained in paragraph 4.1, in order to ascertain the content of custom "the existence of the alleged factual aspects of it, i.e., its material and psychological components", has first to be proved. Only then can the factual aspects thus identified be subjected to the test of the definition of custom. This implies an evidential stage in the ascertainment of the content of custom. With regard to treaties, an analogous stage has to be gone through (proof of authentication, signature, ratification) [18], but it does not seem to be nearly as important as the evidential stage in the identification of custom. And since there is no "interpretation" of custom [19], it may well be said that any attempt to describe the process of such identification takes the place of methods and rules in the interpretation of written RMIL. An interesting question remains as to whether the means of ascertaining the content of custom should one day likewise be codified.

The "factual aspects" of custom which have to be proved are practice and *opinio iuris.* How "factual" are they, in reality, and in particular, how "factual" is an *opinio?* And how can evidence help to inform us about the "existence" of such "facts"? A further question is this: supposing these facts to have been "proved" by one of the parties in a dispute in court, is this tantamount to "proof" of the existence of custom? These and other possible queries give rise to fundamental questions as to the function and object of evidence in general, and with regard to international custom in particular.

17. "Theory and Practice of Treaty Interpretation", p. 10.
18. *Ibid.*, p. 10.
19. *Ibid.*, pp. 9-10.

4.2.1 Eggens' doctrine of evidence

According to the most restrictive of the views of evidence held in the Netherlands in the past, "facts" were the only possible object of proof. By the end of the nineteenth century this doctrine, mainly of German origin, had become generally accepted in this country. In 1918 and 1920, it was overturned on two counts by two important judgments handed down by the Dutch *Hoge Raad* (Supreme Court). Under the former, a written deed not merely proved the fact of the statement made in the deed, but also determined the relevant legal relationship. Under the latter, proof of "rights" was admitted in the sense of proof of facts showing the existence of rights rather than creating them.[20] The total rejection of the doctrine came with J. Eggens' treatise on the law of evidence.[21] Since Eggens' doctrine of evidence as contained in this work is most fundamental in character it deserves to be referred to in any discussion in which considerations of evidence and its legal nature have an essential *rôle* to play, be it with regard to national or international law. The present writer may have more reason than others to remember Eggens' doctrine because of its underlying view of law as a product of thought which appears to be closely related to a number of the basic assumptions in his personal theory of analytical conceptualism.[22] Confining himself to a brief outline of Eggens' doctrine, this writer relies mainly on the author's own brilliant summary offered in his 1951 report to the Netherlands Society of Lawyers *(Nederlandse Juristen Vereniging)* under the title of "The Principles of Evidence in Civil Law Cases".[23]

Looking back at the doctrine of "facts only", Eggens observed that it divorced fact from law, and thus from the legal relationship to be determined by the court.[24] The doctrine, which for this reason was called the "abstract doctrine", was connected with "the materialist, naïvely-realist conception", that nothing but the sensorily perceptible can be the object of proof. Some of its supporters, meanwhile, placed a liberal interpretation on the latter notion by considering some (not all) value-judgments as possible objects of proof: in their eyes, these value-judgments were apparently facts capable of being "perceived!". As an example, Eggens quoted Professor F.G. Scheltema who alleged that the prevalence in some society of some norm with some specific content was a fact capable of proof.[25]

20. Paul Scholten, "Eggens' Bewijsrecht" (Eggens on Evidence), *Weekblad voor Privaatrecht, Notarisambt en Registratie,* 1935, pp. 3-5.

21. Scholten, *ibid.,* p. 16: "a first-rate contribution to legal science" (this writer's translation). The reference is to Eggens' edition of Professor N.K.F. Land's *Verklaring van het Burgerlijk Wetboek* (Commentary to the Civil Code), Vol. VI, the second edition of which was published at Haarlem in 1933. Jannes Eggens (1891-1964) was a Professor of Civil Law in Batavia, Utrecht and Amsterdam, and an Advocate-General at the Dutch Supreme Court.

22. As stated in "Will and Order in the Nation-State System: Observations on Positivism and Positive International Law", N.I.L.R., 1982, pp. 3-31.

23. J. Eggens, *De beginselen van het burgerlijk bewijs,* Handelingen der Nederlandse Juristen-Vereniging (1951), pp. 3-49.

24. Eggens, *op.cit.,* p. 17.

25. *Ibid.,* p. 18.

Instead of divorcing fact from law, Eggens stated, one must realize that in matters of evidence facts should be looked upon as *elements in a process of thought* in the course of which the court has to form an opinion and, finally, to decide on the "existence" of a legal relationship. Facts are never proved for their own sake, and when proved they take their place in the legal process together with other facts. They then assume their own evidential significance in the legal process, each fact depending for its proper evidential significance on the Court's appreciation of it. It is the court which welds all the individual facts together into a whole in which they mutually influence and delimit each other. This is why facts in one particular context may prove something else than in a different context. In general, therefore, it is impossible in advance to determine the evidential value of a fact. But a legislator may, of course, fix that value once and for all, independently of the circumstances of the case. One is put in mind here of the so-called "legal presumptions", i.e., the *praesumptiones iuris et de iure* against which, in contradistinction with the *praesumptiones iuris tantum,* no rebuttal is allowed. But whether a presumption belongs to the first or to the second category, one should always bear in mind that it is but a stage in the court's thought process, and that a *praesumptio iuris et de iure,* therefore, is one of the few stages in that process at which the court's thought is forced into a particular direction, i.e., the court is not free in its evaluation of evidence.

The means whereby facts are proved, such as oral or written statements, should be viewed in the same light. On the one hand, they certainly determine the court's judgment, but the reverse is also true, for it is the court which determines their evidential significance.

As to the "existence" of a legal relationship, which the court's reasoning on the basis of the evidence produced may, or may not, lead it to accept, Eggens' submission was that a legal relationship is not a "fact" which "exists". In his opinion, a legal relationship is "a legally operative product of conscience and thought" [26], and the essence of a judicial decision is to determine, in a manner binding on the parties, that a certain legal relationship does, or does not, obtain between them. The purpose of all evidence, therefore, may be said to be the pronouncement of just such a legal decision. And as "a product of (the court's) conscience and thought", Eggens held that a legal relationship, whatever it might have been before, is in the end whatever the court determines it to be.

The classical problem of judicial "activeness" or "passiveness" also claimed his attention. Should a court be a neutral umpire registering the acts of the parties before it, or should it do more and play an active *rôle* in finding a solution to the legal question before it? Here, the author let his opinion depend on the nature of the case. Though in no circumstances did he think of a court as a "dead applier of the law", he definitely wished to distinguish cases according to the predominance of private or public interests reflected in them. In the defence of the public interest,

26. *Op.cit.*, pp. 8-9: "een bewustzijns- en dus gedachte-inhoud, welke *geldt,* en wel: rechtens, d.w.z. welke geldt naar juridisch – dus normatief – oordeel" (this writer's translation).

he would allow the court a larger measure of freedom than in proceedings in which the interests involved were primarily those of the parties. In the same way, the law of evidence should differ according to the *ius dispositivum* or *ius cogens* character of the applicable rule, just as the attitude taken by one or both of the parties either before or in the course of judicial proceedings should be evaluated differently from one case to another. It is of interest to note the latter point in the context of the doctrines of estoppel and preclusion.

If "facts" and "rights" alike can be proved, could one also assert that a "legal relationship" can be the object of proof? Giving an affirmative answer [27], Eggens understood the question to refer to proof through facts relating to the existence, not the creation, of the legal relationship, just as the Supreme Court did with regard to the proof of "rights".

4.2.2 Its applicability to international law

As postulated above, Eggens' doctrine is fundamental enough to be of interest in any discussion of problems of evidence, whether in national or in international law. Particularly, one should not shy away from it because of the title of his 1951 report which referred to evidence in civil law cases only. At the end of the preceding paragraph, it was shown that in Eggens' opinion a court's latitude in matters of evidence should vary according to the character of the interests or the rules involved in the case, and what he said with regard to private and public interests, and the distinction between *ius dispositivum* and *ius cogens,* appears quite capable of application to other branches of the law than civil law, including international law. As Scholten put it, Eggens' concern in the law of evidence was to open the way to "concrete equity" [28], and there is no good reason for not applying the same principle to evidence in international law cases.

Dealing with proof of custom in international law, the question arises whether in Eggens' doctrine not only facts, rights, and legal relationships may be proved, but also "the law". For proving custom is proving the law. In the context of his report, limited to Dutch civil law in which custom has virtually no *rôle* to play, Eggens had no occasion to enter upon the problem apart from an inconclusive remark about proof of "norms of law" generally.[29] But in fact, proof of custom should never have been a problem for him at all: for if in the "process of thought" finally leading to a judicial pronouncement a legal relationship may be proved, this should be the more so with regard to the norm on which this legal relationship is based. In this sense, even a norm of treaty-law has to be proved. In other words, proof of custom not merely consists in bringing evidence of its material and psychological components (practice and *opinio iuris),* leaving to the court the conclusion to be drawn from them: the conclusion has to be proved as well, for proving is "to bring about a conviction based on experience and reasonable

27. *Op.cit.,* p. 9.
28. Scholten, *op.cit.,* p. 15.
29. Eggens, *op.cit.,* p. 9.

argument".[30] And the conviction a party invoking custom seeks to create is that of the "existence" of a norm of customary law, nothing less. This also applies to situations in which there is no court to decide upon a dispute and the parties themselves make an effort to solve it: one of them then will have to convince the other.[31]

One of the means by which to convince either a court or a party is to provoke a presumption in their minds. A presumption is one stage in the "process of thought" through which a concrete rule of law is elaborated.[32] Obviously, presumptions are of great importance in proving an *opinio iuris.* The emphasis in proving custom is often on practice, and once a certain practice has been proved, the impression may be formed that little or no attention is paid to the necessary *opinio iuris.* However, one should not overlook the fact that a proved practice may legitimately give rise to a presumption as to the *opinio iuris.*

In the end, therefore, one cannot escape the conclusion that not only "the law" may be proved, but that *customary* law may even be proved through presumption. This may shock the professional conscience even more than the absence of *voluntas.* But one thing should be clear, viz., that those opposed to proof of objective law through presumptions have but one way out, namely, to deny custom a place among the RML. However, in order to be consistent with themselves, they should then also reject the general principles of law recognized by civilized nations as a RMIL, to say nothing of complementary natural law.

5. CONCLUSION

The modern citizen living under a legal order not of his own making and confined to statute and its derivatives is very much a "subjected" subject of law. Statute deprived him of his original freedom, and his capacity for private action was taken away from him, especially his capacity to take part in the production of customary law. In the Netherlands, Article 3 of the 1829 General Provisions Act *(Wet houdende algemene bepalingen)* opens the way for custom to re-enter the scene by providing that "no claim arises from custom unless statute refers to it". Reference to custom in statutes is rather exceptional, in this country. To the extent that such references exist, the citizen wins back some of his freedom.

In the international legal order, the State is a "sovereign" subject of law, not a "subjected" one. Consequently, treaty and custom occupy a pre-eminent place in international law, and the *voluntas* and *opinio* of the State in matters of law is of the highest importance. However, under the general concept of law nobody is allowed to frustrate the law by an act of his own volition.[33] The same applies to

30. Scholten, *op.cit.*, p. 8 (this writer's translation).
31. Comp. "Recognized Manifestations", pp. 29-30. Hudson's view as criticized there, like Ch. De Visscher's, is reminiscent of a legal order (the English, *e.g.*) in which statute and judicial precedent are the only RML, and custom leads no life of its own.
32. See p. 17 *supra.*
33. "Recognized Manifestations", p. 38.

frustration of the law through a change of *opinio:* custom, though based on *opinio,* is not at the mercy of a State's whimsical *change* of opinion. Within any legal system recognizing custom as a RML, this is an inescapable limitation of the subject's freedom. And there is another one, also inherent in the nature of custom – namely, that a subject's *opinio* may not always be asked and that it may even be immaterial whether the *opinio* he actually has is in conformity with the opinion of the other subjects of law. The reason for it was suggested above: *opinio* is not *voluntas.*

This is the price of custom in any legal order admitting it among its RML. And as if this were not itself enough, the price is raised even higher by the possibility of proof through presumption. Both points have been stressed in this study, but they are not intended to discourage anybody from recognizing custom as an independent manifestation of international law. However, in acknowledging custom, one should be keenly aware of the properties and implications that have come to light in the two aspects of it studied here.

LIMITATION OF LIABILITY FOR MARITIME CLAIMS

by Robert Cleton*

1. INTRODUCTION

On 19 November 1976 the Legal Conference held in London under the auspices of IMCO (Intergovernmental Maritime Consultative Organization) adopted a new convention on limitation of liability for maritime claims.[1] International unification of private maritime law had thus been carried one step farther. Usually international unification of law is very much a long term matter and this new convention is no exception to this process of slow progress. After 6 1/2 years it has not yet come into force, but there are promising indications that the number of instruments of ratification, acceptance or approval necessary for its entry into force might be reached in 1983.[2]

I will try to give in this contribution a brief picture of the development of the typical maritime concept of global limitation of liability, which has also been introduced in certain legislations within the field of river law. Further I will discuss the main points dealt with in this new Convention which will probably be the future basis for an international legal regime on limitation of liability in maritime law.

There are many ways and means by which a person may limit his liability vis-à-vis another person. The most common way is to include certain clauses in contract exonerating wholly or partially liability or limiting the amount of compensation to a certain ceiling. Particularly in transport law a carrier may be granted this privilege by national law or international convention. In the majority of these cases the person liable will be protected against any claims arising out of the non-

* Head of Division Private Law Legislation of the Ministry of Justice.

1. Convention on Limitation of Liability for Maritime Claims, 1976 (Compilation International Conventions on Maritime Law; Comité Maritime International).

2. Art. 17 of the Convention requires ratification, acceptance or approval by at least twelve States. So far the Arabic Republic of Yemen, United Kingdom, Liberia, France and Spain have acceded to the Convention and it is known that eleven other States, including the Netherlands, Belgium and the Scandinavian countries, are preparing legislation necessary for becoming a Party or have expressed their intention to do so. The rules of the Convention have already been included in section 21 of the new Lloyd's Standard Form for Salvage Agreement (Lloyd's Open Form 1980): "The Contractor shall be entitled to limit any liability to the subject vessel and/or her cargo bunkers and stores which he and/or his Servants may incur in and about the services in the manner and to the extent provided by English law and as if the provisions of the Convention on Limitation of Liability for Maritime Claims 1976 were part of the law of England".

performance of contractual obligations, although his defences may not only be invoked when the action is founded in contract but also when it is founded in tort.[3]

The London Convention however deals with a special kind of limitation of liability, the right of a shipowner and of other persons closely connected with the exploitation of a vessel to limit their liability for all limitable claims (contractual and extra-contractual) arising out of one specific event to one global amount. This right of global limitation can only be granted to a shipowner by statute.[4] The limitation fund must be distributed among the claimants and in this respect there is a similarity between the limitation fund and a bankruptcy fund.

2. JUSTIFICATION OF GLOBAL LIMITATION

The rule which permits a shipowner to discharge all liabilities, originally by surrender of his interest in the vessel that had been involved in a maritime accident and the freight earned in that particular voyage (his "fortune de mer"), in a later stage of the development of this concept by way of a special limitation fund, has always been severely critized and still provokes moral indignation. But so far this rule has survived all attacks and it even has broadened its scope of application to other groups of persons connected with the maritime industry. How can this privilege, not known to other branches of industry and commerce, in any way not in the same broad and general sense, be justified? The only justification given so far is a rather simple and typical maritime one; this privilege is a convenient way to promote the shipping industry and to encourage investments in the risky business of maritime transport and a sound shipping industry is a public interest ("Navigare necesse est"). Often the following words of Lord Denning as Master of the Rolls in *The Bromley Moore* [1964] P. 200, 220 (C.A.) have been cited: "Limitation of liability is not a matter of justice. It is a rule of public policy which has its origin in history and its justification in convenience."[5] The policy of development of maritime transport which made it necessary to encourage investors was the origin of this privilege.

The vicarious liability of the shipowner for the acts of the master and members of the crew proved to be a very heavy burden, probably because not always the most trustworthy persons choose the noble but adventurous profession of seafarer. Due to poor communication facilities in ancient times it was not possible for a

3. See, for instance, Art. 3 of the Protocol of 1968 to the Brussels Bills of Lading Convention of 1924 (new Art. 4*bis* of the amended Convention).

4. In this light the new section 21 of Lloyd's Open Form, cited in footnote 3 is somewhat strange. The Convention has not entered into force and does not yet form a part of the law of England. Being a contractual clause it can only bind the parties to the salvage agreement and one may doubt whether the Court would apply the 1976 rules to an accident where also third parties would be involved. The main purpose of this section is however to neutralize the effects of the decision of the House of Lords in the *Tojo Maru* case, which will be discussed in chapter 4.

5. Michael Thomas, "British Concepts of Limitation of Liability", *Tulane Law Review*, Vol. 53, no. 4 (June 1979).

shipowner to exercise control once the voyage had commenced. This burden of vicarious liability had therefore to be moderated. Moreover the many perils of the sea and the limited technical possibilities to prevent disasters at sea turned every maritime voyage into a maritime venture. However since the introduction of limitation of shipowner's liability in the Middle Ages technology has developed considerably and the invention of modern communication techniques and other navigational aids have improved safety in maritime transport to a large extent. One could therefore question the justification of maintaining this rule, which was perhaps justified in previous centuries when safety conditions were quite different, in modern times. In aviation the benefit of general and global limitation was not introduced to the same extent as in maritime law although the risks in this branch of transport industry may be considerable.[6] Carriage of cargo by truck from Europe to the Middle East will be exposed to many hazards and such a journey might perhaps be considered as a modern version of the old maritime venture. The truckowner may rely as a carrier on the unit limitation of the CMR Convention on international road carriage, but he is not entitled to global limitation. Global limitation has been introduced recently in some other fields but only in respect of certain types of risks and combined with the introduction of a system of strict liability.[7]

Nevertheless the maritime rule on global limitation of liability seems to stand on a firm foundation consisting of two pillars: tradition and public convenience. Tradition is of course not an argument in itself (in any way not on the European continent) but it has the ability to reverse the burden of proof. There must be strong arguments to abolish a rule which has been accepted for a very long time on a world wide basis and on which the shipping and marine insurance industry have based their commercial operations. The striking of this rule could also affect international trade in general because this trade very much relies on the shipping industry. The entire system of distribution of maritime risks is based on a complex legal system which relies entirely on a mechnism to keep these risks insurable. The insurance in the maritime field is to a large extent effected in an international market. First party insurance (cargo and hull insurance) and liability insurance (partly effected by hull insurance for collision risks and for the remaining part by Protection and Indemnity Insurance) are very much interrelated. To disturb this balance would not be a good public policy. On the other hand, however, this balance can only be maintained if the limitation of shipowner's liability is kept on a reasonable level which means that the limitation amounts should be reconsidered if they have been devalued too much by inflation.[8]

6. About the different legal situations in air and maritime law: Neil R. Mc Gilchrist, "Limitation of Liability at Sea and in the Air", *Lloyd's Maritime and Commercial Law Quarterly*, August 1975.

7. In nuclear law and with respect to liability for oil pollution at sea. In air law the Rome Convention of 1952.

8. René Rodière has heavily critized the concept of insurability as the underlying principle for global limitation of shipowner's liability and the British tonnage system as adopted in the 1957 Convention as unjust and unjustifiable. He has proposed to rely on a modernized

This justification is based on economical arguments rather than on legal grounds. The privilege of the shipowner is accepted by the majority of claimants because one way or another they are themselves directly or indirectly involved in the shipping industry. It is much more difficult to accept for those claimants who are "outsiders". For consolation of these claimants one could argue that they are in a better position if they have a limited recourse against a properly insured shipowner than if their claim would be unlimited but perhaps without any possibility of proper recourse.

3. HISTORICAL BACKGROUND AND INTERNATIONAL DEVELOPMENT

3.1 History of global limitation

It is not very likely that the roots of global limitation of shipowner's liability can be found in Roman law.[9] There are better indications that this rule has its origins in the Middle Ages. It developed in the Mediterranean countries, first in Spain, later in Italy and finally in France.[10] The main justification given was also in those times the economic rationale. The concept of limitation spread to Northern Europe, where it was adopted in the statutes of several Hanseatic cities (Hamburg 1306, Danzig 1455, Visby 14th century) and later in Holland during the Golden Age. Promotion of their shipping industry was the very reason for Cities and States to accept the rule. As Sotiropoulos in his excellent thesis *Die Beschränkung der Reederhaftung* has shown the privilege of limitation was at first granted to shipowners with regard to their liability for damage to cargo, mainly because of their vicarious liability for the acts of the master and crew of the vessel. Quite distinctly some statutes afforded him the right of limitation in particular in respect of claims from collision.[11]

Two different systems developed in Nothern and Southern Europe but based on the same philosophy that a shipowner should not put more at risk than the capital he had invested in the maritime adventure of his vessel (the value of his ship and the freight earned on the voyage during which the claims had arisen). The unit of limitation was in both systems the voyage of the vessel in question. According to the Mediterranean system (well known as the French "abandon"-system) the shipowner was personally liable, but he could divest himself of all liability by physical abandonment of the assets of the venture ("bankruptcy of the venture"). Under the Northern European system ("maritime lien"- or "execution"-

"abandon"-system *("abandon en valeur"): Droit Maritime Français,* No. 293, May 1973, pp. 259-267.

9. Sotiropoulos, *Die Beschränkung der Reederhaftung,* (Berlin 1962), p. 4; James J. Donovan, "The Origins and Development of Limitation of Shipowner's Liability", *Tulane Law Review,* Vol. 53, No. 4, p. 999.

10. Fueros de Valencia (1250); Tabula Almalfitana, Italy 12-13th Century; Consulato del Mar, Barcelona 14th Century; Ordonnance of Charles VI, France 1415; Ordonnance de la Marine Marchande of Louis XIV, 1681. See, Sotiropoulos, loc.cit. p. 30.

11. See, in particular, pp. 30 and 31, ibid.

system) the liability of the shipowner was a liability *in rem* and claimants could under that system enforce their claims directly against the assets mentioned, but without personal liability of the shipowner. In both systems the distribution of the assets took place according to the priority of the respective liens attaching to the claims.

It is a remarkable historic fact that the privilege of shipowner's limitation of liability has developed in Great Britain much later than on the European continent. In 1733 a shipowner was held liable for the loss of a cargo of bullion taken on board in Portugal. The cargo had been stolen by the master of the vessel. London shipowners petitioned to Parliament complaining about the serious risks they were running and the insupportable and unreasonable hardships to which the British laws in this case subjected them. They were apparently aware of the more favourable position of their colleagues and competitors on the Continent. Parliament reacted favourably to this petition and passed the Responsability of Shipowner's Act 1734. This Act limited shipowner's liability for loss of cargo by theft by the master or crew of the ship to the value of the ship and the freight. In 1813 a new Responsability of Shipowner's Act extended the rule to claims for collision. For the first time the limitation fund was made available for claims arising out of a specific incident. The voyage was as a unit of limitation replaced by the incident. In the Merchant Shipping Act of 1854 the right of limitation was extended to claims for loss of life and personal injury and a minimum value of £ 15 per registered ton of the vessel's tonnage was set with regard to those claims. This system of a limitation calculated in accordance with a fixed amount per ton of the ship's tonnage and the "incident" criterium was more in line with the requirements of the insurance industry which played at the time already an important role in Great Britain. The continental system was rather based on the idea that the shipowner had no insurance protection.[12] The British system was later to become the internationally accepted system.

3.2 Development of international unification

The international shipping world was faced with different national legal systems, which could basically be distinguished into two regimes:

a. The continental system (also adopted in 1851 in the United States [13]): value of the vessel after the voyage plus freight earned on that voyage and applicable to all limitable claims arising out of the voyage; and

b. the British system: fixed amount per ton of the vessel's tonnage and applicable to all claims per accident.

12. See, in particular, Michael Thomas, loc.cit. pp. 1205-1209.

13. The U.S. Limitation of Liability Act of 1851 as amended in 1935 permits the shipowner to limit his liability, unless the accident occurred with his privity or knowledge, to the value of the vessel at the end of the voyage on which the accident occurred, but with a minimum limitation of US$ 60 per gross ton available with respect to claims for loss of life and personal injury. In practice, however, the U.S. Courts often deny the privilege of limitation on ground of assumed privity or knowledge of the shipowner.

The first international convention on limitation of shipowner's liability was the Brussels Convention of 1924. It tried to compromise between both systems. It limited shipowner's liability with respect of a number of claims enumerated in the Convention (among others claims with respect of salvage awards and contribution in general average which in later conventions would be deleted from the list of limitable claims) and it contained the "per accident" rule. The limitation fund was set at the value of the ship and its accessories after the accident plus the value of the freight which was fixed at 10 per cent of the value of the vessel at the commencement of the voyage. However it was provided that claims for compensation:

a. due to third parties for damage caused;

b. for damage to cargo carried;

c. due by reason of fault of navigation committed in the execution of a contract;

d. for obligations arising out of bills of lading; and

e. for wreck removal

should not exceed an aggregate sum of £ 8 per ton of the ship's tonnage. The Convention provided for a separate limitation fund for personal claims of £ 8 per ton. The unpaid balance of those claims could share in the general fund.

The success of the 1924 Convention was very poor because few States adhered to it. After the Second World War a new convention prepared by the Comité Maritime International (CMI) was adopted in Brussels in 1957. To this 1957 Convention 31 States, among them The Netherlands, have adhered.[14]

The 1957 Convention does not restrict the right of limitation to the shipowner, but includes the charterer, manager and operator of the ship, as well and extends this right even further to the master, members of the crew and other servants of the owner, charterer, manager and operator provided that they have been acting in the course of their employment. The claims subject to limitation have been enumerated in Article 1 of the Convention and include claims for death or personal injury and damage to property (with certain restrictions: see par. 1 *a* en *b*), for wreck removal and for damage to harbour works, basins and navigational waterways (par. 1 *c*). With respect to the latter two categories of claims (par. 1 *c*) the Protocol of Signature to the Convention provides for an admissable reservation to exclude these claims from limitation in national law.[15] The Convention explicitly excludes certain claims from limitation such as claims for salvage and for contribution in general average and claims by the master, members of the crew and certain other servants of the owner, including claims of heirs, personal representatives or dependents of such persons, if national law does not permit limitation or only to an amount greater than foreseen in the Convention.

The 1957 Convention has adopted the basic principles of the British limitation system. The limitation is applicable per accident and amounts to:

14. Australia became a Party to the 1957 Convention only on 30 July 1980, 3 1/2 years after the adoption of the 1976 Convention.

15. The Netherlands have not made use of this reservation.

a. where the occurrence has given rise to personal claims only, 3100 Poincaré gold francs (Pfr.) per ton of the ship's tonnage;

b. where the occurrence has given rise to property claims only (the majority of the cases) to 1000 Pfr. per ton of the ship's tonnage;

c. in case there are both claims for death and personal injury and for damage to property: 3100 Pfr./ton, of which 2100 Pfr. has been reserved exclusively for payment of personal claims and 1000 Pfr. to the payment of property claims and the unpaid balance of personal claims.

Further details of the 1957 Convention will be discussed in connection with the new 1976 Convention.

4. THE 1976 LONDON CONVENTION

4.1 The need for revision of the 1957 Convention

Although the 1957 Convention has been rather widely accepted (but not to the same extent as the 1910 Conventions on collision and on salvage) there was some dissatisfaction with this Convention. The main reason for this dissatisfaction were the limitation amounts since their value had been eroded considerably by inflation and did no longer constitute a reasonable level of limitation. This is a problem common to all conventions providing for limitation of liability and it cannot be considered as a specific defect of the 1957 Convention. So far no solution has been found. A working group of UNCITRAL [16] has taken up this matter and studies the possibility of an acceptable indexation clause or special rapid amendment procedure with respect to limitation amounts.

Application of the 1957 Convention had also caused certain problems of interpretation which had to be solved. The most acute problem arose as a result of a decision of the British House of Lords in the *Tojo Maru* case (Lloyd Law Rep. [1971] Vol. 1, p. 341).[17] Following a collision between the Japanese tanker *Tojo Maru* and the Italian tanker *Fina Italia* the Dutch salvage company Wijsmuller agreed on Lloyd's Open Form to render salvage services to the *Tojo Maru*. In the course of these services a diver employed by Wijsmuller and working underwater (having descended from Wijsmuller's tug *Jacob van Heemskerkck*) negligently fired a bolt through the plating into the tank of the *Tojo Maru* which had not been gas-freed. The resulting explosion caused substantial damage to the *Tojo Maru*. In an arbitration procedure on Wijsmuller's claim for a salvage award the owner of the *Tojo Maru* counterclaimed for damages. One of the issues was whether Wijsmuller being the owner of the *Jacob van Heemskerck* was entitled to limitation of his liability with respect to this counterclaim. The House of Lords denied Wijsmuller this right of limitation because the diver had not been on board of the tug at the time of the accident and neither could his act be regarded as an

16. United Nations Commission on International Trade Law.
17. See also, *supra*, n. 4.

act "in the navigation or management" of the tug. Lord Morris of Borth-Y-Gest, probably realising that the decision would cause serious mi givings with the salvage industry, observed:

"Approaching the matter with every sympathy for salvors, whose right to limitation if applicable must be at least as meritorious as that of other shipowners, it is with regret that I arrive at the conclusion that the contractors are not within the statutory words giving entitlement to limitation of liability."[18]

It is not surprising that the decision did upset salvors and their liability underwriters in particular, in view of the fact that most salvage cases are being put to arbitration in England. The case of the *Tojo Maru* was not an exceptional one because a salvage operation can be a complicated operation involving not only personnel working on board of salvage vessels, but also divers and personnel working on board the ship to which the salvage services are rendered. Even helicopters may be used. It was apparent that something should be done to repair this legal damage done to salvors.

A second problem concerned the relation between the 1957 Convention and other Conventions concluded after 1957 and also dealing with limitation of liability.[19] In this respect the following Conventions should be taken into account: – Athens Convention of 1974 relating to the carriage of passengers and their luggage by sea; – Brussels Convention of 1962 relating to the civil liability of operators of nuclear ships (Trb. 1968, 90); – Brussels Convention of 1969 on civil liability for oil pollution damage (CLC) (Trb. 1970, 196). The 1962 Nuclear Ship's Convention and the CLC include provisions on global limitation with respect to certain types of risks and therefore overlap partially the 1957 Convention. The situation with respect to the Athens Convention is different. The Athens Convention provides only for a unit limitation of liability for claims of passengers carried under a contract of carriage. With regard to passengers' claims not only a double limitation may be applied, first unit limitation and further global limitation (as is also the case for cargo claims), but the limitation system under the 1957 Convention when applied to an average passengers ship results in a very low limitation fund in relation to the number of passengers which may be carried on board. A system based on a fixed amount per ton of the ship's tonnage does not provide acceptable results.

A third problem had been created by the concept of "actual fault and privity" used in the 1957 Convention. Article 1, par. 1 (introductory phrase) of this Con-

18. The House of Lords applied section 2(1) Merchant Shipping Act, 1958 which included among others the provisions of the 1957 Convention. The House of Lords gave therefore indirectly an interpretation of Art. 1, para. 1(b) of the Convention.

19. This creates a conflict between conventions when a State is a Party to both the 1957 Convention and to one or to both of the other Conventions mentioned vis-à-vis another State Party to the 1957 Convention but not a Party to the other Convention(s). This problem has been solved in Dutch legislation in different ways with respect to the Nuclear Ships' Convention and CLC. See: Art. 25, Act of 1973 on civil liability of operators of nuclear ships (Wet

vention deprives the shipowner (or other person entitled to limitation) of the right of limitation if the occurrence giving rise to the claim resulted from his actual fault or privity. According to Article 1, par. 6 the question upon whom lies the burden of proving whether or not this occurrence resulted from the actual fault or privity of the owner must be determined by the *lex fori.* Thus the onus of proof differs in the various States Parties to the Convention. Under English law the shipowner must prove the absence of his actual fault and privity and the English courts seem to be rather strict, using a rather wide interpretation of these words. The situation in The Netherlands is quite different: the claimant who opposes the limitation by the shipowner must prove actual fault and privity and will only succeed in exceptional cases. Uniformity on such an important question is however necessary.

A final item related to the conversion of the limitation amounts expressed in Poincaré Gold Francs into national currency. This problem had been caused by the abolition of the official gold market value by the International Monetary Fund (IMF). Since the value of the gold franc could no longer be based on an official (more or less stable) value the question arose whether the conversion should be made on basis of the free market price of gold which is not only much higher but is also subject to speculation. Meanwhile this problem has been solved by the adoption of the 1979 Protocol to the 1957 Convention introducing the Special Drawing Right of the IMF (SDR) as the new unit of account.

4.2 The preparation of the 1976 Convention

In 1973 IMCO requested the CMI to accept the task of elaborating a proposal for amendment of the 1957 Convention. IMCO did not indicate whether this proposal should be in the form of an entirely new convention or of a protocol to the 1957 Convention. During a Conference held in 1974 in Hamburg the CMI adopted two alternative proposals: a "mini"-draft in the form of a Protocol and a "maxi"-draft (new convention). The Legal Committee choose the "maxi"-draft and this draft was, after several amendments had been made, presented to a Diplomatic Conference held in London in November 1976 under the auspices of IMCO.

The most important and also the most difficult issues to be decided by the Conference concerned the limitation system, limitation amounts and the question in which cases the shipowner should be deprived of his right of limitation (the "breakability" of the limits). These issues are very much interrelated and form the heart of each Limitation Convention. A compromise in the form of a package deal reconciling the views of four different groups in which the Conference had been split up was only reached during the last days of the Conference. The complicated regime of the new Convention can only explained in this way.

van 24 oktober 1973, Stb. 536) and Art. 28 of the Act on the liability of oiltankers (Wet van 11 juni 1975, Stb. 321).

4.3 The main features of the 1976 Convention

4.3.1 Insurability as the underlying principle

In Chapter 2 I already have indicated that the marine industry is operating on the basis of a complex legal system which relies on insurance. These days not only shipowners but many others connected with maritime transport or other users of the sea are being exposed to many types of risks.[20] For shipowners several types of insurance are presently available in the market, which is to a large extent an international market. Hull insurance covers primarily the risk of physical loss of or damage to the vessel and it also partially covers a shipowner's liability arising out of a collision with another ship. Most of the remaining liability risks are being covered by so-called Protection & Indemnity Insurance. For special types of risks special covers are available (for instance against excess liability or against oil pollution).

All these risks have to be covered by the international insurance market and also this market has its capacity limitations. In view of the magnitude of a possible catastrophic accident at sea and the limited insurance cover available it is desirable to set certain limits to liability which are based on a realistic appreciation of the possible insurance cover available. Because of the complexity of this market it is for an outsider not easy to make this appreciation. Sofar I have dealt with insurability in a technical sense, i.e., insurance cover available irrespective of the premium to be paid. However also this second aspect should be taken into account. Shipowners will take out insurance cover if they can obtain such cover against a premium which is still acceptable from a commercial point of view. It is this commercial element which played an important role during the Conference when the general level of the limitation was being debated.

Although the concept of "insurability" is rather vague it has been chosen by the drafters of the Convention as a basic principle. This principle does not only affect the general level of limitation, but also other matters such as the question of "breakability" of the limits, the persons entitled to limitation, etc. This principle of insurability has been severely attacked by Rodière in 1973.[21]

4.3.2 Persons entitled to limitation

Originally maritime law only provided protection by limitation of liability to the owner of the ship. This created an unfair discrimination with respect to other persons who might become liable for damage resulting from their involvement in the operation of the ship. The shipowner is not necessarily always the only person

20. Even cargo-owners or shippers may become liable for damage caused by their cargo during transport to the ship, other cargo on board or even persons outside the ship. The present draft of IMCO for a new convention on liability and compensation for damage caused during transport by sea of hazardous substances (HNS Convention) provides for a strict liability of the shipowner to a certain limit and a supplementary liability of the shipper of the cargo.

21. See, *Droit Maritime Français,* 1973, *supra,* n. 8.

who operates a ship, but in cases of bareboat charter the charterer will employ the master and the crew and will thus have to be considered as the operator. Where under the old systems the owner could limit his liability for the acts of his master or crewmembers, the charterer was deprived of this privilege. The 1924 Convention provided already in Article 10 that "where a person who operates the vessel without owning it or the principal charterer is liable under one of the heads enumerated in Article 1 or Article 7, the provisions of this Convention are applicable to him." This provision presented only a partial solution for the problem, because also a time charterer, voyage charterer or manager of a ship may incur liability because of his involvement in its commercial exploitation. The restriction of the right of global limitation to shipowners seems to have been the reason for inserting into bills of lading socalled "demise clauses" in order to restrict the contract of carriage to one solely between the shipowner and the bill of lading holder in cases where the ship had been chartered. This clause, although no longer strictly necessary, is still being used in bills of lading and remains a source of litigation and uncertaintity for shippers or consignees who wish to claim under a bill of lading.[22]

Another group of persons who need protection by limitation are the master, members of the crew, pilot and other persons who perform duties on board of the ship or in direct connection with its navigation or management. These persons are by their profession in a position that they may make mistakes and consequently become liable. For social reasons they should receive protection against professional liability. If limitation would be denied to them, claimants could very easily circumvent the limitation of the shipowner by acting against those persons in tort, expecting that the shipowners would protect their servants in some way or another (for instance by taking out liability insurance). The limitation could be frustrated and the system would not be "waterproof".

The 1957 Convention extends the right of limitation to charterers, managers, and operators of ships and to the master, members of the crew and other servants of the owner, charterer, etc. provided that they acted in the course of their employment. All these limits are aggregated to the amount determined by the Convention so that by claiming against more than one person liable the claimant cannot receive more compensation than provided for by the Convention. During the elaboration of the 1976 Convention the question arose whether the right of limitation should be further extended to other persons. The CMI draft included any person rendering services in direct connection with the navigation or management of the ship. This formula was very wide and would include an entirely new group of persons who would be only indirectly involved in the operation of the ship. The expression "management of the ship" is well known from the Hague Rules (Art. 4, par. 2a of the Bills of Lading Convention) but has received a dubious reputation in view of its vagueness and it has caused much litigation. IMCO refused to follow this proposal and the final text does not reproduce it any more.

22. See UNCTAD report on bills of lading, United Nations, N.Y. 1971, p. 33.

The 1976 Convention explicitly mentions the salvor. He is defined in Article 1 as any person rendering services in direct connection of salvage operations, which include not only the traditional salvage operations rendered to a ship, but also services in respect of the removal, destruction or rendering harmless of ship's cargo and even preventive measure as defined in Article 2, par. 1*f*.[23] This special rule on salvors is a consequence of the decision of the House of Lords in the *Tojo Maru*. The intention is not to discourage salvors and persons taking preventive masure to undertake action with respect to ships in danger even if such action would involve serious risks. It is no longer a condition that such persons are shipowners or undertake their operations in connection with the navigation or management of a ship.

Also with respect to servants and agents of the shipowner or other persons entitled to limitation the 1976 Convention takes a more liberal attitude. Article 4, par. 4 provides in general that any person for whose act, neglect or default the shipowner or salvor is liable shall also have the right of limitation. As a consequence also independent contractors may rely on this privilege, provided that the shipowner or salvor is liable for their acts, neglect or default. When, for instance, a stevedore used by a shipowner or a charterer in the performance of a contract of carriage would be liable for damage to cargo the (tort) claim of the cargoowner against him would be subject to limitation. In this way the servants and agents receive the same kind of protection as by way of the socalled "Himalaya"-clauses in bills of lading and claimants will be prevented to frustrate the limitation system by acting against other persons than the shipowner. Article 9 provides for an aggregation of claims against all persons entitled to limitation. According to Article 11, par. 3 a limitation fund constituted by one of these persons shall be deemed to be constituted by all of them. This system is similar to that of the 1957 Convention: there is only one fund available.

Article 1, par. 6 even includes the insurer of liability for limitable claims. At first sight this provision would seem to be superfluous since the liability of the insurer (even when by statute the claimant would have a direct action against him) cannot be greater than that of the person whose liability is insured. However some U.S. Courts have denied the right of limitation to the liability insurer in cases of direct action, although the insured shipowner was entitled to limitation of liability.[24]

4.3.3 Claims subject to limitation

Article 2 of the 1976 Convention enumerates the claims which are subject to limitation. Many of these claims were also limitable under the 1957 Convention such as claims for damage to property, for loss of life or personal injury, infringe-

23. Art. 1 of the London Convention.
24. CMI report to IMCO (1974), p. 9 and George E. Duncan, "Limitation of Shipowner's Liability: parties entitled to limit; the vessel, the Fund"; *Tulane Law Review*, Vol. 53, No. 4, p. 1054.

ment of rights other than contractual rights and for wreck removal. But in the new Convention the list has been extended with other types of claims. Claims with respect of loss resulting from delay in the carriage by sea of cargo, passengers and luggage and claims with respect of preventive measures taken by another person than the person liable have been added to the list.

Whether or not a shipowner or charterer in his capacity of a carrier will be liable for delay will depend mainly on national law. The Bills of Lading Convention is silent on this point and national law will decide whether he will be allowed to exonerate himself for this type of damage. There will be liability for delay under the UN Convention on the carriage of goods by sea of 1978 (Hamburg Rules), but this convention has not yet entered into force. With respect to passengers there is no international uniformity either: the Athens Convention, which has not entered into force, does not provide for liability for delay. However this does not exclude the possibility that there might be claims for delay.

The concept of "preventive measures" originates from the CLC. According to Article I, 6 jo 7 of that Convention "oil pollution damage" includes the costs of reasonable measures taken by any person (also the person liable under CLC: the shipowner) after the incident to prevent or minimize oil pollution damage and further loss caused by such measures. The reason for this rule is that persons should be encouraged to take such preventive measures. This idea was also adopted in the 1976 Convention by granting the right of limitation of liability to those persons, but with the exception of the person liable. It was thought that there was no justification to allow the person liable to claim against his own limitation fund because by taking preventive measures the person liable could in any way reduce the amount of compensation to be paid by him if those measures were successful and moreover he has in general an obligation to avert or minimize any further loss. This does not exclude that the person liable may invoke limitation of liability for a claim with respect to preventive measures taken by another person but instituted against him. However he will not enjoy the right of limitation if such claim relates to remuneration for such services rendered under a contract concluded by him (Art. 2, par. 2 final sentence). It would not be encouraging to accept a contract for the rendering of services with respect to preventive measures if the agreed remuneration would be limited by the Convention.

In view of the *Tojo Maru* decision Article 2, par. 1*a* provides explicitly that claims for loss of life and personal injury and for property damage in direct connection with salvage operations shall also be limitable even if those operations were undertaken not from a ship or not in connection with the navigation or management of a ship.

4.3.4 Claims for wreckremoval and for damage to harbourworks, etc.

The Protocol of Signature to the 1957 Convention allows a State Party to exclude application of the rules of the Convention to claims for the removal of wrecks or for damage to harbour works, basins and navigational waterways. Very often such claims will be instituted by public authorities as owners of such works and because they are responsible for keeping navigable waters free of obstacles in the interest of safe navigation. These authorities may try to obtain with all available pressure a more favourable position vis-à-vis other creditors in the limitation fund. The legal regime with respect to such claims varies from one legislation to another and it seems to be very difficult to agree to more international uniformity in this field.[25]

The Protocol of Signature to the 1957 Convention was the result of a compromise between States wishing to grant to public authorities unlimited recourse and those which could not agree to any deviation from the conventional regime in this respect. During the 1976 Conference the controversy continued and a new compromise was necessary. This issue was the last obstacle to overcome and the compromise was only made at the final stage of the Conference. Under Article 6, par. 3 national law may give priority to claims in respect of claims for damage to harbourworks, basins and waterways and to navigational aids over other claims sharing in the limitation fund as referred to in Article 6, par. 1(b) but without prejudice to the right of claims for loss of life or personal injury to share in that limitation fund for the unpaid balance. Article 18 allows a State to reserve the right to exclude from the application of the Convention claims for wreckremoval and for the removal, destruction or making harmless of the ship's cargo.

It is likely that national legislations will continue to follow their own policy in this area.[26] Under the British Merchant Shipping Act 1979 which implements the 1976 Convention no special provision has been made with respect to claims for damage to harbour works, etc. With respect to claims for wreckremoval Article 2, par. 1(d) of the Convention has been excluded until a special fund will be operative which will reimburse harbour and conservancy authorities for the reduction of compensation as a result of said provision (Schedule 4, Part. II, 3 of the Act). The Swedish Maritime Committee has advised the Swedish Government not to give any priority to these claims or to make use of the reservation. One may expect other Scandinavian States to follow the same line.

There is a difference between these two types of claims which might justify a different approach. For so-called harbour claims the 1976 Convention allows States to provide by national legislation for a priority in the distribution of the limitation fund. The position of the person liable will not be affected by this: he will probably not be interested how his limitation fund will be distributed among the various claimants. On the contrary the position of claimants of property damage could be seriously reduced if they would become an underprivileged class. It is doubtful whether the position of public authorities justifies this infringement of the principle of the "paritas creditorum". As far as claims for wreck removal are concerned the possibility of a reservation to the effect that by national law there would be an unlimited liability of the shipowner or a limitation fund to a much higher amount than provided for by the Convention might be justified because the

25. See, Branimir Luksić, "Limitation of Liability for the raising and removal of ships and wrecks: a comparative study", *Journal of Maritime Law and Commerce,* Vol. 12, No. 1 (October 1980).

26. See also, *supra,* n. 15.

public task of authorities to keep navigable waterways free of obstacles for the sake of safe navigation is also in the interest of the "community" of shipowners who should, rather than taxpayers, contribute in the removal of wrecks.

4.3.5 Claims excluded from limitation

Article 3 of the 1976 Convention enumerates under *a - c* claims which have been explicitly excluded from limitation. The claims mentioned under (a) and (e) had already been excluded in Article 1, par. 4 of the 1957 Convention (claims for salvage and for contribution in general average; claims by servants of the shipowner). Claims mentioned under (b), (c) and (d) are new and their inclusion in the list of excepted claims is related to the problem of the relation between the 1976 Convention and other Conventions dealing with global limitation (CLC and Nuclear Conventions). Article 3(b) deals with oil pollution claims, art. 3(c) and (d) with claims for nuclear damage.[27]

The wording of these provisions is wider than would have been strictly necessary for a delimination of the scope of application of the 1976 Convention with the scope of the other Conventions (see also 4.1. "the need for revision of the 1957 Convention"). Several delegations at the Conference wished to leave these matters as much as possible to the discretion of national law. Some delegations also wanted to exclude claims in respect of carriage of other hazardous substances in view of the draft convention which is elaborated by IMCO, but this proposal was rejected by the Conference.

The discussion mainly concentrated on oil pollution claims. The draft prepared by CMI and the legal committee of IMCO excepted only claims *subject* to the provisions of CLC or to national law giving effect to this Convention. Limitation of liability for other oil pollution claims would be governed by the 1976 Convention. This was not acceptable for some States, such as the United States and Canada, which have not accepted the CLC but have introduced national legislation for oil pollution liability with unlimited liability or limitation to a much higher level. Finally the Conference accepted as a compromise the present wording of Article 3(b): "claims for oil pollution *within the meaning of* the International Convention on Civil Liability for Oil Pollution . . .". Consequently this wider wording does not only affect States which have not adhered to CLC but States Party to that Convention as well.

It is without dispute that Article 3(b) means first that claims for oil pollution damage governed by CLC are excluded from the limitation system of the 1976 Convention. Article V of CLC provides for a special limitation system. But the ambiguity of the words "within the meaning of" causes some doubt on the further

27. (c) refers to claims subject to any international Convention or national legislation governing or prohibiting limitation for nuclear damage: Paris Convention of 1960 and Supplementary Protocol of 1962 (Trb. 1964, 176); Vienna Convention of 1963 (Trb. 1964, 175); (d) refers to claims against a shipowner of a nuclear ship: Nuclear Ships Convention of 1962 (Trb. 1968, 90) incl. the Dutch Act giving effect to that Convention (Wet van 23 oktober 1973, Stb. 536).

effects of the exclusion. The CLC does not deal with all oil pollution claims covered by the national law of the States Party but Article II of that Convention restricts the scope of its application to pollution damage caused on the territory (including the territorial sea) of a State Party and to preventive measure taken to avoid or minimize such damage. Claims brought before the Courts of a State Party to CLC and not covered by Article II do not fall under the regime of CLC and are not limitable under Article V. The question arises whether States Party to the 1976 Convention are allowed to apply the provisions of that Convention to such claims or such claims are excluded from limitation in general. In the latter case States which wish to provide for limitation should fill the gap by separate national legislation. The British Merchant Shipping Act 1979 (Part II of Schedule 4, par. 4(1)) takes the view that only claims under the Merchant Shipping Act 1971 (Oil Pollution) are excluded and that all other claims would be governed by the regime of the 1976 Convention. The Norwegian delegate to the 1976 Conference, Professor Selvig, takes the opposite view: his conclusion is that a State ratifying the 1976 Convention should, even if it is a Party to CLC, adopt legislation providing special limitation of liability for oil pollution claims not governed by CLC.[28] His advice is probably the safest course to follow for those States where the Courts must apply the 1976 Convention directly and may overrule any national legislation which they find inconsistent with the Convention.

The concept of "oil pollution claim within the meaning of the International Convention . . ." should be defined according to the CLC. Article I, paras. 1, 5 and 6 of that Convention define "ship", "oil" and "oil pollution damage". Furthermore it should be realized that CLC is only applicable to claims for oil pollution damage against the owner of a ship. These restrictions should be kept in mind when applying Article 3(b) of the 1976 Convention.

4.3.6 Limitation system and amounts; conduct barring limitation

These three interrelated issues have been debated extensively at the Conference as a package deal. Due to the very divergent views which prevailed about these key issues it appeared to be very difficult to find an acceptable compromise. The final package deal is rather complex and the results of the negotiations are of a mainly political character.

The first question raised was the so-called breakability of the limits (Article 4: conduct barring limitation). I have already indicated that the concept of "actual fault and privity" under the 1957 Convention had caused misgivings due to the lack of uniformity with respect to the burden of proof and the interpretation by the Courts. More recent conventions use a stricter formula which concurs with the concept of "wilful misconduct" used in English law.[29] The draft prepared by

28. "The 1976 Limitation Convention and oil pollution damage", [1979] *Lloyd's Maritime and Commercial Law Quarterly*, pp. 21-25.

29. See, Art. 3, para. 4 of the Visby Rules (Protocol of 1968 to Bills of Lading Convention, Trb. 1979, 26) and Art. 13 of Athens Convention on carriage of passengers and their luggage

CMI and IMCO contained this new formula which met however with strong opposition from certain delegations which preferred to stick to the 1957 formula. The breakability of the limits must be considered an important factor with regard to the insurability of the liability risk. The insurance industry can provide cover for higher amounts if the breakability of the limits is low. Consequently there is a relation between the two issues. The new formula was finally adopted by the Conference: the person liable shall not be entitled to limitation only if it is proved that the loss resulted from his personal act or ommission, committed with the intent to cause such loss, or recklessly and with knowledge that such loss would probably result.

The second issue concerned the number of limitation funds to be constituted under the Convention: two separate funds (one for personal claims and one for other claims) or one fund but with priority for personal claims? There was considerable difference of opinion about to what extent this would affect the insurability of the liability risk. Moreover there was the question whether a separate passengers' claim fund should be provided for. The system finally adopted by the Conference is the following: Article 6, par. 1 provides for two different general funds

a. a fund in respect of claims for loss of life or personal injury (passengers' claims excluded); and

b. a fund in respect of any other claims (mainly property claims).

As the balance of unpaid claims under fund (a) shall rank rateably with claims mentioned under (b) there is a spill over from one fund to the other (Article 6, par. 2). Under Article 7 a special fund has been provided for loss of life and personal injury caused to passengers of a ship.

The basis for calculation of the amount of the general limitation funds under Article 6 is rather complicated. The philosophy behind this system is that a limitation fund for a ship with a small tonnage should be relatively higher than for a bigger ship because a small ship is capable of causing relatively large damage. Therefore a minimum-limit combined with a degressive scale has been used.

		(a)	(b)
(i) ships with tonnage not exceeding 500 tons		330,000 units of account [30]	167,000 units of account
(ii) for a ship in excess thereof, the following amount in addition to that mentioned under (i)			
for each ton from	501 - 3,000 tons	500 "	
for each ton from	501 - 30,000 tons		167 "
for each ton from	3,000 - 30,000 tons	333 "	

by sea, 1974 Compilation International Conventions on Maritime Law, Comité Maritime International.

30. The unit of account of the Convention is the Special Drawing Right (SDR) of the IMF (Art. 8).

for each ton from 30,000 - 70,000 tons	250	”	125	”
for each ton in excess of 70,000 tons	167	”	83	”

The passenger's fund of Article 7 is not based on the tonnage criterium but amounts to 46.666 units of account (which is also the unit limitation under the Athens Convention) multiplied by the number of passengers which the ship is authorized to carry. The absolute maximum amounts to 25 million units of account.

Another question to be solved related to the calculation of the limitation of liability of the salvor who is not operating from any ship or is operating on board the ship in respect of which he is rendering salvage services. The outcome of the debates at the Conference should not have disappointed the salvage industry: the limit of liability must be calculated according to a tonnage of 1500 tons (Article 6, par. 4). This must be considered as a moderate level of limitation.

The method of calculation of the ship's tonnage has been changed considerably. The 1957 Convention provided for a special limitation ton which departed from the net tonnage to which the amount deducted from the gross tonnage on account of engine room space had to be added. The 1976 Convention uses the gross tonnage in accordance with the measurement contained in Annex I of the International Convention on Tonnage Measurement of Ships 1969 (Trb. 1970, 122 and 194). This Convention has entered into force on 18 July 1982. However the 1969 Convention obliges States to apply the old measurement systems to existing ships during a transitional period of 12 years which implies that certain ships will not carry certificates indicating the tonnage to be calculated in accordance with Article 6, par. 5 of the 1976 Convention. The same applies to certain ships which have been excluded from the application of the Measurement Convention of 1969. According to technical experts such ships can be easily remeasured in accordance with the 1969 Convention.

4.3.7 Constitution and distribution of the limitation fund

The rules on the constitution and distribution of the limitation fund (Articles 10-14) do not differ considerably from those of the 1957 Convention. Limitation of liability may be invoked notwithstanding that a limitation fund has not been constituted, but a State Party may by national law make the constitution of a limitation fund a condition for invoking limitation. The same system exists under the 1957 Convention. The Netherlands has made use of the possibility under the 1957 Convention to make the constitution of a limitation fund obligatory (see Art. 320*a* W.v.BRv) although in practice the majority of cases are settled outside court.

A new rule is that the fund or funds must be constituted in the amounts set out in Articles 6 and 7 *together* with the interest thereon from the date of the occurrence giving rise to the liability until the date of the constitution of the fund (Article 11, par. 1). It is justified that the person liable should not profit from any delay in the constitution of the fund.

STATUTORY CONTROLS ON STANDARD TERMS EMPLOYED IN AN INTERNATIONAL CONTEXT: IS THE CURE WORSE THAN THE DISEASE?

by H. Duintjer Tebbens*

1. INTRODUCTION

Two of Holland's neighbouring partners in trade and tourism have created new legal instruments for the control of standard terms in contracts. In the Federal Republic of Germany an Act on Standard Terms of Business, known as *AGB – Gesetz,* of 1976, codified and amplified the controls, hitherto created by the courts, on standard terms of business.[1] In the United Kingdom the 1977 Unfair Contract Terms Act [2] was adopted; this also regulates and restricts the effect of certain contract terms. The Dutch legislator also took steps in this direction in 1981 by submitting a Bill on General Conditions to Parliament.[3]

All these texts put standardized contract terms (in general or with particular subject matters) to a twofold test, viz., first, a general test of reasonableness applying to the entire substantive scope of each text, and secondly, more specific and stricter controls in the event of what can be briefly termed a "consumer transaction". Their common aim is to protect "weak" contracting parties confronted with unreasonable standard terms used by "strong" commercial persons or enterprises. (Those parties using standard terms will hereafter be called "proponents" and their contracting partners "adherents".) On the other hand, the various regulations have a different scope in several respects, one of which is examined more closely in this paper. The topic is a comparison of the surprisingly different approaches taken in the three countries as regards the territorial reach of their substantive law provisions in the respective (draft) statutes. Although the solutions essentially have the nature of *unilateral* rules of private international law, the Dutch approach in particular calls for an additional examination of recent codification efforts at an international level. In this context, the *multinational* conflict rules aimed at better protection of consumers, which were drafted in 1980 under the auspices

* Dr. Jur.; Research Office, European Court of Justice, Luxembourg; Member of the Board of Editors.

1. Act of 9 December 1976, regulating the law of standard terms of business, BGBl. I, 3317, entered into force on 1 April 1977.
2. Act of 26 October 1977, c. 50, entered into force on 1 February 1978.
3. Bill no. 16 983 (Tw. K. 1981, 16 983, nos. 1–3), introduced on 28 July 1981.

of the EEC and the Hauge Conference on Private International Law respectively, will be discussed. Before going into these international aspects, it might be useful to mention very briefly some of the main substantive features of each of the three national texts.

2. THE NATIONAL REGULATIONS

The *German Act* deals with standard terms of business forming part of a contract, either through the use of pre-printed standard forms of contract, or through reference to a separate body of such terms. The Act covers any type of clause that deviates from, or supplements non-mandatory rules of law. The Act's control operates both at the stage at which the contract is drawn up and at the stage that the standard terms enter into effect, once they have been validly incorporated into the contract. The emphasis is on the latter stage: by way of a general test *(Generalklausel)* standard terms are ineffective when, contrary to the dictates of good faith they prejudice the adherent in an unreasonable way (s.9). This criterion is elaborated in a "grey list" of terms that are ineffective, subject to judicial appreciation (s.10), and in a "black list" of terms that are prohibited per se (s.11). Those lists, however, do not apply when the adherent is a merchant contracting in the course of his business (s. 24(1)), i.e., for practical purposes they are confined to consumers.

The *British Act* amends the law of England and Wales and Northern Ireland in part I, and the law of Scotland in part II. The Act is not confined to standard terms, but puts restrictions on contract terms whether standardized or individually negotiated. On the other hand, the restrictions operate only insofar as the terms limit or exclude what is called "business liability", which means, essentially, liability arising out of business activities (s. 1(3)).[4] This may be liability for breach of contract, but also – though this is not apparent from the title of the Act – liability for negligence, e.g., when in a sale of goods a notice or written "guarantee" would exclude or limit liability for personal injury towards third persons (s.5). Any adherent to a contract which contains a clause varying business liability is protected by a test of reasonableness: for the application of this test five guidelines are appended to the statute. If the adherent "deals as a consumer" (in Scotland: if a "consumer contract" is involved), certain specified terms are (per se) ineffective. The Act does not tackle the question whether the terms dealt with by it were validly incorporated into the contract (s. 11(2)). Thus the general principles of the English or Scots law of contract apply to that question.

4. With the exception of s. 5 (misrepresentation) and s. 6 (implied terms in sales and hire purchases).

The *Dutch Bill* will insert a separate Title 6.5.2A into Book 6 of the New Civil Code containing the general part of the law of obligations. This Book, including the Bill, is expected to come into force in 1984/1985 together with other important recodifications of the Dutch patrimonial law.[5] General conditions in the sense of the Bill are those which are regularly used, or whose regular use by a proponent may otherwise be anticipated, with the exception, however, of terms which define the essential elements of the contract (s.1). The Bill deals with general conditions which have become part of a contract. Thus, like the British statute, it does not extend to questions of incorporation. Otherwise, the Bill largely follows the pattern of the German Act. It first defines in general terms two grounds on which a particular clause may be annulled (s. 2(2)) for being unreasonably onerous to the adherent in the particular circumstances concerned. Then, in the case of a consumer being the adherent, the Bill gives a "black list" of clauses which are unreasonably onerous clauses per se (s. 3), followed by a "grey list" of clauses presumed to be unreasonably onerous, which presumption may, however, be rebutted by the proponent (s. 4). The grey list may be modified by Royal Decree after consultations with representative organisations of the trades or professions, and of consumers or other adherents' groups (s. 5).

3. INTERNATIONAL SCOPE

In examining the international scope of the three sets of rules and bearing in mind the limited scope of this contribution, I shall concentrate on the sale of movables. Since this type of contract is of paramount importance in commercial dealings and consumer transactions alike, it is very suitable for comparison.

3.1 The German Act on Standard Terms of Business

The German Act contains a specific provision on the effect of a foreign law clause, as one of the many clauses on the "grey list". Section 10 provides in part:

> "In standard contract terms the following clauses in particular are ineffective –
> 8. The choice of foreign law or the law of the German Democratic Republic where there is no legitimate interest in such a choice."[6]

According to the Explanatory Memorandum, a legitimate interest does not as a rule exist when the contract was concluded as a result of business activities in the country, and the domestic adherent also accepted the contract in the country. Such links with

5. See Hartkamp, Vers un nouveau Code civil néerlandais. Rev. int. dr. comp. 1982, p. 319.
6. Author's translation. The English translation of ss. 1–13 of the Act in 26 AJCL (1978), p. 568, has not been followed as it does not appear to be wholly accurate, cf. n. 11 *infra*.

Germany (F.G.R.) correspond to those required for the operation of the second provision dealing with conflicts aspects, section 12, which will be discussed later. Section 10(8) has met with severe criticism from German experts in private international law.[7] Its main weakness can be considered to be the fact that it does not ensure the application of the protective rules of the Act in the absence of a (valid) choice of foreign law by the parties. Indeed, the contract may still be governed by foreign law by virtue of the prevailing general German conflict rules in the absence of such a (valid) choice by the parties, in particular by the law of the seller's domicile under the doctrine of the "characteristic performance".[8] Furthermore, it is not clear how the criterion of a legitimate interest is to be used in less "domestic" contracts than those to which the Explanatory Memorandum refers. According to German conflicts doctrine a reasonable interest is in any case required for a choice of law clause. Therefore, should the test in section 10(8) be implemented along the same lines, then the rule would be superfluous.[9] If, on the other hand, a tighter control should apply since non-professional adherents are involved, the legitimate interest criterion leaves the legal practitioner without guidance in cases where prima facie significant ties both with Germany and with a foreign country exist. Another point of criticism is that the legislator has failed to deal with the preliminary issue, viz., whether a choice of law clause has been incorporated at all in a contract with international aspects. According to this opinion, it is preferable to let the control apply at that earlier stage.[10] Section 10(8) is designed to protect consumers domiciled in Germany against the sudden application of foreign legal rules to a transaction to which they were a party in that country. The rule does not distinguish whether the foreign rules are more or less protective to the consumers than German law. Nor is there a rule in the Act concerning the choice of German law in the contract terms. It may be assumed that, whenever such a choice is accepted within the general limits on party autonomy in German private international law, the Act will apply as part of the chosen law.

The second relevant rule is designed to ensure that in contracts which have important domestic links, the protective German rules are heeded, even though foreign law would otherwise apply. This rule is laid down in section 12, entitled "International scope of application":

7. See among the numerous articles, Drobnig, AGB im internationalen Handelsverkehr, in *Internationales Recht und Wirtschafsordnung* (Festschrift Mann), 1977, p. 591; Landfermann, AGB–Gesetz und Auslandgeschäfte, RIW 1977, p. 445; Jayme, Allgemeine Geschäftsbedingungen und internationales Privatrecht, 142 ZHR (1978), p. 105 (115 et seq.); Sonnenberger, Bemerkungen zum Internationales Privatrecht im AGB–Gesetz, in *Konflikt und Ordnung* (Festschrift Ferid), 1978, p. 377; Stoll, Internationalprivatrechtliche Probleme bei Verwendung Allgemeiner Geschäftsbedingungen, in *Festschrift Beitzke*, 1979, p. 759; Hübner, Allgemeine Geschäftsbedingungen und Internationales Privatrecht, NJW 1980, p. 2601.

8. See Jayme 116; Sonnenberger 381.

9. Cf. Kegel, *Internationales Privatrecht* (4th ed. 1977), p. 296; Sonnenberger 380 and cf. Stoll 776–777.

10. Sonnenberger 382.

"Where a contract is governed by a foreign law or the law of the German Democratic Republic, the provisions of this Act must nevertheless be taken into consideration if:

1) the contract is entered into on the basis of a public offer, a public bid or a similar business activity carried out by the proponent within the territory where this Act is in force, and if

2) the other contracting party, when expressing his acceptance for the contract to be concluded, has his domicile or habitual residence within the territory where this Act is in force, and expresses such acceptance within that territory." [11]

Again, German legal doctrine has been the source of objections, both as regards the substance and the wording of this rule. A major problem is the meaning in the Act of the phrase "to take into consideration" (*berücksichtigen).* The Explanatory Memorandum states that if the applicable foreign law offers an "equivalent protection" to the consumer/adherent, the Act's purpose is satisfied. If not, the Act's protective rules are to be applied by adaptation to the foreign applicable law.[12] This statement fails to make clear whether the required equivalence should exist between the controls on standard terms *in general* of the foreign and German law, or rather as applied to the specific case.[13] Most writers agree that the level of protection afforded by the German Act constitutes a minimum standard, and that the foreign law may not fall short of that level.[14] Meanwhile, the judicial task is far from easy when, in applying the foreign *lex contractus,* certain rules of the German statute have in some way to be given additional consideration. Drobnig observes, not without understatement, that this requires a particularly delicate and discerning approach.[15] On the other hand, it has been recognised that, in real terms the scope of application of section 12 is very narrow. If the formation of the contract is actually so closely connected with Germany as this provision suggests, it will be a rare case where foreign law will nevertheless govern the contract, either by objective localization of the contract in the absence of an effective choice of law clause, or by virtue of such a clause which has successfully passed through the "sieve" of section 10(8).[16] The rather cumbersome formulation of the connection between the Act's territory and the adherent is borrowed from another German statute, viz., the 1968 Act on the Trade in Foreign Investment Shares.[17] We will encounter the same formulation in the international texts, which will be discussed in chapter 4.

11. Author's translation; the translation in AJCL, *supra* n. 6, translates *berücksichtigen* in the opening clause as "to apply", thus disguising one of the main problems inherent in this text. – The Act's territory includes Berlin (s. 29).

12. See the explanatory note, Bundesrat doc. 360/75, p. 41.

13. See Sonnenberger 384 with references.

14. Jayme 119, Palandt- Heldrich, *BGB* (41st ed. 1982), p. 2393, comment 3 on Art. 12; *contra*, e.g., Schlosser *et al., Kommentar zum AGB–Gesetz* (1977), p. 562, Note 8 to Art. 12.

15. Drobnig 610 ("besonderes Fingerspitzengefühl").

16. Landfermann 449.

17. Act of 28 July 1968, BGBl. I, 986.

3.2 The British Unfair Contract Terms Act

In the British Act a long provision (s. 27) is devoted to the impact of choice of law clauses on the Act. The ambit of this provision can however be better appreciated if we first look at another important rule of the Act with an even wider scope. Section 26(1), (3) and (4) essentially provides that the limits imposed by the Act on business liability clauses do not apply to international supply contracts. The definition of such contracts in subsection (4) shows that the description in the Uniform Laws on International Sales is followed here: contracting parties from different States, offer and acceptance in different States, or goods in transit or to be delivered outside the State where the contract was made. The preparatory documents reveal three arguments for this radical exclusion. It should be up to the law of the buyer's country to decide whether his rights are unreasonably restricted; in international transactions the parties normally do not need protection; English exporters would be at a competitive disadvantage in a foreign market, if they were bound by the strict and mandatory rules of the Act.[18] The effects of this exclusion will be further discussed below, see chapter 3.4. Let us look now at section 27, which first deals with a choice of British law, and then with a choice of foreign law. Section 27(1) reads:

> "Where the proper law of a contract is the law of any part of the United Kingdom only by choice of the parties (and apart from that choice would be the law of some country outside the United Kingdom) sections 2 to 7 and 16 to 21 of this Act do not operate as part of the proper law."

The sections referred to contain the main substantive provisions of the Act. The rule quoted above was aptly described by Morris as a "self-denying statute".[19] Its straightforward purpose is that foreign parties should not be hindered by the control provisions of the Act in their agreement on English law either directly or by agreement for arbitration in London.[20] This argument has been challenged by Mann in several papers; he maintains that foreign parties who choose to rely on English law "should take the rough with the smooth", and should not be offered an English law excluding a segment of legislation that is thought to be beneficial to domestic commercial transactions.[21] He also criticizes the phrase "only by choice of the parties", since the choice might also be implied and it will then be rather difficult to discern whether English law applies *only* by the parties' implied choice or would have applied anyway on the strength of the objective elements of the contract.[22]

18. Cf. the Second Report of the Law Commissions on Exemption clauses in Contracts (Law Com. No. 69, Scot. Law Com. No. 39), 1975, p. 80.
19. Morris, Statutes in the Conflict of Laws, in *Multum non multa* (Festschrift Lipstein), 1980, p. 187, at 194, 204; *id., The Conflict of Laws* (2nd ed. 1980), p. 224.
20. See the Report, *supra* n. 18, para. 232.
21. Mann, The proposed new law of exemption clauses and the conflict of laws, 26 ICLQ (1977; Essays in honour of J.H.C. Morris), p. 903, at 908, 911 (quotation); see also *id.*, Unfair Contract Terms Act 1977 and the conflict of laws, 27 ICLQ (1978), p. 661.
22. Mann, 27 ICLQ (1978), at 662.

An entirely different solution is chosen in the converse situation, viz., choice of foreign law in a contract with important links with the United Kingdom, which is covered by section 27(2):

> "This Act has effect notwithstanding any contract term which applies or purports to apply the law of some country outside the United Kingdom, where (either or both)–
> (a) the term appears to the court, or arbitrator or arbiter to have been imposed wholly or mainly for the purpose of enabling the party imposing it to evade the operation of this Act, or
> b) in the making of the contract one of the parties dealt as consumer, and he was then habitually resident in the United Kingdom, and the essential steps necessary for the making of the contract were taken there, whether by him or by others on his behalf."

Criticism has also been made of this. The notion of evasion appears to be novel in an English statute, and the boundary between it and avoidance of English law – i.e., the legitimate choice for another, also connected, legal system – is far from clear.[23] This is even more the case, since section 27(2) does not require that, apart from the choice of foreign law, English law would be the proper law of the contract.[24] Another point is the interpretation of "the essential steps necessary for the making of the contract" when the adherent is a consumer. Does this phrase relate to steps taken by either party [25] or by the consumer alone? [26] Furthermore, when is a contract term "purporting to apply" foreign law? If this comprises jurisdiction or arbitration clauses, the scope of the rule would become very large and even extend to instances where the foreign law applies as objectively applicable law. However, it is open to doubt whether that consequence conforms with the real purpose of the rule.[27] Leaving aside these doubtful points, section 27(2) at least contains an overriding rule against foreign law clauses in contracts made in the United Kingdom by consumers residing there.

3.3 The Dutch Bill on General Conditions

Yet another approach is taken in the Dutch Bill. There is no specific rule in it concerning the impact of a choice of law clause, whether for Dutch or for foreign law. The only provision on the international scope of application of the Bill is a straightforward rule in Article 6.5.2A.13:

23. See Cheshire and North, *Private International Law* (10th ed. 1979), pp. 234–235; Mann, previous note.
24. Cheshire and North, previous note, at 235 and n. 4.
25. Mann, 27 ICLQ (1978), at 663.
26. Triebel, Das englische Gesetz über unbillige Vertragsklauseln von 1977, RIW 1978, p. 353, at 358.
27. Cheshire and North, *supra* n. 23, at 235 and n. 5, do not allow for that consequence.

"1. Irrespective of the law governing the contract, this Chapter [i.e., the substantive provisions of the Bill] applies to contracts between parties who do business in the course of their profession or trade, and who both have their principal place of business in the Netherlands.

2. Irrespective of the law governing the contract, this Chapter does not apply to contracts between parties who do business in the course of their profession or trade, and who do not both have their principal place of business in the Netherlands." [28]

The most obvious point about this rule is that it is explicitly confined to business and professional dealings. It does not deal with the consumers. This aspect is dealt with in the Explanatory Memorandum to the Bill: the Minister expects that Article 5 of the EEC Obligations Convention of 19 June 1980 [29] will have an anticipatory effect on Dutch private international law, even before its ratification. Thus, consumers residing in the Netherlands would be sufficiently protected.[30] The special conflicts rule for consumer contracts in that Convention, to which the Minister refers, will be examined below, in chapter 4. According to the Explanatory Memorandum, the Dutch rule is based on two arguments. First, legal certainty requires that the applicability of the Bill be clearly defined when a contract is governed by foreign law, but is also connected with the Netherlands. Reference is then made to the celebrated *Alnati Case*[31] and Article 7 of the above-mentioned Obligations Convention. Secondly, the interests of international trade should be safeguarded: neither foreign firms doing business on the Dutch market nor Dutch exporters should be obliged to comply with the Bill. In other words, the Bill should be reserved for domestic transactions only. The approach is comparable to that of section 27(1) in the British Act, to which the Explanatory Memorandum explicitly refers.[32]

3.4 Interim comparative remarks

In a brief evaluation and comparison of the rules governing the national scope of the legislation, various similarities and dissimilarities come to light. As to their substantive ambit, two major restrictions must be emphasized: the British Act exempts international supply contracts from the scope of its application and the Dutch Bill's overriding rule is confined to commercial transactions. In contrast, the German rules governing the international scope apply only to contracts to which a consumer is a party.

28. Author's translation.

29. OJ of the EC of 9 October 1980, No. L 266/1; see further *infra*, ch. 4.1.

30. Doc. 16 983 No. 3, at 66–67.

31. HR 13 May 1966, NJ 1967, 3, 15 NILR (1968), p. 82 note Deelen, Rev. crit. d.i.p. 1967, p. 522 note Struycken, Clunet 1969, p. 1010.

32. See *supra*, n. 30. The memorandum mistakenly refers to s. 26 of the British Act, instead of s. 27.

The three texts all contain an *overriding rule,* which cancels a choice of foreign law by the parties. Furthermore, all these rules supersede foreign law that applies in the absence of a choice of law by the parties. The overriding rules apply, as regards the German and British Acts, if the case is connected with the respective country through the consumer's residence and the location of a substantial part of the formation of the contract. The Dutch Bill, in its turn, requires that both parties be established in the Netherlands.

In addition to overriding rules, the British and Dutch texts contain a *self-denying rule.* Both seek to free parties to a commercial contract, which has only slender ties with the country, from the burden of complying with the protective legal rules, a burden that would otherwise fall on them. The British regard an uncorroborated choice of the law of the United Kingdom per se as an insufficiently strong tie, the Dutch self-denial presupposes that neither of the parties has his principal place of business in the Netherlands. No such self-denying rule is contained in the German Act, which can be explained by the fact that the Act, in defining its international scope, is concerned with consumer adherents only.[33]

Another borderline has to be drawn in the case of the separate treatment of choice of law clauses, namely between the United Kingdom and Germany on the one hand, and the Netherlands on the other. The British overriding rule also prevails if a foreign law clause "evades" the Act. Similarly, under the German Act a foreign law clause is ineffective if it lacks a justifiable interest – a situation that, however confused its outer limits may be, certainly includes evasion of the Act itself.

A striking feature of all these rules is that they do not make any extra-territorial claims where *commercial transactions* are involved. In Britain and in the Netherlands the legislator feared a deterrent effect on international trade; hence the substantial exclusion of the control provisions. Both texts have gove too far, in my opinion, by also excluding hypotheses which do have a significant connection with the domestic economy. This applies to the British Act in that *all* international supply contracts are excluded from its ambit, [34] even if, e.g., a UK buyer is involved and a seller in the Netherlands, with delivery to be made from the latter's works to a port in England, as is the case in section 26(3) and (4)(a). Similarly, the Dutch Bill relinquishes its control if only one of the parties does not have its principal place of business in the country. Thus a Dutch party sells to a multinational company whose principal place of business is in Germany, when the contract is concluded in the Netherlands and the goods have to be transported from a Dutch warehouse to the Dutch subsidiary of the buyer. In a case like this, it is not easy to understand why the domestic standard terms controls should not be applied. At the very least the general test of reasonableness in either text

33. S. 24(1) provides, inter alia, that ss. 10 and 12 do not apply to commercial transactions.

34. Cf. the analysis in Imhoff-Scheier, *Protection du consommateur et contrats internationaux* (Etudes suisses de droit international, vol. 22), 1981, pp. 65–67, whose discussion of s. 26 and its relationship to s. 27(2) is, however, not entirely clear to me.

could have been retained, for this is flexible enough to be adapted to the special circumstances inherent in the international branch of trade concerned.

In the German Act the matter is somewhat different. Under section 24(2) the general test of unreasonable prejudice seems to apply to all commercial transactions and might then eventually render a choice of foreign law ineffective. Yet it had been argued that this section should be interpreted to apply only to contracts governed by German law.[35] Even if it were restricted in this way, this solution seems preferable to that of the two other texts, since it ties the applicability of the special control rules to the ordinary choice of law rules, instead of creating fresh self-denying rules. Where legislative intervention in standard contract terms is taking place nowadays in most of the surrounding countries, it cannot realistically be argued that international trade should be entitled to immunity. The Dutch self-denying rule is particularly striking, since it implies that compliance by all competitors with the control rules is not even attempted on the Dutch market. Why should a foreign-based competitor on that market be exempted from those rules, which the Dutch merchant is obliged to follow? (The Explanatory Memorandum would prefer this to be the case.)

The British exclusion of international supply contracts has yet another conseqence, namely that of excluding a range of *consumer transactions* with a foreign element, from the Act's protective rules. Indeed, whenever a consumer residing in the United Kingdom enters into a supply contract with a supplier whose place of business is in a different country, there is a fair chance that one of the cross-frontier elements listed in section 26(4) applies.[36] This is the case even if the contract simultaneously falls under the overriding rule of section 27(2), e.g., when the consumer took the essential steps for making the contract in the United Kingdom. In other words, in the absence of a clear indication in the Act to the contrary, it must be assumed that the exclusion in section 26 overrules the "overriding" rule in section 27(2).[37] If this interpretation is correct, it is a heavy blow to the underlying purpose of consumer protection in the Act. In my opinion, a similar situation under the 1973 Supply of Goods (Implied Terms) Act has therefore been justly criticized.[38] Whether the exception in section 26 can be regarded as being very narrow in scope, because it covers only contracts for the international supply of goods [39], is a matter of opinion. I would argue that it affects a major category of contracts in a way which is at odds with the general purpose of the Act.

The effect of the German conflict rules on consumer transactions was summarized earlier in this paragraph. Unfortunately, the overriding section 12 of the German Act does not explicitly claim that it applies to "foreign" contracts, but

35. Drobnig, *supra* n. 7, at 611–612.
36. See Cheshire and North, *supra* n. 23, at 233–234.
37. In this sense apparently Imhoff-Scheier, *supra* n. 34, at 67 and n. 51.
38. Hall, International sales and the Supply of Goods (Implied Terms) Act 1973, 22 ICLQ (1973), p. 740, at 744.
39. Thus Mann, 27 ICLQ (1978),at 664.

requires a sort of "cocktail" of the foreign law, in combination with parts of the Act to make the contract (at least) as fair as regards consumer interests as a "German" contract would be. Whether this exercise will really lead to a balanced contract remains to be seen.

In the Dutch Bill the regulation of conflicts aspects as regards consumer contracts is entirely omitted, bearing in mind the EEC Obligations Convention. Let us, therefore, turn to the international instruments.

4. CONVENTION RULES

The recently elaborated texts drawn up under the auspices of the EEC and the Hague Conference respectively, do not specifically deal with standard contracts in an international context. On the other hand, they do separate consumer transactions from commercial contracts for choice of law purposes. The texts were drafted more or less simultaneously and they reveal a mutual influence on each other. Both have a narrow substantive scope, confined to "certain" consumer contracts (in the relevant EEC rule), and sales (Hague Conference). This convergence is very desirable indeed, since all EEC countries are also members of the Hague Conference.

4.1 EEC Obligations Convention

In 1972 when a Preliminary Draft Convention on the law applicable to contractual and non-contractual obligations was prepared under the auspices of the EEC no specific provision was made for contracts concluded by consumers. During the additional preparations the need for such specific rules was voiced in academic writings [40] and eventually led to the insertion of a fresh rule, which is now Article 5 of the final text adopted in Rome on 19 June 1980.[41] The central paragraphs of this article state:

"2. Notwithstanding the provisions of Article 3 [freedom of choice of law by the parties], a choice of law made by the parties shall not have the result of depriving the consumer of the protection afforded to him by the mandatory rules of the law of the country in which he has his habitual residence
– if in that country the conclusion of the contract was preceded by a specific invitation addressed to him or by advertising, and he had taken in that country all the steps necessary on his part for the conclusion of the contract, or
– if the other party or his agent received the consumer's order in that country,

40. In particular see Lando, The EC Draft Convention on the Law Applicable to Contractual and Non-Contractual Obligations, RabelsZ 1974, p. 6; von Hoffmann, Uber den Schutz des Schwächeren bei internationalen Schuldverträgen, *ibid.*, p. 396.

41. Convention on the Law Applicable to Contractual Obligations, OJ of the EC of 9 October 1980, No. L 266/1; Report by Giuliano and Lagarde, OJ of 31 October 1980, No. C 282/1.

or
– if the contract is for the sale of goods and the consumer travelled from that country to another country and there gave his order, provided that the consumer's journey was arranged by the seller for the purpose of inducing the consumer to buy.

3. Notwithstanding the provisions of Article 4 [closest connection principle in absence of choice by the parties], a contract to which this Article applies, shall, in the absence of choice in accordance with Article 3, be governed by the law of the country in which the consumer has his habitual residence if it is entered into in the circumstances described in paragraph 2 of this Article."

The first paragraph of this Article defines the notion of a consumer contract. The formulation in paragraph 2 "shall not have the result of depriving the consumer of the protection afforded to him" shows that the aim of the rule is to provide a minimum legal protection. Thus, the extent of protection by the chosen law has to be compared to that of the mandatory rules laid down in Article 5 – a comparison that would be made in a specific case; this is shown by the use of the words "the consumer".

The Obligations Convention contains another provision that is also relevant in the present context, viz., Article 7, entitled "Mandatory rules":

"1. When applying under this Convention the law of a country, effect may be given to the mandatory rules of the law of another country with which the situation has a close connection, if and in so far as, under the law of the latter country, those rules must be applied whatever the law applicable to the contract. In considering whether to give effect to these mandatory rules, regard shall be had to their nature and purpose and to the consequences of their application or non-application.

2. Nothing in this Convention shall restrict the application of the rules of the law of the forum in a situation where they are mandatory irrespective of the law otherwise applicable to the contract."

A previous formulation of this rule in the 1972 Draft had provoked much criticism from experts in private international law.[42] It may be true, as the Explanatory Report states, that the wording has been considerably improved, but even as it stands now, the rule is open to a number of criticisms.[43] It is significant, in this respect, that at the last moment before the Convention was opened for signature in Rome, a reservation regarding the application of this Article 7 had to be provided for.[44]

42. See above all, Lando, von Hoffmann and Siehr (eds.), *European Private International Law of Obligations* (1975), passim, and especially Drobnig, Comments on Art. 7 of the Draft Convention, p. 82; Batiffol, Le project de Convention CEE sur la loi applicable aux obligations contractuelles et non-contractuelles, Rev. trim. dr. eur. 1975, p. 181.

43. See, among others, Pocar, Kodification der Kollisionsnormen auf dem Gebiet des Vertragsrechts im Rahmen der Europäischen Gemeinschaften, RIW 1979, p. 384, at 391; North, The EEC Convention on the Law applicable to Contractual Obligations, J.Bus.L. 1980, p. 382, at 387; Haak, Nieuw internationaal overeenkomstenrecht, WPNR 1980, p. 865, at 902.

44. Art. 22(1)(a).

4.2 Hague Conference

On the initiative of the Scandinavian countries, the Hague Conference recommended at its Thirteenth Session in 1976 that the 1955 Convention of the law applicable to international sales be reconsidered, especially in view of a separate treatment of consumer sales.[45] On the basis of a preliminary draft elaborated in 1979, the Fourteenth Session, held in October 1980, adopted a set of articles on the law applicable to certain consumer sales, but left for a future decision the question whether these articles should be incorporated into a revised general sales convention, or whether they should be incorporated in a separate convention.[46] Article 5 exhaustively defines the situations in which the special rules apply, and it does so in a similar way to Article 5(2) of the EEC Obligations Convention. The first situation is where

> "the negotiations for the sale were conducted mainly in the country in which the consumer then had his habitual residence and the consumer there took the steps necessary on his part for the conclusion of the contract;"

The other three situations correspond to the second section (order received in the consumer's country), first section (marketing and acceptance in consumer's country) and third section (sales promotion trip) of Article 5(2) of the Obligations Convention.

The first choice of law rule, Article 6, provides for party autonomy but adds that this shall not "deprive the consumer of the protection afforded by the mandatory rules" of the law of his habitual residence. Again, this is in complete harmony with the opening words of Article 5(2). However the second paragraph of Article 6 is a new provision: "The choice of law must be express and in writing". This marks a departure from the 1955 Convention, which allows an implicit choice of law as well as an explicit choice in writing. The Explanatory Report to the 1979 Draft (also containing this requirement) by von Mehren, states on this matter: "[t]he experts were of the view that stipulations for governing law were more problematical in consumer contracts than in contracts generally, and, therefore, should never be implied."[47]

If the parties have not chosen the applicable law, the law of the consumer's habitual residence applies, just as in Article 5(3) of the Obligations Convention.

5. IS THERE A NEED FOR SPECIAL RULES ON INTERNATIONAL SCOPE?

The above survey of special rules on international scope may well raise various questions of interpretation, of delimitation and, indeed, of possible interaction.

45. *Actes et Documents*, 1976-I, p. 36.
46. See the Final Act, p. 34, reproduced in 27 NILR (1980), p. 408.
47. Prelim. Doc. No. 2, June 1979, p. 28.

The national rules vary considerably, from the overriding German ones, to their partly self-denying British counterparts and the Dutch anticipation of the EEC Obligations Convention: *tot leges, quot solutiones.* While the EEC and Hague Conference rules do not differ materially in their structure, the substantive scope of the former is much larger than that of the latter.

By way of conclusion, I will go into one question here, concerning the merits of special rules on international scope in standard terms control statutes, which derogate from the ordinary conflict rules. As indicated above, I do not welcome this separate treatment for *commercial contracts.* When a contract of this type can be considered as "foreign" or "international" this should not result in abandoning the application of the domestic controls. It would be better if attention were paid to that eventuality *when applying the rules,* e.g., in the case of the British Act, by means of the appropriate guidelines prescribed by the legislator.[48] In the Dutch Bill too the general criterion for the appraisal of standard terms refers to "the circumstances of the case" [49], which may well include, for instance, the question whether a foreign party could anticipate a typically "Dutch" contract term, common only among Dutch traders.

The case of *consumer contracts* containing unreasonable terms is different. Here too, it would be preferable, on principle, to let the application of the control legislation follow a general conflict rule for consumer contracts, but such a rule has not yet actually come into existence in the three countries concerned. It is true that in academic literature growing opposition is found to the full application of the general contractual choice of law rules – i.e., party autonomy or the law of the most closely connected country – to typical consumer contracts, such as sales for private use or consumption, small loans and insurance contracts, contracts to hire services.[50] The same line of thought is being applied to standard contracts more generally (therefore including standardized commercial contracts), as it is based on the assumption of unequal bargaining power.[51] It is equally true, however, that even in those countries where the case for consumer or, for that matter, adherents' protection is fostered most strongly in domestic law, case law concerning transnational consumer transactions, whether or not also they involve adhesion contracts, is almost completely absent. For example, Drobnig noted that

48. See Schedule No. 2, under c: "(regard is to be had) whether the customer knew or ought reasonably to have known of the existence and the extent of the term (having regard, among other things, to any custom of the trade and any previous course of dealing between the parties)".

49. Art. 2.2(a) of the proposed new title.

50. See von Hoffmann, *supra* n. 40; Vischer, The Antagonism between Legal Certainty and the Search for Justice in the Field of Contracts, 129 Recueil des Cours (1974 II), p. 1, 42–44; Lando, *International Encyclopedia of Comparative Law,* III, ch. 24 (Contracts), ss. 249–252; Kropholler, Das kollisionsrechtliche System des Schutzes der schwächeren Vertragspartei, RabelsZ 1978, p. 634.

51. See Ehrenzweig, Adhesion Contracts in the Conflict of Laws, 53 Colum.L.Rev. (1953) 1072; Jessurun d'Oliveira, Internationaal overeenkomstenrecht, Mededelingen Ned. Ver. Int. Recht no. 71 (1975), p. 71, 104, also in "Characteristic Obligation" In The Draft EEC Obligation Convention, 25 AJCL (1977), p. 303, 318; Vitta, *Diritto Internazionale Privato,* III (1975), pp. 429-435.

the German case law on the incorporation of standard terms relates to commercial contracts only[52]; some fifteen years of documentation of mainly unreported Dutch conflicts cases on contract law by the TMC Asser Institute has not discovered any case that can properly be classified as a consumer transaction[53]; a recent Swiss study on consumer protection and international contracts could only cite three or four relevant cases, decided in three different countries.[54] In attempting to explain this situation, a major point appears to be that disputes between consumers and their suppliers often do not reach the courts at all[55]; in fact they are settled out of court or simply not pushed through because of the small sum of money at stake.[56] Such practical considerations have an impact at the domestic level, but may be even more significant when an adherent to a standard consumer contract is faced with an adversary abroad, let alone when he also has to bring his action abroad.

If we exclude, for the moment, the element of the forum or fora where litigation could eventually follow, the question remains what types of contract we actually have in mind when speaking of (standard) consumer contracts with international aspects. In general terms, three types can be distinguished; first, the "home deal", where the consumer contracts in his own country with a foreign supplier who presented himself there; secondly, the "traveller's deal", where the transaction is local as seen from the supplier's position, the consumer being abroad when contracting; and thirdly, the "correspondence deal" where the transaction is concluded *inter absentes.*[57]

What would happen if no special rules existed either at a national level or on an international scale? In the first two categories, the transaction would, as a rule, appear to be most closely connected with the consumer's or the supplier's country, respectively. When a home deal is made, the supplier or his agent comes to the consumer and it is probable that the law of the latter's country of residence is suitable for application if no choice of law clause for another legal system is contained in the (standard) contract.[58] If, on the other hand, another law is chosen, probably the law of the supplier's place of business, I consider that, once the forum's conflict rules permit the choice of that law, it would primarily be for that law (i.e., its relevant provisions on the formation and effects of contracts) to say whether the clause was validly incorporated

52. Drobnig, *supra* n. 7, at 609 n. 77.
53. Based on the author's research.
54. Imhoff-Scheier, *supra* n. 34, at 56-58.
55. In this sense also see Sealy, The Unfair Contract Terms Act 1977, 37 Camb.L.J. (1978), p. 15, at 20.
56. Cf. on the settlement by arbitration Hondius' contribution to this volume.
57. Cf. for the first two types, Lombois, Report on French private international law, in La protection du consommateur, 24 Travaux de l'Association Henri Capitant (1973), p. 441, at 456; Duintjer Tebbens, *International Product Liability* (1979), p. 367; Sauveplanne, Het toepasselijk recht op de internationale koop van roerende lichamelijke zaken, NJB 1979, p. 693, at 699.
58. Cf. Art. 3(2) of the 1955 Hague Sales Convention.

into the contract and is enforceable.[59] Should the contract eventually give rise to a dispute that is decided by litigation in the consumer's country, the forum would in any event have the public policy weapon at hand, enabling it to substitute its own standard terms control rule for the foreign provisions, where these fall short of the forum's fundamental standards.

Conversely, when it is the consumer who travels abroad to the supplier's country, one may readily assume that the latter's law will prevail, either by a choice of law clause or as objectively applicable law. For it seems reasonable that a person who takes advantage of a foreign market to buy, should expect to be subject to that market's legal standards, irrespective of whether such a person is a consumer or not.

It is particularly the third category of correspondence deals which is neglected in the existing choice of systems of national law. In addition, it was this type of (sales) contract that emerged in a preliminary study for the revision of the 1955 Hague Sales Convention, as being most in need of regulation.[60] Accordingly, all the national and international rules reviewed in this paper provide for a rule on this type of contract, with the sole exception of the Dutch Bill.

In the EEC and Hague Conference texts the special rules also extend to yet another activity, falling outside the tripartite distinction outlined above, viz., organized trips abroad for the purpose of inducing the party to purchase certain goods.[61] This sales practice is probably peculiar to Germany, where it is known as "*Kaffeefahrten*", and little known elsewhere.[62] In my opinion, such commercial practices are more appropriately regulated by legislation in the country whose consumers are affected.

Surprisingly, the three national texts pay hardly any attention to choice of court clauses in standard terms. Only the Dutch Bill has such clauses on its black list, but is doubtful whether derogation from the jurisdiction of Dutch courts in favour of a foreign court, is included in this rule.[63] Nevertheless, choice of court clauses form a serious potential obstacle for the consumer adherent to enforce his rights under the contract, particularly where the courts in the various countries are so differently guided by their respective legislators as is demonstrated by the German, British and Dutch examples. However, the problem will be considerably reduced for the Common Market countries when the amended EEC Judgments Convention enters into force.[64] Under the amended Section 4 of the Convention, entitled "Jurisdiction over consumer contracts", it will be practically ensured

59. Cf. Duintjer Tebbens, *supra* n. 57, at 168 and Stoll's discussion, *supra* n. 7, at 767-772; see also Arts. 3(4) and 8(1) of the EEC Convention.

60. See Prelim. Doc. No.1, January 1979, by Pelichet, p. 18-19, 24.

61. Art. 5(2) *in fine* of the EEC Convention, Art. 5(4) of the Hague text.

62. The term is referred to in the commentaries on the AGB-Gesetz.

63. Art. 3 sub p of the proposed new title.

64. See for the text of the amended Convention, OJ of the EC, No. L 304/77 of 30 October 1978.

that the consumer is always entitled to bring proceedings in the country of his domicile.[65]

6. CONCLUDING REMARKS

Where do the doubts, briefly outlined in the previous chapter, leave us with regard to the special rules which aim at maximizing the protection of adherents to standard contracts? The rules abound, but cases are very few. In examining the ways in which the national legislators seek to reach the contract adherents whom they wish to protect, one cannot help feeling that little credit is given *a priori* to the potential ability of a foreign legal system to protect those persons. In Western Europe, where the nations live so close together and share many of their economic and social vicissitudes, such enlightened xenophobia would be regrettable. Where, in addition, the choice of law rules for contracts are being harmonized and rendered more flexible in themselves, as in the case of the EEC Obligations Convention, this might lead us to rely more on the substantive law to which we are thus referred. If that law – *ex hypothesi* foreign – is not sufficiently strong with regard to its consumer or adherent protection, then a court in that party's country may justly use the shield of public policy and substitute its own law.

Zweigert's appeal to remedy the lack of social values in the conflict of laws,[66] echoed by many others [67], has certainly proved influential and is repeated, inter alia, in the EEC and Hague Conference texts. Yet, the multilateral special rules for consumer contracts have such a limited scope, that their practical significance is bound to be rather restricted.[68] The deviation of such special rules from the general conflict of laws rules for contracts – even when the latter have already been supplemented by escape devices such as contained in the EEC text [69] – raises various fresh problems of interpretation and application. The above survey of national standard terms statutes has shown that similar problems can arise when special scope rules are drafted in a national context.

However laudable it may be to enhance the protection of weaker parties in the conflict of laws, we should at the same time remember that "Law is not only made for deciding cases in the court, but also for avoiding court suits. Conflict law, too, must serve this goal."[70] It appears particularly appropriate to conclude on this practical note, for the eminent judge in whose honour this contribution was written, sought over so many years to match theoretical soundness with practical solutions of international disputes.

65. Art. 14(1).
66. Zweigert, Zur Armut des IPR an sozialen Werten, RabelsZ 1973, p. 435.
67. See the writers cited in n. 50.
68. Cf. North, *supra* n. 43, at 388, who considers the special rules for consumer contracts to be "a new and not wholly desirable development".
69. See, e.g., Arts. 3(3) and 4(5) of the EEC Convention.
70. Vischer, *supra* n. 50, at 53.

TOWARDS A SYSTEM OF EQUITABLE STANDARDS IN THE NEW DUTCH CIVIL CODE

by J.L.M. Elders*

After the Second World War, the Dutch civil code, dating from 1838, was generally considered to be outdated. In the course of its existence, many gaps, particularly in the field of civil obligation law, have had to be filled by the judiciary. The result was that Dutch civil law could no longer be understood from the existing civil code as its authors originally intended, but only by studying a comprehensive number of judicial decisions over a long period. Therefore, by a decree in council of 25 April 1947, the famous Leyden civil lawyer, Professor E.M. Meyers was commissioned to draft a new civil code. After his death in 1954, his work was continued by a triumvirate and later completed, with the exception of the books concerning special contracts. On 1 January 1970, the first book of the "new code", hereafter referred to as NBW *(Nieuw Burgerlijk Wetboek)* concerning personal and family law, entered into force, followed in 1976 by Book 2, containing the new corporation law. In 1980, Books 3, 5 and 6, containing general principles of property, possession, obligation law, contract and tort, were enacted by parliament and are expected to enter into force in 1985. Equitable standards as a kind of open texture rules are not unknown in the present civil code. Concepts like "good faith" in contractual relations[1] and "unlawful conduct" as a ground for tort liability[2] have been given a much broader application by the judiciary in this century than in the first sixty years of the code's existence. It should not be forgotten that in Dutch statute law, law and equity are united into one system though priority is given to rules of strict law. On the other hand, the judiciary has been elaborating a significant number of new rules to supplement the legal system. The introduction, however, of Books 3, 5 and 6 of the NBW will bring about a considerable extension of the scope and the application of equitable principles, as we will see below. [3] From this it follows that the task of the judge in litigation will be considerably complicated because the courts will have to balance the interests of the parties in a growing number of cases before rendering judgment, while the decision itself will be subject to a far greater variety of possible solutions. When comparing the present

* Former Vice-President of the District Court of Rotterdam, currently Professor of Civil Law at the University of Maastricht.

1. See: sections 1374 and 1375 of the present civil code, hereafter referred to as CC.
2. See: *Onrechtmatige daad,* Kluwer, Deventer, containing a comprehensive review of case law in this field.
3. Hartkamp, *Compendium van het vermogensrecht volgens het nieuwe burgerlijk wetboek,* Kluwer 1977; Schoordijk, *Het algemeen gedeelte van het verbintenissenrecht naar het nieuw burgerlijk wetboek,* Kluwer 1979; Hartkamp, Open normen, in het bijzonder de redelijkheid en billijkheid in het nieuw BW, WPNR 5559.

code and the new one with regard to the effect of the above mentioned equitable principles, we will have to ask which are the differences with regard to the rules as such, and with regard to the range of their application. Until now, the equitable principles underlying the concepts of "good faith" and "unlawful conduct" have been regarded by some authors as being more or less in the same vein.[4] When the new code enters into force, the judge will meet with a greater variety of equitable standards and this means greater difficulty in formulating the grounds to justify his decision. Even now it is sometimes asserted that an equitable decision cannot be justified by legal reasoning.[5] Therefore, in view of the increasing importance of open texture rules in the new code, it might be useful to examine the question whether a distinction can be made among these standards when they are applied. If it can, the danger of an arbitrary judgment could possibly be reduced and the process of judicial reasoning improved. When the legislator restricts himself to open rules, the judge will sometimes have to formulate minor rules by which he may reach his final judgment and which at the same time may justify his conclusion.[6] Possibly the different equitable standards will be united into one system in order to maintain a better balance between law and equity.

1. ABUSE OF POWER

The first new legal rule of conduct refers to the exercise of rights by forbidding the abuse of legal rights, be it a proprietary right or a procedural right, and it is to be found in section 8 of the preliminary title of the NBW. This rule belongs essentially to the general moral principles of human conduct. Section 8 reads: "The abuse of power is prohibited. A power is presumed to be abused if it is used with the sole intention of damaging another person or for a purpose other than it was granted for, or if it is used in such a way that considering the disproportion between the interest to be served and the damage to be caused, a reasonable man would not have exercised his power or right. A power, which is by definition discretionary, cannot be abused." With this new legal provision, although it is not yet in force, the important court-created law concerning the abuse of rights has been codified in a comprehensive way. The principle behind this provision can be qualified as the standard of reasonableness and it may be applied in every situation where a person is entitled to make use of his right or power in accordance with the law in a case where no special relationship of confidence exists between the parties concerned. One cannot expect that the entitled party will put his interests to be served by the right in question on a level with the interests of strangers who might be injured by his acting in conformity with his right, because

4. Hage, Over de betekenis van vage termen als goed trouw, redelijkheid en billijkheid, WPNR 5579.

5. Van Schendel, Toerekening, doorwerking, partij, WPNR 5561 et seq., p. 256.

6. Van Schellen, Adequaat causaal verband en toerekening naar redelijkheid, in: *Non sine causa*, p. 342; J.H. Nieuwenhuis, *Drie beginselen van contractenrecht*, Kluwer 1979, p. 40 et seq.

this right is the source of his privilege. Only when the interests to be served are considerably inferior to the damage to be caused to a third person, a man will have to abstain from acting, unless where possible, due compensation can be offered. The standard of reasonableness demands that the entitled person acts with a lawful purpose and that his action can be conceived as a proper means to realise his purpose. A good example of this can be found in the decision of the Supreme Court in the *Kuipers* v. *de Jongh* Case. (HR 17-4-70, NJ 1971, 89). The owner of a garden sued his neighbour, who by mistake had built his garage partly on the adjacent grounds of the former, and he asked for the garage to be demolished. The Court considered that his claim should be dismissed if the damage caused by demolition considerably outweighed the value of the lost area, in which case the injured owner should have to be satisfied with a financial compensation if this were offered to him. Abuse may also occur in civil proceedings as such, the standard of reasonableness in this respect being enacted in section 3.11.8 NBW, which reads: "Without a sufficient interest nobody is allowed to sue in court". For example, the seizure of goods as a conservatory measure with permission of the President of the court, although formally legal, shall be lifted on request of the debtor if the seizure appears to lack reasonable interest. In all of the above-mentioned situations, the judge will have to balance the lawful interests of the parties concerned before he is able to decide, which means that the law is involved in the case. The most recent elaboration of the standard of reasonableness has been enacted in the draft law 16983 of 1981, completing chapter 5 of Book 6 NBW with regard to standard form contracts. A clause in a standard form contract may be declared void by the court when the said clause would bring forth other consequences than the contract would have had without the presence of the clause in such a degree that, taking into account the nature and purpose of the contract, the mutual interests of the parties and the circumstances of the case, it has to be regarded as an unreasonable aggravation for the customer. Therefore, not every inequality in the terms of a standard form contract will give grounds for a claim, but only such terms as are incompatible with reasonableness. From this it follows that unreasonableness does not mean the same as unfairness or injustice, because measured by the standards of strict equity or fairness, every clause by which the interests of just one of the parties are favoured ought to be subject to voidability. This draft law, however, does permit a businessman to protect his own interests by making standard terms which are more favourable to his interests than to those of his customer. In sections 3 and 4 of the law, there is a summary of the terms which are considered unreasonable. Generally speaking, the terms mentioned are wholly incompatible with the legal interests of the other party, for instance, by denying him the right to take evidence or to dissolve the contract.

2. PRINCIPLE OF REASONABLE IMPUTATION

Closely related to the standard of reasonableness, but different in its application and consequences, is the principle of reasonable imputation in case of tort. Section 1401 of the present code provides that every unlawful act causing damage to another makes the man by whose fault the damage has been caused, liable without any limit. Originally, the term "unlawful act" was understood as being contrary to written law, but in 1919 the Supreme Court adopted a broad conception of "unlawful" by considering as unlawful every act or omission contrary to propriety in commerce or social intercourse. In present law, tort liability has a strict character and is based (with a few exceptions) on fault, not on risk. Therefore small faults can produce unlimited liability, no moderation being allowed. Since the decision of 20 March 1970, NJ 1970, 251, the Supreme Court has no longer expounded a special theory of causality because the former doctrine of "foreseeability" proved to be unconvincing. One could argue that in legal reasoning, any causal theory may work as long as it is not contrary to common sense. The new code includes the results of some fifty years of court-created law. Section 6.3.1.1. reads: "He who commits an unlawful act against another person which is his fault, has to compensate for the damage caused by him." Unlawful acts are considered to be violations or rights, acts or omissions contrary to legal duty or to propriety in social intercourse pursuant to generally accepted rules of conduct, unless there are grounds for justification. The tortfeasor shall be liable if he can be blamed for his act or if it is due to a cause which legally or judged by common standards may be imputed to him. What is new in this provision is the reference to common standards of conduct, the introduction of risk liability and the possiblity of justification. [7] It seems clear that the task of the judge will become even more complicated because tort law will be less strict than it used to be. In a case of liability based on risk, the question is who shall be considered to bear the risk when both of the parties have taken risks, while the ascertaining of common standards by the judge seems open to many interpretations. No doubt, judicial practice will find its own way. In case of damage, caused by a motorcar for instance, in the present law, the fault of the driver has to be proved; in the new law, the driver of the car which made a wrong manoeuvre will be held liable unless he proves that the accident is exclusively due to an act of God. An important question is the care which may be required to prevent damage to other people in connection with the new possibility of justification of acts by which lawful interests are injured. In case of interests on the same level, the standard of conduct to be enforced may be based on strict reciprocity, a principle expressed in section 4 of the Dutch constitution, namely the right to equal protection of person and property. In case of special responsibility more extensive care may be required in proportion to the interests concerned. Section 6.3.1.5b reads: "the judge may dismiss a claim for an injunction to abstain from a proposed measure if the latter has to be allowed on the ground of important social interests. The injured person retains his claim for damages." Thus the decision by which justification is accepted, can (only) be given after a thorough weighing-up of the interests of both the litigants. Some authors have qualified the new system of tort liability as reasonable imputation, [8] because it is characterised by a larger degree of

7. Hartkamp, op. cit. no. 316.

8. Köster, *Causaliteit en voorzienbaarheid,* Bloembergen, *Schadevergoeding by onrechtmatige daad,* 1965; Van Schellen, *Juridische causaliteit,* Kluwer 1972.

judicial discretion. In this connection, another provision has to be mentioned, namely section 6.1.9.4, which provides that damages have to be paid if there is a close connection between tort and damage and this damage may be imputed to the tortfeasor regarding the nature of the damage and the character of his responsibility. Thus, if the connection between act and damage is not close enough, no obligation will be imposed, while when the injured person has contributed to the damage himself, the damages to be paid will be ordered proportionately. Section 6.1.9 12a allows the judge to mitigate a legal duty to pay compensation in case of tort, if the payment of complete damages would lead to unacceptable results in view of the nature of the responsiblity, the relation between the parties and their financial situation, but as this provision is an application of the standard of fairness, it will be dealt with later. According to Van Eikema Hommes, the new doctrine of reasonable imputation extends the limits of liability to a considerable degree and he would therefore like to maintain the present criterion of foreseeability of the damage as a strict condition for liability.[9] It must be admitted that the standard of reasonable imputation, being rather vague, does not in itself imply clear criteria for liability, but it should not be overlooked that section 6.3.1.1. of the new code implies strict conditions for tort liability. Where the new law permits the judge to limit liability on reasonable grounds in favour of the tortfeasor, it does not warrant criticism. On the other hand, where liability is based on risk, the same causality is required as in the case of fault. Apart from the fact that the tortfeasor need not necessarily be blamed for it, his conduct remains the *conditio sine qua non* for the damage caused, while this conduct, according to generally accepted standards of behaviour, has to be more closely connected with the risk of damage than the conduct of the victim. One could say that the authors of the new code chose a more pragmatic solution than that in the present code, where small faults (even when there is only the slightest question of moral reproof) may cause unlimited liability.

However, as we saw above, section 6.1.9.4 allows the judge to mitigate liability. One could therefore say that this provision is an application for a flexible version of the "thin skull" rule. The justification for this new provision is that if a man on his own behalf is risking damage which exceeds the normal risk of people in his position, he has to take measures to insure himself against this abnormal risk instead of assigning it to others, for there ought to be a proportionality between conduct and result. When the extent of responsiblity for damage has been assigned, it might transpire that the liable person is unable to pay the damages. In that case, section 6.1.9.12a permits the liability to be mitigated, as we mentioned above, but since this rule is an application of the principle of fairness per se, it will be dealt with below.

9. Van Eikema Hommes, Juridische causaliteit, redelijke toerekening en enige nieuwe rechtspraak van de Hoge Raad, in: *'t Exempel dwinght,* Zwolle 1975; Nuis, Differentiatie van de causaliteits/aansprakelijkheids criteria bij de onrechtmatige daad, WPNR 5555.

3. REASONABLENESS AND FAIRNESS

In the present law of contract, namely sections 1374(3) and 1375 BW, the term "good faith" expresses the principle of due performance of contractual obligations. Section 1374(3) reads: "Lawfully made contracts shall be performed in good faith". Section 1375 reads: "Contracts create obligations not only by virtue of their terms but also by virtue of the obligations to perform everything demanded by the nature of the contract, custom or equity." For many years, it has been disputed if good faith could suspend all or part of a contract. The Supreme Court held that good faith could fill the gaps in a contract, but not modify the agreed obligations of the parties. Since the decision of 1967, *Saladin* v. *H.B.U.* (H.R. 19-5-67, NJ 1967, 261) it is generally accepted that in particular circumstances, contractual clauses, though not illegal, can be put aside on grounds of equity. In the new code, the term "good faith" has been replaced by the words "reasonableness and fairness" which according to the official explanation, have the same meaning as the term "good faith".[10] This equitable standard has been enacted in section 6.1.1.2 which reads: "Parties to a contract are bound to behave in accordance with the demands of reasonableness and fairness", hereafter abbreviated as "r.a.f.". One might ask whether the words "reasonableness" and "fairness" each have a meaning of their own or if they have more or less the same definition. Sometimes it is argued that these concepts can only be defined arbitrarily, but I do not think this is the case.[11] In dealing with the concept of reasonableness as expressed in legal terminology, it seems to be possible to define it, because reason is the foundation for all law. To summarise what has been said above, reasonableness by definition excludes arbitrariness because it is closely akin to common sense in daily life. Reasonable conduct is acting on behalf of legitimate personal interests without completely ignoring the legitimate interests of other people. However, the question whether an act or omission in law can meet the demands of fairness cannot be answered in general terms but has to be related to the results of the act or omission and it may also depend on the legal relation existing between the parties concerned. Generally speaking, people will then consider themselves to have been treated unfairly or unjustly only when they had grounds to expect different behaviour towards them, but it is especially the unfair result which will affect them. By using a hendiadys, i.e., "reasonableness and fairness", both concepts acquire a somewhat different meaning, something more than plain reasonableness and a little less than complete fairness. Langemeyer, a former Attorney General, said that the standard of "r.a.f." between contracting parties demands from both a stronger respect for their mutual interests than may be required between strangers.[12] The application of the expression "r.a.f." in the new code, particularly in sections 6.1.1.2, 6.5.3.1. and 6.5.3.11, indicates that this standard governs the relations of confidence, pre and post contractual relations and partnership. There-

10. Parlementaire geschiedenis van het nieuwe burgerlijk wetboek, ad 6.1.1.2.
11. Hage, op.cit.
12. Langemeyer, *De Gerechtigheid in ons burgerlijk vermogensrecht*, p. 111.

fore we may state that by virtue of this principle (in the above-mentioned relations), people have to behave according to a reasonable standard of fairness. In other words, parties in relations of confidence, have to take care of each others' interests in a more specific way than they would have to if they were only exercising their own rights. It would be going too far to say that their relations and obligations are ruled completely by equity. That would be more than could be expected from the average contracting parties who are (only) motivated by their own considerations when entering into a contract. Another argument for this is to be found in the general section of the new code. This applies insofar as the so called "justum pretium" doctrine has not been enacted, although the application of equitable standards has been broadened a good deal. As in the present law, people remain free within the limits of the law to decide about the contents of their agreements without observing proportionality between performance and the service in return. Whether a party in a contract receiving the agreed consideration derives any profit from it or whether it is adequate compared with the consideration he is giving, is immaterial as long as he entered into the contract itself in a legal manner. Section 6.1.1.2. expresses a twofold rule which can be defined as the positive and the negative function of r.a.f. As noted above, the first paragraph of this section states that both the creditor and the debtor are to act in conformity with the demands of reasonableness and fairness, which is the positive function of this rule. In determining the degree of effort required by the interests of a partner in a contract, the interests of the latter have to be taken into consideration, where it is not on equal terms. The second paragraph of section 6.1.1.2. reads: "A rule or clause between parties, based on statute law, custom or contract shall not be applied if this would be unacceptable on grounds of r.a.f.". This may be called the negative function of this standard.[13] The use of the word "unacceptable" in this paragraph clearly shows that this provision may be applied only to marginal cases where reasonable people would agree that the result for one of the parties is such that no one could be expected to accept it. The judge must decide in every individual case if there are sufficient grounds for applying the limiting force of r.a.f., but how can he avoid arbitrariness? In the present code, section 1486 provides that in case of loss of consideration, no one may ask to be discharged from his obligations except in cases of duress, error, fraud or undue influence, i.e., when there was no free consent. The Roman law action "laesio ultra dimidium vel enormis", the classical remedy if a party to an onerous contract had been injured to the extent of more than one half of the contractual interest, has never been accepted in Dutch law. However, since the new code introduces the limiting force of r.a.f., the "laesio enormis" rule could be used as a standard to decide whether an agreed performance has to be accomplished when the interests are out of balance. According to this remedy, losses which exceed one half of the interest in question may be reduced to one half of the countervalue of the original consideration. The justification of this limitation can be based on the

13. On the limiting force of r.a.f. see: Abas, *Beperkende werking van de goede trouw*, Kluwer 1972, pp. 177 – 203.

argument that if losses amounting to half of the value of the consideration have to be accepted, there are no grounds for restoring more than half of the loss of the original value. Of course, this "emergency" standard has to give way in cases where the law or the terms of the contract provide otherwise. This may be the case when the performance is indivisible or when a more favourable solution has been agreed upon. The importance of this standard becomes clear when claims for debts are concerned. According to section 6.1.9a, an obligation to pay a certain amount of money has to be settled nominally unless statute law, custom or contract provide otherwise. From this it follows that inflation, unless one of the above-mentioned exceptions exists, even in case of long term monetary obligations, is not regarded as a sufficient ground for changing the terms of the contract. However, the limiting force of r.a.f. may play a part if the loss can no longer be accepted; this might be the case when less than half of the original value remains. The justification for this intervention can also be based in a number of cases on section 6.5.3.11 which reads: "The court may on the request of one of the parties adapt, or partly or wholly dissolve a contract on the ground that there has been no foresight as regards fundamental change in circumstances, so that the creditor may not hold the debtor to the terms of the contract when this would be contrary to r.a.f." The following example clarifies this. Inflation as such has become a never ending process in most economies, so that when people lend money, they have to take into account the decrease in value of the loan over the years. However if inflation increases beyond reasonable expectation, the hard and fast rule of nominalism which takes no account of inflation may be put aside by the equitable standard of r.a.f. In balancing the interests of creditor and debtor, the judge could use the so-called "comparative" method, introduced by Justice G.J. Wiarda, former president of the Supreme Court. In this method fictional results are compared which would either be accepted or no longer accepted (according to general standards). The result of the case if no modification took place, is then compared with these fictional cases. If the former most resembles the non-accepted result, the judge will adapt the obligation in question. [14] We may conclude by stating that the standard of r.a.f. constitutes a fair compromise between party autonomy and equity.

4. THE EQUITABLE STANDARD OF FAIRNESS

A legal definition of fairness can be found in section 7 of the preliminary title of the new code which reads: "In determining what corresponds to fairness one has to consider the generally recognised principles of law, common opinions about law held by the Dutch people, and the social and personal interests involved in the case." Although this definition will not be enacted into the new code, one cannot deny its importance for the judicial process in civil law. The areas where

14. Wiarda, *Drie typen van rechtsvinding*, Tj. Willink 1980, p. 97 et seq.

fairness must play a part, are indicated in this definition where reference is made to objective criteria and adherence to the facts, considered from an intersubjective point of view. Finally, fairness requires an exact balance of the interests in question and the harmonisation of the results in an equal manner. In a number of cases this equitable standard is expressed in a specific way. Thus, section 1576t CC provides that when a hire-purchase contract is dissolved, a complete settlement has to take place to prevent the seller from having more profit in case of dissolution than he would have had if the contract had been performed pursuant to its terms. According to section 38 of the Land Lease Act, the judge has to decide when the parties disagree about prolonging the contract, by balancing the social and economic interests of the farmer and the landlord. The contract has to be prolonged when a dismissal of the farmer's claim would affect the basis of his economic existence while the loss of the personal use of the land would not have the same consequences for the landlord. From this it becomes clear that a decision, exclusively based on fairness, depends on the results for the parties in dispute and not on their conduct. Formerly equitable decisions were regarded as exceptions to a legal rule in a special case to mitigate its severity, but in the new code, some general rules of equity have been enacted. The first can be found in section 6.4.3.1., and deals with unjust enrichment. This new provision has created an obligation to repay when a person has unjustly obtained a benefit at the expense of another person. Repayment is due to the amount of financial gain to the extent that this is considered reasonable.

The use of the term "reasonable" applies in cases where the enriched person played no part in his enrichment. This may justify a smaller restitution, if any at all.[15] In other cases, complete restitution will be ordered. Section 6.1.9.12a provides that if granting complete damages in tort liability would lead to unacceptable consequences, with regard to the nature of the responsibility, the relation between the parties and their respective financial resources, the judge may moderate the obligation to pay damages. In this provision too, the new code has not elaborated a standard of reference but the judge will have to decide in a fair manner. This might imply that the damages will have to be levelled until both the tortfeasor and injured party are in an equal position. If this equal position appears to be contrary to fairness, the basic needs of the tortfeasor still have to be safeguarded provided that the same interests of the injured person in this respect are safeguarded.

5. SUMMARY

From a comparison of the different equitable standards discussed, namely reasonableness, reasonable imputation, reasonableness and fairness and fairness per se, it transpired that they should relate to situations which can be distinguished

15. Parlementaire geschiedenis ad 6.4.3.1.

in law. In this serial order, they represent a number of standards which increasingly promote actual equality. The greatest contrast seems to be between reasonableness on the one hand and fairness per se on the other hand, while proportionality in liability, as a result of reasonable imputation and reasonableness and fairness in contracts, falls between the two. Thus, when they are combined into one system of open texture rules, an interaction may take place which enables us to say that in the new code equity is not embodied by merely one rule but by the system of law itself.[16]

16. Crombach, *de Wijkerslooth;* Cohen, *Een theorie van rechterlijke beslissingen,* especially p. 91 where the authors state that equity corresponds with the consistence of the legal system.

INTERNATIONAL LAW AND SUBNATIONAL INTERGOVERNMENTAL LAW: SOME RELATIONSHIPS

by Wesley L. Gould*

Is it possible that public international law has relevance for the relations among entities other than those endowed with international personality? This matter is explored below with limited attention to normative content, since dealing therewith entails a far-reaching search into reports of national judicial decisions and other legal materials that cannot be compressed into available time and space.

Whenever two or more collectivities, each capable of exercising some measure of autonomous decisionmaking, aim their policymaking or administrative activities at the same target, the potential for conflict or cooperation is likely to transform itself into one of these relationships or into a mixture of both. A mixture is possible in both internal and external forms because the several agencies within one complex organization (e.g., a state, a corporation, a supranational organization) may cooperate with or struggle against each other individually or in coalitions,[1] just as can happen between two organizations and their agencies. In the latter case, there may or may not be an umbrella organization possessing at least nominal and/or rhetorical authority over the subject-matter in actual or potential dispute.

Despite empires and despite the old papal claim to be arbiter between princes, most of the history of international relations is the history of autonomous governments, jealous of their unfettered authority, often exercised without wisdom for which a lengthy trail of vanished sovereign entities provides evidence. The historical system of international relations was characterized by Charles Dupuis as an "anarchy of sovereignties."[2] It is likely that, despite various international and transnational organizations, Dupuis's phrase is even more pertinent today in circumstances of (a) bigness, specialization of function and knowledge, (b) even unitary systems displaying effective decisionmaking at a level lower than the theoretically supreme hierarchical authority,[3] and (c) territorially restricted governments attempting to

* Professor, Wayne State University, Detroit, Michigan.

1. See T. Mathiesen, *Across the Boundaries of Organizations* (Oslo, 1971), esp. pp. 97 - 103 on the problems of those engaged in external communications when they attempt to disseminate information within an agency.

2. Ch. Dupuis, *Le droit des gens et les rapports des grandes Puissances avec les autres États avant le pacte de la Société des Nations* (Paris, 1921) p. 7.

3. For a conceptualization of legal systems as reflections of a society's subgroups so that a multiplicity of legal systems exist, perhaps in conflict, with no guarantee that the center of power is at the level of the most inclusive social group, see L. Pospisil, "Legal Levels and Multiplicity of Legal Systems in Human Society," 11 *Journal of Conflict Resolution* 1967 pp. 2 - 26.

set bounds to the decisionmaking capacities of multinational corporations, labelled "nonterritorial governments" by the geographer, Robert B. McNee.[4]

Anarchy, whether that arising in part from slow and too little transportation and communication or, more recently, that attributable to speed and information overload combined with complexity and technical specialization, need not necessarily be a nonsystem. As long as there is a network of more than occasional, *ad hoc*, relationships and even if for practical (or, perhaps, accidental) reasons important internal decisions and/or external communications, negotiations, and agreement-making occur at lower hierarchical levels or, in the case of states, at subnational levels, there exists a system of relatively durable relationships among actors performing functions in separate entities with decisionmaking capacity. Durability both gives rise to and is a product of rules regulating behaviour – rules that need not have their origin in acts of governments, territorial or nonterritorial, but can arise from private actions and expectations to which governments react prohibitively or permissively. Some of the resultant rules take on, with time (e.g., custom) or upon completion of formal legislative procedures, the characteristics of law. Public international law is one such set of rules and in the present context should be seen as the form of intergovernmental law formulated out of the longest experience with and study of the relations among autonomous governments.

Public international law need not be the only segment of law that deals with relations among entities possessing some measure of autonomy. Confining attention to public entities, one finds that not only international relations but also interstate, interprovincial, inter-county, and intermunicipal relations are components of that field of study known as "intergovernmental relations." The inclusion of international relations goes beyond the usual usage of the term "intergovernmental relations" as employed in studies of interactions of subnational entities either with each other or with a senior level of government within or outside the hierarchy to which a particular junior level belongs. Nevertheless, as indicative of the propriety of including international relations, and so international law, in the field of intergovernmental relations, F. Kenneth Berrien's examination of conflict between systems relied largely upon studies of international relations.[5]

Since, among interacting autonomous entities, there arise rules for behaviour effective within the range of autonomy, it would seem that there is such a thing as intergovernmental law of which public international law is a segment potentially applicable but, in a particular jurisdiction, not necessarily applied in disputes among subnational governments.[6] Moreover, Berrien's resort to studies of international relations while analyzing conflict in general and social systems suggests that there may be such a thing as intersystem law, that is, a law generalizeable to a variety of non-

4. R.B. McNee, "Central-Centripetal Forces in International Petroleum Regions," 51 *Annals, Association of American Geographers* 1961 pp. 124-138.

5. F.K. Berrien, *General and Social Systems* (New Brunswick, N.J., 1968), ch. X.

6. On the possibilities in Australia, despite judicial decisions seeming to suggest that there are no rules peculiar to intergovernmental relations other than those relevant to the exercise of political or governmental powers, see Enid Campbell, "Suits Between the Governments of a Federation," 6 *Sydney Law Review* 1971 pp. 326, 331, 334.

hierarchical relations among human systems. Lord Stowell seemed at least to recognize the possibility when he accepted the validity of a law of nations among the Barbary States that, within their region, differed from the law of nations applicable to inter-European transactions.[7] However, the possibility of thinking in terms of intersystem law will not be pursued here because to think in such terms would overextend the topic to embrace the private sector.

At this point the question ought to be asked on what basis, other than the common factor that governments have decisionmaking capacities, can international relations and law be linked with subnational relations and law. Today's subnational units exist in systems that have both supreme authorities who speak for the whole and superior levels of law that, presumably, take precedence over the laws, ordinances, and by-laws of subnational units except in so far as constitutional law assigns control of certain functions to subnational units as, for example, the Canadian constitution does in respect to municipal affairs and resources within the provinces. In such cases, agreements reached through bargaining and negotiation become necessary if national policy and related law are to emerge. The outcome of internal diplomacy can be something akin to treaty law. Furthermore, where gaps in the law exist or arise through an evolution productive of unanticipated activities, it may be that an internal law derived from international law may emerge to control certain subnational intergovernmental relations. Thus, the Federal Constitutional Court of West Germany could comment: "Even in a federal union, relations between member states are governed, in the absence of federal constitutional regulation, by the rules of international law."[8]

What this seems to mean is that law as a process exists in structures not necessarily hierarchical and not necessarily complete even when some units are supposed to be subordinate to a larger system. Moreover, it means that because legal systems are attached to and operate within structures of relationships, some of them intergovernmental, conflicts between governments can take on the character of conflicts between laws. For processes, as distinguished from procedures which are the formalized ways of doing things, operate within structures with the peculiarities of structures being significant among the variables productive of outputs. In a simplified example, digestion in a dog produces different results from digestion in humans.

Turning to structure while bearing in mind that legal system structures essentially parallel governmental and broader political structures, note can be taken of some types of system structure within which law functions. At the national level, unitary systems, federal systems, and confederations have been sufficiently discussed in the literature to render recapitulation here unnecessary. So have the variations within each of these classifications and the changes within particular systems in response to changing economic, sociological, and technological environments. The direction of change may be in one direction in one system and in the

7. *The Hurtige Hane* (1801) 3 C. Rob. 324; *The Helena* (1801) 4 C. Rob. 3 at 6; *The Madonna del Burso* (1802) 4 C. Rob. 169 at 172.
8. 1973 *Neue Juristische Wochenschrift* p. 1539 at 1542, col. 2.

opposite direction in an otherwise similar system. For example, an examination of the British North America Act and the United States Constitution could lead one to the belief that Canada would have become increasingly centralized while the United States, in light of the Tenth Amendment, would have become increasingly decentralized, especially as new problem areas were perceived. But in both countries, with the help of judicial decisions rendered amid competition between governments for primacy, the evolution has been basically in the opposite direction from what the respective constitutions suggest.

What has just been said about federations is not wholly without relevance to unitary systems. Aside from the fact that even in a unitary system, such as that of England, both hostile and cooperative relationships develop among counties, municipalities, and other units of local government, at any stage of their history subnational units may, under organic acts of constitutional quality, enjoy considerable authority, albeit at the risk of greater central government encroachment in response, for example, to gross overspending by local authorities [9] that can be countered only by effective political action at the national level.[10]

Moreover, whatever the degree of autonomy accorded local governments by an organic act such as England's Local Government Reorganization Act of 1972, a court challenge could raise the issue of whether a particular local government action, perhaps a by-law, is *ultra vires.*[11] Even if the question of prevalence is pre-determined in favor of national law, it still lies within judicial discretion to ascertain whether a conflict between rules of two legal systems exists. It is not beyond the competence of courts to read seemingly obvious conflicts out of existence.[12]

Confederation, however formally titled, bears the closest resemblance to the traditional structure of international relations in that, although organizations, most of the vital policy and lawmaking decisions are taken not at the center but at what, for the sake of generality, may be termed the regional level. Of the three basic types of governmental organization, this is the only one, other than historical empires, that has been established among nations. The international law approach to the problems of conflicts of legal systems would seem to be appropriate for confederations were it not for three factors: (1) the constitutive agreement is not an ordinary treaty but one with constitutional authority, assuming no intention to dissolve the league, community, organization, or otherwise titled confederation;

9. N.P. Hepworth, *The Finance of Local Government* (4th ed., London, 1978) pp. 36 - 37; *The Economist* (8-14 March 1980) p. 67, (15-21 March 1980), pp. 60-61, (7-13 November 1981) pp. 71-72,(14-20 November 1981) p. 65.

10. E.g., the "Keep It Local" campaign of the Association of Metropolitan Authorities, coordinated by Roger Neville seconded from Newcastle upon Tyne, was announced through press releases dated 13 October 1981.

11. Lord Redcliffe-Maud and B. Wood, *English Local Government Reformed* (London, 1974) ch. 10.

12. L. Erades and W.L. Gould, *The Relation Between International Law and Municipal Law in the Netherlands and in the United States* (Leiden, 1961) pp. 351, 358, 368 - 369, 393 - 413, 455, 457. The types of United States treaties that were held to be in conflict with and superseded by subsequent Acts of Congress were bilateral treaties dealing with commerce, aliens, Indian affairs, custom duties and taxation.

(2) the constituent members' courts derive their jurisdiction from national constitutions and national legislation; (3) it is possible that an organ of a supranational confederation, such as the Council or the Commission of the European Economic Community, could take a lawmaking action that conflicts with a self-executing international agreement to which the confederation is a party. Obviously, these three considerations require a working out in practice of modifications of the traditional approaches of international tribunals and Article 27 of the Vienna Convention on the Law of Treaties and those of national courts. The former give supremacy to international law, while the latter may or may not, in regard to their internal effects, accord supremacy to treaties, especially in cases of conflict with subsequent statutes. The approaches of national courts differ as national constitutions and legal traditions differ.

That the above-mentioned considerations can create complex situations at the supranational level is evidenced by some of the difficult questions faced by the Court of Justice of the European Communities, e.g., in *International Fruit Co. NV* v. *Productschap voor Groenten en Fruit* (1972),[13] involving the issue of whether Regulations of the EEC Commission were invalid as contrary to Article XI of the General Agreement on Trade and Tariffs. In response to two more generalized questions submitted by the Netherlands Appellate Tribunal for Trade Matters, ("College van Beroep voor het Bedrijfsleven") the Court held that the validity of acts of Community institutions could be examined for conformity with rules of international law other than Community law, provided that the Community is bound by such law and that the nature of the rule is such that it entitles subjects of the Community to assert it in a national court (i.e., is self-executing). It may be noted that the question of whether EEC is bound by GATT rules is complicated by the requirement that only states can be members of GATT and so possess formal voting powers but, after 31 December 1969, the power to conclude customs and other commercial agreements has belonged exclusively to the Community. The Court met this problem by characterizing EEC "as a partner in the tariff negotiations and as a party to the agreements." The case illustrates the difficulties and dilemmas that can arise when a group of governmental entities is bound by both a constituent document and consensual rules valid in relations with third parties.

Turning to the subnational level, it is evident that the three major forms of governmental organizations can be found in a variety of combinations. Within federal systems one can find unitary subsystems as in the Canadian provinces where local government (municipal, county, and other forms) are as subject to provincial control as English local government is subject to central government control. Having a mixed system in which a unitary system is at the middle rather than the national level introduces certain legal and political complications, e.g., when a

13. 67 *AJIL* (1973) p. 559, with commentary by S.A. Riesenfeld at pp. 504 - 508. For a systematic approach to the general problem, see H.F. van Panhuys, "Conflicts Between the Law of the European Communities and Other Rules of International Law," 7 *Common Market Law Review* (1965 - 66) pp. 420 - 449.

municipality wants to persuade the national government to bind itself to assist in a project such as railway relocation on its terms rather than those of a senior provincial government claiming to be the spokesman or negotiator with the national government.

Moreover, national or middle level unitary systems can establish unitary, federal, or confederative systems at the local level, perhaps formally quite uniform throughout the area as in Scotland and England (ignoring the somewhat different allocation of functions in the six English metropolitan counties and Greater London) or perhaps in some mixture of unitary and either federal or confederative systems. The unitary city is the more traditional form and may itself become a subnational regional government either by annexation of adjoining territories or whole suburbs or by amalgamation. Or there can be a two-tier system, sometimes referred to as municipal federalism but more likely to be a confederation [14] if neither English county nor district and neither Ontario regional municipality nor area municipality is superior to the other but (to say the same thing in a different way) each has its vertical relationships directly with the same senior level of government and conducts its horizontal relationships with its partners by negotiations and agreements or, in hostility, by name-calling and other vituperative practices. Such local confederations can be established or replaced by the competent senior level of government as Manitoba created two-tiered Metropolitan Winnipeg in 1960 and replaced it with a single tier, "Unicity" Winnipeg, in 1972.

What happens in two-tiered subnational regional systems is that bargaining and negotiating procedures become vital to the conduct of governmental activities – vital in ways different from interagency bargaining within a single tier. Having more than one government legislating for the same people living in a given area presents the same situation as when a treaty rule and a municipal statute relate to the same private persons, e.g., importers. Needed is some means of harmonizing activities and harmonizing laws or, in the absence of harmonization which is far from an easy accomplishment, some means, including controlling norms, for resolving the conflict.

Negotiation and resultant agreement, highly dependent upon opportunities for and the quality of communication [15] including that embodied in law, are usually considered the most desirable means of resolving conflict. Institutions, formal and informal, sometimes successful and sometimes not, have been established in hope of facilitating negotiations. Indeed, how seriously intergovernmental relations are now taken and how much they have become a day-to-day thing is demonstrated by the fact that at national state, and local levels can be found ministeries (in Québec in 1982, headed by a specialist in international law, Jacques-Yvan Morin),[15a]

14. But not in the sense of a body with voluntary membership and right of withdrawal (secession) as in the case of the League of Nations and its American local analogue, Councils of Governments of which cities, counties, and possibly school districts can be members. M.B. Mogulof, *Governing Metropolitan Areas* (Washington, 1971); N. Wikstrom, *Councils of Governments* (Chicago, 1977).

15. See, e.g., *Report of the Royal Commission on Metropolitan Toronto*, vol. 2, *Detailed Findings and Recommendations* (June 1977) pp. 127 - 133.

15a. Morin is Vice President of the Canadian Branch of the International Law Association.

offices, or committees established to specialize in intergovernmental relations, while in the United States, for certain purposes related to federal funding of certain types of projects, Councils of Governments came into being in the 1960's.[16]

Personal observation of negotiations in county-district entities in two northern English metropolitan counties revealed some of the ways in which competition between governments to display some jot or title of sovereignty can manifest itself. One group was composed of administrators – chief planning officers of the county and its districts. To the extent that the group reached agreement on a matter before it at that stage of the structure planning process, the achievement resulted not from direct agreement but from much hemming and hawing and alleged lack of understanding which clever leadership transformed from indecision into specific agreement in the absence of identifiable specific disagreement.

The second planning institution was composed of councillors from another northern English metropolitan county and one of its districts. All were from the same political party, hypothetically disciplined but keenly aware of juridictional boundary lines that were largely meaningless in terms of constituents' daily activities. The scene was reminiscent of rhetorical conflicts at the United Nations as county councillors lectured district councillors on their duties while the district councillors similarly lectured the county councillors – the substantive issues and decisions needed apparently being secondary to the competition for primacy.

In these types of policy formulating situations, one way out of the impasse is for a senior level of government to impose a policy to be administered by local units. But the situation in which an agreement is reached but a local by-law diverges from the agreement is similar to a conflict between treaty and statute and would call for the application of some sort of decision rule about which of the two prevails.

Whether or not a local federation is involved, it is also possible for the relations among subnational entities to have an international dimension.[17] After all, problems of agriculture, health, water quality, and flood control, among other things, are not confined by national boundaries and are quite immediate concerns of subnational governments.

Article III, section 5, of the Michigan Constitution reads:

> "Subject to provisions of general law, this state or any political subdivision thereof may enter into agreements for the performance, financing or execution of their respective functions, with any one or more of the other states, the United States, the Dominion of Canada, or any political subdivision thereof unless otherwise provided in this constitution".

16. D.S. Wright, *Understanding Intergovermental Relations* (North Scituate, Mass., 1978) pp. 7-8, 237-244; Gérard Veilleux, "L'évolution des mécanismes de liaison intergouvernementale," in R. Simeon (ed.), *Confrontation and Collaboration – Intergovernmental Relations in Canada Today* (Toronto, 1979) pp. 35 - 77; Don Stevenson, "The Role of Intergovernmental Conferences in the Decision-Making Process," *ibid.*, esp. pp. 94 - 95 on provincial-municipal liaison in Ontario.

17. R.F. Swanson, "Intergovernmental Relations at the State/Provincial Level," in Swanson (ed.), *Intergovernmental Perspectives on the Canada - U.S. Relationship* (New York, 1978) pp. 221 - 265.

A Michigan statute of 1941 established House, Senate, gubernatorial, and state commissions on interstate cooperation charged, among other things, with advancing interstate cooperation by means of compacts.[18] Act 89 of 1954 enacted the Great Lakes Basin Compact with seven other states and, if it became a party, Ontario, while Act 28 of 1955 rendered the compact itself (which made provision for Quebec to adhere) a part of Michigan law.[19] Interestingly, these statutes reflect at the subnational level the well-known Anglo-American doctrine that international law is part of the law of the land.

These Michigan examples are presented as demonstrations of possibilities for bipartite and multipartite relations among subnational governmental units across international boundaries. That subnational boundary relationships, arising out of functional needs, can be far more numerous than is generally realized is shown by the fact that in the early 1970's the Department of State's Office of Canadian Affairs had little knowledge of the nature and extent of the procedures of state-provincial relations and so the Department issued a research contract to Roger Frank Swanson. Swanson's study in 1973-74 revealed 766 interactions which, to bring some order to the variety of activities, were classified as agreements, understandings (correspondence, resolutions, communiqués, or memoranda, not jointly signed), and arrangements ("any other written or verbal articulation of a regularized interactive procedure").[20] The total number of interactions would be far greater if the sum included the instances in which the interacting subnational party on at least one side of the border were not a province or a state.[21]

Legal questions, essentially of a constitutional nature, can arise and have arisen, although outside the courts, in respect to the capacities of subnational units to enter into agreements, understandings, or arrangements with their cross-border counterparts. Apparently, care is taken to defer to the relevant law, including the avoidance of arrangements subject to international law, although in some circumstances, such as disaster emergency situations and preparedness therefor (e.g., flood control, forest fire), there may be need to rely on hope that federal authorities will be understanding.[22]

It would seem that subnational agreements, understandings, and arrangements would be free from subjection to the norms of public international law except when so subordinated by a combination of a treaty and constitutional allocation of legislative power to act in the functional area (or issue area) concerned.[23] Certainly subnational intergovernmental undertakings do not themselves constitute formal treaty law, for the subnational units do not possess the treaty-making

18. *Michigan Compiled Laws, 1970,* vol. I, secs. 3.31 - 3.41.

19. *Michigan Statutes Annotated,* 1977 revision, secs. 4.128, 4.129.

20. Swanson, *op.cit.,* pp. 235 - 236, 248 - 249, 265.

21. For an example of extended bargaining proceedings, in this case between the City of Seattle and the Province of British Columbia over raising the height of a dam and flooding 5000 acres of the Skagit River Valley in British Columbia, see *The Globe and Mail* (Toronto), February 16, 1982.

22. Swanson, *op. cit.,* pp. 225 - 231, 261 - 262 notes 3, 7, 9.

23. The constitutional problem for a federal government is illustrated by *Attorney General for Canada* v. *Attorney General for Ontario* [1937] AC 326.

power.[24] It will be noted that the framers of the Michigan Constitution took care to use, in Article III, section 5, the word "agreement" instead of "treaties".

However, it is not impossible that the norms emerging from the acts of subnational governmental units might indirectly, either through custom or through subsequent treaty-making, become part of international law, just as the actions of such private persons as sailors and fishermen gave rise to an international law of the sea.[25] Conversely, norms of international law might become part of the law among subnational governments either through conscious borrowing or through internalization by judges, legislators, or executives who subsequently have occasion to give expression to such norms. In such instances, while formally the internal and external systems of law may remain separate, in content there may be a number of important similarities. Indeed, it should be possible to find norms of intergovernmental law that correspond to norms of international law even when the intergovernmental relations involved do not have an international dimension. Using the law of contracts as an example, might not the progress of a norm have been from municipal contract law to international law to internal intergovernmental law?

That borrowings by international law from Roman Law and other municipal law systems have occurred is evident from a reading of any good history of international law. In the other direction, borrowing has also occurred. As Justice Byron White, for the majority of the United States Supreme Court, said in *Texas* v. *Louisiana* (1973) concerning a dispute over the boundary of the two states along the Sabine River:

> The argument that the middle of the main channel was intended rests on the line of cases in this Court beginning with *Iowa* v. *Illinois,* 147 U.S. 1 (1893), which held that in normal circumstances it should be assumed Congress intends the word "middle" to mean "middle of the main channel" in order that each State would have equal access to the main navigable channel. The doctrine was borrowed from international law and has often been adhered to in this Court, although it is plain that within the United States two States bordering on a navigable river would have equal access to it for the purposes of navigation whether the common boundary was in the geographic middle or along the thalweg, *Id.,* 7-8, *New Jersey v. Delaware,* 291 U.S. 361, 380-385 (1934).[26]

Regardless of the direction of borrowing, that is, by international law from municipal law or *vice versa,* one finds that, in addition to boundary issues, norms similar to those discoverable in international law have been brought into play among subnational entities to deal with such matters as title by prescription,[27] air and

24. See J. - G. Castel, *International Law* (3rd ed., Toronto, 1976) pp. 923 - 929.

25. W.L. Gould and M. Barkun, *International Law and the Social Sciences* (Princeton, 1970) pp. 200 - 205.

26. 93 S. Ct. 1215 at 1219 - 1220.

27. *Rhode Island* v. *Massachusetts* (1846) 4 Howard 591; *Indiana* v. *Kentucky* (1890) 136 U.S. 479, supporting the precedent of *Rhode Island* v. *Massachusetts* by using quotations from Vattel and Wheaton.

water pollution,[28] appropriation of river waters,[29] and the validity of the *clausula rebus sic stantibus.*[30]

In how many issue areas comparable norms have been applied at both the international level and the subnational intergovernmental level is a question that cannot be answered without further research. Certainly, we should be aware of the Supreme Court's suggestion in *Texas* v. *Louisiana* that a rule of international law may not be essential in internal intergovernmental affairs. Circumstances may be different or, as in the matter of use of a river's main navigable channel, certain safeguards may not be as necessary internally as internationally. Although in the matter of the Texas-Louisiana boundary along the Sabine River there was no difficulty comparable to the dilemma that exists when what is functional at one organizational level is dysfunctional at another level, *Texas* v. *Louisiana* still implies that in some, perhaps most, issue areas no harm is done to the functioning of subnational governmental units and no negation or limitation of the validity of an international rule of law, as international law, occurs when a deviation therefrom occurs among subnational entities. But, to my knowledge, there is no comprehensive study distinguishing the issue areas in which international norms are applied from those in which they are not applied in subnational intergovernmental relations that display the same bargaining, bickering, and defense of local autonomy that one finds in international relations.

As for the problem area of conflicts between intergovernmental law and national law, a simple analysis is probably not possible. It may be doubted that such all-embracing concepts as monism and dualism reflect reality even though, hypothetically, the legal structure in a unitary state should be monistic and that in a federalism, particularly one like Canada's in which Section 91 of the BNA Act assigns certain exclusive powers to Ottawa and Section 92 assigns others to the provinces, the legal system should be dualistic. But, even in such systems there is room for concurrent jurisdiction and a resultant competition for primacy that could create conflicts of laws with settlement thereof taking place issue area by issue area. This means that research, like that of Lambertus Eradus on conflicts between international law and municipal law, must focus upon what courts and law makers do, not upon their rhetoric except in so far as the rhetoric serves in some issue areas to avoid invalidating one or the other of the conflicting rules of law.

28. Convention between Baden-Württemberg, Bavaria, Austria, and Switzerland concerning the Protection of the Waters of Lake Constance, October 10, 1960; *State of Georgia* v. *Tennessee Copper Company and Ducktown Sulphur, Copper and Iron Company, Limited* (1907) 206 U.S. 230, in which the Supreme Court, describing Georgia's capacity as that of a "quasi-sovereign", noted that the state had tried in vain to obtain relief from the State of Tennessee; *New Jersey* v. *City of New York* (1931) 283 U.S. 473.

29. *Wyoming* v. *Colorado* (1922) 259 U.S. 419; *Washington* v. *Oregon* (1936) 297 U.S. 622.

30. *Bremen* v. *Bavaria*, 3 Annual Digest (1925-6), np. 266.

INTERNATIONALISM ABOVE FREEDOM OF CONTRACT

The Rotterdam District Court's view on the scope of the Hague Rules Convention. A lesson for the Hague-Visby era.

by Mr. W.E. Haak*

1. INTRODUCTION

Specialized judges are in principle unknown to the Dutch legal system. A judge or president of a chamber need not sit in the same chamber for more than four years.[1] It is quite remarkable, therefore, that Erades presided over the Rotterdam District Court Chamber dealing with actions relating to the carriage of goods, in particular carriage by sea, from 1958 until the end of 1981. This was based on both policy and voluntary agreement. The District Court of the world's largest sea port has deliberately decided to confine jurisdiction over cases relating to the carriage of goods to one chamber, although several chambers of the Court deal with civil matters. As President, Erades appeared to be prepared to carry this policy with good results, for the period of his uninterrupted presidency saw the growth of case law which has provided an element of legal security in international trade, and this cannot be valued too highly. It may safely be said that Erades has given the judgments of the Rotterdam District Court a reputation reaching far beyond national frontiers.

The President of a Chamber is of course one member in a court of three judges, and the secrecy of judges' chambers makes it impossible for us to find out how a judgment has been made.[2] However, the fact that Erades was the one constant element in an everchanging cast during all those years justifies the conclusion that he had a significant influence on his Chamber's decisions. This influence, incidentally, also appears from his publications.

I should like to confine myself in this paper to one aspect of the international carriage of goods by sea which particularly appealed to Erades, namely, the law applicable to international carriage under a bill of lading. In 1969, Erades gave a lecture in Willemstad, Curaçao, on the carriage of goods by sea and the conflict of laws.[3] I will discuss the trend that may be discerned in his Chamber's decisions involving the application of the 1924 Brussels Bills of Lading Convention on the basis of a statement he made during this lecture that international carriage under bills of lading should, whenever possible, be governed by uniform rules.

* Judge in the Supreme Court of the Netherlands.
1. Art. 22 a (2), Regulations I, Royal Decree of 14 Sept. 1838, Stb. 36.
2. Art. 28 of the Act on the Organisation of the Judiciary.
3. For a report on this lecture (unpublished), see NJB 1969 pp. 776-777.

The early stages of Erades' period of service as President of the Law of Carriage Chamber were characterized by the Netherlands' accession to the Brussels Bills of Lading Convention, and later on by the signing of the Act approving the intention to denounce this Convention and the Act approving the Amended Bills of Lading Convention, the Hague-Visby Rules.[4] The judgments relating to the application of the Bills of Lading Convention made during these years cannot be described more aptly than they were by Kahn-Freund when he referred to the Hague Rules as "a testing ground for the struggle between internationalism and freedom of contract."[5]

It is well known that the Hague Rules in the Bills of Lading Convention provide rules for a division of liability between the carrier and the cargo owner which enjoys a worldwide reputation. Article X of the Bills of Lading Convention provides that the Hague Rules shall apply to all bills of lading issued in any of the Contracting States. A final Protocol leaves these states the option of either giving the Convention the force of law or including the Hague Rules in their national legislation in a form appropriate to that legislation. The Dutch Commercial Code was amended in 1955 to incorporate the Hague Rules after a minor modification was made in the already revised maritime law, to bring this law in line with the Hague Rules dating back to February 1927. This newly amended law came into effect on 26 August 1956. A few months later, on 1 February 1957, the Netherlands officially adopted the Hague Rules; on that day the Bills of Lading Convention entered into force for the Netherlands.

The international problem of the scope of Article X, which also applied in the Netherlands,[6] will not be discussed here. It should suffice to mention that, before the 1956 Amendment, Article 517d of the Commercial Code provided that Articles 468-480, dealing with liability in the carriage of goods by sea, should apply to the carriage of goods by sea *from and to* Dutch ports. In 1956 these Articles of the Commercial Code were amended to incorporate the basic Hague Rules. The mandatory Article 517d of the Commercial Code was on that occasion reduced (as stated during parliamentary discussion) "in anticipation of a possible regulation by treaty" to a provision that made the application of the Hague Rules thus incorporated in the Commercial Code mandatory in respect of carriage of goods *from* Dutch ports,[7]

4. Act of 11 March 1981 for the approval of the intention to denounce the Brussels Convention of 25 Autust 1924 for the unification of certain rules relating to bills of lading, with the annexed Protocol of signature, Stb. 204, entered into force on 8 May 1981; State Act of 11 March 1981 for the approval of the Brussels Protocol of 23 February 1968, amending the International Convention for the unification of certain rules relating to bills of lading, signed at Brussels, 25 August, 1924, Stb. 205, entered into force on 8 May 1981. See further n. 32.

5. Kahn-Freund, The growth of internationalsm in English private international law; The Hebrew University of Jerusalem, Lionel Cohen Lectures, Sixth Series, January 1960, p. 40.

6. See W.E. Haak, De Hague Rules en het Alnati-arrest, Studiekring 'Prof. Mr. J. Offerhaus' 1969, with references to the literature.

7. Report of the Standing Committee for Justice, Chamber Documents, session 1953-1954, Bill 3520.

and no longer to Dutch ports. An additional complication for the Netherlands was the question to what extent the Hague Rules of the Bills of Lading Convention were self-executing. The Constitution provides that provisions of agreements with a content which might be universally binding shall have this binding effect from the date of publication.[8]

So there was the Convention, on the one hand, and the national legislation, on the other, and of the two, there was never any doubt as far as the Rotterdam District Court was concerned as to which should prevail: the Hague Rules contain internationally uniform laws, provisions with universally binding contents. Therefore, the Convention would take precedence over national legislation, were a conflict to arise. This was not the case, if only because carriage to Dutch ports and carriage "by-passing" them were not covered by the mandatory provisions incorporated in the Netherlands legislation and, on the whole, the substance of the Dutch Hague Rules was actually very similar.

Even before the Bills of Lading Convention took effect for the Netherlands, the Rotterdam District Court favoured the supremacy of the Hague Rules as global uniform law, which should be considered more important than the parties' freedom to determine the law by which a contract of carriage should be governed. In the 1950's, the Court expressed this view in a bilateralizing interpretation of Article 517d of the Commercial Code. By regarding this provision as a mandatory general conflict rule, the Convention, although not yet operative for the Netherlands, could be made to apply as long as the port of loading was situated in a Hague Rules country.[9] Gradually this kind of decision disappeared; the Court of Appeal did not accept this interpretation. In itself it is obviously quite correct to say, as the Court of Appeal did, that Article 517d of the Commercial Code does not necessarily imply that "a mandatory provision was intended to make the carriage from and to a foreign port in different countries subject to the law of the port of loading"[10], for Article 517d dealt with special law which did not apply to every port of loading. Subsequently, the District Court proceeded to attack decisive importance to the Hague Rules of the port of loading on the basis of connecting factors, considering in particular the nature and intended scope of this uniform law, and the fact that the Netherlands' accession to the Convention was imminent. Thus the Court considered the choice of law made by the parties to be of secondary importance.[11]

This is the background against which the 1963 judgment in the Alnati Case must be viewed.[12] The action concerned the carriage, in 1954, of potatoes from Belgium. In pursuance of Article 91 of the Belgian Commercial Code the application of the Hague Rules were compulsory for this carriage; the bill of lading contained a contracting-out provision that went further than the Bills of Lading Convention permitted, but was still possible under Dutch law, which the parties had agreed to be

8. Art. 65(1) of the Constitution, as revised in 1972.

9. See e.g. Hoogkerk, District Court of Rotterdam, 23 April 1954, NJ 1954, 770; for further case law see RMTh. p. 104 n. 2.

10. Cf. Aagtekerk, Court of Appeal of The Hague, 17 October 1958, S & S 1958, 77.

11. Cf. Alnati, District Court of Rotterdam, 23 April 1963, NJ 1963, 458; see also the cases referred to in RMTh. 1971, pp. 104-105.

12. The Alnati Case is also reported in S & S 1964, 16.

applicable and which at that time allowed 'contracting out' of the Hague Rules to a certain extent. In accordance with established case law, the Court reached the conclusion that "the choice . . . of Dutch law is only relevant to the extent that it does not result in infringement of the above-mentioned mandatory provisions of Belgian law". The Court of Appeal shared this view.[13] This case, of which the facts and circumstances occurred before the Netherlands acceded to the Bills of Lading Convention, was concluded in 1966 with a Judgment of the Supreme Court that was characterized by a high degree of internationalism in terms of the international law of contract in general.[14] It was not because the principle of complete party autonomy in this branch of law was expressly recognized – it can be argued that this principle had already been established in earlier judgments [15] – but because the judgment expressed the following important principle, viz., that Dutch courts should in appropriate circumstances give precedence to provisions of a foreign State's law the observance of which affects vital interests of that state even outside its own territory, over the law selected by the parties. It is the principle which appears in a weaker form in Article 7 of the EEC Convention on Contractual Obligations and allows for *'règles d'application immédiate'* such as currency regulations and other rules of a semi-public character which are not easily incorporated in the traditional conflict rules.

For all its internationalism, the Alnati Judgment gave no support for the Rotterdam District Court's similarly motivated policy relating to the international carriage of goods under bills of lading. According to the Supreme Court, the Belgian Hague Rules were not included in the abovementioned category of rules which may affect the parties' autonomy. Even after sixteen years, many people feel that the result could have been different. There is no need to regard Article 91 of the Belgian Commercial Code (the Belgian equivalent of Article 517d) as a *règle d'application immédiate* in the restricted sense of the term to recognize that the intended effect of this rule is the same. One possible decision would have categorised the mandatory provisions of article 91 of the Belgian Commercial Code as belonging to the rules, the observance of which involved such vital Belgian interests, even outside its territory. One should have taken this into acccount and therefore should have given precedence to these provisions over the rules chosen by the parties. This possibility was based on similar consideration which had consistently led the Rotterdam District Court to compulsory application of the Hague Rules of the port of loading. In this kind of decision, the international motivation referred to by Kollewijn would have been one of these Belgian interest, "because this precedence over the parties' choice of law ensures the required international unity of law that would otherwise be lacking"[16]; an international unification, incidental-

13. Court of Appeal of The Hague, 11 December 1964, S & S 1965, 13.

14. Supreme Court, 13 May 1966, NJ 1967, 3, NILR 1968, 82 n. Deelen; see Lagarde, Travaux 1972, p. 160 and H. Gaudemet-Tallon, Rev. trim. dr. eur. 1981, p. 261.

15. See J.E.J.Th. Deelen, Rechtskeuze in het Nederlands Internationaal Contractenrecht, een jurisprudentie-onderzoek, diss. 1965.

16. See Vier Jaren Nederlandse Rechtspraak Internationaal Privaatrecht (1964-1968), p. 158.

ly, to which the Netherlands was not opposed and in which it was about to take part.

This was the situation before the Netherlands became a party to the 1924 Convention. After the Netherland's accession, the District Court took the view that whenever carriage took place under a bill of lading issued in a contracting state, irrespective of the parties' choice of law, the Hague Rules were applicable on the grounds of the Convention's direct effect, in conjunction with Article X. Therefore the Hague Rules of the foreign state claiming application should have precedence, as they are "incorporated law in pursuance of an agreement of public international law for the unification of law."[17]

In cases involving carriage from a non-Hague Rules country to a Hague Rules country, or a State which had in any way incorporated these Rules in its national legislation, the District Court proceeded initially on the basis of decisive connections in order to arrive at the applicability of the law of the port of discharge, in consideration of the international motive referred to above. One such case concerned the carriage of fishmeal by the m.s. Portalon from Peru to the Netherlands and Germany.[18] In this case the Court declared that the Hague Rules of the ports of discharge should apply, this time in accordance with a clause in the bills of lading. The Court also considered that "the differences which emerged when the Netherlands and Germany became partners to the convention in question and incorporated its rules into their national legislations . . . (were) irrelevant to this part of the action." Earlier in the same judgment the Court had referred to "the applicability in this case of the Hague Rules as laid down in . . . the Brussels Convention." On appeal in cassation, these words began to assume a special significance. The Supreme Court made a statement in this case about the direct effect of the Hague Rules of the Bills of Lading Convention without relating them to the *Dutch* Hague Rules.[19] The Supreme Court considered that the Hague Rules of the Convention had no direct effect since the Protocol annexed to the Convention gives the option either to give the Convention the force of law or to incorporate its rules into the national legislation. The Netherlands has opted for incorporation of the rules into the Commercial Code. This implies that only the Hague Rules incorporated in the Commercial Code can be reviewed on appeal in cassation. Thus the Supreme Court.

It goes without saying that the result of this judgment was not encouraging for the policy hitherto adopted by the District Court. This is not necessarily because of the abovementioned principle contained in the constitution that provisions from a convention which can be universally binding have binding effect from the date of publication of the convention. Nor is it because of the dwindling character of this uniform law when the binding effect of the Bills of Lading Convention is not accepted. Whatever one's opinion of this the Supreme Court in this case adopted the view of the Government who, when introducing the Act of Approval of the Convention,

17. Cf. Risa Paula, District Court of Rotterdam, 28 November 1967, S & S 1968, 11.
18. Portalon, District Court of Rotterdam, 6 April 1965, S & S 1965, 53; for judgment of the Court of Appeal, see S & S 1967, 28.
19. Supreme Court, 8 November 1968, NJ 1969, 10; see Erades, NILR 1969, p. 97.

explained that its ratification was a question of international courtesy in order to avoid misunderstanding with other contracting states, but considered that "the question whether the present Convention was to provide rules only for the contracting states or to provide rules binding also on private individuals [must be answered] in the former sense".[20] In fact, I am now concerned with the critical observation made by Struyken, at the end of 1981,[21] when he considered that in this case the carrier's grounds of appeal in cassation included not only a complaint about the District Court's interpretation of the Hague Rules of the Convention as such (not self-executing, in the Supreme Court's view) but also a complaint about the incorrect interpretation of the Hague Rules as incorporated in the Commercial Code of the Netherlands where one of the ports of discharge was situated.
In Struyken's view, the Supreme Court should have seized this opportunity to examine the case by referring to the Dutch Hague Rules as incorporated in the Commercial Code; the District Court's policy of applying the law of the port of discharge in the appropriate circumstances could then have been judged by referring to a complaint of the opposing party that was partly based on the Dutch Hague Rules.

After the Portalon Judgment the District Court continued to apply the mandatory Hague Rules of foreign ports of loading, regardless of the choice of law made by the parties; the motivation, however, is not very clear. The guiding principle seemed to remain, if not Article X, then the desirability for the carriage of goods by sea to be governed where possible by uniform law, a consideration which has also motivated application of the Hague Rules of the port of discharge.[22]

In the Portalon Case carriage did not involve bills of lading issued in a contracting state. Strictly speaking, it may be said that Article X – not one of the Hague Rules which the final Protocol gives the option of being incorporated in national legislation, but a rule on the scope of the Convention which includes the Hague Rules – had not been affected by the Portalon Judgment.[23] Erades correctly contended that Article X should be ascribed direct effect on the basis of the Constitution.[24] Article X was only partly incorporated in Article 517d of the Commercial Code. If the final Protocol to the Convention left parties the competence to incorporate the whole of the Convention in their national legislation, it is also allowed the parties to incorporate them in part. Article X was not a provision directed at legislative or executive organs of the State of the Netherlands. The "remaining" part of Article X, which was not incorporated in Article 517d of the Commercial Code, was therefore self-executing, in Erades' view. It is not necessary, however, to go as far as this to derive an obligation from Article X for contracting states to apply "foreign" Hague Rules when a bill of lading has

20. Cf. MvT 3520, No. 3; for further comments, see also NJB 1970, pp. 298-299.
21. Contractenrecht-X-274, 275; see also P.J. Swart, Het Cognossementsverdrag en rechtstreekse werking, Annex to S & S 1971, No. 4 p. 4.
22. Cf. the cases referred to in RMTh 1971, p. 105.
23. See Snijders, NILR 1971, pp. 141-142; Haak, NJB 1970, pp. 350-351.
24. NILR 1961, p. 375 et seq; NILR 1964, p. 67 et seq.; NILR 1979, p. 97 et seq.; see also RMTh 1982, p. 56.

been issued in another contracting state. Contracting-out of the Hague Rules is not only contrary to the mandatory rules of the Bills of Lading Convention in force in the country of the forum, but is also contrary to these mandatory rules as applied in any of the contracting states. Therefore, although it is not self-executing from this point of view, Article X implies a treaty obligation for a judge in a contracting state to consider his country in a state of violation of such an obligation should a choice of law allowing contracting out of the Hague Rules be accepted; an argument which had been advanced before by Kahn-Freund.[25]

The latter view is important with regard to the judgment of the Supreme Court delivered in 1971 in the Katsedijk Case[26], in which a Dutch conflict rule was found to exist, viz., that contracts for carriage of goods by sea under a bill of lading are governed by the law of the country of loading. This rule is certainly not intended to be mandatory in the sense that it should prevail over the autonomy of the parties. If that were the case, it would imply a reversal of the Alnati Judgment, and this would be unhelpful. It may be recalled that in practice a bill of lading often refers to one or other of the Hague Rules by way of a choice of law, since carriage by no means always has its origin in a Hague Rules country. However, the question arises whether in the case of carriage from a Hague Rules country this conflict rule allows contracting out of the Hague Rules by choice of law of a non-Hague Rules country. Choice of law takes precedence over this conflict rule. Why is it therefore not possible to make the choice of law of a non-Hague Rules country? A case of this kind has not yet been submitted to the Supreme Court.

The Rotterdam District Court holds the view, even after the Katsedijk Judgement, that it is impossible to do this. The reasoning since the Katsedijk Judgement has been that contracts for carriage of goods by sea under a bill of lading are governed by the law of the country of loading if the State where the port of loading is situated is a party to the Convention, or has incorporated the Hague Rules in its legislation.[27] Choice of law is possible insofar as the Hague Rules of the port of loading permit. This reasoning may be based on the opinion that according to the principle derived from Article X, the Netherlands is bound to apply the foreign Hague Rules, notwithstanding the choice of a different law. In addition, the international motive, as well as the nature and intended application of the uniform law are likely to play a part, for the District Court also continued in subsequent years where possible to apply the Hague Rules of the port of discharge, if the port of loading was not situated in a Hague Rules country. This application was no longer based on the grounds of decisive connections. For the application of the Hague Rules of the port of discharge, the Court initially referred to the version of Article X drafted by the *Comité Maritime International* at Rijeka in 1959 and at Stockholm in 1963, but not amended to the same extent at the 1968 Diplomatic Conference on Maritime Law at Brussels; the extended version had not been opposed by the Netherlands Government delegation to the Conference.[28] The subsequent

25. Loc. cit. pp. 43-44.
26. Supreme Court 19 February 1971, NJ 1971, 299; see Verheul, NILR 1974, p. 322.
27. Cf. Giancarlo Zeta, District Court of Rotterdam, 25 Oct. 1976, S & S 1977, 96.
28. Cf. Kimovsk, District Court of Rotterdam, 24 March 1970, S & S 1970, 87.

motivation was that, according to Dutch conflict rules, contracts for carriage of goods by sea under a bill of lading are governed by the law of the country of loading or by the law of the country of delivery, according to whether the state of the port of loading, or only the state of the port of discharge is a party to the Convention or has incorporated the Hague Rules in its national legislation.

3. THE MORAL OF ERADES' POLICY

An assessment of Erades' policy over the past twentyfive years leads to the conclusion that internationalism has prevailed over freedom of contract for the benefit of international trade. Where possible, the Rotterdam District Court has applied the Bills of Lading Convention on defensible grounds. By applying another of his favorite theories, viz., that the law must be in harmony with socio-economic realities, in which it has to play a part [29], Erades demonstrated the fictitious character of autonomy in carriage by sea under an adhesion-contract such as the bill of lading, a view that has gained ground in consumer law, but not yet in the law of carriage.[30]

This story has a moral. It is the lesson which is interwoven in Erades' policy. On 26 April 1982, the Netherlands denounced the Brussels Bills of Lading Convention of 1924 and simultaneously ratified the Bills of Lading Convention as amended at Brussels in 1968; we are therefore back where we started. History has repeated itself and we can learn from previous periods.

4. THE HAGUE-VISBY ERA

The Amended Bills of Lading Convention was signed at Brussels in 1968. It consists of a number of amendments (the Brussels Protocol) to the former 1924 Convention, which together with the former Convention form an amended Bills of Lading Convention, the Hague-Visby Rules. One of the amendments concerns Article X, which in its amended version makes these Hague-Visby Rules applicable not only to any bill of lading issued in a contracting State or to any carriage under a bill of lading from a contracting State, but also to any bill of lading that refers to the Amended Bills of Lading Convention or to Hague-Visby Rules incorporated in any national legislation.

This has given rise to a conflict of treaties. Should a country accede to the Brussels Protocol containing the amended Article X, but at the same time continue as a party to the 1924 Convention? This country could then find itself in a situation requiring simultaneous application of the Hague Rules under Article X of the 1924 Convention, and of the Hague-Visby Rules under Article X as amended. Not all the Hague Rules countries became a party to the Amended Convention at the

29. This theory is also found in judgments; cf. e.g. Evie W., District Court of Rotterdam, 27 Oct. 1970, S & S 1971, 18.

30. See the report of his lecture in Curaçao, NJB 1969, p. 777.

same time.[31] A number of countries continue, and will perhaps continue even for a substantial time, to maintain the old Convention without acceding to the new Convention. It would be very difficult to apply the new Convention to these countries without violating the international obligation to maintain the old Convention. In order to avoid this dilemma, the Netherlands decided, following the example of the United Kingdom, to denounce the 1924 Convention.

In some respects, particularly with regard to the limitation of liability, the Hague-Visby Rules differ considerably from the Hague Rules. By denouncing the 1924 Convention a country is entirely free vis-à-vis the 'old' Hague Rules countries, as it is bound only as regards the Hague-Visby countries. The Hague-Visby Rules are distributed throughout the Commercial Code, shortly to be embodied in Book 8 of the New Civil Code. [32] In addition, and this is very important, the Amended Bills of Lading Convention is "ascribed" direct effect in order to avoid any misunderstanding. The new Article 467a of the Commercial Code, which has been substituted for Article 517d, provides that the articles of the Amended Convention shall be applicable to any bill of lading relating to the carriage of goods by sea between ports of two different States, if

(a) the bill of lading is issued in a contracting State

(b) the carriage is from a port in a contracting State, or

(c) the contract contained in or evidenced by the bill of lading provides that the rules of the Amended Convention or any legislation declaring these rules to be operative, or has incorporated them in another form or wording, are to govern the contract, whatever may be the nationality of the ship, the carrier, the shipper, the consignee or any other interested person.

In its recommendations on the ratification of the 1968 Brussels Protocol, the State Commission on Private International Law has expressed a preference for denunciation of the 1924 Convention. At the same time the Commission recommended extending the scope of the Amended Convention to cover carriage of goods by sea under a bill of lading to a port of discharge situated in a Hague-Visby Rules country including the Netherlands.[33] The 1968 Protocol did not extend the Convention's scope in this way, but granted the parties powers to that effect. After weighing up various arguments, the State Commission reached the Conclusion "that it is advisable to adopt some of the current views in the field of private internation-

31. In February 1982, the countries which ratified or approved the Amended Bills of Lading Convention include: Belgium, Sri Lanka, Denmark, Fed. Rep. of Germany, Ecuador, France, United Kingdom, Lebanon, Norway, Poland, Singapore, Syria, Tonga, Sweden and Switzerland.

32. See the Act of 11 March 1981, amending the Commercial Code in connection with the ratification by the Netherlands of the Brussels Protocol of 23 February 1968, amending the International Convention for the unification of certain rules relating to bills of lading, signed at Brussels 25 August, 1924, Stb. 206; the Act entered into force on 26 July 1982. The Hague-Visby Rules entered into force for the Netherlands on 26 July 1982 as well. The Brussels Bills of Lading Convention will cease in force for the Netherlands on 26 April 1983, a year after its denunciation. See W.E. Haak, Het Gewijzigd Cognossementsverdrag en zijn werkingsomvang: NJB 1982, p. 717 et seq.

33. See MvT 15948 (R1132), No. 3, p. 21.

al law in which increasing attention is also given to interests which applicable provisions of substantive law aim to protect." [34] In the light of the above view it is appropriate, the Commission considers, for the Amended Convention to be made applicable also to carriage to a state which is party to this Convention. The Government has not adopted this recommendation.

It seems to me that the extension of the scope of the Amended Bills of Lading Convention to inward carriage would be desirable, in particular since the 1924 Convention has been denounced, for another dilemma has now arisen. Readers should judge for themselves on the basis of the following situation which is likely to arise in the future:

Carriage takes place from a state party to the 1924 Bills of Lading Convention to a port in the Netherlands where the cargo appears to have sustained damage. The carrier is sued for damages, but claims exemption from liability; he refers to a clause in the bill of lading which makes the choice of law of a country that has incorporated neither the Hague Rules nor the Hague-Visby Rules.

Under the new Article 467a of the Commercial Code, the Amended Bill of Lading Convention is not applicable to this inward carriage. Nor is there an international obligation under Article X of the 1924 Convention for the Netherlands to apply the Hague Rules of the port of loading, since the 1924 Convention has been denounced.[35] According to the Katsedijk rule it would be possible to apply the Hague Rules of the port of loading. But according to the Alnati Judgment, choice of law takes precedence. Or does it? This is a crucial question.

I would suggest that this situation is very similar to the 1954 Alnati Case, both involving carriage from a Hague Rules country and contracting out of the Hague Rules, with the Netherlands neither a party to the 1924 Convention, nor opposed to it.

History repeats itself. Quid juris?

Erades provides us with the answer.[36]

34. Loc. cit. pp. 20-21.

35. See further n. 36.

36. A direction for application of the (old) Hague Rules law in cases of this kind could perhaps also be derived from Art. 6, last sentence of the Brussels Protocol; see also Struycken, Contractenrecht X, No. 55.

ARBITRAL CLAUSES / some comparative observations

by E.H. Hondius*

1. INTRODUCTION

On 1 September 1981 the local court *(kantongerecht)* of Alphen aan den Rijn decided on a case in which a contracting party, a commercial enterprise, invoked an arbitral clause in order to prevent the court from deciding the case on its merits. In accordance with Dutch case law, the defendant's reliance on the arbitral clause was allowed and plaintiff's claim was denied.[1]

The local court decision may be in accordance with the law as it is, but it might well be contrary to the law, as set out in the New Civil Code, which will enter into force by 1985.[2] However, the way in which the new law will treat arbitration clauses is still uncertain. In this contribution, I shall try to present the arguments advanced in favour of or against legislation on standard arbitral clauses. The discussion in The Netherlands with regard to this question has recently been enlivened by the proposed legislation on unfair contract terms.

Since similar legislation on standard contract terms has already been enacted in several other European countries, it seems worthwile to study how these countries have approached the specific problems related to arbitration clauses. Sweden provides us with the most interesting development in this respect. In the United Kingdom, it is not the Unfair Contract Terms Act, but rather the Arbitration Act 1979 which is of interest: some recent cases reveal how arbitral clauses can be constructed. The construction of such clauses constitutes the second subject of this contribution.

The German Federal Republic, which produces by far the largest number of court decisions and especially legal publications in the area of standard contract terms *(Allgemeine Geschäftsbedingungen)*, has surprisingly little to teach us with regard to arbitral clauses and will therefore not be dealt with in this contribution. Nor will French law be considered, though for a different reason. In France, arbitral *(compromissoire)* clauses have long been considered unlawful except in commercial cases. Development there has been in a different direction: towards more freedom[3]; so far, the legislation on unfair contract terms has not had any influence in this respect.

* Professor of Civil Law, Utrecht University; Member of the Board of Editors.

1. Kantongerecht Alphen aan den Rijn 2 September 1981, *Praktijkgids* 1981 no. 1652 (Zorab v. B.V. Koetsier Hekman van Zutphen).
2. See my article on 'Recodification of the law in The Netherlands' in NILR 1982, 348.
3. Decree of 14 May 1980 JO 1980, 1238-1240. Cf. Thomas E. Carbonneau, The elaboration of a French court doctrine on international commercial arbitration; a study in liberal

In Italy, a draft bill on standard contract terms [4], which was presented at a conference in Fiuggi in 1981, provides an interesting analogy to the Dutch bill, at least with regard to arbitration.[5] The future of this draft is still uncertain, however, and the Italian provision on arbitration will therefore not be dealt with.

The Dutch discussion on how to handle arbitral clauses necessarily reflects the approach to arbitration itself. I shall therefore first try to give a summary of the advantages and disadvantages of arbitration, as set out in Dutch legal writing.

Before going into the advantages and disadvantages of arbitration and other forms of settlement of disputes out of court, I will suggest the relative importance of Dutch arbitration as compared with the settlement of conflicts through the courts.

2. ARBITRATION: THE PRESENT SITUATION IN THE NETHERLANDS

What role does arbitration play in The Netherlands at present? No comprehensive statistics are available on the exact number of arbitrations, but we do possess some figures which give an indication of its use.

Modern commercial arbitration dates back to the second half of the nineteenth century.[6] Among the aims of many of the then newly-formed trade associations was the foundation of private arbitration tribunals for the settlement of conflicts. These tribunals were very welcome to Dutch commerce, since – unlike countries such as Belgium and France – the Netherlands did not have any *tribunaux de commerce* comprising both judges well versed in the law and trade experts.

Arbitration became very popular in the first two decades of this century. In the period from 1900 to 1913, the number of commercial cases settled by the Rotterdam District Court remained on average 300 per year, whereas the number of arbitral awards deposed at the same court rose from 20 to 1,330 per year.[7]

---

civilian judicial creativity, *Tulane Law Review* 1-62 (1980). Regarding the Decree of 12 May 1981 JO 1981, 1380 see B. Goldman, La nouvelle réglementation française de l'arbitrage international, in: *The Art of Arbitration*/Liber amicorum Pieter Sanders, Deventer 1982, pp. 153-174.

4. Testo-base di discussione per il convegno di Fiuggi sulle condizioni generali di contratto del 5-6 giugno 1981.
Regarding binding recommendations see also C.M. Barone, Considerazioni sul procedimento arbitrale e sugli aspetti processuali dell'arbitrato irrituali, in: *I processi speciali,* Napels 1979, p. 57 et seq., especially p. 68 et seq.; G. Collura, Manifesta inequità e arbitrato irrituale, *Revista trimestrale di diritto e procedura civile* 1981,pp.89-139; and Corte di cassazione 12 December 1981, *Foro italiano* 1982, I, p. 1062.

5. According to the draft art. 1341/2 'Sono nulle, anche se approvate specificamente per iscritto, le clausole che alterano l'equilibrio del contratto in pregiudizio dell' aderente senza giustificarsi obiettivamente nell' economia dell'affare e, in generale, le clausole non conformi alle regole della correttezza, anche professionale, o all' equità'.
The draft art. 1341/2 proceeds with a 'grey' list of clauses – 'A titolo esemplicativo sono reputate nulle, salvo che risultino giustificate obiettivamente nell' economia dell' affare . . .' among which the arbitration clause.

6. Some authors give 1872 as the starting point – B.D.H. Tellegen, *Handelingen Nederlandsche Juristen-Vereeniging* 1872, II, p. 152 and A.S. Fransen van de Putte, *Handelingen Nederlandse Juristen-Vereniging* 1968, I, p. 79, 88. Others sometimes mention an earlier date.

7. W. Nolen, Zijn wijzigingen in de bepalingen van het Wetboek van Burgerlijke Rechts-

After 1919, however, the annual number of arbitral awards settled at a much lower level and was rapidly overtaken by the number of court decisions. By 1968, the number of arbitral awards was estimated to be some 5% of all district court decisions in civil matters – family law, bankruptcy, and expropriation cases are not included – (in Rotterdam, this percentage was estimated to be 10%).[8] Since 1968, the number of arbitral awards appears to have grown once again, not only in the area of trade, but also through the spread of arbitration to areas other than the traditional ones, in particular to construction.[9]

However, another development is taking place which from a purely quantitative viewpoint is even more important. The growth of consumer protection had led to the foundation of a steadily increasing number of *geschillencommissies* (complaints boards), usually composed of a member appointed by trade or industry, a member appointed by a consumers' organisation, and an independent president. These *geschillencommissies* do not lay down their decisions in the form of an arbitral award, but as a *bindend advies*. The literal translation of this peculiarly Dutch concept will be obvious to English-speaking readers: it is a binding recommendation. "Binding" in the sense that the parties to a contract who have submitted the settlement of their dispute to the *geschillencommissie*, are contractually bound and not bound by way of civil procedure: a *bindend advies,* unlike arbitration, does not entitle the creditor to an execution; it is a recommendation to the parties on how to solve their dispute.[10]

In theory therefore, arbitration and *bindend advies* are two distinct concepts, the one belonging to civil procedure, the other being of contractual origin. In practice, arbitration and *bindend advies* are not so far apart. Although a binding recommendation does not by itself constitute an executory title, a court will usually consider it binding and demand its enforcement.

It should be remarked that the *bindend advies* concept is not an invention of the consumer protection movement, nor is it a recent phenomenon. Like modern commercial arbitration, it originated during the second half of the nineteenth century in the construction industry.[11] By the 1970's, the construction industry had almost wholly moved from binding recommendations to arbitration, but then the *geschillencommissies* came into being. In 1979, as many as 2,715 binding recommendations were submitted to the five *geschillencommissies* operating under the auspices of the *Stichting Consumentenklachten.*[12]

---

vordering omtrent de rechtspraak door scheidslieden, mede in verband met de toeneming van vaste scheidsgerechten, wenschelijk? Zoo ja, welke? *Handelingen Nederlandsche Juristen-Vereeniging* 1919, I, p. 1, 154.

8. A.S. Fransen van de Putte, Dient de wettelijke regeling omtrent arbitrage te worden gewijzigd? *Handelingen Nederlandse Juristen-Vereniging* 1968, I, p. 79, 153 (data collected by J. Knottenbelt).

9. See M.A. van Wijngaarden (ed.), *Vijfenzeventig jaar bouwarbitrage 1907 - 11 april - 1982,* Zwolle 1982.

10. See P.A. Stein, Chapter 14, Civil Procedure, in: D.C. Fokkema *et al. Introduction to Dutch law for Foreign Lawyers.* Deventer 1978, p. 231, at p. 256.

11. M.A. van Wijngaarden, *De Nieuwe A. V.,* thesis Vrije Universiteit, Deventer 1979.

12. Stichting Consumentenklachten, *Jaarverslag* 1979, p. 5.

In the New Civil Code which is expected to enter into force in 1985, the *bindend advies* will have a *permanent* basis. Title 7.15 on the *vaststellingsovereenkomst* [13] is explicitly meant to apply to binding recommendations as well.

One form of arbitration which is not now prevalent in The Netherlands is compulsory arbitration or arbitration provided for by law. A French law of 1790 for instance provided for compulsory arbitration in family and commercial matters [14], but this law was not introduced in the Netherlands in the nineteenth century, nor was the German concept of *Schiedsmann* [15] or the modern form of arbitration by a court registrar as applied in the United Kingdom.[16]

3. ADVANTAGES AND DISADVANTAGES OF ARBITRATION [17]

Why should two contracting parties submit their disputes to arbitration or to other forms of settlement out of court, instead of to a state-appointed judge? Several reasons are usually advanced, such as the expertise of arbitrators, the swiftness and the informality of the arbitration procedure and the alleged possibility of reaching more equitable settlements. On the other hand, the high cost of arbitration, the (usual) absence of appeal, and the surprise element of arbitration clauses are often seen as disadvantages of settlement out of court. In this paragraph, I will set out these advantages and disadvantages in some detail, illustrating them with some recently compiled data.[18]

One advantage, which arbitration almost undoubtedly has, is the technical expertise of arbitrators in their trade. This expertise does not only relate to such matters as the composition, the nature and the quality of goods or services, but also to the usages in the branch of trade concerned. The ordinary court does not possess this specialised knowledge and therefore will often have to call in outside experts.

Against the advantage of expert knowledge of technical matters, we should set the possible disadvantage of a lack of legal knowledge. Unlike the courts, an arbitration tribunal is not necessarily equipped with a member or a registrar who is learned in the law. In practice, however, most arbitration tribunals have a

13. See the contribution by W. Snijders in this volume.

14. See I. Delbrouck, Arbitrage in historisch perspectief, in: A. Boehlé *et al.*, *Arbitrage*, Ghent 1973, p. 81, at pp. 93-94.

15. G. Bierbrauer, J. Falke, K.F. Koch, Conflict and its settlement: an interdisciplinary study concerning the legal basis, function and performance of the institution of the Schiedsman, in: M. Cappelletti, J. Weisner (eds.), *Access to Justice*, II, Promising Institutions, Alphen aan den Rijn/Milan 1978, I, p. 39 at p. 48.

16. G. Appleby, Small Claims in England and Wales, in: M. Cappelletti, J. Weisner (eds.), *Access to Justice*, II, Promising Institutions, Alphen aan den Rijn/Milan 1978, II, p. 683 at pp. 743-754.

17. This paragraph is partly based on my contribution 'De toekomst van de arbitrage', in: *Advocatenblad* 1981, pp. 151-156.

18. *Harmonisatie van Standaardvoorwaarden in de Bouw*, Rapport van de Werkgroep Standaardregelingen in de Bouw (hereafter cited as *Rapport)*, Deventer/Alphen aan den Rijn 1981, Appendix 6 by J.M. Schoenmakers.

registrar who is learned in the law. The statutes of the *Stichting Consumentenklachten* require that the president of a *geschillencommissie* is learned in the law. Conversely could an ordinary court be supplemented with lay judges who are expert in a specific trade? Belgian and French experience shows that this should be possible. Dutch experience with lay judges is less positive. As has been pointed out, such lay judges will often be appointed on the recommendation of a professional organisation and will therefore often be more likely to represent professional interests than to be mere experts.[19]

A second advantage which is attached to arbitration is the informal procedure and the possibility of equitable judgments. Although this advantage does still exist, it no longer seems of primary importance, as court procedures have become far less formal than they were previously.[20] Arbitrators are not bound by the rules of evidence, but these rules have become so flexible that the difference in this respect between court adjudication and arbitration is now rather small. Finally, arbitrators should apply equity [21], but once again practice shows that this makes little difference, as common law has developed so many constructions to reach equitable judgments that the harsh *pacta sunt servanda* is no longer considered to be the last word on the matter.[22]

Rapid procedure is the third advantage which is usually ascribed to arbitration. Statistics are now available, which support this contention at least in some areas of arbitration. In the construction industry, the average time between bringing a case before the arbitration tribunal and receiving the arbitral award ranges from eight to fifteen months for the various arbitration tribunals.[23] For the *geschillencommissies* of the *Stichting Consumentenklachten,* the number of months varies from 3.5 to 7.5.[24]

Corresponding statistics on court adjudication are unfortunately not available. Some years ago, some 70% of all defended actions – family affairs excepted – were dealt with within twenty-two or twenty-four months.[25] It is not possible to compare these figures with any great precision. Moreover, one should always reckon with the (theoretical) possibility that an arbitral award will be annulled by a court.[26] Nevertheless, the available data do at least suggest that arbitration is more rapid than court procedure.[27]

19. O.A.C. Verpaalen, *Hart en nieren van de Nederlandsche Burgerlijke rechter,* Zwolle 1974, pp. 95-96.

20. J.L.M. Elders, The use of conciliation for dispute settlement in Dutch civil procedure, in: Netherlands Report to the Xth International Congress of Comparative Law, Budapest 1978, Deventer 1978, pp. 159-170.

21. According to art. 636 *Wetboek van Burgerlijke Rechtsvordering* arbitrators should either apply the law or equity. The law sees the latter possibility as an exception, but in practice the terms of reference always provide that arbitrators should apply equity.

22. See the contribution by J.L.M. Elders in this volume.

23. *Rapport* (see footnote 18), p. 280, 287, 293.

24. Stichting Consumentenklachten, *Jaarverslag* 1979, p. 9.

25. P. Zonderland, *Privaatrechtspleging in grondtrekken,* Zwolle 1977, p. 255.

26. N.A. Koedam, *Tijdschrift voor arbitrage* 1980, p. 65, at p. 70.

27. This experience does not seem to be universal. Cf. for instance the Chairman of the (English) Law Commission, Mr. Justice Kerr, in *Journal of Business Law* 1980, p. 178: 'The

A final advantage of arbitration which I should not omit to mention (there are, of course, several other advantages) is that the procedure and outcome may be kept secret. From the point of view of legal development such secrecy is a disadvantage, though this can be overcome by anonymous publication.[28]

Is arbitration also cheaper? Here, a distinction should be made between arbitration proper and non-arbitral conflict settlement out of court. There is some evidence that the former is more expensive – at least for the parties concerned – than court procedure, and the latter less expensive. Arbitration is often more expensive for the parties concerned, because the costs of the arbitration tribunal must be borne by them. In the construction industry for instance the average costs of arbitration itself (usually to be paid by the loser, costs of legal aid not included) some years ago varied from f. 3.600,-- for the *Raad van Arbitrage voor de Bouwbedrijven in Nederland* to f. 2.000,-- for the *Arbitrage-Instituut Bouwkunst.*[29] These costs are high compared to the cost of litigation before an ordinary court (most of the expenses of which are furnished by the State). On the other hand, the arbitration tribunal will rarely have to call in the testimony of experts. Secondly, arbitration does not necessarily require legal counsel (although in practice many contracting parties retain an attorney in arbitral litigation).

In contrast, the settlement of conflicts by means of binding recommendation is often quite inexpensive for the contracting parties. Usually, no more than f. 50,-- is demanded from the consumer (this will only be forfeited if he loses). In practice, the costs of maintaining a *geschillencommissie* will be far higher, but these costs are mainly borne by the state and by trade and industry.

A major disadvantage of both arbitral and *bindend advies* clauses is that they are often concealed in the small print of a contract and then take the other party by surprise. This problem does not only occur with regard to arbitral and binding recommendation clauses. What makes these clauses even harder to accept for the other party, however, is that from his point of view the enterpreneur not only drafts his own law (the standard form contract), but he also decides on the conflicts as to this "law". This point of view is of course erroneous, in the sense that the private tribunals involved are most often unbiased, quite representative and of high quality. Nevertheless, the suspicion of a biased attitude will persist, especially when the arbitral or *bindend advies* clause does not offer the other party the possibility of opting for settlement of the conflict by an ordinary court.

Finally, arbitration often does not allow appeals to be made. Appeal from arbitral awards to the courts is virtually unknown in The Netherlands (unlike in the United Kingdom) and appeal to appellate arbitration tribunals exists only in some trades and industries. In the construction trade further problems arise when,

---

only merit of many arbitration clauses currently in vogue, if one is cynical about them, is the fact that they provide a great incentive for settlement. Indeed, in many cases it ultimately turns out that it is virtually impossible to obtain an enforceable award within a reasonable time at reasonable cost'.

28. Thus, for instance, the T.M.C. Asser Institute for International Law in The Hague collects and classifies arbitral awards resulting from international trade in anonymous form.

29. *Rapport* (see footnote 18), p. 276, 286, 291.

in a conflict involving three or more parties various arbitration tribunals may be called upon to settle the conflict between two of the parties concerned.[30]

The balance of the several advantages and disadvantages of conflict settlement out of court will differ, according to the importance one attaches to these elements. In my opinion, this method of conflict settlement has some obvious advantages in several areas, such as international trade and consumer contracts. Some disadvantages seem difficult to overcome, but others might conveivably be set aside. The latter category includes the problem that arbitration is often 'agreed' upon in a surreptitious way.

4. THE SWEDISH RECORD

Sweden was among the first of the European countries to enact legislation in the area of unfair contract terms. The control system, with its Consumer Ombudsman and Market Court, has proved to be effective. Swedish substantive law, however, is much less specific than more recent legislation on unfair contract terms, such as the German *AGB-Gesetz* and the Austrian *Konsumentenschutzgesetz.* When dealing with arbitral clauses, Swedish courts have therefore had to resort to the general clause *(Generalklausel)* contained in the unfair contract terms legislation, rather than to a more specific provision dealing with arbitral clauses.

Some recent cases illustrate the Swedish approach to arbitral clauses in standard form contracts. In *Designern Carleric Göranzon* v. *Skandinaviska Aluminium Profiler Aktiebolaget*[31] the *Högsta Domstol* (Supreme Court) held that a company could not make use of an arbitral clause contained in its general conditions. The other contracting party was a freelance graphic designer, who himself acted in a professional capacity. This was probably the reason why in two lower instances the company was held to be entitled to invoke the arbitral clause, when the designer sued the company in court. The *Högsta Domstol,* however, decided in favour of the designer, on the grounds that he was inexperienced, needed the goods ordered, and had no alternative but to order them from the company in question.

In a more recent case, *Tureberg-Sollentuna Lastbilcentral ek.för* v. *Byggnadsfirman Rudolf Asplund Aktiebolaget,*[32] the *Högsta Domstol* decided in favour of the company which invoked its arbitral clause. Although the said company had neglected to send the other party a copy of the general conditions which contained the arbitral clause, it was nonetheless considered to be entitled to avail itself of the clause, one of the major considerations being that the other party it-

30. *Rapport* (see footnote 18), p. 206 et seq.

31. *Högsta Domstol* 1 November 1979, *Nytt Juridiskt Arkiv* 1979, 666, *Nordisk Domssamling* 1980, 616.

32. *Högsta Domstol* 12 February 1980, *Nytt Juridiskt Arkiv* 1980, 46, *Nordisk Domssamling* 1981, 167.

self used general conditions containing an arbitral clause in its commercial dealings.[33]

On what ground was the arbitral clause considered to be inapplicable in the first case while it was applied in the second case? The Swedish Contract Law *(Avtalsvillkorslagen)* contains a provision, which gives ordinary courts the power to adjust or declare unenforceable any contract term which is found to be unreasonable (para. 36).

Although the wording of this provision is in general terms, it is clear from its legislative history [34] that it was introduced in the aftermath of an important piece of consumer protection, the Act prohibiting improper terms of contract *(Lag om förbud mot oskäliga avtalsvillkor).* [35] Under section 1 of this Act, the Market Court may issue an injunction prohibiting a tradesman from henceforth using an improper contract term. The court has used this power, inter alia, to prohibit the further use of arbitral clauses in consumer contracts. The Swedish Arbitration Act *(Lag om skiljemän)*[36] contains a mandatory provision with regard to consumer contracts. Para. 3a provides that arbitral clauses are not enforceable against consumers when the amount in litigation is less than the jurisdictional amount of the Small Claims Act *(Lag om rättegang i tvistemal om mindre värden).*[37] The purpose of this provision is to ensure that the simplified procedure available under the Small Claims Act is not denied to consumers.[38] As a result, in the case of *Kvissberg & Bäckström Byggnads AB*[39], a supplier of prefabricated housing materials was forbidden to use the term "Disputes arising from this contract shall, if the seller so desires, be resolved by arbitration according to the law".

What makes this case interesting, is that the Market Court based its injunction on two separate grounds. The second was the supplier's failure to comply with the Arbitration Act and the ensuing deception of the consumer regarding his legal rights. The first ground given by the court was that arbitration procedures are more expensive for consumers than judicial procedures because the Legal Aid Act provides for financial help only in the latter instance. The court was afraid that such clauses would discourage consumers from asserting their rights and from having them legally established. As a result of the court's reliance on this more general reasoning, its decision has an impact exceeding the area covered by para. 3a of the Arbitration Act. It may suggest that arbitral clauses are unreasonable in all consumer transactions to which the Legal Aid Act applies. The decision is also an

33. The two Supreme Court decisions are discussed by Nils Mångard, Ogiltighet av skiljeavtal i affärsforhållanden, in: *Svenk och internationell skiljedom* 1981/Arsskrift från Stockholms Handelskammares Skiljedomsinstitut, Stockholm 1981.

34. Generalklausul i förmögenshetsrätten, SOU 1974: 83, pp. 33-39.

35. SFS 1971: 112, as amended.

36. SFS 1929: 145, as amended. An English translation can be found in Arbitration in Sweden, published by the Stockholm Chamber of Commerce, Stockholm 1977, p. 192-201.

37. SFS 1974: 8.

38. Prop. 1976/77: 110, p. 45.

39. *Marknads domstolens avgöranden* 1975: 5.

example of unreasonableness *per se* of any term which gives the tradesman the unilateral right to call for arbitration.[40]

The effect of consumer protection law on the development of the law as applied between businessmen is obvious [41], cf. the two Supreme Court cases discussed at the beginning of this paragraph. Moreover, a government commission has recently proposed the enactment of a bill which would extend the jurisdiction of the Market Court to (improper) terms in contracts between business enterprises.[42]

5. SOME ENGLISH CASES

Although the United Kingdom has recently enacted a statute on improper contract terms, the Unfair Contract Terms Act, it is not this act which has provided the courts with the possibility of setting aside arbitral clauses.[43] It is rather the Arbitration Act 1979, which has given rise to some interesting cases.[44] The Arbitration Act 1979 was intended to change arbitration practice in England. It had been observed that, although many arbitrations were still held in London, other centres such as Paris, Geneva, New York and Stockholm had come to be regarded as more suitable for major international arbitration. The basic reason for this "emigration" of arbitration lay with the British courts' application of the Arbitration Act 1950, under which they exercised wide-ranging powers to supervise arbitration proceedings, particularly through the "case stated" procedure. This procedure allowed either party to request the arbitrator to state a question of law arising in the course of the arbitration for the decision of the High Court. If the arbitrator declined, the requesting party could nevertheless apply to the Court, which almost invariably directed that a special case be stated.

Under the 1979 Act, the "case stated" procedure was abolished. An appeal to the High Court arising out of an arbitration's award was only to be made on a point of law, and such an appeal might be made either with the consent of all parties or where the Court gave leave (subject to an exclusion agreement). Section 1 (4) provides that the Court shall not grant leave unless "it considers that, having regard to all the circumstances, the determination of the question of law concerned

40. Ulf Bernitz and John Draper, *Consumer Protection in Sweden/Legislation, Institutions and Practice,* Stockholm 1981, pp. 238-239.

41. Ulf Bernitz, when discussing the question whether small businessmen might rely on para 36 of the Contract Act, argues that the reflex effects of the new consumer legislation are evident: U. Bernitz, Chapter 8 on Market and consumer law, in: Stig Strömholm, *An Introduction to Swedish Law,* Deventer 1981, I, p. 231, at 252.

42. Avtalsvillkor mellan närigsidkare, Delbetänkande av Konsumentköpsutredningen, Statens offentliga utredningar 1981: 31, Stockholm 1981. On the subject of arbitration clauses see p. 50.

43. More in general terms, the virtual absence of reported cases concerned with the Unfair Contract Terms Act is striking. The Act was described by L.S. Sealy, 37 *Cambridge Law Journal* 15 (1978) as follows: 'Not since the Statute of Frauds three centuries ago has there been an enactment which threatens to have so profound an effect on the law of contract . . .'

44. Regarding the following text see the instructive note by C.J.B. Bloomfield in *International Legal Materials* 1981, p. 1099 and also C.M. Schmithoff, in *Yearbook Commercial Arbitration* V, 1980, pp. 231-239; VI, 1981, pp. 155-161; VII, 1982, pp. 179-188.

could substantially effect the right of one or more of the parties to the arbitration agreement".

Some cases decided shortly after the 1979 Act entered into force have raised doubts as to whether the Act will achieve this objective. In *The Nema Case*[45], the Court of Appeal presided over by Lord Denning MR suggested that in this aspect a distinction should be made between "one-off clauses" in a "one-off" contract and arbitral clauses in a standard form. In the *Oinoussion Virtue Case*[46], Robert Goff J.[47] flatly rejected this distinction, but on appeal in *The Nema*[48], the House of Lords, although reproving Lord Denning for his 'somewhat less than tactful phrase' that an arbitrator might just as likely be right as a judge – in fact was probably more likely to be right – upheld his decision. Lord Diplock's views on arbitral clauses in standard contract terms are relevant here. He begins by observing that "the great majority of international maritime and commercial contracts which contain a London arbitration clause . . . are made on standard printed forms on which the particulars appropriate to the contract between the actual parties are inserted, and any amendments needed for reasons special to the particular contract are either made to the printed clauses or dealt with in added clauses, which sometimes may themselves be classified as standard. Business on the Baltic, the insurance market and the commodity markets would be impracticable without the use of standard terms to deal with what are to be the legal rights and obligations of the parties upon the happening of a whole variety of events which experience has shown are liable to occur, even though it be only rarely, in the course of the performance of contracts of those kinds".[49]

Lord Diplock then continues by considering that "when contracts are entered into, which incorporate standard terms, it is in the interests alike of justice and of the conduct of commercial transactions that those standard terms should be construed and treated by arbitrators as giving rise to similar legal rights and obligations in all arbitrations in which the events have given rise to the dispute do not differ from one another in some relevant aspect. It is only if parties to commercial contracts can rely upon a uniform construction being given to standard terms that they can prudently incorporate them in their contracts without the need for detailed negotiation or discussion. Such uniform construction of standard terms had been progressively established up to 1979, largely through decisions of the courts upon special cases stated by arbitrators. In the result English commercial law has achieved a degree of comprehensiveness and certainty that has made it acceptable for adoption as the appropriate proper law to be applied to commercial contracts wherever made by parties of whatever nationality. So in relation to disputes involving standard terms in commercial contracts, an authoritative ruling of the

45. [1980] QB 547; [1980] 3 All ER 117; [1980] 3 WLR 326.
46. [1981] 2 All ER 887.
47. The very same High Court judge, who had already had to decide the Nema Case, before it came before the Court of Appeal.
48. Pioneer Shipping Ltd. v. B.T.P. Tioxide Ltd. (The Nema), [1981] 3 WLR 292, applied also in Italmare Shipping Co. v. Ocean Tanker Co. Inc. (Court of Appeal), [1982] 1 WLR 158.
49. [1981] 3 WLR 292, at 298.

court as to their construction, which is binding also upon all arbitrators under the sanction of an appeal from an award of an arbitrator that has resulted from his departing from that ruling performs a useful function that is lacking in that performed by the court in substituting for the opinion of an experienced commercial arbitrator its own opinion as to the application of a "one-off" clause to the particular facts of a particular case."[50]

Although Lord Diplock does not say so explicitly, it seems clear from his opinion that the maxim of uniformity in construction of standard arbitral clauses may be placed on a higher level than the sacred *contra proferentem* maxim.[51]

6. DUTCH IUS CONSTITUENDUM

To return to Dutch law, I must first briefly outline the law regarding arbitral clauses as it stands. Unlike French law, Dutch law has always been liberal in allowing arbitral clauses. In legal writing it has long been argued that, especially when incorporated in standard contract terms, arbitral clauses should not be considered to apply as automatically as other clauses. A legal basis for this contention was found in Article 170 *Grondwet* (Constitution) – 'Nobody may against his will be abstracted from the court, which law allots him' – or in Article 620 *Wetboek van Burgerlijke Rechtsvordering* (Code of Civil Procedure) – 'One may even commit oneself in advance to submit to arbitration conflicts which might arise in the future'.[52]

In 1967 the *Hoge Raad* (Supreme Court) rejected this theory unequivocally.[53] This decision, however, has not been accepted by all writers [54] and a counter trend may be observed. There is some evidence that under modern international arbitration conventions, arbitral clauses should be dealt with more strictly than other standard contract terms.[55] This is also the case with regard to the related choice of forum clauses.[56] The heaviest attack on the arbitral clause, however, comes from the present government bill on standard contract terms.[57] This bill

50. *Ibidem.*

51. The maxim *verba cartarum fortius accipiuntur contra proferentum* is often used in common law to construct standard contract terms against the party who has drafted the terms.

52. See P. Sanders, *Aantasting van arbitrale vonnissen,* thesis Leyden, Zwolle 1940, pp. 46-47; the same, Dutch national report, in *Yearbook commercial arbitration* VI, Deventer 1981, pp. 60-85.

53. HR 27 October 1967 *Nederlandse Jurisprudentie* 1968, 3 (Menne v. Van Nunen).

54. See A.R. Bloembergen and W.M. Kleyn, *Contractenrecht* VII, No. 291.

55. Regarding the possible voidness of a compromissory clause by virtue of art. II/section 2 of the New York Arbitration Convention, see for example, A.J. van den Berg, *The New York arbitration convention of 1958/ Towards a uniform judicial interpretation,* thesis Rotterdam, The Hague/Deventer 1981, pp. 170-232.

56. See for instance art. 17 EEC Execution Convention and its application by the European Court in Estatis Salotti di Colzani Aimo c.s. v. RÜWA Polsteraimaschinen, [1977] 1 CMLR 345 and Galeries Segura v. Rahim Bonakdarian, [1977] 1 CMLR 361.

57. *Bill* 16,983. See also the contribution by H. Duintjer Tebbens in this volume. At the end of 1982, the Ministry of Justice published a draft bill on arbitration itself. This draft also refers to arbitral clauses in standard contract terms. According to art. 1000 of the draft, the

is to be incorporated into the New Civil Code, which presumably will enter into force in 1985. The bill provides for a control system of standard contract terms, which is quite similar to the German system: one of the five *gerechtshoven* (courts of appeal), i.e., the one in The Hague, will be given the power to issue an injunction with regard to any further use of standard contract terms which contain unreasonably onerous clauses. The injunction will be issued only upon the request of a trade organisation or a consumers' organisation (Article 6.5.2A.6, para. 2). The general clause, which should provide a guideline to the court and to the parties concerned (Article 6.5.2A.2, para. 2 under a) and which shall also be applicable in individual disputes, is supplemented in consumer contracts by two lists of clauses, which will either be held to be unreasonably onerous and therefore null and void (Article 6.5.2A.3), or be held to be unreasonably onerous unless the contrary appears to be the case (Article 6.5.2A.4). Among the clauses which are listed in the 'black list' of Article 6.5.2A.3 is the arbitral clause, at least the arbitral clause which does not leave the other party the possibility to opt for the ordinary court once the conflict has arisen.

An earlier draft outlawed the standard arbitral clause outright, but apparently the government paid heed to the comments of the construction trade in particular with regard to this clause. It is apparent that Dutch trade interests are very concerned about the present prohibition article, even though it is somewhat diluted, and the outcome of the parliamentary debate which will ensue is uncertain.

In my opinion the present government approach is correct. Arbitration and other methods of the settlement of disputes out of court are not inherently bad; often the advantages outweigh the disadvantages. But if arbitration is beneficial to both parties, it should be able to sell itself. It should not be imposed upon one party, who is unaware of the arbitral clause.

If, under special circumstances, an arbitral clause should be made binding without the consumer being offered a possibility to take the case to court, the bill provides for a procedure to arrive at such a result. Under Article 6.5.2A.5, para. 4 both of the lists of clauses may be set aside, insofar as a consumer's organisation declares a clause to be not unfair. This leaves room for negotiation – the principal aim of the bill. It should also be observed that the scope of the two lists is limited to consumer transactions and that the bill contains several exceptions. Thus, the *kantongerecht* case which was cited in the first paragraph might fall under two exceptions: first, it is not clear whether it was a consumer contract and second, being a shipping contract, it would fall under the exception of Article 6.5.2A.11, para. 2. Both exceptions would result only in the two lists of clauses not being directly applicable. This would not prevent a court from applying the general clause of Article 6.5.2A.2, which in turn might lead to the avoidance of the arbitral clause, even in a commercial contract. The Swedish experience may turn out to

existence of an arbitration agreement shall be proven by a document. This includes a document issued by one of the parties which refers to standard contract terms providing for arbitration'. Although this provision does not appear to be exactly in line with the government bill on standard contract terms, it is not clearly in conflict with the proposed art. 6.5.2A.3 either.

provide some guidelines to Dutch courts regarding the way in which this discretionary power should be used.

As to the construction of standard arbitral clauses, or rather standard contract terms in general, the question has been raised in Dutch legal literature whether any importance should be attached to the avowed wish of trade and industry to have their standard contract terms applied in a uniform way. This wish may be thwarted by other construction maxims, such as the *contra proferentem* rule. When a private party comes across standard contract terms, which have been drafted bilaterally by two organisations, neither of which, however, can be deemed to represent the said party, the two constructions may result in conflicting outcomes. In a recent report it is argued that in such a case the uniformity of construction should prevail.[58] Lord Diplock's opinion in *The Nema Case* may contribute to a better understanding of this argument.

58. *Rapport* (see footnote 18), p. 56.

INTERNATIONAL ISSUES ON COLLECTIVE AGREEMENTS OF SEAFARERS

by L.F.D. ter Kuile *

1. INTRODUCTION

During the course of several decades collective labour agreements (CAOs) have shown their importance as a stabilizing factor in the constantly fluctuating balance between employers and their employees. The collective agreements were intended to have a stabilizing influence which would be in the interests of both of the social partners. The relations between them, the trade unions and the employers' associations, and consequently between their individual members, are regulated to a great extent. An adequate organization for each party is a prerequisite for this regulation. In addition, there must be a fixed system of rules. Thus the strike, the oldest positive form of communal action, is used as a last resort and becomes an industrial sanction rather than an industrial action. All of these factors form an important part of the infrastructure of the labour market.

The above cannot really be considered to be a correct description of seafarers and their social antagonists, referred to hereafter as "shipowners", for the sake of simplicity. The infrastructure does not seem to extend beyond national boundaries. It certainly does not always meet the requirements of this particular labour market and the international issues at stake. It does not take much imagination to identify the main obstacle: the various discrepancies between the socio-economic conditions of the different countries from which seamen are recruited. The developing countries in particular are not self-sufficient as regards the employment of their own national seamen and are forced to depend on vessels flying a foreign flag. In these countries the primary objective is the fight against domestic unemployment, poverty and privation. Their seamen are not in a position to act in a similar way to their fellow seamen in the traditional seafaring countries of Western Europe and the USA, when it comes to negotiating their employment contracts.

While the above-mentioned socio-economic conditions slow down the development of international collective agreements, the freedom of organization has achieved a considerable recognition; this entails the freedom of both workers and employers to form local, national or international organizations for the protection of their economic and social interests and to join those organizations; similarly the freedom of negotiation, including the right to organize an international framework for such negotiation, e.g., the right of trade unions to establish national federations or confederations and the right of the latter to form or join international trade unions, as well as the right of trade unions to function freely and the

* Vice-President of the District Court at Rotterdam.

right to strike, provided that it is exercised in conformity with the laws of the particular country.[1]

This certainly amounts to considerable, though not universal, recognition. This is hardly suprising in view of the above-mentioned discrepancies. The need for regulations or control by public authorities is not compatible with freedom.

In fact many areas of conflict have arisen when these various autonomous developments meet at an international level. In a large number of cases the courts have been consulted for specific conflict situations, especially in the conflicts mentioned below regarding collective agreements for seafarers. These conflicts are not concerned primarily with the collective agreement as the result of bargaining, but, and this is characteristic of these problems, with questions regarding the obligation to conclude a collective agreement to replace or adapt another still valid collective agreement. They are also concerned with questions regarding the consequences resulting from the acceptance of this sort of obligation.

1.1 The duty to bargain

It is generally accepted that there is no obligation to enter an agreement unless such obligation has a specific basis. If this is formulated as a principle of the freedom of contracts, further precision is required with regard to international labour relations. In an international industrial relations system where the employers and their organizations meet the workers and their unions, how does this principle relate to other equally important principles such as the freedom of negotiation and the right to function freely, which in my opinion includes the right to use democratic forms of power, and finally, the right to strike.[2]

With regard to the principle of the freedom of contract, this refers to freedom as it exists in a democratic system. In this system the duty to bargain must be created before the collective bargaining by way of democratic interaction.

1.2 Interactions at an international level

The possibility of participating in collective bargaining depends primarily on representativeness. However, there is no international "Tariffähigkeit", to use the German term, "a norm to determine the capacity to participate in bargaining".[3] The right to form an international organization supports any international federation of national unions of various countries, each of them "tariffähig" under their own national law and together forming a representative workers' interest, in initiating a democratic interaction at an international level. In this context

1. Special reference has to be made to the European Social Charter (Trb. 1962, 3) and to the International Covenant on Economic, Social and Cultural Rights, New York 19 December 1966, of the U.N., Trb. 1969 no. 100.

2. See on this subject W.J.P.M. Fase, *De botsing tussen de contracts- en vakverenigingsvrijheid* (Deventer 1981).

3. See on this subject Rolf Birk, "Internationales Tarifvertragsrecht", *Festschrift Günther Beitzke*, (Berlin 1979) p. 839 et seq.

the recommendations of the ILO on wages and conditions of employment constitute a well-known example, but they are not the result of collective bargaining and are not binding. On the other hand, the International Transport Workers Federation (ITF) has played an important role for a long time. In an attempt to reach acceptable wages and conditions the ITF has unilaterally formulated regulations for a collective agreement, the so-called ITF Collective Agreement. Unlike the ILO recommendations, which form a standard for reference, this is a collective agreement proposing normative wage scales and conditions to be adopted wherever the ITF can exert an influence. Nevertheless, there is no duty to bargain. The current aim of the ITF is to enforce the ITF Collective Agreement on individual ships. In practice such enforcement boils down to industrial action or threats that similar measures will be taken in the event that the shipowner should continue to refuse to negotiate with the ITF.

In fact, under such circumstances there is no negotiation in the normal sense of the word, because the contents of the current ITF Collective Agreement are not open to negotiation. The shipowner can choose whether to accept or not. If he accepts, he has to sign a so-called Special Agreement obliging him to employ all seafarers in accordance with the terms and conditions of the current ITF Collective Agreement, to incorporate these terms and conditions into the individual contracts of employment of each seafarer, to pay contributions to a fund of the ITF on behalf of each seafarer, and to grant the representative of the ITF and of its affiliated trade union organizations free access to all seafarers. On the other hand, the ITF is entitled to change the rates in the ITF Collective Agreement at two months' notice, after which the new rates come into force from the specified date.

So far the modus operandi of the ITF and its adopted role in the collective bargaining for seafarers from the developing countries has not been accepted by its social opponents. What is more, experience has shown on several occasions that the conduct of the ITF as manifested in the industrial actions it has organized, is not endorsed by the national trade unions of these countries and the individual members concerned. The following case is an example of this.

In September 1978 the ITF organized a boycott in Glasgow of two ships flying the Liberian flag, the *Camilla-M* and the *Anna-M* for the purpose of imposing an ITF wage structure for the Indian crew members. These crew members were employed on conditions agreed upon by their own national trade union, the National Union of Seafarers of India (NUSI) and did not wish the ITF to interfere. As the ITF nevertheless continued the action in spite of this, the shipowners then dismissed the Indian crew members and replaced them by Greek seamen. The boycott was continued, this time to demand the payment of ITF wages to the Greek seamen. However, the Greeks also appeared to be content with their wages. The shipowners then took legal action to obtain the termination of the boycott. The Court of Appeal considered:[4]

4. Star Sea Transport Corp. of Monrovia *v.* Slater c.s., Lloyd's Rep. 1979 (1) p. 26.

"What the Court had to deal with was a new situation. The Indian and Greek crews were content with their wages and conditions and their unions were content; and then the ITF came along and said, 'We don't think these men are being paid enough. They should be paid on ITF rates.' That might be a legitimate claim . . . but the IFT went further. They made demands virtually impossible for the owners to fulfil – that the crew should sign the ITF agreement, when the men said they would not sign."

The Court ordered that all instructions preventing the *Camilla-M* from sailing should be withdrawn. A month later the NUSI was suspended from the ITF on the grounds that it had acted against ITF policy.

In the opening address to the Conference of Asian Seafarers' Unions in Singapore in April 1979, the spokesman said:

"The net result of all this (i.e., ITF policy: author's note) is that thousands of Asian seamen from developing countries will be priced out of their jobs."

A similar discrepancy between national trade union policy and ITF conduct was revealed in court proceedings in the Supreme Court of South Africa in March 1980. It was stated that in the Philippines, employment contracts of national seamen concluded as a result of industrial action by a third party, such as the ITF, which compels the shipowner to agree to an alteration of its original employment contracts with the crew, are unenforceable on the grounds of duress.[5]

Similarly the President [6] of the Rotterdam District Court, judging the third *Saudi Independence* case (hereafter *Saudi Independence* III), considered that it would be contrary to Philippine law as a reflection of national labour policy for the shipowner to be compelled because of the influence of the strike to alter his original employment contracts.[7]

The absence of a duty to bargain, the absence of what has been described above as an infrastructure for the international labour market and the conflict of rights, such as the freedom of negotiation, the right to function freely, the right to strike and the right to use democratic forms of power, together constitute a labyrinth in which it is hard to find the way.

2. IN COURT

2.1 Conflicts regarding collective agreements for seafarers

The procedures initiated by a conflict regarding a collective agreement are often introduced by the attachment of a ship in a foreign port or by industrial action against such a ship. The requirement of the declaration of value of this attachment

5. Pres. Rb. Rotterdam, 12 June 1981, S & S (Schip en Schade) 1982, 5.
6. The author of this contribution functioned as President in the three *Saudi Independence* Cases.
7. See note 5.

or the termination of the industrial action are submitted to the courts of a state which does not necessarily have any connection with the basic conflict. In practice, the following questions arise: questions concerned with the basic conflict and questions regarding the legality of industrial action.

In cases falling under the first category the judge must form an idea of how the collective agreement was created, e.g., if use was made of unacceptable pressure (lack of genuine intent). For example, in July 1978 the ITF instigated an industrial action (boycott) in Redcar, an English port, against the MS *Pacifico,* flying the Liberian flag, in order to force the shipowner, a Liberian company with its management in New York, to act in accordance with the ITF Collective Agreement. This industrial action had resulted in the shipowner signing a special agreement with the ITF at the office of his local agent in Redcar in which he undertook to apply the ITF wage scales for his crew. However, the shipowner did not keep to this agreement. The members of the crew, who had meanwhile been paid off, had the *Pacifico* attached in Rotterdam in order to achieve the payment of back pay.
The first case put forward by the shipowner was based on the fact that the Special Agreement had not been implemented by him due to lack of genuine consent and was therefore voidable. One relevant factor was that the ITF had not been involved in ratifying the collective agreement between the shipowner and the crew: the Collective Agreement Concerning Greek Cargo Vessels Over 4,500 TDW (hereafter, "GCA"). This GCA, as well as the individual contracts of employment of the crew members, were applicable in accordance with Greek law. In its decision of 18 December 1981 [8] the Rotterdam Court considered that the shipowner had no duty to bargain with the ITF, which had not been involved in the creation of the GCA nor the individual contracts of employment and that there was certainly no obligation to invalidate a still valid collective agreement; the fact that the parties nevertheless negotiated and that the shipowner signed a Special Agreement was solely a consequence of the pressure exerted by the boycott of the ship on the instigation of the ITF; in accordance with the Greek law applicable in this case – in accordance with the legal choice made by the parties to the valid GCA – the shipowner was in principle free to determine himself whether to negotiate with any third parties, and if so, with which, outside the existing framework of organized discussion. However, the boycott made this an unreal choice; Greek law should determine whether the shipowner should be bound to the Special Agreement. Even before the Court came to a final decision, the case went into higher appeal, and this is still pending.

Let us limit ourselves for the moment to the lack of genuine consent, and which law should apply to decide this. Is it logical that for the effect of an agreement drawn up in England between an English party (the ITF) and a Liberian company with management in the USA, dealing with the conditions of employment on board a Liberian ship with a crew of various nationalities, other than Greek, Greek law is relevant to the question of lack of genuine consent? Are any

8. Rb. Rotterdam, 18 December 1981, S & S 1982, 104; it has gone to higher appeal.

of the other legal systems concerned logically more relevant? For example, if the Special Agreement had not been signed on shore but on board ship, the connection with England would be more tenuous; as regards the ITF, which acts mainly for third parties, the domicile is hardly relevant; the same applies for the place where the ship was registered when the ship has no genuine link with this place; and finally, the nationalities of the crew members change as rapidly as the crew members themselves. In this case the contracts of employment at stake were subject to Greek law, and the Rotterdam Court turned to Greek law from the multiciplicity of possibilities.

It is possibly less correct to suppose that a more recent special agreement can in principle intervene in the individual contracts of employment, either directly or indirectly. In fact, it is more likely that these individual contracts of employment and the older GCA on which they are based would have a limiting effect on the freedom of contract of the parties bound by them. The latter certainly concurs with the objective of the collective agreement as such. If this assumption is not made [9], problems arise when the employee changes membership from one union to another or becomes a member of both unions during the course of two collective agreements with which the employer is simultaneously involved.

Obviously problems such as these have been recognized for a long time; many collective agreements contain prohibitive provisions against becoming a party to other collective agreements. However, an organization such as the ITF, which is not bound, does not have to pay any attention to this sort of prohibition.

Meanwhile it is conceivable that the *Pacifico* procedure was carried out, while the order in which the various agreements were signed was the reverse. In fact, special agreements had already been made between the ITF and the same shipowner regarding the same ship – at that time called the *Argo Pollux* – but their validity had already expired before being implemented. In this case, the question of what scope should be attributed to a prohibition against becoming a party to other collective agreements could be of importance; the boundary seems to lie at the exclusion of organizations other than the CAO partners ("closed shops").

In each of the above-mentioned examples the question arises whether individual employees derive any rights from the special agreement. In English law, which does not recognise direct rights deriving from provisions in contracts for persons who are not parties to them, the answer is "no". However, the crew members of the *Pacifico* argued that the Special Agreement had been drawn up by the ITF as a collective representative of its members (the crew members).

Direct representation, as argued in the *Pacifico* case, would mean that all the ITF members employed at the time the special agreement entered into force, or who enter employment while it is in force, can derive individual rights from this special agreement. As regards the first category – members who are allready employed – we have already pointed out that the earlier agreement should have priority. As regards the second category, it depends on whether, at the time he enters employment, the employee is or becomes a member of the ITF, and whether

9. E.g., J. Mannoury, *De collectieve arbeidsovereenkomst* (Alphen aan den Rijn 1961) p. 67.

he refers to the special agreement. If he signs an individual contract of employment on different conditions, the conditions of his employment are in almost all cases subject to a different collective agreement than the ITF agreement. The Special Agreement is not replaced by this other collective agreement but in fact has never applied with regard to this employee.

2.2 Industrial action

Korthals Altes [10] concluded that a judge may not invervene in a strike on board ship when the flag state has not requested this; he came to this conclusion in conjunction with his statement that in public international law the judge of a port state has no right to judge the conditions of employment on board a foreign ship unless these are such that they affect the legal order of the port state. Nevertheless, Dutch judges have several times declared their competence to judge a case without such a request. Their lack of competence has not always been pleaded.

Thus the President of the Amsterdam District Court considered in the case hereafter referred to as the *Tropwind* case, that the question of his legal competence regarding the manner in which the case was submitted to him did not affect his legal competence, but that it only affected forcible execution of his judgment.

Legal competence featured more as a principle in the summary proceedings before the President of the Rotterdam District Court in the *Saudi Independence* III case, and on appeal before the Court of Appeal in The Hague in the same case.[11] The President considered that his legal competence, which had been tacitly accepted by the parties in the case, could be based on the fact that the strike on board the ship in the Rotterdam port was taking place within the Dutch legal system. During appeal both parties and the Court went further into this issue. The Court scorned the idea that a ship really constituted part of the flag state. According to the Court, this could mean at most that in principle the law of the flag state applies on board ship, while it does not act as an obstacle to the assumption of legal competence of the coastal states entered by the ship, as soon as the conflict on board also affects the legal order of these coastal states. According to the court this was the case, particularly as the Dutch inspector of the ITF played an important part in the strike conflict.

This decision is entirely in line with what Geffken [12] has to say on the subject: he points out that conflicts concerned with conditions of employment on board foreign ships should in principle be considered to be internal in character. In accordance with customary public international law, the court of the coastal state remains detached from these conflicts, with the exception of the English courts, which fall outside this customary law. However, these conflicts soon acquire

10. A. Korthals Altes, "De weg tot het water: bevoordeling van de nationale vloot mede in het licht van het volkenrecht", Preadvies *Nederlandse Vereniging voor Internationaal Recht* (1979) p. 87 et seq.
11. CA The Hague, 23 April 1982, S & S 1982, 79; the appeal has gone to cassation.
12. Rolf Geffken, Neue Juristische Wochenschrift 1979 p. 1739 et seq.

external aspects because of the consequences arising in the port: at this point the court of a coastal state can be considered competent to intervene.

We are inclined to restrict the area in which conflicts can be considered to be internal in character, if only because of the effect of employment conflicts taking place on foreign flag vessels on international labour relations. However, if there is a strike resulting from dissatisfaction about the food provided on board ship, this is a conflict with a predominantly internal character, and the courts of the foreign coastal state will feel reluctant to intervene. There is even less ground for intervention in cases in which consular officials of the flag state have been appointed and have even been assigned legal competence.[13]

In this case the following ought to be pointed out: In the ILO Convention, no. 147 concerning minimum standards in merchant ships [14], Article 2 provides that each member state which ratifies this Convention undertakes to verify by inspection or other appropriate means that ships registered in its territory comply with applicable international labour Conventions in force which it has ratified, with . . . *etc.* and, as may be appropriate under national law, with applicable collective agreements. This means that the foreign judge should be more aware of his intervention in cases where this Convention applies. When the Court of Appeal in the *Saudi Independence* III case endorsed the decision of the President to terminate the strike, it considered that with regard to the help of the "strong arm of the law" for the execution of this decision, it is not conceivable that the "strong arm" should not be used because the flag state might object. In the light of the above, this decision has turned out to be insufficiently subtle.

The discussions discussed so far were concerned with strikes on board ships. It ought to be mentioned that during the strike on board the *Saudi Independence* in Rotterdam, the President of the District Court and the Court of Appeal [15] were called upon to pronounce upon side issues arising from the strike. Thus in the summary proceedings of the *Saudi Independence* I the question arose whether the competence of the shipowner to withhold the crew's wages during the strike could also apply to the provision of food. In both instances the shipowner was considered to be in the wrong. The Court considered that the vulnerable position of employees in this sort of strike meant that the employer would be going too far if he attempted to break the strike by withholding the normal food allowance from the striking crew, in view of the principle of equality of the parties involved in the strike. The principle of equality used by the Court in this case also played a role in the *Saudi Independence* II case. After the President had decided that the strikers could block the entry from shore to ship, the Court came to an identical conclusion.[16]

13. See Art. 409 Wetboek van Koophandel (Netherlands Commercial Code) for the study of victuals on board and Arts. 383 and 439 for the rescinded declaration of the individual service of captain and crew.

14. I.L.O. Convention no. 147, Geneva 29 October 1976, Trb. 1977, 108.

15. Pres. Rb. Rotterdam, 22 May 1981, S & S 1982, 3; CA The Hague, 23 April 1982, S & S 1982, 80.

16. Pres. Rb. Rotterdam, 27 May 1981, S & S 1982, 4; CA The Hague, 23 April 1982, S & S 1982, 81.

It considered that the principle of equality of weapons of the parties involved in the strike entailed that in this case the means of blockade could be permitted as an exception, as the right the strike would otherwise be jeopardised. The shipowner actually had a replacement crew on shore ready to go on board to take over the work of the striking crew. This consideration had weighed heavily on the President as the shipowner's aim to bring in a replacement crew would have had further reaching consequences than simply breaking the strike, as the strikers would actually completely lose their position as employees on the ship. Thus in contrast to the Court's decision, the breaking of a strike was not used as a criterion.

The decision of the President in the *Tropwind* case [17] is in line with the Hague Court of Appeal. It too wished to prevent the strike action from losing any effect it might had. Should not the principle of equality mean precisely that in contrast to the right to strike there should be a right to minimise the effect of the strike, provided that acceptable means are used? Can the means no longer be considered acceptable if they break the strike, or render it ineffectual? Or are the means unacceptable because of other consequences?

In the *Tropwind* case decision other factors deserve attention. This vessel, flying the flag of Singapore, was moored in the port of Amsterdam while being loaded. The majority of the crew was of Philippine nationality. Their contracts of employment with the shipowners were accepted by the National Seamen's Board, Department of Labour, Philippines. The wage scales applied on board had not been adjusted since September 1974. The crew asked the local ITF representative to intervene on their behalf. The shipowners were given the choice of adopting the ITF Collective Agreement or facing a strike ("industrial action") on board. When the ITF ultimatum was not accepted, the Philippine crewmembers, who in the meantime had joined the ITF as individual members, proceeded to strike. The shipowners dismissed the striking crew and gave orders that they should disembark. When this order was ignored, the shipowners tried to obtain an interim injunction to get the ship cleared. The President of this Court observed that starting from the assumption – as pleaded by the shipowners – that the question whether the shipowners had the right to dismiss summarily the Philippine crew, is to be judged according to the law of Singapore, the outcome might be denied its effect, in any event as far as the issue of this injunction is concerned, with a view to the ruling considering opinions in the Netherlands about employment law and the right to strike. The injunction was dismissed with no explicit explanation given by the President on this point. As regards the strike as such, the President held that according to the ruling, considering opinions in the Netherlands about employment law, a strike is generally allowed when it is organized by an organization of workers which was involved in the negotiations for the collective agreement; that such a strike can be unlawful when it is an unreasonable weapon for the intended goal, or when it is used prematurely; that these rules, which are attached to the existing relations system in the Netherlands between the employers and the workers, do not lend themselves for application to strikes, a) when only alien parties are

17. Pres. Rb. Amsterdam, 30 November 1978, S & S 1979, 75.

involved in the strike, b) when the parties were not negotiating with each other, c) when the labour relations in their native countries do not really allow the seamen, who are employed on ships sailing under a flag of convenience, to strike, and d) when the strike is characterised by elements of industrial occupation.

The exception given under c) indicates that the judge was inclined to give more substance to the right to strike of this category of seamen. He was prepared to favour the strikers by changing the rule that a strike is allowed when it is organized by an organization of workers which was involved in the negotiations on the collective agreement. In his judgment he refers to the general familiarity which already exists in shipping circles with ITF aims – the acceptance of its Collective Agreement by shipowners – and with the overall content of its Collective Agreement. He also refers to the nature, the international character of the shipping companies as well as the special relations in the labour market of the countries where seafarers for ships sailing under a flag of convenience are recruited, making industrial action more difficult. The President considered that in judging the lawfulness of the strike under these circumstances, it was necessary to maintain a great deal of reserve.

The applicability of Dutch law to the strike had priority in the *Tropwind* case; the parties were in agreement on this.

In the *Saudi Independence* III case, this did not happen. In this case the Court did not follow the argument put forward by the strikers that Dutch law should be applied, as the law of the place where the ship was located at the time the strike was called; the effect would be that strikes would only be held in ports where the ITF knew that the law was on their side ("forum shopping"), so that the trial would contain an unfair element (or was the Court thinking in terms of a conflict of power?). In principle, in labour conflicts on a ship, the applicability of the law of the flag state should be taken as starting point, according to the Court. The strike in question concerned Philippine crew members whose contracts of employment were controlled by Philippine labour law, and the Court considered that this entailed the application of Philippine strike law, despite the Saudi Arabian flag of the vessel.

The Philippine Labour Code contains a number of provisions in Article 264, including the following:

> "(b) Any legitimate labour union may strike and any employer may lock out in establishments not covered by General Order No. 5 only on grounds of unresolved economic issues in collective bargaining, in which case the union or the employer shall file a notice with the Bureau of Labor Relations at least thirty (30) days before the intended strike or lockout. . . ."

The Court used the criteria "legitimate labour union" and "unresolved economic issues" as well as "shall file a notice". It considered that the strike was not in line with these criteria and was therefore not a lawful strike in the eyes of Philippine law. The Philippine law would not have been applied, according to the Court, if the Dutch public order ("openbare orde") had protested against this. However, the contracts concerned were one year contracts which had only two months left to run and the strike was called suddenly with no prior warning when the strikers had initially complained about their food. They started to complain about their wages only after contacting the ITF and the Dutch "openbare orde" did not therefore oppose this strike being terminated on the basis of Philippine law.

The provisions of the Philippine labour code and strike law have a (semi) public law character. In principle, provisions of this nature have only a territorial effect. This means that outside his own territory, the judge who is called upon to make a decision concerning these foreign provisions does not have to apply them. They are not applicable when they conflict with the fundamental legal principles which apply within the legal order of the forum; this is the negative limit.[18] On the other hand, it may happen that such important factors are at stake for a state when provisions applicable in that state are taken into consideration, that the foreign judge should take these into account;[19] this is the positive limit. There are intermediate cases in which the judge has a discretionary freedom of decision. It is not clear what standards guided the Court in the *Saudi Independence* III case in applying the foreign provisions. However, compared with the decision of the President in the *Tropwind* case, there are some obvious differences. Not only did the judge fail to apply the foreign law in this case, but he even derived an argument from the labour relations in the native countries to apply provisions from his own legal system less stringently or not at all. Thus no attempt was made in the *Tropwind* case to ascertain the law with which the case was most closely connected by means of rules of private international law (connecting factors). Nor did the approach used have a substantive nature in which the degree of validity of the conflicting legal norms from the different legal systems connected with the case are weighed against each other.[20] Instead of this, an open social norm was employed; the strike as a socially acceptable weapon without the restriction "that it is exercised in conformity with the laws of the particular country."

This list of decisions should include the actions brought before the District Court at Middelburg concerning the *Bernhard Oldendorff* which sails under the Panamanian flag.[21] After the shipowner had been forced to sign the Special Agreement in June 1979 in Nantes, France, because of a strike on board his ship, the French judge discussed the legal validity of this Special Agreement in summary proceedings. The result of the proceedings was that the shipowner guaranteed to implement the Special Agreement for the duration of six months. After the shipowner had terminated this Agreement on 19 June 1980, the crew went on strike again in January 1981, this time in Flushing. The summary proceedings resulting from this industrial action concluded with an agreement of compromise, in which the shipowner signed a new Special Agreement. The legality of the strike and its consequences were deliberately not discussed. The valid complaints of the members of the crew were then submitted to the court, based, amongst other things, on

18. See also Luc Strikwerda, *Semipubliekrecht in het conflictenrecht,* (Alphen aan den Rijn 1978) p. 18 et seq.

19. See also HR, 13 May 1966, S & S 1966, 50 and NJ (The Netherlands) 1976, 3 ("Alnati").

20. Cf. Th.M. de Boer, "De vermaatschappelijking van het internationaal privaatrecht", NJB 1980, p. 794.

21. Pres. Rb. Middelburg, 17 February 1981, S & S 1981, 115; Rb. Middelburg, 24 June 1981, S & S 1981, 116.

the fact that there had been a one-sided and premature termination of the contracts of employment by the shipowner. The alleged illegality of the strike was influential in this. In order to deal with these complex matters the court required more information regarding the question to which legal system the labour relations were subject.

On 30 June 1982 [22], this Court decided in a subsequent interim decision that, on the one hand, the labour relations were subject to Panamanian law and, on the other hand, the law of the flag state should be applied to the strike which had broken out in the Netherlands – thus, likewise, Panamanian law. The Court considered, in addition, that it was following, in this regard, the opinion of the Hague Court (in the '*Saudi Independence)* concerning the applicability of the law of the flag state to labour conflicts on board ship: however, with the cautious addition that the Supreme Court had not yet been handed down an opinion on this question.

3. FINAL OBSERVATIONS

The legal decisions discussed above do not seem to have clarified the situation very substantially. Perhaps this is due to the fact that in most of the proceedings the strike itself was central. The fundamental questions were hardly touched upon. Thus the question whether the ITF has the right to put itself forward as the representative of seafarers of developing countries remains undecided. This is also true of the question whether there is a duty to bargain on the part of the shipowner if the ITF has this right: the question whether the industrial action taken can be classified as a democratic means of power if no duty to bargain is assumed, or if it is, the question whether the ITF should in principle offer the opportunity of bargaining instead of proposing a unilaterally elaborated regulation of a collective agreement; the question whether the stipulation that in future the rates in the ITF Collective Agreement can be reviewed by the ITF after a single notification of notice is in conflict with the freedom of negotiation; the question whether the ITF from a juridically dogmatic point of view can intervene in a CAO even in cases where it was not involved in creating this collective agreement; the question whether in the event that the ITF Collective Agreement conflicts with the legal system to which the labour relations on board ship are subject, or whether the former has priority over the latter. Only one decision (the *Pacifico* decision) indicates which legal system applies in an appeal to duress. There is more available about the legal system which is used to judge the legality of a strike when special considerations may play a role, such as the freedom of negotiation, the right to function freely, the right to strike, the safeguarding of rules of public order such as the prohibition on discrimination, as well as examples of less fundamental but nevertheless essential rules concerned with negotiations, etc.

Korthals Altes' article elsewhere in this publication sheds more light on the problem of the correct law to be applied.

22. Rb. Middelburg, 30 June 1982, S & S 1982, 114.

SEAMEN'S STRIKES AND SUPPORTING BOYCOTTS:
Recent case developments abroad

by A. Korthals Altes *

> "This case is of interest to all those who go down to the sea in ships. It is about flags of convenience. They are much disliked by a trade union, called for short the ITF, the International Federation of Transport workers".

Thus summarised the Master of the Rolls the case of the *Camilla M.* when it came before the British Court of Appeal in 1978.[1] It can hardly be said more simply, and I will endeavour to keep matters simple in my contribution to this Liber Amicorum, where limited space is a very effective way of avoiding lengthy complicated and detailed discussion: though in avoiding the Charybdis of unnecessary complication one must also steer clear of the Scylla of oversimplification. The critical reader will probably consider that I did founder in one or other of these ways.

1. INTRODUCTION

A ship is a movable chattel by right of birth (or more appropriately: right of berth?). Therefore it is not surprising that both strikes on board seagoing vessels and more particularly, the secondary actions in support of these strikes, were the subject of court opinions in various countries in North and Nortwestern Europe. In the contribution preceding mine, Mr. Ter Kuile discussed the disputes judged by Dutch courts. For my part, I will review cases in foreign countries, in an attempt to establish some guidelines for handling these cases. 'Trooping the colour' is a parade of ten ships, each of them with a slightly different background, but all have in common that they fly a flag of convenience, and all of them were in some way involved with the ubiquitous ITF. The first aspect to become apparent is that most of the cases are concerned only with the ITF's position. However, few also deal with the legality of the strike on board. A brief introduction will suffice as most of the basic issues have been set out in Mr. Ter Kuile's contribution, to which this writer gratefully refers. We may distinguish two catagories of cases coming up in court:

a) in the *first* case, no agreement has been signed between owner and seamen (frequently represented by the ITF); such an agreement is then more or less forced upon the owner by a strike of the crew, usually supported by a boycott of the workers, organised in unions affiliated with ITF;

b) at a *subsequent* stage, when such an agreement has actually been signed, the

* LL.B. (Leyden); LL.M. (Cornell, U.S.A.); LL.D. (Amsterdam); Professor of Commercial Law (Utrecht), res.-judge (Arnhem, D.Ct).

1. C.A., 13 October 1978, 1979 (1) Ll.L.R.26; *European Transport Law* (ETL) 1979, 870.

seamen have their ship attached in order to obtain their wages, by now increased but still unpaid.[2]

In the cases under review here we will come across both categories; even at this stage it is obvious, apart from a single maverick case, that the judge had little difficulty assuming his competence as a point of departure. In a Report published three years ago [3], I observed on this particular point: "... it could also be argued that the judge has to declare himself not competent to give judgment on a strike on board, because international law would not allow a judge of a riparian or port state to intermediate in the internal management of the vessel as long as this was not requested by or on behalf of the flag state, in particular the local consular official of that state. The judge is only allowed to give orders or injunctions without such a request if the actual happenings on board also have repercussions on the law and order within his own territory. Without such a request a judge would not be allowed to render a judgment." This point of view, as we will more specifically state below (part 2), though based upon the opinions of leading authors, should now be updated, as it lags behind major new developments. Before arriving at a conclusion in part 3, we will, as indicated above, first review our small armada of cases, hardly a dozen ships all told. The review begins with three French decisions; followed by a brief Norwegian interlude, four British cases, and finally a German and several Belgian decisions. Then there is a very brief comparison with some recent Dutch cases as these have already been discussed in the preceding contribution.

2. DECISIONS ABROAD

2.1 France

One of the rare examples where the judge did not consider himself competent to take cognizance of a case may be found in the *Astros* case. This ship flew the Liberian flag, had a London based owner and an Indian/Egyptian crew. The prelude to the Court of Dunkirk's decision for incompetence was a case brought in summary proceeding ('référé') before the Dunkirk Tribunal of Land and Maritime Commerce.[4] The crew's action was based upon a 'special agreement' signed by the owner in December 1978 during the *Astros'* stay in a Swedish port. The owner argued that he had signed only because a boycott had been organised in Sweden against his ship, so that, to avoid the risk of the *Astros* being frozen in, he was simply compelled to do so. First the owner argued that the plaintiffs

2. See this writer in *Deinend Zeerecht* (Oratie Utrecht University), 1977 , published 1978, pp. 30-32.

3. Report (preadvies) Neth. branch of the International Law Association, *De Weg tot het Water: bevoordeling van de nationale vloot mede in het licht van het volkenrecht* (1979), pp. 47-103, in particular p. 89; hereinafter abbreviated *De Weg tot het Water* (English summary in NILR 1979, pp. 347-354)

4. 3 December 1979, ETL 1981, 233.

the defendants CFDT and the ITF, had two viewpoints. On the one hand, it considered that French law explicitly was applicable to the actions of the defendants, and additionally, implicitly also to the question of the legality of the strike on board. The court reasoned, prima facie, that a strike is legal unless it interferes with the right of property or with the freedom to work (L. 412 French Labour should withdraw the attachment, which they had made to obtain their back pay, because they had exerted pressure to obtain their claim under pressure. Secondly, he requested the plaintiffs to accept a bond. His first move was fruitless. The judge did not consider himself, sitting in 'référé', competent to undertake a substantive investigation into the alleged background of the agreement with the ITF. A judge in référé was only empowered to consider such a document at face value. Thus there was at least an apparent maritime claim which justified the arrest according to art. 2 of the Brussels Convention on Maritime Arrests (1952); as a result, Fr.frcs 470.000.– had to be deposited in court as a security, pending the ultimate decision. However, the main issue came to a dead-end. The crew sued after an amicable settlement ('reconciliation') had proved abortive, and the payment of arrears was the cause of their action. This suit clearly belonged to category b) set out above, sub 1). The defendant/owner maintained that the Dunkirk Court had no jurisdiction and that only a British judge could take cognizance of the complaint. The court upheld this defence.[5] The 1959 Decree, which vested competence in maritime matters, either in the court of embarkation or the court of disembarkation, formed part of the Maritime Labour Code which declared itself non-applicable to seamen engaged in France serving on board a foreign vessel. The plaintiffs had implicitly agreed to this because they had accepted the non- applicability of the conciliation procedure compulsory under this Code. Could the *general* Labour Code (in particular R.517) then apply? The answer was no. The Labour Code with its R. 517 (giving a French court jurisdiction with regard to wages earned by either French persons or foreigners as soon as their contract was made on French territory) is a *general* rule which is excluded by operation of the Maritime Labour Code as a *specific* rule. Nor did the general Civil Code apply; this would give competence only if the contract was made in a foreign country between parties, one of which was French, or by foreigners in France. Therefore the Court dismissed the case on the basis of its own incompetence.
The second case also concerned a Liberian vessel, the *Global Med.* She had a completely Indian crew, engaged in Bombay: each of her officers had an individual contract, and all the able seamen together had a collective contract applicable to all Indian seamen and approved by the President of the Indian Republic. The officers and crew went on strike during a stay at Boulogne sur Mer, after a visit from representatives of the CFDT (Confederation Francaise Démocratique du Travail), an affiliate of the ITF. CFDT-members resorted to the occupation of the ship to assist in preventing replacement crew from boarding the vessel, tearing up warning messages from the owner, etc. Moreover, the occupants, who

5. 6 June 1980, ETL 1981, 228.

might almost be considered squatters, blatantly ignored a court order to leave the vessel, and the owners ultimately signed a Special Agreement with CFDT representing the ITF. Subsequently, however, the owners presented each of the unions with their bill for all damages accrued in consequence of their role in encouraging the strike. The Court [6], deciding in favour of the plaintiff/owner against Code). The Court only marginally tested the labour conditions on board (as did the Amsterdam President in the *Tropwind* case [7], see Mr. Ter Kuile's preceding contribution): it could not consider the wages "miserable", as the defendants alleged, on the face of it. On the other hand, the Court did not go into the merits of the strike itself, as it took place on a foreign ship and was held by workers who were not subject to laws and agreements that were part of French law: one has to keep in mind here that the owner's action was not against the strikers, but only against the Unions. Without any hesitation the Court declared their behaviour unlawful on various grounds and even went so far as to observe: "the methods used by the ITF smack of downright blackmail" in that the ITF simply *demanded* that the owner would sign a contract; if he failed to do so, an all-out boycott of his ship would follow. These methods, the Court held, were unlawful and rendered the Unions liable under art. 1382 CC. Therefore they had to make good the damages; only the suit for restitution of the wages paid as arrears by the owner to the defendants, was dismissed. The last French case is related to the Middelburg Court case mentioned in the preceding contribution [8] because it concerns the same vessel of the same beneficial owner in Germany, the Oldendorff company. The *Bernhard Oldendorff,* registered in Panama, nominally belonging to a Liberian corporation was threatened, while berthed at Nantes, by the CGT, representing the ITF, to sign an agreement for the usual increase of wages. Subsequently pressure was put on the captain to have this agreement operate with retroactive effect and also to be applicable to overtime. Upon his refusal, a boycott was threatened. The owners then sued both the CGT and the ITF, alleging not only that they had obtained the contract under duress, but also that their subsequent actions were contrary to the understandings in the agreement. The judge in chambers (référé) left both these issues undecided.[9] He considered that it was not his responsibility but that of the court in the main procedure to examine the facts underlying the agreement. However, as the arrears were obviously a matter of dispute, the agreement could not now serve as a basis for further detention of the ship. All the parties concerned preferred to make a preliminary settlement in court; Egon Oldendorff, inter alia, giving a guarantee of payment of whatever amount would either be settled amicably or adjudged by the Nantes Court. An injunction was granted against both defendant Unions to refrain from any actions which might delay the *Bernard Oldendorff's* departure. From the Middelburg District Court's decision we know that the parties concerned did have difficulties in implementing

6. Trib. Boulogne, 28 November 1980, ETL 1981, 201
7. NJ 1979, 75.
8. See L.F.D. Ter Kuile, Interference in collective agreements of seafarers, above, p.
9. Trib. Nantes, 28 June 1979, ETL 1981, 243.

their understanding, but, as the final judgment is still pending, this prevents us from commenting here.

2.2 Norway

Just as the Oldendorff's ships found themselves harassed by the ITF in various ports, so the path of the m.s. *Nawala* was dogged by industrial action both in Norway (mid-1979) and in England. The *Nawala*, registered in Hong Kong, was beneficially owned by the Skaarup Shipping Company, essentially a Norwegian company, but having its place of business in the United States. The actions against this ship gave rise to proceedings by the shipowners as plaintiffs against the Norwegian Seamen and Transport workers Unions, their federation and the Longshoremen's Association. In two instances [10] the defendants were ordered to make good the *Nawala's* damages incurred by their actions, amounting to U.S. $240.000. The overriding fact in this case was that there was no question of a strike on board the ship itself. On the contrary, its owners produced written statements from the crew as evidence that they were content with their present wages and did not desire the collective Agreement with the ITF for which the unions' activities had been organised. Therefore the only question of law relevant for the Court was whether or not the "sympathy" boycott by the Norwegian longshoremen was unlawful. On this question Norwegian law was undoubtedly applicable. Four elements were relevant for the Court to decide on the boycott's legitimacy. On two of them (see below, i and ii) the Court gave a negative reply; the other two, however, (see below, iii and iv) were deemed sufficient to declare the boycott to be in violation of the 1947 Norwegian Labour Disputes Statute.

i) The fact that the crew had a negative attitude towards the "sympathy" boycott was considered to be irrelevant. In this respect the Norwegian judgment is at variance with the British decision in the *Camilla M.* case: see below, sub 2.3. The Court considered that before 1947 the Law had contained a prohibition in such a situation; but in the amended statute this was not maintained, and the parliamentary history of this change was inconclusive. More important was the Court's assumption that "in the case of a boycott with demands for an ITF Agreement against vessels sailing under a flag of convenience, it is not unusual for the crew to express its satisfaction with the existing pay and working conditions". The Court referred to a decision of the Hoyesteret in a similar context, two decades previously.[11] "Hence, the statements made by the Nawala's crew members are not facts which, taken in isolation, imply that the boycott appears to be improper in the sense of art. 2 of the Statute . . . If labour conflict is approved in order to obtain the implementation of ITF agreements in respect of vessels sailing under a flag of convenience the effectiveness of boycott actions will be seriously re-

10. Narvik Municipal Court, 22 January 1980; C.A. Halogaland, 2 November 1981: a translation was given to the author by Mr. F. Meeter, Rotterdam.

11. Hoyesteret in *The San Dimitris* case, 1959: see *Deinend Zeerecht*, p. 28 and note 152.

duced if they are not allowed when the shipping company has obtained declarations from the crew that no action is desired."

ii) Similarly the owner's argument was rejected that the boycott "would prejudice vital public interests" in the sense of the above-mentioned art. 2(c). Although as the owners contended, the Norwegian authorities accepted free competition in international shipping and in consequence permitted foreign registration of vessels to allow for competition, this did not imply, according to the Court, that the relevant statements by government officials, "kept in general and imprecise terms" "provide a basis for concrete deductions as to whether the boycott of the Nawala has prejudiced vital public interests."

iii) However, the Court rejected the demands for a collective wage agreement, because they were understood to include a demand for *back pay* for the crew from the date they started their work on board the ship. The Unions pleaded that this depended on further negotiations, but the Court dismissed their argument as being contradictory to the usual ITF demands, in which backpay was important. At the time of the boycott, the owners were not, in any event, made aware of a different practice in this respect.

iv) The second element which made the Court declare the boycott unlawful, was based on art. 5 and concerned the rights of the ITF (or the Norwegian Seamen's Union) to change the rates upon two months' notice to the shipping company. The Court considered this stipulation an unreasonable burden on the employer.

As elements iii) and iv) were sufficient to enable the Courts to declare the boycott improper, the other elements were only cursorily dealt with. In particular, the Court left undecided the question whether it was unlawful to demand a collective agreement contribution/affiliation fee and contribution to the Welfare Fund. The fact that this contribution was the same amount as the usual membership fee did not imply that the ITF/Seamen's Union actually obliged the crew to become compulsory members. This Welfare Fund contribution was also discussed in the British decision regarding the *Universe Sentinal* (see below, 2.3). One important consideration remains to be discussed. How strong must the connection be between Norway and the vessel and crew for the unions to take offensive action? The Court first stated that "the more a vessel with a flag of convenience with a foreign crew makes regular freight runs to Norwegian ports, the more defensible a demand can be for a collective agreement with a Norwegian seamen's organisation". The fact that the vessel is also owned and/or managed by persons or companies with little connection with the flag state is also a point in favour of accepting a boycott action when the ship sails to Norway. This applies in particular if the owner's interests are Norwegian (as was the case). However, a sufficient connection was only formed when the *Nawala* arrived in Narvik and this fact contributed to make the boycott supporting demands for backpay unlawful because before this time there was "no immediate interest in action in Norway by the defendants to get an ITF Agreement implemented." Before the ship's arrival in Narvik, the Unions did not have any connection with the vessel of the sort which would give them any reasonable claim to have an ITF Agreement implemented. In my view this argument is an intriguing aspect of the case: as noted above, the beneficiary ownership was in Norway. One could say, with regard to the initially desired connection with Norway, that the Court's decision takes back with one hand what it had given with the other. However, in this case I am unable to discover another element to justify the legality of the boycott.

2.3 United Kingdom

Recent British case law has dealt with four ships. We will only deal briefly with the first of these, because, as we will see, the decision was overruled shortly afterwards. In the *Camilla M.*, a Liberian vessel with a Greek management in London, the Court of Appeal considered the fact that first the Indian crew, backed by its own (Indian) Union and government, and subsequently the replacement crew, did not agree to a change in pay. For the British Court [12] (unlike its Norwegian counterpart a year later; see above 2.2) this was a vital factor in judging the ITF's action to be unlawful. The Court used as a basis for its preliminary decision, comparable with a 'référé' in France, the 1974 Trade Union and Labour Relations Act (TULRA) which was amended in 1976. The officers of the ITF were immune from legal action by the owners, seeking an injunction against their boycott, if their actions were "in contemplation or furtherance of a trade dispute." But in this case, where the ITF obviously did not represent the wishes of the crew, the Court granted the injunction against the ITF officers, which had been refused the owners by the lower court. It considered the demand so unreasonable that a court, hearing the case in full, might consider the ITF to be "meddling" and their antipathy towards flags of convenience a mere extraneous motive. The ITF licked its wounds and waited for the next opportunity. This time its action was successful. In the *Nawala* case – the vicissitudes in Norway are already familiar to us (see 2.2. above) – the injunction by the lower court was lifted by the Court of Appeal [13] and this decision was upheld by the House of Lords.[14] In essence it considered that the TULRA's formula "in furtherance . . . of a trade dispute" covered not only a dispute between an employer and his own employee, but also a dispute between an employer and a *trade union.* The wording of the Statute does not exclude the union officials from immunity if the dispute in reality is not predominantly the improvement of terms and conditions of the workers to whom their demands relate, but perhaps rather to drive crews of convenience from the seas, unless they serve on ships (beneficially) owned by their own nationals. Nonetheless the threat of industrial action if the demands were not met, was an act made "in furtherance . . . of a trade dispute" because it was connected with terms and conditions of employment. With this decision the *Camilla M.* was overruled, in favour of the ITF. The outcome of the *Nawala* case produced quite an outcry from shipowners against the interpretation of the House of Lords of what was caustically nick-

12. See note 1, above, and *De Weg tot het Water,* p. 88, note 139 a.
13. C.A. 12 November 1979 (2) Ll.L.R. 317.
14. H.L. 1980 (1) Ll.LR. 1.

named the TULRA's "golden formula", whose protection the ITF could continue to enjoy – unless the law were changed. The International Shipping Federation, *inter alia,* (uniting the shipowners, also in their role as employers) made representations to the Secretary of State for Employment. This provoked the U.K. government to take action. At the moment a Bill is pending in which the "golden formula" has been drastically narrowed down:

i) immunity should only arise when the trade dispute relates "wholly or mainly" to a number of specific industrial relations matters (rather than being merely "connected with" them;

ii) the term "trade dispute" will only apply to disputes between an employer and his own employees and action on behalf of a dispute between the employer and a trade union would be unlawful;

iii) the trade union itself would be liable for such actions organised by its officials unless such actions were repudiated by more senior officers or authoritative body of that union.[15]

Such legislation would obviously impede action by the ITF as soon as the crew stated that they were satisfied with their wages and/or other conditions, and the *Camilla M.* ruling would be restored. Another important issue in curbing secondary action was decided by the Court of Appeal in the *Antama* case. Had it not been for the most recent changes in the employment legislation, the owners would have lost this case. The *Antama* was Panamese owned but sold to a Turkish beneficial owner and was now flying the Maltese flag, obviously for the sake of convenience. When she arrived in Hull crew members complained to the ITF about their pay. Subsequently, in November 1980, when the owner refused the ITF level, the ship was blacked by the Unions. Port Authority employees blocked her exit by refusing to operate the locks. In this case the owner was held in two instances to be entitled to injunctory relief [16], because it was not the owner but the *Antama's* charterers (who did not employ the crew) who had a contract with the Port Authority. What would normally be allowed by virtue of Sect. 17(3)(a) TULRA, was unlawful in this case because of Sect. 17(3)(b), which had only recently come into force. The secondary action had to satisfy the subsequent subsections. Sect. 17(3)(a) would allow such action if its purpose were specifically to prevent the supply during the dispute, of goods or services between an employer who was *a party to the dispute* and the employer *under the contract of employment* to which the secondary action relates. However, section 17(6)(a) provides that the "supply of goods or services" as intended above is the "supply of goods or services by one to the other in pursuance of a contract between them subsisting at the time of the secondary action." Since the Port authorities had a contract with the charterers, and not with "the employer who was a party to the dispute", the ITF tried in vain to invoke the TULRA's immunity. After losing its case the ITF did not request a further appeal.

15. Information sheet I.S.F. 82/2 (7 January 1982).
16. (1982) 2 Ll.LR 112.

The last case which deserves to be mentioned here came before the Court of Appeal and, ultimately, the House of Lords; [17] it concerned the payment of $ 6.480 as a contribution to the ITF's Welfare Fund. The owners of the Liberian ship *Universe Sentinel* had paid a total of $ 80.000 when their vessel was 'blacked' in Milford Haven and thus prevented from sailing. About $ 71.000 had been paid as wages in arrears and $ 6.480 as said contribution. The crewmembers had, for the first item, assigned their claim to the shipowner. One might wonder whether these assignors, indeed, had afterthoughts about the ITF's activities on their behalf, or whether they in their turn were pressed to make the assignment just as their principal had been pressed to pay up to the ITF. This issue, however, was not raised by the ITF in the present case: the assignments were not contested. The lower Court was of the opinion that the owners had paid under duress (illegitimate commercial pressure), but upon appeal the Court denied the owners the recovery of their $ 6.480 contribution to the Fund. That payment, the Court said, had a connection "albeit perhaps a tenuous one", with the trade dispute, since it might result in "fringe benefits" (e.g., better port amenities) for the seamen. Hence the ITF in this respect did enjoy the TULRA's protection against actions in tort. Upon further appeal, the House of Lords, in a 3 to 2 majority opinion, allowed the owners' claim. To be more specific, the owners' first argument was dismissed, but three of the Lords did agree with the cause of action based upon *money had and received* (our Article 1395 CC). For clarity's sake: it was not disputed that the payments were made under such economic pressure as to amount to duress. But the ITF maintained its immunity under the TULRA. The majority opinion did not consider the ITF to be entitled to such immunity. The owners' contribution to the Welfare Fund was *not* made in furtherance of a dispute in connection with terms and conditions of employment of this particular crew. Its payment had nothing to do with them as members of the crew. "There is nothing whatever,"Lord Diplock held, "to suggest the entitlement of a member of the crew of the Universe Sentinel to take advantage of any benefits that might be provided for out of the fund, would be in any way dependent upon the existence or non-existence of a relationship of employee and employer between the crewmember and the shipowners." "(The crew's) chance", so held Lord Cross, "of receiving some benefit from the Welfare Fund is just the same whether or not the appellants contribute to the fund or whether or not they remain in the employment of the appellants. (. . .) I cannot bring myself to think that even in this day and age a demand that an employer shall make contributions to union funds at rates 'fixed from time to time by the Union' is a demand which can be legitimately enforced by duress." In this way another cornerstone of the ITF's normal bill presented to shipowners was removed from its already stricken premises; and this time by the authority of Britain's highest court. In all these cases we see only one case clearly being won by the ITF, and in that case it proved to be Pyrrhic victory because it gave rise to a reform in legislation which would henceforth curb the TULRA's ambit.

17. CA 10 July 1980, (1980) 2 L1.LR 523; HL 1 April 1982 (1982) 1 L1.LR. 537.

2.4 Germany; Belgium

It was only in a German Court that the ITF won an outright victory. Moreover this was the only case abroad I discovered in which the strike itself passed the test of the Court. In Hamburg the crew of the Panamese m.s. *Khoobchand* went on strike to obtain an ITF Agreement which would include backpay. The owners sued the crew, the ITF and its representative Schmeling. The Labour Court (Arbeitsgericht) [18] held the Panamese Labour Code applicable on the issue. However, the Court rejected its application insofar as it made compulsory an arbitral and reconciliation procedure. This part of the Panamese Code would be against German 'ordre public', as it would lead to considerable delay and probably even make the furtherance of a labour dispute illusory because the ship by that time would normally have left the port of action. Thus "the autonomy of collective bargaining" would be impaired and the Court disregarded the Panamese procedural provisions as they jeopardised the German "right of labour conflict" (Recht auf Arbeitskampf). The Court also upheld the strike as far as back pay was its aim, because improvement of labour conditions 'is not necessarily limited to the future'. Once the strike was held not to be unlawful, the owner's action against the ITF and Schmeling failed as well. Schmeling had to have access to the ship as it was the residence of the crew. This decision is most surprising, as it is (to put it mildly) at variance with German authors like Wintrich [19] – who stated that generally even a foreign prohibition to strike must be recognised by a German court – and Geffken [20] – who wants to limit the German 'ordre public' from operation beyond the case where application of the foreign law would forthwith be intolerable, taking into consideration the German legal order: this would only be the case if such application would 'directly affect the pillars of German public or economic life.' Geffken goes on to say: "It cannot be seriously argued that this should be the case when there is merely non-conformity with the often corrected and frequently criticised – by the circles concerned – "judge-made law" of the Bundes Arbeits Gericht." Hardly a stronger contrast with this lone German decision can be imagined than the findings of the Antwerp Tribunal. On a former occasion[21] this Court had already condemned a boycott against the *Caroline Oldendorff* as the action hampered the free navigation which the port of Antwerp had the duty to guarantee its users; in the *St Marcos*-case, this Tribunal, judging in summary proceedings (référé) on the legality of a sympathy boycott, even went into the merits of the ITF's policy, condemning it in rather strong terms.[22] It doubted the honesty of

18. Arbeitsgericht Hamburg, 29 May 1981, re Indramar Shipping: text submitted to the author by Prof. dr. M. Bos.

19. Wintrich, *Die rechtliche Beurteilung von Steiks mit Auslandberührung* thesis 1970, p. 142.

20. Geffken, *Seeleutestreik und Hafenarbeiterboykott,* thesis 1976, reprint in comm.ed. 1979, p. 1 and in Neue Juridische Wochenschrift (NJW) 1979 Internationales Recht im Seeleutenstreik, pp. 1739 et seq., in particular p. 1740.

21. Trib. Comm. Antwerp, 21 January 1977, ETL 1978, 64; see also *Deinend Zeerecht* note 170 and *De weg tot het water,* p. 88, note 138.

22. E. du Pontavice, Les pavillons de complaisance, in Droit Maritime Français, pp. 503-512, 567-582, in particular pp. 510 and 573.

the ITF's fight against "flags of convenience" as "it does not seem entirely self-evident that workers on (the ships concerned) are ipso facto underpaid". The *St. Marcos'* crew was engaged in Spain under a Spanish contract, receiving a basic wage of $ 333 a month, which should be, according to ITF standards, $ 395 a month, i.e., 40% higher than the wages of British seamen. Quoting a recent study by Prof. Du Pontavice [23], the judge mentioned that the wages on many Liberian vessels compared favourably with payment under some 'national flag' ships and wondered, as did Prof. Du Pontavice, why boycott actions are directed against vessels under flags of convenience only, and not against ships sailing under the Indian, Turkish, Russian or even the British flag. Apparently approving of Du Pontavice's argument, the judge observed: "He suggests that trade union federations want to encourage a process which is intended to make national ships sail under their national flag. It is certainly worth considering whether such a policy should be followed, but the question arises whether there are no other ways of achieving this. The study quoted previously notes that by implementing certain financial policies, Greece has succeeded in persuading a large number of Greek ships sailing under flags of convenience, to sail under the national flag. However, provided that previously determined requirements are not imposed on vessels of a foreign nationality, e.g., by general regulations in the field of nationality, the above-mentioned aim of the trade union federations, which perhaps is justified, cannot constitute a legal ground to justify the present (boycott)". It is useful to compare the German Court's use of the 'ordre public' with the rejection of this doctrine in the *Saudi Independence* case by the Hague Court of Appeal, though this rejection was based upon the facts of that particular case. Furthermore, it is interesting to note that the same Court, in rejecting the 'balance of interests' argument of the ITF, touched upon the general background of the ITF's policy but did not consider the ITF's interests of such an overriding nature that the shipowner's action should fail for this reason, "considering the background most difficult to judge" . . . "which is not free from political aspects and in which in particular the relationship between rich and poor countries appears to play a not altogether comprehensible rôle." In comparison with the Belgian observations on the general background, the reasoning of the Hague Court of Appeal appears to be couched in Sybilline terms. However, as the *Saudi Independence* will be considered again by our Court of Cassation, we must refrain from commenting on the matter here.

3. APPRAISAL AND REAPPRAISAL

When summarising the cases above, we saw the task of the great majority of the courts limited to dealing with the legitimacy of the ITF's supporting activities, and that issue was invariably judged according to the lex fori. This in itself is not in the least surprising as these actions were secondary actions, supplementary to activities on shore. It was usually the legality of *these* actions and not the instigation

23. See *De Weg tot het Water,* pp. 66, 80.

of a strike on board of the ship itself which formed the core of the case. Either directly – an attempt to obtain an injunction against a boycott (threat), or indirectly, by means of a suit for repayment of allegedly unlawfully obtained money – the Unions' actions constituted the matter under consideration. There were two notable exceptions to this general rule: The *Astros,* where the French judge did not consider himself competent to take cognizance of the crew's suit for unpaid arrears; and the *Khoobchand* in which the strike on board did indeed come to court. In this context it may be observed that in the Netherlands the FWZ (Federation of Employees in Seatrade) prefers to refrain from organising secondary actions, as it is still under the influence of the Court of Cassation's decision in the *Pan-Hon-Lib* case of 1960 [24], and limits itself to encouraging strikes on board, in most cases with not unfavourable results. The Dutch courts have therefore been faced, in a situation different from almost all the cases dealt with above sub 2), with the problem of giving a judgment on the legitimacy of the strike on board itself. The preliminary question is whether the court should give its opinion on the merits of that issue, or rather declare itself, according to the rules of international law, forum non conveniens? My own opinion, which I formed three years ago, is stated in paragraph 1. At that time it was based upon opinions of leading writers on international law.[25] However, a *caveat* seems fitting here. The authors at the time of writing, were imagining a situation which was vastly different from what developed afterwards when the ITF "came of age". Those writers probably had no more in mind than a mere isolated strike on board a vessel concerning labour conditions which were relevant only within the particular ship's internal relations, a conflict between a specific employer and a specific (set of) employee(s). At that time they could hardly envisage the possibility of a worldwide policy against "flags of convenience", and still less, actions against "crews of convenience", the latter concept coming into general use only in the last decades. This policy has its roots *on shore,* in accordance with the masterplans of an international organisation and its local affiliates, laid down in a certain strategy to which neither the shipowners nor the crews are privy. This strategy is developed entirely independently from the internal ship's management, in line with a particular social-economic concept. So far the strikes on board have usually not been isolated issues but have had a very close connection with the internal order on shore. This is true even when they were unaccompanied by sympathy actions in the port concerned – as is the case in Dutch ports of call – and the strike is encouraged and supported by an organisation on shore, if not instigated by it. As far as these propositions are concerned I am inclined to submit my former point of view that there should be a reappraisal. First of all: I think it still holds for the isolated, single strike which is entirely limited to the ship and in which no organisation on shore in the port of call is involved. In general, the requirement should be made that the conflict on board must be of such a nature that it affects the order and peace of the port of call. The single fact that an organisation based in that country plays a material rôle in the issue,

24. See *Deinend Zeerecht,* p. 29 (information given to the writer by FWZ, W.C. van Zuylen and C. Roodenburg).

25. See above, note 7 and the observation quoted in *De Weg tot het Water* pp. 89-90.

is sufficiently important to meet this requirement. Under these circumstances a court may ordinarily assume its jurisdiction without hesitation. In fact it appears from Dutch practice (in particular judgments in summary proceedings of the Rotterdam, Middelburg and Amsterdam District Courts, some of which have not been published) that our judges do not have many reservations about this. Our case law is full of decisions very unlike those that are made abroad. This jurisdiction, however, is normally limited to the question of the legality of the strike. It may only marginally extend itself to the merits of the actual labour conflict underlying the strike: see the prudent observations in the *Astros* (above, 2.1.) and in the *Tropwind* and *Saudi Independence* cases. Given the court's competence, the second question to be answered is: which law should be applicable to the strike itself?

First of all we have to qualify the strike. Rather than calling it a tort, I would prefer to characterise it as, prima facie, an interruption by the employee of his *contract of employment* with the employer. I do not think that the question whether a strike is an individual or collective act is of much relevance at this stage. As a collective act it does not sufficiently enter the sphere of public law to deprive it of its predominantly civil law nature. This brings us back to the law of contracts, and to the general rule that the law which governs the contract, also governs the strike on board. The contract of employment, by virtue of its nature as contract, will in my opinion primarily be governed by the law *chosen* by the parties. This party autonomy has also been assigned the primary function in the EEC Treaty of Rome (19 June 1980) on the Law applicable to Obligations in Contract. The Tre and its accompanying Report provide an important lead, as they may be seen as a com mon denominator of prevailing rules of private international law. Although the group of delegates and experts preparing the treaty did not explicitly attempt to create rules for contracts of employment for crews on board seagoing ships [26], nevertheless the provisions of Art. 6 of the Treaty may serve as an indication of which method is best for determining the applicable law. As regards contracts of employment, the Treaty puts party autonomy first, but the choice of law in this contract cannot put the employee in a less favourable position than he would have been under the cogent provisions of the law which would have been applicable to the contract without such a choice. If the contract of employment does not contain a choice of law, art. 6.2 *a* of the treaty provides that the law of the place where the employee usually performs his work, will govern. In the case of seagoing ships this would lead us to the law of the *flag.* I would submit that the exception, embodied in Art. 6.2 *b* is not present here, i.e., when an employee does *not* usually work in the same country. However, Art. 6.2 ends with the final proviso that if circumstances suggest that the contract of employment is more closely connected with another country, the law of that country will be applied. In the case of flags of convenience this rule would, however, put us in a delicate position. Is the mere flying of a flag, the mere fact of registry in such a country, a sufficient-

26. Treaty of Rome 19 June 1980: not yet in force; text and report of explanation by M. Giuliano and P. Lagarde, in *Contractenrecht,* ed. Kluwer, X Internationaal Privaatrecht, ed. A.V.M. Struycken, X. See his plea for anticipatory application, loc. cit., 1.

ly genuine connection with the law of that country? To treat ships in this category as being "stateless" as Geffken contends, [27] would lead to a cure worse than the illness. However, as far as this radical point of view is concerned, one may allow that in cases like this the country of the ship's registry is a point of connection which might become secondary if stronger connecting points present themselves. In the case of labour conflicts this will not often occur. However, it does explain why, for instance, in the *Tropwind* case the President of the Amsterdam District Court was hesitant about applying the law of Singapore, where the ship was registered. There was simply no stronger connecting point available in this case.[27a] If, for that matter, the crew's nationality had been considered as a connecting point, we would have been at a loss in the *Tropwind* case. Apart from the law of Singapore, the crew members had *eight* different nationalities: on the *Bernard Oldendorff* twenty-seven seamen had *twelve* different nationalities. In this respect the *Saudi Independence* was much simpler; all the striking crew members were Philippine nationals. Moreover, the overriding factor in this case was that there was an explicit choice of law, i.e., Philippine law, a choice approved by the National Seamen Board of that country. In two instances the Court decided with little hesitation that Philippine law was applicable not only to the contract, but also to the strike itself, which was closely connected with that law because it was an interruption of the labour contracted for. One might wonder, however, whether the Court should not have considered the question whether the application of Saudi law would have been more favourable to the employee, in consequence of art. 6 of the Rome treaty.

So far, so good. However, as noted above, even though in this particular case the facts provided a clear choice for the judge for Philippine law, one might well imagine that it could be otherwise. In cases where the contracts for employment determine the applicable law, and this choice of law is such that it offers hardly any connection with the crew members and their various nationalities, the judge might feel obliged to disregard such a choice; it may well amount to a mere evasion of the cogent law of a country which has more connecting factors. This move towards another law is reinforced by the Rome Treaty. This Treaty requires one to determine whether the law which would have to be applied when no choice of law had been made, does offer the crew a more favourable position. It was already submitted above that – given the lack of an explicit and/or acceptable choice of law, a judge should not as a general rule resort to the law of the flag; in particular if the flag is one of mere convenience: he could then resort to the law of the true owner's principal place of business. However, I would object to application of the flag law as much as to the viewpoint that the law of the port state – the lex fori – should apply. This might well lead the Unions, in encouraging and supporting strikes on board, to "forum shopping". Moreover it would make the crew very uneasy as their right of action would be subject to the vicissitudes of their ship's

27. See Report at art. 6 (in fine), loc. cit., X, 74.

27a. The President merely observed: "the law of Singapore which governs the contracts of employment": Information from the shipowners, later received by me, revealed a rather itinerary. In that imbroglio it would be better for the judge to try to find internationally representative standards. He might find these in the Wage Recommendations issued under no. 109 by the International Labour Organisation (ILO).[28] Though these Recommendations and their implementing Resolutions are not binding upon the member states of the ILO, they have to report to the Organisation when they do not comply with the minimum wage standards set out in the Recommendations,[29] and if they do not, give the reason why not. These standards are certainly the product of mutual agreement between representatives of employers, employees and national authorities. This is not true of the standards unilaterally laid down by the ITF. I would therefore be inclined to give the ILO's standards priority over those of the ITF. I do not agree with Verheul's view that the latter are 'international minimum standards . . . guidelines, a kind of semi-manufactured law'.[30] In this respect it may be remembered that the ILO standards are currently under review and that the minimum of $ 187 a month for an able seaman, as advised in 1976, was raised in October 1980 to $ 276 a month (compare this with the ITF standard of $ 570 a month). Unlike those of ILO, ITF standards are a source of considerable friction between this organisation and its affiliates, especially in Asian countries. The ITF, it must be granted, did admit to this controversy in its most recently published Report of Activities covering 1976–1979. In three conferences of Asian seafarers in 1979 the ITF's policies and practices on flags of convenience were "violently attacked" and a "review of the ITF flag of convenience policy, together with a restructuring of the Fair Practices Committee" was demanded. The latter committee, in which no developing countries were represented at that time, only industrialised countries, attacks the falsification of competition by Western shipowners who are seeking refuge under a flag of convenience, or resort to crews of convenience, and, by so doing, are making the position of Western seamen more difficult.[31] One could question whether such an attitude seems to have more of a political nature because its intention is to get the ships back to their own proper law; this was Du Pontavice's argument when quoting another author.[32] This would give us a clearer view of the background to the controversy between the ITF and the Asian Seamen's Unions of various countries. As Lord Denning stated in the *Nawala* case: "The competitiveness of Asian seafarers as candidates for manning the merchant navies of the world depends upon their cheapness. Their natural fear is that if their competitiveness is reduced by forcing shipowners who employ them to pay to them wages at the middle rate

chameleonic clause in the contract: the law of Singapore was applicable merely as "law of the flag"; this implied that, in the event that the employee would transfer to a sistership flying another flag, the law of that latter flag would apply to his contract.
As to the applicable law, the *Tropwind* judgment is not cristal clear. However, we can read nowhere that Singapore law was applied as the law of the parties' *choice.* Maybe the Chameleonic nature of the contract clause made the President disinclined to follow that line.

28. For texts of ILO Treaty resp. Recommendation no. 109 (1958), see *British Shipping Laws*, vol. VIII (ed. N. Singh), 1973, pp. 1203 et seq. resp. 1213 et seq.
29. See loc. cit., note 28, p. 1135.
30. See NILR 1979, p. 126.
31. Report on Activities ITF 1977-1979, pp. 76, 85-86, 141 et seq., 147.
32. DMF 1979, p. 573.

paid to European seamen, their chances of seafaring employment will be very much reduced." This observation is completely in line with what was said in the extensive British Dell Report of 1977 concerning 'non-domiciled seamen' which I used at length on a former occasion.[33]

To what extent does the multiplicity of the views on case law abroad suggest criteria to test the legality of strikes on board ship and the demands made by the employees?[34] As noted above, a court should refrain from going too deeply into the material background. In this respect the Norwegian Court (see above, 2.2 under ii) behaved in very much the same way as the Dutch Court of Appeal in the *Saudi Independence* case; this was otherwise in the Belgian *St. Marcos* case and the British *Nawala* case, although the relevant observations in the latter two did not actually form the basis of the judgment. Secondly, a court should exercise caution in considering demands for backpay (unless previously agreed upon) and for a contribution to the ITF Welfare Fund: for the former, see the Norwegian decision (2.2 under iii and in fine), for the latter see again the Norwegian decision in fine, and the *Universe Sentinel* (2.3). On the other hand, a judge may marginally investigate the validity of the owner's contention that the crew does not want to have anything to do with the ITF: see the Norwegian judgment above (2.2 under i), in contrast to the previous British decision concerning the *Camilla M.*: it should be made clear whether or not the crew acted under pressure from the employer.[35]

To summarize: the judge should be wary of declaring a strike legal merely because the ITF's standards were not accepted. It might be an indication that the ITF was also taking these factors into account; last February, it supported a strike on board the Singapore registered *Neptune Sapphire,* berthed in Rotterdam. The strikers were from Sri Lanka and had demanded an increase in wages not in accordance with the ITF standards, but with those of the ILO.[36] In my view – though the ITF denies it – this is more indicative of a trend than the declaration of war, brought by a majority vote in a Resolution by the Shipping Committee of UNCTAD, June 1981, against flags of convenience (49 for, 18 against, 3 abstentions and Panama not participating).[37] This Resolution instigated an Intergovernmental Preparatory Group to make recommendations to a Conference of Plenipotentiaries, but it will be a long time before a mere majority vote succeeds in effectively banning flags of convenience from the sea: it is by now an established necessary evil in shipping economy that the owners use flags and crews of convenience.

33. See *De Weg tot het Water,* pp. 90-91.

34. The British decisions as far as they deal with the TULRA's immunities, must be left out of consideration here, as they apply only to the British national situation.

35. Compare with the *Wonder Venture, Deinend Zeerecht,* p. 32.

36. According to the *Volkskrant*, 11 February 1982. NRC-Handelsblad, 24 June 1982 stated that the crew of the Greek-owned Panamanian ship *John M.,* as far as they threatened to strike, were forced to repatriate by the owners. In this case, the ITF inspector contended that the owners did profit from the CA Hague's view that the owners of a ship have to be notified of a strike before a ship gets to its next port.

37. UNCTAD Doc. 2 June 1981 (TD/B/C.4/L.152).

One question of law now remains to be dealt with. If the strike on board is governed by the law of a particular country, not that of the riparian state, would this be of consequence for the law which would govern the question of the legality of the secondary actions on shore?

On this question, the Hague Court of Appeal in the *Saudi Independence* case puts forward an important consideration. The Court considered that the ITF, operative at an international level, in trying to improve conditions for the crew members on foreign flag vessels, will in general have to take into account "the strike law of the systems of foreign law in which ITF penetrates". In other words: the law which governs the strike and is decisive for the question of its legality, is at least *relevant* to the question of the legality of the Union's support of this strike. In the *Saudi Independence* case the Court did not go as far as to say that Philippine law was applicable to this support for the strike. It was sufficient for the Court that according to Dutch law, supporting an unlawful action constitutes a tort per se. Nevertheless, I would be inclined to interpret the Court's reasoning as an implicit resort to a method known in private international law as "accessory attachment' *(accessoire aanknoping).*[38] Its supporters maintain that this kind of attachment will influence the outcome of a case if an alleged tort is connected with a different type of legal relation (e.g., a contract) in which the *same* parties are involved. Whether this may be extended to cases where a third party is involved is doubtful; a doubt which I would be inclined to deplore. However, the limited scope of my contribution does not permit me to dwell upon the merits of this method. Suffice it to say that as 'akzessoire Anknüpfung' the term was coined by a German lawyer, Jan Kropholler, who used it in 1969.[39] Twelve years later it found another protagonist in the Swiss lawyer Adolf Heini.[40] *How* close the connection should be between a certain act – as it is not a contract itself – and the contractual relation, is difficult to state in general terms. A mere connection with the contract is clearly insufficient. But the example given by Heini [41] is too far fetched to be capable of indicating where the line should be drawn. In an article publiched some years after his thesis, Geffken intimated that a sympathy boycott bears a 'Akzessoritätsverhältnis' to the principal labour conflict, and was inclined to consider that the law governing the latter was also applicable to the boycott action.[42] In his thesis he also made a point of this accessory relationship, but observed that one then has to take into account the fact that the crew, because of the pressure of internal forces, simply does not dare to strike, [43] and this leads Geffken to make another suggestion. The riparian state's law should also be applied to the strike on board because of the boycott action

38. See *Onrechtmatige Daad,* ed. Kluwer, III, nr. 74, par. 4 with literature and Dutch case law.

39. Kropholler, Ein Anknüpfungssystem für das Deliktsstatut, RabelsZ, 1969, pp. 601 et seq.

40. Heini, *Festschrift F.A. Mann,* 1977, pp. 193 et seq.

41. Loc. cit., p. 197: two parties in a contract go rock climbing in their spare time; one of them makes a mistake and injures the other.

42. Geffken, NJW 1979, p. 1744.

43. Geffken, thesis, pp. 385-389, compare above, note 35.

on shore.[44] In my view, Geffken has got the wrong end of the stick; his line of thinking is retrogressive. The application of the riparian state's law would give rise to all the difficulties discussed above. As we noted above, the judge should be chary of applying his own national law, and should resort to that law only if there is an obvious lack of any other point of connection. This, of course, would not imply that one should be too ready to discover the desired connection required for 'accessory attachment': in these strike cases one might see it by defining the Unions in their activities as mere *representatives* of one of the contracting parties, and not as a third party. Some Dutch cases did offer an opportunity for the application of this method, but we also find notable examples where it was not applied. The Rotterdam District Court twice refused to recognise such a connection where a stevedore invoked the protection of a Himalaya clause in a contract of carriage embodied in a Bill of Lading, and the cargo interests pleaded in vain that the stevedore's right to profit from this clause should be tested by the law governing the contract of carriage.[45] The Court, in both cases presided over by Dr Erades, rejected this argument in identically worded decisions, which quite convincingly made clear why the stevedore's right of protection had to be tested by Dutch law. One of the arguments also relevant here, was that in so doing the socio-economic reality would best be served. With this the man in whose honour this contribution is written, points out the direction for us through the rocky channel of the applicable law: let us bear in mind, when making a choice, that this socio-economic reality is omnipresent in virtually all legal decisions.

44. Loc. cit. note 43, pp. 398, 416-417.

45. Rotterdam D.C., 12 January 1971, S & S 1971, 20 resp. 9 January 1978, S & S 1978, 56: See Duintjer Tebbens' note in WPNR 1980 , pp. 736-737 – apparently in favour of the limited (same parties) view on this attachment.

Rolf BIRK, "Internationales Tarifvertragsrecht" *Festschrift Günther Beitzke*, (Berlin 1979)

Jos DUMORTIER, Arbeidsverhoudingen in het internationaal privaatrecht, (Antwerpen 1981)

W.J.P.M. FASE, De botsing tussen de contracts- en vakverenigingsvrijheid, *Reeks Studiekring Drion* nr. 5 (Deventer 1981)

Rolf GEFFKEN, Seeleutestreik und Hafenarbeiterboykott *Schriftenreihe für Sozialgeschichte und Arbeiterbewegung*, Band 18 (Marburg 1979)

E.P. DE JONG, Een inleiding tot het denken over arbeidsconflictenrecht (Deventer 1975)

T. KOOPMANS, De internationaalrechtelijke aspecten van de arbeidsovereenkomst, *Mededelingen van de Nederlandse Vereniging voor Internationaal Recht* nr. 53 (Baarn 1966)

A. KORTHALS ALTES, "De weg tot het water: bevoordeling van de nationale vloot mede in het licht van het volkenrecht", Preadvies *Nederlandse Vereniging voor Internationaal Recht* (1979)

G. LYON–CAEN, La convention collective de travail en droit international privé, Clunet 1964

Jacques ROYOT, International collective bargaining (Deventer 1978)

THE NATIONALITY OF SHIPS IN YUGOSLAV LAW WITH REFERENCE TO PRESENT INTERNATIONAL DEVELOPMENTS

by Emilio Pallua*

In this contribution we will not consider the rules of law concerning the nationality of ships on the Yugoslav Littoral in medieval times, but will limit our brief historical *aperçu* to the laws in force from the 18th century.[1]

The first Austrian law which comprehensively treated maritime matters, and *inter alia* the nationality of ships, was published in 1774 under the title *Editto politico di navigazione* and in German *Politisches Navigations Edict.*[2] This law admitted to the Austrian Register of Ships only those ships that were entirely owned by Austrian nationals. The ship's master was obliged to declare any change of ownership that contravened this rule, and failure to do so incurred heavy penalities, including death. Additionally, master, officers and crew all had to be Austrian subjects.[3]

This 18th century law was fundamentally modified by an Austrian law of 7 May 1879 (Gaz. 65) concerning the registration of merchant ships and by a Hungaro-Croatian Law (Art. XVI ex. 1879) of identical text.[4]

This Austro-Hungarian legislation limited the requirement of national ownership to two-thirds. The master and first officer on board and two-thirds of the crew also had to be Austrian or Hungaro-Croatian nationals.

After the constitution of the Yugoslav state (until 3 October 1929 called the Kingdom of the Serbs, Croats and Slovenes and from that date the Kingdom of Yugoslavia) the Yugoslav law concerning the registration of merchant ships of 30 March 1922 largely reproduced the Austro-Hungarian legislation, of course substituting Yugoslav nationals for Austrian or Hungaro-Croatian.[5]

* Scientific Counsellor, Adriatic Institute of the Yugoslav Academy of Science and Arts.

1. For the legislation preceding the Austrian domination of the Littoral see V. Brajković, *Etudes historiques sur le Droit maritime privé du Littoral Yougoslave*, Marseilles 1933, pp. 110 et seq.

2. See A. Gertscher and P. Schreckenthal, "Österreich-Ungarn, Seerecht", in *Handelsgesetze des Erdballs*, 1906, XIII, 413-627, especially p. 543 and *Sammlung der Gesetze und Verordnungen betreffend den See- und Hafendienst in der Österreichisch-Ungarischen Monarchie*, herausgegeben von den Seebehörden in Triest und Fiume, vol. I 1883, p. 339.

3. See Gertscher-Schreckenthal, op.cit., p. 555.

4. See *Sammlung und Verordnungen* etc., vol. I pp. 270 et seq. By the Austro-Hungarian compromise of 1867 some matters concerning legislative and operational activities were common to both halves of the monarchy, and in some matters only the legislation was common. Maritime private law was common until 1908, after which it ceased to exist. Thus the nationality of ships ceased to be a common matter but the text cited remained in force until the dissolution of the monarchy.

5. See M.J. Perić, "L'inscription maritime en Yougoslavie", *Journal de la Marine Marchande*, 1925, pp. 1045 et seq.

After the Second World War and the Constitution of the new Yugoslav state, with a political and economic structure very different from the old one, it was also necessary to reform maritime legislation, and in the first place the law on the nationality of ships, so that socio-economic changes could be reflected in the new rules. The *Decree Concerning the Registration of Yugoslav Ships and Barques,* 12 May 1951 (Gaz. 25/51) admitted to the Yugoslav Register only ships totally owned by Yugoslav legal entities, or by Yugoslav citizens residing in Yugoslavia, or under foreign ownership but with a Yugoslav operator. The Federal Minister of Maritime Affairs could at his discretion allow the registration of ships under foreign ownership and with a foreign operator.[6] This decree was slightly modified by the *Law Concerning the Registration of Seagoing Ships,* 1965. Finally a codifying law on maritime and internal navigation was passed (Gaz. 22/1977) which entered into force 1 January 1978. We will limit our consideration of this law to seagoing ships only.

Under the 1977 law it is mandatory to register in Yugoslavia a ship which is entirely in social ownership; or under the ownership either of a citizen of the Socialist Federal Republic of Yugoslavia (hereafter Yugoslavia) residing in Yugoslavia, or of private law legal individuals residing in Yugoslavia (Art. 174). As a result of these rules the link between the flag of the ship and the Yugoslav state is genuine from the personal and economic point of view. Articles 119 and 128 rule that the ship's master and the entire crew must be Yugoslav citizens, with the proviso that the operator and the master may in case of need, but only in case of need, replace part of the crew by foreign nationals. This rule is valid for all ships under the Yugoslav flag. Optional registration of ships in the Yugoslav Register of Ships is possible for seagoing vessels only in two cases (Art. 175, para. 1, 3): ships under foreign ownership with a Yugoslav operator, and yachts under foreign ownership.

The first case, 'social ownership', is when a Yugoslav organization of associated labour or some other legal entity, or a physical person of Yugoslav citizenship residing in Yugoslavia is operator of a ship under foreign ownership, the owner being a foreign citizen, a stateless person or a Yugoslav citizen residing abroad. For registration of this type the agreement of the shipowner must be produced in the correct form. A condition for the registration of ships in the Yugoslav Register is removal from a foreign register (Art. 178). The documents to be produced for such registration must be in accordance with the different procedural rules of the 1977 Law (Part IV, chapter 4, of the Law regarding the procedure on the registering of ships, Articles 239-377). This possibility for optional registration has been utilized in some cases of demise charter ships, the Yugoslav party being a demise charterer. There is no involvement of the Yugoslav administrative authorities in the completion of these operations, except for those stipulated in the above articles concerning procedural rules.

6. For a more detailed account of this see B. Jakaša and E. Pallua, "La Nationalité des navires de mer en droit Yougoslave", *Jugoslavenska Pevije za Medjunarodno pravo (Yugoslav Review of International Law,* hereafter JRMP), 1964, 36-48 (in French).

No authorization by Yugoslav administrative bodies is needed in cases either of mandatory or of optional registration or de-registration in the Yugoslav Register of Ships. The person having the right to dispose of a ship in social ownership is authorized in his own right to sell or otherwise alienate the ship, mortgage it or abandon it to the insurers, and to conclude all contracts for the utilization of ships, including demise charters (Art. 188).[7]

De-registration takes place if the ship is lost (including presumed lost), if the conditions prescribed for the Yugoslav nationality of ships (Art. 175, 175) cease to be valid, or if the ship is withdrawn from navigation. If de-registration of a Yugoslav ship is the result of transfer of registration to another Yugoslav register this has no effect on the ship's nationality (Art. 179).

In cases of an optional Yugoslav registration a genuine legal and economic link is created because the Yugoslav operator guarantees the observance of the rules of Yugoslav domestic law and of international conventions concerning maritime public and private law ratified by Yugoslavia, so much the more as the rules concerning the composition of the crew, including the master, apply to all ships under the Yugoslav flag, and also to ships under foreign ownership but with a Yugoslav operator.

Very different from this optional registration of ships that are not of Yugoslav ownerships is that of the second case, the registration of yachts that are entirely or partially owned by foreign citizens, stateless persons or Yugoslav citizens residing abroad. In such cases registration is accorded upon request of the owner of the yacht, but the Federal Committee on Transport and Communication must give it its approval (Art. 175, para. 3). The right to give this permission is discretionary and reasons for refusing need not be stated (Art. 175, para. 4). This has been made possible purely for reasons of tourism, which makes it understandable that the supreme maritime administrative authorities can refuse such registration without revealing their motives in cases where reasons for such registration would not be in accordance with the exception to the rigid rules of the nationality of ships in Yugoslavia.

In the *Law on the Registration of Ships and Barques* of 1965, and in the Law of 1977 the general clause concerning the discretionary authority of the ministry to permit the registration of ships (other than yachts) without a Yugoslav owner or operator does not appear. It was abolished because the reasons for its existence were no longer valid.

Yugoslav regulation of the nationality of seagoing ships has reverted almost entirely to the original rigidity of conditions for registration contained in the Law of 1774 (and also in medieval times) in which total national ownership was prescribed. It is not therefore surprising that Yugoslav doctrine considers that fixed rules on the character of the link between a ship and its state flag should be clearly defined.[8]

7. We have not reproduced the rules concerning alienation between Yugoslav Socialist organizations within Yugoslavia because it has no relevance for our topic.

8. See V. Brajković - E. Pallua, "Les conditions dans lesquelles les Etats accordent aux

We will now attempt to give a general outline of the problems of the international regulation of the nationality of ships. Before the First World War such a problem was practically non-existent.[9] Thus the otherwise excellent Rules established by the *Institut de Droit International* at its conference in Venice in 1896 did not take account of what were to be much later developments. The ship's operator was not mentioned at all as a possibly vital element in search of a reasonable solution to the problem.[10]

These well-known Rules[11] demanded that national legislation should enforce the domestic majority ownership of a ship, taking into account the different kinds of companies. The construction of ships in national yards and the nationality of master and crew were not specified as conditions-precedent for the nationality of ships. The Rules were limited to defining conditions of ownership. The Institute considered that the fulfilment of these conditions was necessary for international cognition of the ship's nationality. Therefore the Institute considered, and also produced, a model for rules concerning loss of nationality and the procedure for striking off ships from a national registry.

The United Nations Commission on International Law (ILC) was obliged, in drawing up a draft convention concerning the high seas, to provide a solution to the problem of the nationality of ships.[12] The *rapporteur,* Professor François, and the majority of the Commission, accepted as the basis of their work the Rules established in Venice in 1896, considering the fulfilment of those conditions to be necessary if the nationality of a ship was to be recognized by other states. Some of the members of the Commission challenged this view, believing that only one rule of international law existed in this matter, namely that a ship registered in one country could not be entered in the register of another state.[13] The ILC adopted the Venice Rules at its seventh session by a majority vote, but completely reversed its point of view at its eighth session (1956). In the interval between the seventh and eighth sessions a survey of the nationality laws of sixty-seven states had been published and replies received from governments commenting on the pro-

---

navires le droit d'arborer le pavillon national", in *Rapports généraux au Ve Congrès international de droit comparé,* Brussels 1960, pp. 670 et seq.

9. See G. Dumke, "Die Flagge des Heiligen Landes" (The Flag of the Holy Land), *Jahrbuch für internationales Recht,* VIII 2, 101 et seq. This flag ceased to exist in 1916 and it seems that it never had any commercial value.

10. The CMI tried to arrive at a definition of "operator" *("armateur")* and the Yugoslav and Italian Maritime Law Associations supported this attempt. A draft convention was presented by G. Berlingieri to the Twenty-fourth Conference of the CMI (Rijeka 1959, pp. 161-162), but the responses of the national maritime law associations did not encourage a continuation of the study, *ibid.,* 144-166.

11. See "Règles relatives à l'usage du pavillon national pour les navires de commerce", *Annuaire* XV, (Session de Venise 1896) pp. 201, nouvellement approuvé à la Session de Lausanne en 1927, *Annuaire* XXXIII, 103 et seq. especially 139 the proposal of M. Lemonon to give solution to the problem "sous forme de convention internationale, de manière que la matière soit réglé de façon uniforme et non de façon multiple comme elle l'est à présent."

12. For an analysis of the role of the nationality of ships see E. Pallua, "La nationalité des navires de commerce en doit international public et privé", JRMP 1958, 1, 81-95 (in French).

13. See A/CN. 4/SR 121, pp. 7 et seq. for the opinions of Hudson and Amado.

posed draft convention. Most governments proposed only slight modifications of the text.

The Yugoslav government proposed an addition to the draft: that registration of a ship should be permitted when the operator of the ship *("armateur")* was a national of the flag state.[14] The governments of the Netherlands and of the United Kingdom asked for a complete revision of the draft rules on the nationality of ships. The Netherlands demanded that states should be at liberty to fix the conditions of registration, but that for international recognition of the ship's nationality a genuine link *("lien réel")* should exist between the flag state and the owner of the ship. In commenting on this proposed amendment the government of the Netherlands gave some examples of a genuine link, such as the nationality of the owner, the master and the crew.[15] The United Kingdom proposal was in the same vein as that of the Netherlands. It considered that for international recognition of the nationality of a ship on the basis of a genuine link it is supposed that the flag state is able effectively to submit the ship to its jurisdiction and control in accordance with its own national law and international law.[16] The ILC adopted a text that incorporated the proposed Netherlands and UK amendments.

In this text the ILC maintained the rule regarding the recognition of a ship's nationality by other states only if the condition of the genuine link was satisfied. In the interval between the eighth session of the ILC and the first UN Conference on the Law of the Sea many had doubts about the application of such a sanction on the basis of vague criteria.[17]

The Geneva Conference of 1958 eliminated the said sanction concerning lack of a genuine link between the ship and the flag state. This facilitated the development of a situation in which a quarter of the world's merchant fleet is under a flag with which its ships have no link at all, except registration in that country's registry of ships.

The situation especially deteriorated after the International Court of Justice gave its "advisory opinion" on the Constitution of the Safety Committee of the Inter-Governmental Maritime Consultative Organization (8 June 1960). The conflicting views were, as is well known, on the interpretation to be given in the IMCO convention to the words "the largest ship-owning nations" for the purpose of electing eight members of the maritime safety committee with this qualification. The choice was between Panama and Liberia on one side, France and the Federal Republic of Germany on the other. The majority of the court adopted the view that these words mean the merchant fleets that are the largest in Lloyd's Register of Shipping, not entering into the question of ownership or other connecting circumstances between ship and flag. The governments of the UK and the Netherlands considered that "the expression largest ship-owning nations" has no apparent

14. See A/CN. 4, pp. 85 et seq.
15. See A/CN. 4/99, Add. 1, pp. 39 et seq.
16. See A/CN. 4/99, Add. 1, pp. 53 et seq.
17. See E. Pallua, "La nationalité des navires de commerce dans le Projet de la Commission du droit international", *Annual of the Association of Attenders and Alumni of the Hague Academy of International Law,* 1957, No. 27, pp. 67 et seq.

"clear cut or technical meaning", and they thought that the Assembly of IMCO should rely on its own judgement as to whether some nations should be regarded as being amongst the "largest ship-owning nations" in a real and substantial sense. Registered tonnage was not by itself a sufficient basis for the application to a country of the term "largest ship-owning nation". They declined to enter into the question of ownership, but insisted on the freedom of the IMCO Assembly to determine, weighing all relevant circumstances, which are the "largest ship-owning nations".

It seems that for these two governments the "genuine link" formula had merits less easily discovered by others. The United States insisted on the literal interpretation of the words "genuine links" as meaning the largest ship-owning nations. The Court found, by a majority judgment, (9-5) that the words "largest ship-owning nations" referred to "registered tonnage". Dissenting opinions were appended only by the President, Klaestadt, and Judge Moreno Quintana. President Klaestadt, in an analysis of Article 28a that contains the words at issue, argued his case very pertinently, but did not touch on the interpretation of the question of the link between state and ship. He solved only the problem of the interpretation of the powers of the IMCO Assembly in the sense that the Assembly had an electing power that should not be exercised in an arbitrary manner. Judge Moreno Quintana adopted the interpretation of Article 28a of the IMCO convention given by President Klaestadt, but he expressed his opinion on the "genuine link". That opinion is very interesting today because it coincides exactly with the interpretations of the present situation. His words, in the English translation given by the Court, were: "The registration of shipping by an administrative authority is one thing, the ownership of a merchant fleet is another. The latter reflects an international economic reality which can be satisfactorily established only by the existence of a genuine link between the owner of the ship and the flag it flies. This is the doctrine expressed by Article 5 of the Convention on the High Seas which was signed at Geneva 29 April 1958 by all the eighty-six states represented at the Conference that drew it up. This provision, by which international law establishes an obligation binding in national law, constitutes at the present time the *opinio juris gentium* on the matter".[18]

This advisory opinion was criticised and it was possible to foresee that an opposite point of view would develop, as proved to be the case with the judgment by the Permanent International Court of Justice in the *Lotus* Case.[19] With time it became evident that a solution to the problem of the genuine link could only be found by a new unification convention. The *rapporteur* at the Geneva Conference

18. ICJ Rep. Advisory Opinion 1960, of 8 June.

19. See E. Pallua, "Savjetodavno misljenje Medjunarodnog suda od 8.VI 1960. i drzavna pripadnost brodova" (The Advisory Opinion of the International Court of Justice 8 June 1960 and the nationality of ships) JRMP 1962, pp. 44-53 (with résumé in French (pp. 53-55). In this article the view is expressed that "the advisory opinion was not a judicial precedent for the interpretation of the contents of the notion of "genuine link" at all, and also that it missed the possibility of taking a standpoint on the question". As is well known the *Lotus* decision was followed by trade union reaction that eventually led to the signing of an international convention for the unification of certain rules relating to penal jurisdiction in matters of collision or other incidents of navigation, Brussels, 10 May 1952.

of 1958 had indeed foreseen that the insufficient way in which the problem had been solved in Article 5 of the High Seas Convention would require a new international convention.[20] It seems that it will perhaps be achieved through the initiative of UNCTAD. The Third UN Conference on the Law of the Sea leaves this task to UNCTAD because the rules established by it in its drafts are essentially the same as the old formula of 1958, the only relevant difference being that jurisdictional and supervisionary duties are enumerated.[21]

The title of the introductory paper circulated by UNCTAD drew attention to the economic character of the study.[22] It is evident that an economic study must eventually give rise to a legal solution. The Secretariat of UNCTAD concluded that the ownership of a ship must, for the greater part, be invested in the state or in companies or citizens belonging to that state (reserving the question of ships belonging to multinationals), and articulated detailed rules about the residence and the citizenship of the owners. The shipping enterprise should be taxed in the flag state and this state should exert full control over the application of adequate standards for the ship and for its crew and the terms of their employment.[23]

The Intergovernmental Working Group, discussing this paper, arrived at the following conclusions (10 February 1979) with regard to the genuine link question: that the merchant fleet has to contribute to the development of the economy of the flag state; that the expenses and the profits of shipping, including the buying and construction of ships, must enter into the balance of payments of the flag state; that citizens of the flag state must be employed on its ships and last (but we would argue not least) ownership must be related to the flag State.[24]

The UNCTAD Committee on Shipping, at its third session (27 May - 6 June 1981) discussed the results of the *ad hoc* intergovernmental working group. This discussion was very interesting as the confrontation between the developed and the developing countries continued.[25] It was especially characteristic, as was rightly stressed by the developing countries, that the states which were most strict about the ownership conditions for the registration of ships in their countries were at the same time protecting, and pleading for, the continuation of the present situation with respect to flags of convenience. (The US and the UK have, as is well known, the strictest ownership conditions concerning ships registered in their countries.)

20. The opinion of Professor François (R/Conf. 13/C2/L. 14, p. 10) was consistent with his view that the right of states to fix the conditions for the nationality of their ships is not unlimited. But see Gidel, *Le Droit international publique de la mer,* 1932, vol. I, p. 349, the case *Virginius* and H. Meijers, *The Nationality of Ships,* The Hague, 1967, pp. 99 et seq. for the case *I am Alone.*

21. See A/Conf. 62/VP 10/rev. 3.

22. See "Economic Consequences of the Existence or lack of a Genuine Link between Vessel and Flag of Registry". *Report of UNCTAD Secretariat,* TD/B/C.4/168.

23. *Ibid.*

24. See the Report of the Committee on Shipping of UNCTAD at its third special session, 27 May - 6 June 1981 to be published under TF/B/1855 - TD/B/C. 4/227.

25. *Ibid.* pp. 10-27.

The UNCTAD committee on shipping adopted, by a majority vote, a resolution asking for the convening of an inter-governmental preparatory group, in order to prepare for a Diplomatic Conference, and recommended to such a group the following basic principles which, in the opinion of the Committee, should be taken into consideration as possible conditions for the nationality of ships: a) the manning of vessels; b) the role of flag countries in the management of ship-owning companies and vessels; c) equity of participation in capital; d) identification and accountability of owners and operators.[26]

The concurrent draft proposals of the Federal Republic of Germany, on behalf of Group B, asked only for the convening of an inter-governmental working group to shed some light for the Committee on Shipping upon "a set of non-mandatory guide lines" relating to the conditions under which vessels should be registered and asked the Secretary-General of UNCTAD to organize, along with IMCO, a joint programme to study: "a) the data that might be required by the port states relating to ownership and operation of ships i.e. certificates of nationality, ownership and registration; a list of successive owners of the ship; identity of the legal person under whose auspices the shipowner is domiciled in the State of registry; a list of mortgages on the vessel; bare-boat charter parties or time-charter parties in excess of six months (to the extent that the information is not a matter of confidentiality); the name and location of the person operationally responsible for the vessel; . . ." combining these with other requirements always directed to port States.[27] In these draft proposals it was recommended that developed countries should "urge their shipping companies to involve, whenever possible, the nationals of developing countries in the ownership, management, and crewing of their ships, by joint ventures, management arrangements or other means". The last sentence invited developing countries to adopt such legislative measures as would attract foreign investment in their shipping industry.

A third draft proposal, presented by France in a slightly different form, contained many elements of the proposal of the Federal Republic of Germany, with emphasis on the role of the port authorities in the control of the genuine link, but specially demanded that the responsibility "of shipowners and managers could be engaged, in particular, by greater transparency of the organization of shipping companies". This reflected the very strong French concern with problems analogous to the *"Amoco Cadiz"* disaster.[28]

It seems that the developed countries rely very heavily on the port authorities implementation of internationally accepted standards concerning ship and crew, and that the developing countries, and the Secretariat of UNCTAD, rely much more on the efficient supervision of the flag state in this respect.

The ILO Convention 147 on the minimum standards to be observed on merchant ships (Geneva, 29 Oct. 1976) entered into force on 28 November 1981.

26. *Ibid.* Annex I, p. 30 especially 31. 49 delegations voted in favour, 18 against and 3 abstained. Panama gave reasons for her absence (p. 22).
27. *Ibid.* Annex II, p. 33 et seq.
28. *Ibid.* Annex III, p. 35.

Its rules can now be applied to contracting and non-contracting states and it will soon be possible to arrive at clear conclusions concerning the effectiveness of the supervision of foreign ships in ports with respect to security and social questions. Thus, before the end of the discussion on the genuine link question, it will be established, which of the two groups of states were right in their expectations – those relying on the flag state, or those relying on the port state.

From the point of view of customary international law one point of delimitation of jurisdiction between flag state and port or coastal state was not controversial: internal discipline on board ship was submitted to the jurisdiction of the flag state only, not just on the high seas but also in territorial waters and internal waters, including ports. The new ILO Convention changes the delimitation of competence a great deal between the two state authorities, flag and port. It seems that normally all competencies concerning relations between shipowner (or ship operator) on the one side and crew, including the master, on the other, could be much better dealt with by the flag state's authorities, but this supposes that the flag state has the means to impose its authority. The countries of open registry obviously lack this means, and so almost a quarter of the world's merchant fleet depends on diligent port authorities alone to ensure conformity with international standards. This development has been made possible only because special, mostly economic, circumstances have induced the flight of some shipowners from the flag of their country to the flag of open-registry countries. As the representative of ICFTU [29] put it in his concluding statement at the meeting of the UNCTAD Committee on Shipping in June 1981: "... flags of convenience were an unmitigated disaster" and their abuse (such as "exploitation of seafarers") could not be eliminated as long as the system itself existed.[30] It must be said that the criteria recommended by the Committee on Shipping in its aforesaid resolution are not all of the same practical value as to ensure the efficacy of the jurisdiction of the flag state. So the manning of a vessel cannot be an independent condition because the manning can always be changed. The role of the flag state in the management of vessels could be a point of departure for finding a solution to the problem, but only if this role can be described in such terms as comply with the legal terms used in the legislation on the nationality of ships. It is not always easy to insert economic facts into laws but the legal concepts that derive from such facts as ownership, operator, company, and company board, can with some ingenuity be fixed fairly well.

From the point of view of Yugoslav legislation on the nationality of ships it can be said that the rules suggested by the Committee on Shipping in this matter are in principle acceptable as a basis of discussion for international unification.

29. ICFTU stands for International Confederation of Free Trade Unions. Its intervention p. 26.

30. Industrial action taken by ICFTU in ports in England against the ship ... *"The Nawala"*, registered in Hong Kong, was recognised by the House of Lords as having all the legal immunities which pertain to such actions in English law, in its Judgment 25 September 1979, see Lloyd's Rep. 1980, 1, p. 1. But see the limits set to that immunity in the later judgments of the Court of Appeal in *The Antama* (1982) and in *Merkur Island Shipping Corporation* v. *Laughton and others* (1982) *Times Law Report*, 5 November 1982.

Both mandatory and optional rules of registration insure that ships are integrated into the national economy, and obliged to use only Yugoslav seamen as crew. Yugoslav regulations on this matter seem to be well balanced and ensure to the maximum the efficacy of the jurisdiction of the flag state.

There is a great difference between some states of open-registry which have no possibility of applying coercive measures to their ships, and those open-registry states which are British dependent territories, such as Hong Kong, or in states of the Commonwealth, such as Singapore. British legislation is applied there, directly or indirectly, through reception and authorities of the registry can, in great ports in different parts of the world, apply coercive or supervisionary measures.

It seems to us that the very wise rules recommended by the *Institut de Droit International* in 1896 in Venice, and in 1927 at Lausanne, and adopted as a basis for the preparatory work of the ILC, have now reappeared in a more imprecise form. The critics of the present situation, who deplore the economic consequences of the open-registry flags of convenience are, perhaps, not well documented in every detail, but an obviously deplorable fact is that the open-registry ships are totally independent of any truly sovereign power over them, so that only very energetic and concerted operations by the port authorities in the developed countries can remedy the most flagrant abuses of the possibilities offered by such fleets to unscrupulous shipowners.[31]

It is difficult to understand why the states which impose the most rigid conditions for ships under their own flag (UK and USA) are in favour of the open-registry flags, and that the states which proposed a resolution of an intermediate character did not go further than merely suggesting guide lines. These contradictory attitudes have been underlined many times in international meetings. The rule of Article 5 of the Geneva Convention on the High Seas 1958 was a guide line that should not have been misinterpreted, albeit in good faith, as giving limitless power to states in conferring their nationality on ships. However some states and certain authors, encouraged by the evasive Advisory Opinion of the ICJ of 1960, sustained this opinion concerning the interpretation of the genuine link.

It appears to us that with the imposition of more and more responsibilities on the flag state in security matters, social matters, pollution and ecology, it is becoming increasingly anachronistic to permit registration alone to be the link in international law between the ship and the flag state. It also seems that the conditions precedent that must be fulfilled before registration, e.g., national ownership and/or national operator, should be well defined, bearing in mind, however, the

31. See on ships without a nationality, Ripert, *Droit maritime*, 1929, I p. 427: "S'il ne se rattachait à aucun Etat il serait lui-même un Etat indépendent et souverain". Ships registered in open-registry countries are almost in this situation. But see Myres S. Dougal, William T. Burke and Ivan V. Vlasić, "The maintenance of public order at sea and the nationality of ships", AJIL, vol. 53 (1960) pp. 26-116 which considers registration a sufficient link with the flag state. For the opposite point of view see Peter Mander, The Nationality of Ships – Politics and Law, *Arkiv for Sørett* 1961, p. 267 et seq. But see H. Meijers who in his exhaustive monograph on the nationality of ships, op.cit., considers the registration of ships as sufficient link only on condition of effectivity of the exercise of jurisdiction and control by the flag state. On p. 297 he is very benevolent towards the flag of Liberia.

needs of landlocked states to exercise their right to a merchant fleet as laid down in the Barcelona Declaration 21 April 1921. None of these states is an open-registry country, and one of them. Switzerland, has the most rigid registration rules: owner and operator must both be resident nationals. Perhaps this stipulation would not be generally acceptable to all landlocked countries, much less to all other countries, but it might, *mutatis mutandis,* serve as a basis for the finding of a more flexible formula.

The international rule *de lege ferenda* could demand a substantive part of national ownership (perhaps more than fifty per cent, perhaps something less) or alternatively a national operator. No clear formulation has been produced to date by the different bodies of UNCTAD.[32]

A combination of the proposals in the resolution adopted by the Committee on Shipping at its third special session, June 1981, and some of the proposals of the Federal Republic of Germany, transmuted from guide-lines to actual rules of international law, might be the way out of the present deadlocked situation[33].

Whatever economic advantages or disadvantages merchant fleets of the open-registry countries bring to states of the different groups, it is very difficult to conceive that a country without any link with the ship, with the exception of registration (which is in fact a *petitio principii ...),* should be the country whose laws are pertinent for the solution of many private international law problems, and for the internal discipline on board.

32. In the resolution adopted by the Committee on Shipping it is *inter alia* recommended: "... the present régime of open registries be gradually and progressively transformed into one of *normal registries* (italics mine E.P.) by a process of tightening the conditions under which open-registry countries retain or accept vessels on their registers . . .", so that the existence of normal registries is there affirmed, which was the point of departure of the Institut de Droit International in 1896 and 1927, and of the ILC until 1956.

33. The first session (doc. TD/B/AC. 34, 10 June 1982) of the Intergovernmental Preparatory Group on Conditions for the Registration of Ships was held after this article had gone to press. The third annex of its report contains a "Draft set of basic principles concerning conditions upon which vessels should be accepted on national shipping registers". This draft set allows grounds for optimism on the outcome of future work. The second session of the group was held in November 1982 and no report has as yet been published.

SUBSEQUENT CHOICE OF LAW AND COMPROMISSORY AGREEMENT *(VASTSTELLINGSOVEREENKOMST)*

by Mr. W. Snijders*

The *Theo* case was before the District Court of Rotterdam in the spring of 1963. The *m.s. Theo,* flying the Costa Rican flag, had been moored in the port of Lagos (Nigeria) for some time in 1955 when it was time-chartered by De Craecker, Antwerp. In Lagos a branch office of the plaintiff, a Dutch company, acting as agent for De Craecker, had incurred costs in respect of the ship which De Craecker had never repaid nor could be expected to repay because of its subsequent bankruptcy. On the basis of these facts the plaintiff requested a declaratory judgment against the Costa Rican owner and the Rotterdamsche Bank N.V. to the effect that the plaintiff had a claim against De Craecker for these costs and that this amount was recoverable against the *Theo,* which on the plaintiff's instructions had been attached in the port of Rotterdam, though the attachment had been withdrawn on receipt of a guarantee from the Rotterdamsche Bank N.V. The plaintiff based its claim on the plea that the debt in question was due 'in respect of the business carried on by the ship' within the meaning of Article 318r read in conjunction with 318q of the Dutch Commercial Code.

Understandably, the judges raised their eyebrows when counsel did not address themselves to the question of what law was to apply to this case, but this difficulty was resolved in classic Rotterdam style. The submissions were interrupted by the Court requesting an opinion on this point. When counsel replied that they wished to confine their pleadings to Dutch law, the Court advised them to enter a joint statement that by way of compromise *(dading)* they had agreed to request the Court to decide the case exclusively on the basis of Dutch law. So it was done.

It is not without reason that I recall this incident in this *Festschrift:* the president of the Court to which I refer was Erades, with Van den Biesen and myself as judges. I remember quite clearly that before we made our suggestion, there had been no consultation between us other than the words spoken by one of us: "I cannot think why it could not be done". The arrangement was reflected, naturally, in the judgment (Rotterdam District Court, 2 April 1963, S & S 1963, 52).

It was the first time that a Dutch court had unambiguously recognized a subsequent choice of law *(rechtskeuze achteraf)*, and we got what we deserved: a fine essay by Kollewijn in the Netherlands International Law Review [1], in which he

* Counsellor, Supreme Court *(Raadsheer Hoge Raad);* Government Commissioner for Books 3, 5, 6, New Civil Code.

1. *Netherlands International Law Review* (1964) p. 225 et seq. where reference is made

rightly rebuked us for the technically incorrect use of the term *dading* [2] and in a well-constructed argument, carefully analysing all the difficulties we had ignored, finally agreed with our view.

Almost twenty years have passed since then. The possibility of a subsequent choice of law has become the general practice in the Netherlands, even though its limits are not yet settled. The present collection seems to me to provide an appropriate opportunity to reconsider the question, and I do so in particular in order to relate it to a quite different matter: the new Dutch Civil Code. This, too, fits well into this collection, since it is my work on this Code that caused me to leave Rotterdam, and the paths of Erades and myself to diverge.

The relation that may be established with the new Civil Code is to be found in Title 7.15 concerning the compromissory agreement *(vaststellingsovereenkomst).* It has been repeatedly suggested in Dutch literature that a subsequent choice of law must be regarded as a compromissory agreement.[3] One gathers the impression that these authors intended their remarks as a kind of reassurance: the compromissory agreement is a familiar object, so it seems obvious that the subsequent choice of law may be similarly regarded as permissible. This may perhaps be understandable, certainly to the extent that compromissory agreements do not fall into the category of ('specified') contracts regulated by statute, but it would be over-optimistic to believe that the difficulties are thereby resolved. On closer consideration of the problems connected with such an agreement, it becomes clear that there are few areas in Dutch law so thorny and so highly controversial.

In the meantime, the compromissory agreement is to be regulated in the new Civil Code, namely in Title 7.15, which forms part of the draft text of Book 7 published in 1972 (the first five Articles of which are reproduced hereafter in an Annex). It has already been announced that this Title as well as a few others are due to enter into force together with Books 3 - 6, and that this will occur in 1985. However, Title 7.15 has met with a good deal of criticism in legal literature, and will be introduced as a Government Bill only after substantial alterations. Remarkably enough, the problems attaching to choice of law are ignored in these criticisms, which clearly illustrates the distance existing in the Netherlands between practitioners of substantive civil law and those of private international law. Nevertheless, in the current redrafting of Title 7.15, it will be necessary to consider its implications for the international choice of law. It may be assumed that, in practice, a subsequent choice of law in proceedings before a Dutch Court will be a choice in favour of Dutch law, made in a situation where the agreement on this choice of law will itself be governed by Dutch law. It is this particular case that will be given special attention in the present essay.

---

to what may be regarded as precursors to the Rotterdam Judgment, e.g., Court of Appeal, The Hague, 4 May 1936, NJ 1936, 826.

2. A *dading* within the meaning of Art. 1888, Civil Code is an agreement by which the parties terminate or prevent proceedings. It is valid only if made in writing. Neither of the two conditions was fulfilled in this case.

3. Deelen, *Rechtskeuze in het Nederlands Internationaal Contractenrecht* (Choice of law in Dutch International Law of Contract) Thesis, Amsterdam 1965, p. 219; Santen, W.P.N.R. 5545 (1980) p. 886.

The first Article of Title 7.15 circumscribes the compromissory agreement as follows: "By means of a compromissory agreement the parties, in order to terminate or avoid uncertainty or dispute as to their respective rights and duties, accept an agreed determination thereof intended to be of binding effect even where it deviates from the legal position obtaining in the absence of such agreed determination".

Where this provision includes the words 'in order to avoid uncertainty or dispute', the first question that arises is whether this definition does not cover *any* choice of law, including the choice laid down in the contract itself. In my opinion, the answer must be in the negative. When the choice of law is made in the contract, the parties employ a conflict rule with the result that the law designated by them is applicable under the rules of private international law. Its application is not founded on an "agreed determination" by the parties, but arises from this rule of private international law, irrespective of the question whether there would have been uncertainty in the absence of their choice of law[4].

At first sight it might be thought that the question will become academic as soon as the EEC Convention on the Law Applicable to Contractual Obligations enters into force (Official Journal of the European Communities 1980, No. L 266/1). For this Convention contains in Article 3 separate provisions relating to choice of law that cannot be prejudiced by Title 7.15. Two things should, however, be borne in mind. In the first place, the Convention applies only to contractual obligations, whereas a choice of law may be incorporated also in other agreements and juristic acts. In the second place, the question arises whether the Convention regulates the whole field of contractual obligations, and also, for example, the effect of such an obligation on third parties whose position may be affected by the choice, a question to which I will return hereafter.

The next point to consider is the question whether the above definition of a compromissory agreement includes the *subsequent* choice of law. It seems to me that, in principle, this is quite defensible. But, again, a reservation must be made. Once the parties have brought their dispute before the Court and made their choice of law after the Court has drawn their attention to the uncertainty of what is to be the proper law, there is certainly an agreed determination whereby a previously existing uncertainty between the parties is removed by the new legal position created by them.[5] But the situation may also be different.

4. See Art. 3 (1) of the EEC Convention on the Law Applicable to Contractual Obligations as well as the report on this Convention in the Official Journal of the European Communities, 1980, C 282; Th.M. De Boer, in *Partij-invloed in het internationaal privaatrecht,* Opstellen ter gelegenheid van het 25-jarig bestaan van het Centrum voor buitenlands recht en internationaal privaatrecht van de Universiteit van Amsterdam, (1975) p. 55 et seq. Supreme Court, 13 May 1966, NJ 1967, 3 (Alnati) expressing the view that, according to *Dutch conflict rules*, the choice of law brings with it that the agreement is in principle governed only by the chosen law.

5. A slightly different distinction, although not incompatible with the text, is made by Kollewijn, *loc.cit., supra,* n. 1, who terms a subsequent choice of law a choice of the "right of decision".

Thus, it is not inconceivable for persons who have entered into a contract to supplement it with a choice of law that, although made subsequently, is just as conclusive for the question what law is to govern the contract as is an immediate choice of law, so that the situation referred to in Title 7.15 is not reached for the reasons set out above. This view seems to be implicit in Article 3 (2) of the above-mentioned EEC Convention, in which a special provision for the validity of a contract and the protection of third parties is deemed necessary only in cases where the parties change their previous choice of law.

Another reason why a subsequent choice of law may not come within the scope of the definition referred to above arises where the parties never intended to remove any uncertainty, nor differed in opinion as to what was the proper law, but for some reason prefered a law other than the law which they knew was applicable. Also this possibility is implied in Article 3 (2) of the EEC Convention, namely, in the case contemplated in this Article, when the parties' choice of the law to be applied is subsequently varied, a possibility which the Convention permits. But quite apart from such a case, it may easily occur that parties to an action before a Dutch Court wish their dispute to be decided by Dutch law. The reason may be found in an understandable fear that the application of foreign law, with which counsel and judges are not familiar, might well result in an irresponsible decision. Another possibility may be that the parties wish to benefit by a favourable Dutch regulation that would not otherwise be applicable to them, which is the underlying idea of Article 1 (4) of the Act of 25 March 1981 regulating the conflict of laws relating to the dissolution of marriage and separation, which precribes the application of Dutch law at the joint request of the parties or at the uncontested request of either party. It appears from its parliamentary history that this rule is intended to enable the parties, also in default cases, to make use of the new divorce regulations which entered into force in the Netherlands in 1971.[6]

So the situation, briefly summarized, is that Title 7.15 applies to a subsequent choice of law in some cases, but not in others. Therefore, every care will have to be taken to prevent arbitrary differences arising out of this. Article 3 of the EEC Convention is even less likely to provide the solution to all difficulties, than would be the case where the choice of law is laid down in the contract itself. For the subsequent choice of law covers, in principle, the whole field of private law. Thus, the Rotterdam judgment referred to at the beginning of this essay, to take just one example, fell, as for recovering against the *Theo,* outside the scope of the contractual obligation and, consequently, of Article 3.

The first point calling for attention here is the choice, in the draft text of Title 7.15, in favour of the declaratory effect of an agreed determination laid down in Articles 2 and 3 of Title 7.15. This principle, which is the subject of controversy in current law[7], is opposed to the principle of dispositive effect. The latter implies that the new legal position envisaged by the agreed determination, and based

6. *Bijl. Hand.* II, 1980-1981, 16 004, Provisional Report, p. 3 and Memorandum of Reply, pp. 3-4.

7. See, the explanatory note to the draft text of Book 7, p. 1122, and Asser-Kamphuisen, *Bijzondere Overeenkomsten,* p. 810 et seq.

on the various assumptions concerning the previous situation as to which there was uncertainty or dispute, must be brought about in the usual manner by means of passing of title, waiver of rights or whatever further acts may be required to bring about this new legal position. By contrast, under the principle of declaratory effect, the dispute or uncertainty is directly removed, without regard to the previous legal position, by means of a specific juristic act to that effect, which in principle requires no further implementing act. It will be clear that this is of particular importance in cases involving the law of property. The declaratory principle has found acceptance particularly in France and Belgium where it fits into the municipal systems of these countries, under which, e.g., in sales contracts, the transfer of ownership is effected by the mere contractual obligation without any separate act of delivery being required. Dutch law, however, does require such an act; therefore, the declaratory principle conflicts with the Dutch system. Although Articles 2 and 3 of Title 7.15 make certain corrections, these provide only for the case where the creation of the envisaged legal position requires the permission of a Government body or the consent of a third party, or where the agreed determination concerns the legal status of registered property (immovable property, ships and aircraft and the rights attaching thereto).

Thus, Title 7.15 could be expected to give rise to criticism in this respect.[8] This is not the place for further discussion of this aspect. But it may be remarked that a change in the dispositive system is under serious consideration. Various arguments may be advanced in its favour. One such argument is that, especially in cases where the agreed determination concerns the choice of applicable law, this system seems to lead to better results, provided that it is not applied too dogmatically and that it is recognized that an agreement may have a certain effect on third parties. The Dutch courts already recognize this with regard to compromissory agreements without legal basis. In the new Civil Code this may be inferred from the fact that the strictly formulated Article 1376 has been cancelled.[9]

Examples are provided by the agreed determination of the extent of a preferential debt, or a debt secured by a lien or mortgage, which is of importance to other, lower-ranking creditors[10], the admission of a right of recovery, as in the case of the Rotterdam judgment referred to above, which is important to the other creditors of the ship-owner, and the determination of the substance of a contract which by its nature is liable to be invoked by a third person.[11] In a dispositive system the effect on a third-party of an agreed determination may also be based on a third-party agreement, for which the new Civil Code makes ample provision.

8. *Rapport Koninklijke Notariële Broederschap,* W.P.N.R. 5451 (1978), p. 607; Aaftink van Van Zeben, NJB (1973) pp. 112-113; Schoordijk, W.P.N.R. 5283 (1974) p. 739; H. Stein, *Advocatenblad* (1981) p. 437.

9. See, Memorandum of Reply on Book 6 in section 6.5.3. under *'Algemeen',* also included in Van Zeben-Du Pon, *Parliamentary History of Book 6,* p. 917 et seq.

10. Supreme Court, 7 February 1941, NJ 1941, 934, and 23 May 1980, NJ 1980, 502.

11. See, Supreme Court, 26 June 1964, NJ 1965, 170, 7 March 1969, NJ 1969, 249, and 12 January 1979, NJ 1979, 362, as well as Artt. 6.1.2.5., 6.1.9.12., para. 3, 6.5.3.8*a*., 7.7.3.3. and 7.7.3.4. new Civil Code, and many provisions of Book 8 which allow reliance by or against third parties to a contract of carriage.

Further, an agreed determination may well have direct third-party effect, particularly in cases where passing of title, although not coinciding with the contractual obligation, can be effected by simple agreement between the parties, as is the case in the Netherlands in the sale of movable goods.[12] Where the agreement has been made in writing, further examples include all goods transferable by a simple deed.[13] It seems obvious to regard such an act of delivery as implied in the dispositive determination, unless the parties have expressed an intention to the contrary.

It would not, in my view, be desirable for a subsequent choice of law to ensure more than this, and break through mandatory provisions concerning acquisition under the laws of property, succession or matrimonial property regimes. If differentiation is advisable in this connection, a view gaining ground both in and outside the Netherlands [14], it requires a caution which already seems to have been abandoned in the fundamental choice in Title 7.15 in favour of the declaratory principle, even though Article 5 of this Title does not allow reliance on an agreed determination except against the parties and their successors by universal or special title.

This view is reflected in the development of choice of law in the international law on matrimonial property. Dutch court decisions are restrictive in this respect and seem to suggest that choice of law is allowed only before marriage.[15] The 1978 Hague Convention on the Law Applicable to Matrimonial Property Regimes allows something like a subsequent choice of law only within the narrow limits of Article 8 (2) which, by reference to Article 13, requires the form prescribed for marriage contracts either by the chosen law or by the law of the place where the choice is made.

In all this it should be noted that the direct production of a particular result – the clarification of the substance of a marriage contract to which the parties give divergent interpretations, or the transfer of ownership of which the completion or validity is contested – is not the same as the subsequent choice of law, in which the result in question is achieved indirectly through the application of the law chosen. The latitude between these two forms of agreed determination provides the possibility, where the dispositive system is adopted for compromissory agreements generally, to be less strict in attaching consequences in terms of property to a subsequent choice of law than would follow from a direct

12. Art. 3.4.2.5. combined with Art. 3.5.9., new Civil Code.

13. Artt. 3.4.2.7., 3.4.2.7*a*. para. 2 and 3.9.2.2. and 3.9.2.3. new Civil Code, and Artt. 2 (2) of the Copyright Act and 38 (1) of the Patents Act.

14. Deelen, *De toepasselijkheid van materieel vreemd recht in de Nederlandse rechtssfeer, preadviezen Koninklijke Notariële Broederschap* (1980) p. 20, No. 17; Stille, WPNR 5530 (1980) and the discussion of the above-mentioned *preadvies* in WPNR 5545 (1980) passim. Outside the Netherlands: Flessner, RabelsZ. 34 (1970) p. 547 et seq., Weber, RabelsZ. 44 (1980) p. 510 et seq., and the Swiss draft for a *"IPR-Gesetz"* published in RabelsZ. 42 (1978) p. 718 et seq., in particular Artt. 50-52 (the law of matrimonial property), 60 para. 3 (divorce) 91 paras. 2 and 3 (succession), 106 and 107 (law of property), 130 (tort) and 143 (cession).

15. Supreme Court, 10 December 1976, NJ 1977, 275; cf. also Supreme Court, 25 May 1979, NJ 1979, 549.

determination of the final result. Thus, where necessary in practice, the courts need not deny the choice of law any significance in terms of property even in a dispositive system.[16]

A further important point is that, as has already been observed, in a subsequent choice of law before a Dutch court, the parties will usually designate Dutch law. That implies that the cardinal question will be whether it is possible in this way to set aside the *foreign* rules governing the transfer of ownership, the variation of a marriage contract, etc. I will not here discuss the question whether Dutch courts – with due regard to the circumstances, such as the nature of the goods concerned and the question whether Dutch law is more favourable for the continuation of the act in question – ought to do so more readily than in cases where Dutch mandatory rules are to be set aside. But Title 7.15, if applicable, would not exclude this, even if a dispositive system were adopted. All this leads to the conclusion that, at least from the angle of subsequent choice of law, there is no objection against adoption of the dispositive system.

We now arrive at the relation between the compromissory agreement and *jus cogens* in general. In this respect Article 4 of Title 7.15 includes a very generous rule: an agreed determination to terminate uncertainty or dispute relating to patrimonial rights is valid even should it transpire that it is inconsistent with a mandatory rule, unless additionally the substance or tenor of the agreement is contrary to good morals or public policy. This important provision, which is derived from Dutch court decisions involving the relation between arbitration and *jus cogens* [17], also affects the subsequent choice of law. It means that a choice of law arising from uncertainty or dispute on the question what law is applicable, may set aside Dutch mandatory rules, unless that would be contrary to the Dutch conception of public policy.

The rule provides no answer to the question what is to apply when Dutch law is designated by the parties and, consequently, mandatory rules of foreign law are involved. In that case the answer must be given on the basis of private international law, with reference to, e.g., Article 3 (3) of the above-mentioned EEC Convention or the principle of 'direct effect'.

In this context it should be borne in mind that mandatory rules play a smaller part in the subsequent choice of law than they do in the case of choice of law in the contract itself. The difference lies in the fact that, especially in the law of contract, a mandatory rule will often bar only previous waiver of reliance on the rule in question and not also subsequent waiver, after the obligation concerned has been created. Thus, a worker cannot, in the employment contract, waive reliance on mandatory rules created to protect him, but he can subsequently waive a resultant claim for, e.g., continued payment of salary after unlawful dismissal. In that situation, even Article 6 of the EEC Convention on the Law Applicable to

16. For the general aspects of this question, see in particular, Weber, *Parteiautonomie im Internationalen Sachenrecht?* RabelsZ. 44 (1980) p. 510 et seq.

17. Supreme Court, 27 December 1935, NJ 1936, 442. The explanation (p. 1140, note 25) establishes in addition a relationship with public policy in the conflict of laws.

Contractual Obligations will not, in my view, exclude a choice of law other than the applicable law. However this may be, difficulties in connection with Article 4 of Title 7.15 are not likely to arise since in any case the Convention prevails. Nor are there difficulties to be expected from the fact that the Article is confined to determinations relating to patrimonial rights, which, as it appears from the commentary on the draft of Book 7, include cases where an agreed determination is based on facts pertaining to the law of persons or family relationships, but takes effect only in the sphere of patrimonial law. It will be clear, however, that a subsequent choice of law should not lead to the result that a question concerning, for example, the legitimacy of a child or the validity of a marriage would be answered differently from what would have been decided under the law applicable thereto. But there, too, a certain differentiation may be appropriate where foreign rules are involved. Thus, the same Article 1 (4) of the Act regulating the conflict of laws relating to the dissolution of marriage and separation allows the choice of Dutch law for divorce or separation proceedings. However, Article 4 of Title 7.15 does not refer to foreign mandatory rules.

The picture emerging from Article 4 combined with the dispositive system discussed above is, briefly summarized, that the rules of the law of property as well as the law of persons and family law may not, or only to a certain extent, be set aside, whereas there is a wider discretion in respect of mandatory rules in the field of contract. This result, which does not exclude the applicability of stricter rules to certain kinds of contract, such as the provisions relating to consumer and employment contracts in Articles 5 and 6 of the said EEC Convention, seems to be acceptable.

Article 5 of Title 7.15, which was already referred to in connection with the declaratory system, provides that an agreed determination relating to previously existing rights cannot be invoked against persons other than the parties and their successors by universal or special title. Clearly, this provision belongs to the declaratory system. In a dispositive system, from which it follows as a matter of principle that the rights of third parties cannot be affected, the situation is different. Nevertheless, it is obviously prudent to maintain Article 5 even in a dispositive system, since this system does not exclude every third-party effect and the provisions of Article 5 contain a rule of practical importance. It should be noted, incidentally, that 'third-party rights' are something different from 'third-party interests'. There is no reason to deny an agreed determination such third-party effect as occurs in the above examples. It is rather a question of describing the limits of such an effect. In my opinion, the line must be drawn where the third person can rely on a right acquired before this determination, and which would be affected by this determination. Therefore the question arises whether the Article is not in this respect drafted too strictly.

The protection of third-party rights corresponds with what is usually assumed with regard to choice of law in the Netherlands.[18] This might seem to be hardly

18. Kollewijn, *loc.cit., supra* n. 1, p. 238, Haak, W.P.N.R. 5545 (1980) p. 884, and the discussion in W.P.N.R. 5545, p. 887. Third party protection may be obtained also by means

compatible with the final sentence of Article 3 (2) of the EEC Convention referred to, where the rights of third parties are respected only in the event of variation by the parties of a previous choice of law. This might be so construed as to imply that the Convention allows third-party rights to be affected in other cases. But I doubt whether this interpretation is correct, since the effect of the agreed determina tion on persons other than the parties is not included in the list of matters governed by the Convention under Article 10. This argues for the assumption that this point has remained an open question, so that Article 5 of Title 7.15 will not in this respec lose its importance even when the Convention has entered into force.

The other provisions of Title 7.15 are less relevant to the subsequent choice of law. Applicability of Articles 7 - 11 is hardly conceivable; nor does Article 6 relating to error call for much discussion. The crux of this Article is that error cannot be relied upon in respect of uncertainties or disputes which the parties have discounted in the agreed determination. Obviously, this also applies with regard to choice of law. The technical elaboration of this Article is now outdated since it was drafted on the basis of the general rules relating to error in Book 6, which have been subject to substantial alteration since. Therefore, Article 6 may be taken to be superfluous.[19]

The end of my reflections comes in sight. They result in the provisional conclusion that, as far as the subsequent choice of law is concerned, Title 7.15 raises difficulty only in respect of the fundamental choice in favour of the declaratory system, and the perhaps too generous third-party protection in Article 5. Fears of arbitrary differences arising from the fact that this Title would in some cases be applicable to choice of law whereas in other cases it would not, have proved to be unfounded.

One final remark in conclusion. This essay may be regarded as a by-product of the work on the new regulation of the compromissory agreement, which at the time of writing is still in full progess. But it was a pleasure to look back and dwell upon the good old times when I was given an opportunity under Erades' presidency to help in giving the Rotterdam case-law its 'couleur locale'.

---

of a restrictive interpretation of the choice of law itself, as in Court of Appeal, The Hague, 14 February 1973, NJ 1973, 415, S & S 1973, 42.

19. Cf. Schoordijk, W.P.N.R. 5284 (1974) p. 763 and Numann in *Non Sine Causa, Opstellen aangeboden aan G.J. Scholten* (1979) p. 279 et seq.

ANNEX: First Five Articles of Title 7.15 of the New Civil Code

Title 15

Compromissory Agreement

Article 1. (1) By means of a compromissory agreement *(vaststellingsovereenkomst)* the parties, in order to terminate or avoid uncertainty or dispute as to their respective rights and duties, accept an agreed determination *(vaststelling)* thereof, intended to be of binding effect even where it deviates from the legal position obtaining in the absence of such agreed determination.
(2) The agreed determination can result from a settlement between the parties as well as from a decision entrusted to one of the parties or to a third person.
(3) An agreement relating to evidence is equivalent to a compromissory agreement to the extent that it excludes counter-evidence.

Article 2. (1) The agreed determination operates without any further juristic act being required to substitute its substance for the legal position as that would exist according to the different assumptions to be taken into account in the absence of the agreed determination.
(2) Should, however, juristic acts as referred to in the previous paragraph be required, one of which could be performed only with permission of a Government body or with the consent of a third party, then a comparable requirement applies to the agreed determination.

Article 3. (1) Without prejudice to section 3.1.2., an agreed determination may be entered in a public register if what otherwise appears from such register must be considered to be incorrect, not clear or incomplete when compared with the agreed determination. The agreement on which the agreed determination is based may be registered at the same time.
(2) Should registration such as is provided for in paragraph 1 be lacking, incomplete or incorrect, the substance of the agreement can be invoked against third parties only within the limits peculiar to the register concerned.

Article 4. Without prejudice to Article 2, paragraph 2, an agreed determination to terminate uncertainty or dispute relating to patrimonial rights is valid even should it transpire that it is inconsistent with a mandatory rule, unless additionally the substance or tenor of the agreement is contrary to good morals or public policy.

Article 5. An agreed determination relating to previously existing rights and duties cannot be invoked against persons other than the parties and their successors by universal title and those persons who, after the agreement has become operative, have become their successors by special title.

QUOD LICET IOVI . . . .
The Precarious Relationship between the Court of Justice of the European Communities and Arbitration.*

by Paul Storm[1]

1. THE ISSUE

May arbitrators request a preliminary ruling from the Court of Justice under Article 177 of the EEC Treaty? In the Sixties this was a question to which quite a few of the sharpest legal minds in Europe applied themselves. Why should it be raised again? The debate was inconclusive inasmuch as neither side appeared to be able to convince the other. Both agreed, however, that the definitive answer could only be given by the Court of Justice. This it did recently. Or did it?

The issue of the controversy is well known: under Article 177(1) the Court of Justice is competent to make a preliminary decision concerning, *inter alia*, the interpretation of the Treaty and the validity and interpretation of acts of the institutions of the Community. Paragraph 2 of Article 177 provides:

> "Where any such question is raised before a court or tribunal[2] of one of the Member States, such court or tribunal *may* if it considers that its judgment depends on a preliminary decision on this question, request the Court of Justice to give a ruling thereon" (emphasis added).

The third paragraph reads:

> "Where any such question is raised in a case pending before a domestic court or tribunal from whose decisions no appeal lies under municipal law, such court or tribunal *shall* refer the matter to the Court of Justice" (emphasis added).

The key question is: do arbitrators fall within the definition of "court or tribunal of one of the Member States"? In this connection, it seems useful to define "arbitrators" and in particular to distinguish arbitration from pseudo-arbitration, which has played a major part in the debate, as will be seen. Arbitration could be defined as the resolution of a dispute between two or more parties by a third person who is appointed by the parties and derives his powers from an agreement

* I am most grateful to Andrew Frei for his careful reading of the manuscript and correction of the English.

1. Member of the Rotterdam Bar.

2. "Juridiction d'un des Etats membres", "Gericht eines Mitgliedstaates", "rechterlijke instantie van een der Lid-Staten".

between the parties, and whose decision is binding upon them and enforceable by virtue of the law.

True arbitration is based upon an agreement between the parties. This is the main feature distinguishing it from pseudo-arbitrations such as the procedure in the case of the *Scheidsgerecht van het Beambtenfonds voor het Mijnbedrijf* (see *infra*). In the United Kingdom such procedures are referred to as "statutory arbitration" or "compulsory arbitration".[3] True arbitration should furthermore be distinguished from other procedures which are also based upon an agreement between the parties such as the German *Schiedsgutachten,* the Dutch *bindend advies,* the Belgian *avis obligatoire,* the British "valuation" or "appraisal" and the Italian *arbitrato irrituale.* Although there are considerable differences among these procedures, in general they are not subject to the same procedural safeguards that apply to arbitration. The decisions which are made also merely have the force of a contract between the parties. Thus they cannot be enforced in the same way as an arbitral award, but rather only by way of an action to seek performance of a contract, which may to some extent give rise to judicial review on the merits of the decision. It is first and foremost on these procedural grounds that I would deny such procedures the status of "court or tribunal" required by Article 177 EEC Treaty[4]. However, there may be exceptions where there are rules providing proper procedural safeguards. Such safeguards would allow these procedures to meet the requirements of "administration of justice". Even if all procedural requirements are met there is yet another obstacle to application of Article 177 – such procedures may concern issues which cannot generally be submitted to arbitration or even to courts (such as the mere appraisal of a loss or the filling of gaps in contracts deliberately left open by the parties). Again, however, in view of the very pragmatic approach taken by the Court, indicated below, this need not be an absolute obstacle in all cases.

As to true arbitration, I do not propose to reiterate all the arguments put forward over the years to answer the question in the affirmative or in the negative[5]. Some of them will be dealt with below. Obviously, those who feel that arbitrators

3. In the UK quite a few special statutes provide that certain disputes shall be determined by arbitration to the exclusion of the ordinary courts. Certain provisions of the Arbitration Act 1950 may apply to such statutory arbitrations. See, e.g., A. Walton, *Russell on the Law of Arbitration,* 19th ed. (1979), p. 10.

4. See the decision dated 2-3-'66 of the *"Beroepscommissie RAI"* in Amsterdam, *Arbitrale Rechtspraak* (AR) 1967, p. 280.

5. Reference is made to the surveys in the opinion of Advocate General Reischl in the *Nordsee* case dealt with in 4 *infra,* and in the annotation by Louis Dermine under the judgment dated 15-10-75 of the *tribunal de Bruxelles* in *Journal des tribunaux* 1976, p. 493. See also R.H. Lauwaars, "Prejudiciële beslissingen" in *Rechtsbescherming in de Europese Gemeenschappen* (Kluwer, Deventer 1975), p. 37 at p. 49; B. Goldman, *Droit commercial européen* (3rd ed. 1975), p. 461; P. Schlosser, *Das Recht der internationalen privaten Schiedsgerichtbarkeit,* Vol. 1 (1975), p. 496; J. Lew, *Applicable Law in International Commercial Arbitration* (1978), p. 425; J.J. Burst, L'arbitrage dans ses rapports avec les Communautés européennes, *Revue de L'Arbitrage* 1979, p. 105; H.G. Schermers, *Judicial Protection in the European Communities* 2nd ed. (Kluwer, Deventer 1979), § 569; G. Bebr, *The Development of Judicial Control of the European Communities* (1981), p. 371. There is a clear majority of writers who are in favour of arbitrators being authorized to refer questions to the Court.

should be permitted to request preliminary rulings emphasize the purpose of Article 177, which is to ensure the uniform interpretation and indeed the effective application of Community law throughout the Community. Since arbitrators may have to apply Community law, the proper functioning ("effet utile") of that law could be enhanced by allowing them to request preliminary rulings.

On the other hand, it should be kept in mind that within the Community basic attitudes vis-à-vis arbitration are widely divergent. In this respect, reference can be made to the old controversy[6] about the nature of arbitration. Many consider it to be purely contractual. Many others view arbitration as "jurisdictional", that is, although based on the parties' contract, it must nevertheless be subject to certain procedural rules which emanate from a state. The jurisdictional view is often linked to the increasing role played by institutional arbitration where the arbitrators are sometimes very professional and the rules are well-established.

One could imagine that those who hold the purely contractual view are not inclined to see a role for arbitrators in developing authoritative case-law and thus furthering one of the main purposes of Article 177, uniform interpretation and application of Community law. Such a role fits better in the "institutionalized" jurisdictional view of arbitration. I do not wish to suggest, however, that all those who are of the opinion that arbitrators should not be allowed to request preliminary rulings are inspired by the purely contractual view. Nonetheless, this view still prevails among many lawyers and may even have had some influence on recent case-law from the Court of Justice.

2. THE SCHEIDSGERECHT BEAMBTENFONDS CASE

The first decision of the Court of Justice that should be mentioned in connection with the question posed in the first lines of this contribution is the preliminary ruling dated 30th June 1966 in Case 61/65 given at the request of the *"Scheidsgerecht van het Beambtenfonds voor het Mijnbedrijf"*[7]. Apart from the name *"Scheidsgerecht"* (Dutch for arbitral tribunal) this case had nothing to do with arbitration. It is a typical case of pseudo-arbitration. The *Scheidsgerecht* had been created by the bye-laws of the *Beambtenfonds*, a body set up to administer certain matters regarding social security insurance. Those who were insured had to be members of the *Beambtenfonds* by virtue of a regulation of the *Mijnindustrieraad*, a public corporation. Under the bye-laws of the *Beambtenfonds*, members had to submit any disputes with the corporation's Board to the *Scheidsgerecht*. The powers of the *Scheidsgerecht* were by no means based on any agreement between the parties.[8] On the other hand, it was also clear that the *Scheidsgerecht* was

6. See, e.g., Ph. Fouchard, *L'arbitrage commercial international*, Vol. II (Paris; 1965), p. 7.

7. In a dispute between Mrs. G. Vaassen-Goebbels and the Board of the said *Beambtenfonds* (Fund for Non-Manual Workers employed in the Mining Industry), European Court of Justice Reports (ECR) 1966, p. 258.

8. For this reason I cannot agree with the opinion that the decisions of the *Scheidsgerecht* are *"bindende adviezen"* as described above. This opinion was put forward by the Board of the *Beambtenfonds* and the Dutch Government (ECR p. 265 and 268) and also by W.L. Haardt in his note in *Common Market Law Review* 1966-7, p. 443/444, and A.S. Fransen van de Putte, AR 1967, p. 196.

neither part of the ordinary judiciary of The Netherlands nor created by a formal Act of Parliament[9].

This case is nevertheless interesting since it showed the Court's rather pragmatic approach to the question of what consitutes a "court or tribunal" within the meaning of Article 177. The Court enumerated a number of characteristics of the *Scheidsgerecht,* the cumulative force of which led to the decision that the *Scheidsgerecht* was a "court or tribunal".

The main characteristics enumerated were:

- the *Scheidsgerecht* had been instituted in accordance with Netherlands law (this is rather doubtful, see note 9);
- there was a certain statutory basis and Government approval for the bye-laws of the *Beambtenfonds;*
- the Minister for the Mining Industry had appointed the members of the *Scheidsgerecht* and determined its rules;
- the *Scheidsgerecht,* as a permanent body instituted to settle disputes described in a general way by the bye-laws, had to observe procedural rules similar to those for the ordinary judiciary;
- membership in the *Beambtenfonds* was compulsory for all people insured, each of whom was obliged to submit any dispute with the Board to the *Scheidsgerecht;*
- the *Scheidsgerecht* had to decide in accordance with the rules of law.

Some of these characteristics can also be found in the subsequent decisions of the Court which are discussed below. Suffice it to point out here that this case concerned the exercise of rights granted by Community law, such rights being the counterparts of obligations imposed on the Member States. In the field of these rights and obligations there is a general system of public administration in each Member State, which in The Netherlands is supplemented by certain special elements, including legal protection.

3. THE BROEKMEULEN CASE

The second decision of the Court to be mentioned in the context of the question posed in this article is the preliminary ruling dated 6th October 1981 in Case 246/80[10] at the request of the *"Commissie van Beroep Huisartsgeneeskunde"* (Appeals Committee for General Medicine, which will be referred to as "CvBH").

Mr Broekmeulen, a Dutch national, had obtained the diploma of Doctor of Medicine, Surgery and Obstetrics from the University of Louvain in Belgium. On the strength of this diploma the Dutch Secretary of State for Health and the Environment (applying EEC Directive 75/362 on the mutual recognition of

9. This latter fact has given rise to serious doubts about the legality of the *Scheidsgerecht* as a decision-maker in view of Article 170 of the Dutch Constitution, which states that nobody can involuntarily be kept away from the court whose jurisdiction is based on a formal Act of Parliament. See Fransen van de Putte, AR 1967, p. 262.

10. In a dispute between Mr C. Broekmeulen and the *Huisarts Registratie Commissie* (General Practitioners Registration Committee), [1981] ECR, 2311.

diplomas in medicine) authorized him to practise medicine in The Netherlands. However, in order to be able to act effectively as a general practitioner in The Netherlands one has to be registered with the *Huisarts Registratie Commissie* (hereafter referred to as "HRC") as a recognized general practitioner. The HRC is a committee of the Royal Netherlands Society for the Promotion of Medicine, an association under Dutch private law, but one can register with the HRC without being a member of the Society. In order to be registered one has to meet certain requirements laid down under the supervision of two Government Ministers by another committee of the Society. These requirements include one year of special training in general practice after one has obtained a medical diploma from a university. In view of the EEC Directive, an exception had been made for nationals of other Member States who had obtained a diploma in another Member State. However, the HRC made no exception for Mr Broekmeulen on the ground that he was a Dutchman, and refused him enrolment. He appealed to the CvBH, which is also a subordinate body of the Society. The CvBH requested a preliminary ruling from the Court of Justice.

Although the CvBH did not ask a ruling on whether it had power to request a preliminary ruling[11], the Court examined this question *ex officio* and did so again in a very pragmatic manner. It established first of all that the Dutch public authorities had a major say in the composition of the CvBH and that the CvBH determined disputes on the adversarial principle, i.e., having heard the HRC and the doctor concerned. It then repeated the following observations by the Dutch Government (without expressly endorsing them): that the CvBH could not be regarded as a court or tribunal according to Dutch law, but that this was not decisive for the interpretation of Article 177, and that the question whether the CvBH was entitled to request a preliminary ruling had to considered "in the light of the function performed by that body within the system of remedies available to those who consider that their rights under Community law have been infringed".

After analysing the system of admitting general practitioners to the Dutch register, the Court concluded that applicants who wished to avail themselves of the right of establishment and the freedom to supply services conferred upon them by Community law were obliged to apply to the HRC and, in the event of their application being refused, to appeal to the CvBH.

The Dutch Government had stated that non-members of the Society could challenge a refusal before the ordinary courts, but this had never actually happened. The Court made a point of this and mentioned expressly that in practice all doctors, whether members of the Society or not, appealed to the CvBH in the event of a refusal.

The last two paragraphs of the Court's reasoning are interesting and therefore it is useful to quote them in full, noting that the first of the paragraphs has particular significance in view of the next Court decision to be discussed:

11. The *Scheidsgerecht* in the *Beambtenfonds* case had not done so either.

"16. In order to deal with the question of the applicability in the present case of Article 177 of the Treaty, it should be noted that it is incumbent upon Member States to take the necessary steps to ensure that within their own territory the provisions adopted by the Community institutions are implemented in their entirety. If, under the legal system of a Member State, the task of implementing such provisions is assigned to a professional body acting under a degree of governmental supervision, and if that body, in conjunction with the public authorities concerned, creates appeal procedures which may affect the exercise of rights granted by Community law, it is imperative, in order to ensure the proper functioning of Community law, that the Court should have an opportunity of ruling on issues of interpretation and validity arising out of such proceedings.
17. As a result of all the foregoing considerations and in the absence, in practice, of any right of appeal to the ordinary courts, the Appeals Committee, which operates with the consent of the public authorites and with their co-operation, and which, after an adversarial procedure, delivers decisions which are in fact recognized as final, must, in a matter involving the application of Community law, be considered as a court or tribunal of a Member State within the meaning of Article 177 of the Treaty. Therefore, the Court has jurisdiction to reply to the question asked."

A few observations should be made. First, there is little doubt that the CvBH does not act as an arbitrator within the meaning of the Dutch Code of Civil Procedure. There is absolutely no doubt that this is so where non-members of the Society lodge appeals with the CvBH, because in such cases there is never any agreement to go to arbitration[12].

But what about an appeal by a member of the Society? By joining the Society the member has agreed to abide by its rules, which provide, *inter alia,* for appeal to the CvBH. Then the question is how one classifies the procedure: is it arbitration, or *bindend advies,* or something else?

Insofar as the choice lies between arbitration and *bindend advies* Netherlands legal doctrine does not seem to provide a clear answer to this question. There is a certain area where arbitration and *bindend advies* overlap. In fact, in one dispute the same persons may act as arbitrators on some questions and as *bindend adviseurs* on others. Examination of the internal rules of the Society shows that the only function of the CvBH is to hear appeals against 5 categories of decisions of the HRC, to refuse enrolment or certain recognitions, or to strike a general practitioner off the register. The internal rules contain no indication whether the CvBH acts as arbitrator or as *bindend adviseur.*

There are a number of reasons not to classify the CvBH as an arbitral tribunal. First, it may make decisions with an even number of members present, whereas Dutch law requires an odd number of arbitrators. More importantly, the CvBH is an organ of the Society. Thus any agreement forming the basis for arbitration (or, for that matter, for *bindend advies)* is between the Society and its member and not, for example, between the HRC and a member of the Society. Consequently the

12. In fact, here the decisions of the CvBH are subject to the same objections based on Article 170 of the Constitution as those set out in note 9.

CvBH, however impartial and independently appointed its members may be, is not a third party and can therefore not be considered an arbitrator or a *bindend adviseur*[13]. This does not of itself mean that the CvBH could not validly decide appeals by members of the Society. In making decisions the CvBH will have to observe the requirements of good faith applying to the performance of any contract (Article 1374 (3) Civil Code). Its decisions would in any event be subject to review by the ordinary courts, which would probably be a full review on the merits.

The Court's decision does not disclose whether Mr Broekmeulen was a member of the Society at the time he appealed to the CvBH. He may have been. If so, the basis of the procedure was purely contractual. In that event it would seem rather remarkable that the Court should have accepted that the CvBH was entitled to request a preliminary ruling, particularly if one compares this case with the *Nordsee* case (discussed later), where one of the main reasons why the Court did not accept the arbitrator's request seems to be the voluntary (and therefore purely contractual) basis of the procedure. Admittedly, the Court said that the general practitioner *must* appeal to the CvBH and that, in practice, there was no right of appeal to the ordinary courts, but it may have accepted this rather too easily. I respectfully submit that the mere fact that no doctor had challenged a registration refusal by the HRC in the ordinary courts prior to the date of the case is insufficient ground for saying that in practice no right to do so exists. The Court mentions this in the context of the exercise of rights granted by Community law. It may well be that this was the first case where Community law was involved and that in all other cases the refusal was based on assessments of a purely professional nature which do not lend themselves to review by ordinary courts. I would express the same doubt about the significance which the Court attaches to the fact that the decisions of the CvBH have never been challenged in the ordinary courts.

Nevertheless, it is interesting to note that the Court apparently attaches great significance to factual situations rather than to the formal legal situation. When it is called upon to decide whether a reference for a preliminary ruling comes from a "court or tribunal" within the meaning of Article 177, there can be no doubt that the Court has power to make a full investigation of the facts.

4. THE NORDSEE CASE

The third and last decision of the Court of Justice to be discussed here is the preliminary ruling in *Nordsee* dated 23rd March 1982[14]. It was given at the request of the President of the *Hanseatische Oberlandesgericht* (an ordinary court of appeal) who acted in this case as an arbitrator[15] despite his name, Walther Richter.

13. That is to say, *bindend adviseur* in the ordinary sense of this term. There are some lawyers who call a decision given by one of the parties to a dispute a *"bindend advies"*. This term is confusing; *"partijbeslissing"* (decision by a party) is better.

14. Case 102/81, "Nordsee" Deutsche Hochseefischerei GmbH *v.* Reederei Mond Hochseefischerei Nordstern AG und Co KG and Reederei Friedrich Busse Hochseefischerei Nordstern AG und Co KG.

15. To my knowledge, The Netherlands is the only Member State where Judges are pre-

4.1. Background and Reasons

The case concerned an agreement among three groups of German shipowners to pool any aid to be received from the European Agricultural Guidance and Guarantee Fund (EAGGF) for the building of a number of factory-ships for fishing. The agreement contained an arbitral clause according to which the sole arbitrator had to be appointed by the *"Handelskammer Bremen"* if the parties could not agree among themselves. A dispute arose between Nordsee and two other shipowners, with Nordsee claiming more than DM 2 million from the other two under the pooling agreement. The defendants claimed that the agreement was void for violation of certain EEC Regulations. Because the parties could not agree on an arbitrator, the *Handelskammer* appointed Judge Richter. This resulted in the very first request for a preliminary ruling by a real arbitrator. Judge Richter did not only refer a question concerning the interpretation of the Regulations which had allegedly been violated, but also a question regarding his own authority to request a preliminary ruling.

It was the latter question in particular that provoked three Member States and the Commission to intervene and submit rather divergent observations to the Court: the UK and Italy opposing an arbitrator having authority to request a preliminary ruling; Denmark also opposing in principle, but supporting if the request is made by a permanent arbitral tribunal or if certain requirements are met; the Commission (in this case) supporting such authority.

The Court of Justice denied this authority. Upon close analysis, the reasons stated by the Court seem to be somewhat puzzling. It is by no means certain that the decision will have been published by the time this *Liber Amicorum* for Judge Erades appears. The reasons are relatively short. Quotation of the full text of the decision thus seems justified. I have added some footnotes to compare the English version with the French and German ones. The versions referred to are the mimeographed ones; they may be slightly amended before being printed in the official Reports.

> "9. It must be noted that, as the question indicates, the jurisdiction of the Court to rule on questions referred to it depends on the nature of the arbitration in question.
> 10. It is true, as the arbitrator noted in his question, that there are certain similarities between the activities of the arbitration tribunal in question and those of an ordinary court or tribunal inasmuch as the arbitration is provided for within the framework of the law, the arbitrator must decide according to law and his award has, as between the parties, the force of *res judicata,* and may be enforceable if leave to issue execution is obtained. However, those characteristics are not sufficient to give the arbitrator the status of a "court or tribunal of a Member State" within the meaning of Article 177 of the Treaty.

---

vented by law from acting as arbitrators (see Article 29 of the Code of Civil Procedure). Because this rule is an exception in the EC, there was every reason to interpret it restrictively so as to enable Judge Erades to act as arbitrator in a couple of major international cases.

11. The first important point to note is that when the contract was entered into in 1973 the parties were free to leave their disputes to be resolved by the ordinary courts or to opt for arbitration by inserting a clause to that effect in the contract. From the facts of the case it appears that the parties were under no obligation, whether in law or in fact, to refer their disputes to arbitration.
12. The second point to be noted is that the German public authorities are not involved in the decision to opt for arbitration nor are they called upon to intervene automatically[16] in the proceedings before the arbitrator. The Federal Republic of Germany, as a Member State of the Community responsible for the performance of obligations arising from Community law within its territory pursuant to Article 5 and Articles 169 to 171 of the Treaty, has not entrusted or left to private individuals the duty of ensuring that such obligations are complied with in the sphere in question in this case.[17]
13. It follows from these considerations that the link between the arbitration procedure in this instance and the organization of legal remedies through the courts [18] in the Member State in question is not sufficiently close for the arbitrator to be considered as a "court or tribunal of a Member State" within the meaning of Article 177.
14. As the Court has confirmed in its judgment of 6 October 1981 *(Broekmeulen,* Case 246/80 [1981] ECR 2311), Community law must be observed in its entirety throughout the territory of all the Member States; parties to a contract are not, therefore, free to create exceptions to it.[19] In that context attention must be drawn to the fact that if questions of Community law are raised in an arbitration resorted to by agreement the ordinary courts may[20] be called upon to examine them either in the context of their collaboration with[21] arbitration tribunals, in particular in order to assist them in certain procedural matters or to interpret the law applicable, or in the course of a review of an arbitration award – which may be more or less extensive depending on the circumstances – and which they may be required to effect in case of an appeal or objection, in proceedings for leave to issue execution or by any other[22] method of recourse available under the relevant national legislation.
15. It is for those national courts and tribunals to ascertain whether it is necessary for them to make a reference to the Court under Article 177 of the Treaty in order to obtain the interpretation or assessment of the validity of provisions of Community law which they may need to apply when exercising such auxiliary or supervisory functions.
16. It follows that in this instance the Court has no jurisdiction to give a ruling."

16. In French "d'office"; in German "von Amts wegen".
17. In French "n'a pas confié ou laissé à des personnes privées le soin de faire respecter ces obligations dans le domaine dont il 's agit en l'occurrence", in German "nicht Privatpersonen damit betraut oder es ihnen überlassen, für die Beachtung dieser Verpflichtungen in dem hier fraglichen Bereich Sorge zu tragen."
18. In French "l'organisation des voies de recours légales"; in German "dem allgemeinen Rechtsschutzsystem".
19. In French "libres d'y déroger"; in German "frei, davon abzuweichen".
20. In French "pourraient"; in German "können".
21. In French "concours qu'elles prêtent; in German "der Hilfe die sie . . . . gewähren".
22. In French "en cas de saisine en appel, en opposition, pour exequatur, ou pour toute autre . . . ."; in German "im Wege der Aufhebungsklage, durch einen Einspruch. zur Vollstreckbarerklärung oder mit irgendeinem anderen . . . .".

4.2. Analysis and Some Comments

As in the two decisions discussed above, the Court's reasoning is of a very pragmatic nature. The Court enumerates a number of characteristics which it declares insufficient to qualify the arbitrator as a "court or tribunal of a Member State", and the lack of some characteristics which it finds sufficient *not* to qualify the arbitrator as such.

The substance of the reasons lies in points 11 and 12 and can be summarized in four points (the last three of which belong together):

a) the parties were not obliged, either *de jure* or *de facto,* to choose arbitration as the method of settling their disputes;

b) the public authorities were not involved in the decision to opt for arbitration;

c) the public authorites could not intervene *ex officio* in the arbitral procedure; and

d) the German public authorities had not entrusted or left to private individuals the duty of ensuring that obligations arising from Community law were complied with in the sphere in question in this case.

Point 13 seems to contain the essence of the Court's reasoning. For the arbitrator to be considered as a "court or tribunal of a Member State" the Court requires a "sufficiently close link" between the arbitration procedure and "the organization of legal remedies through the courts in the Member State in question". This requirement is presented as a conclusion from preceding considerations.

It is interesting to note that all the reasons stated in points 11, 12 and 13 are formulated in a negative way. However, the very fact that the Court mentions four different elements (which it does not find to be present in this case) seems to indicate that none of these could of itself be considered as an absolute requirement for the power to refer questions under Article 177[23].

Points 14 and 15 contain only *obiter dicta,* but these are interesting enough to deserve some detailed comment.

When reading the reasons stated by the Court (and in particular their negative formulation) one cannot help being reminded of the two other cases discussed above. In points 11, 12 and 13 this case seems to be distinguished from the *Scheidsgerecht Beambtenfonds* and *Broekmeulen* cases. In point 14 the latter case is even explicitly referred to, although there did not seem to be any need to do so since what the Court says in that point goes well beyond the ruling in point 16 of the *Broekmeulen* decision, which is the only point to which the reference could apply.

In point 12 the Court seems to compare the situation in the *Broekmeulen* case with the present case. In fact, the words used in the last sentence of point 12 are very similar to those used in point 16 of *Broekmeulen*[24]. However, the way in

23. This applies in particular to element (c). In practice, intervention *ex officio* by public authorities in civil proceedings before any court or tribunal (except the Supreme Court in a number of Member States) rarely occurs. *Ex officio* intervention in arbitrations is a rather unusual concept. There was certainly no question of such intervention in *Scheidsgerecht Beambtenfonds* and *Broekmeulen.*

24. This is particularly evident in the French versions. In *Nordsee* "entrusted or left to private individuals the duty of ensuring that such obligations are complied with" is the trans-

which the Court expresses itself in point 12 is so concise that it could give rise to some misunderstanding. For someone unfamiliar with the *Broekmeulen* case the second sentence of point 12 is very difficult to understand. In the context of a discussion about the arbitral procedure, the Court suddenly remarks that the duty of ensuring that certain obligations imposed by Community law are complied with (which duty rests upon the Member States) has not been assigned to private individuals. In this context, "private individuals" must be understood to mean arbitrators. If that duty has not been entrusted to arbitrators, has it been entrusted to the ordinary courts? Are the parties not entirely free to settle any disputes among themselves without submitting them to courts or arbitrators? Neither ordinary courts nor arbitrators are public watchdogs seeing to it that the citizens are complying with Community law.

Clearly the Court did not intend to put such thoughts in the minds of its readers. What then could the Court have meant with the last sentence of point 12? The only reasonable answer lies in a comparison with point 16 of the *Broekmeulen* decision. Apart from the similarity of wording referred to above, the words "in the sphere in question in this case" give every reason to make such a comparison. In the last sentence of point 12 the Court apparently wishes to make an exception for such cases as *Broekmeulen* where a Member State has assigned its task of implementing Community law *in a specific area* to a professional body.

In point 16 of the *Broekmeulen* decision the Court made a clear distinction between the assignment of the task of implementing Community law to a professional body on the one hand and the creation by that body of appeal procedures on the other. The former is clearly an administrative matter and the latter is a judicial one. Unfortunately, in its very succinct reasoning in point 12 the Court seems to refer to this latter aspect only, but I feel it is much more likely that the Court referred to both aspects of the *Broekmeulen* case. The reference to Articles 5 and 169 to 171 EEC Treaty seems to confirm this feeling. These provisions are of a public international law nature imposing obligations on the State as such. The fulfilment of such obligations may involve both administrative and judicial activity.

The comparison with the *Broekmeulen* case leads me to what I feel is a weakness in the *Nordsee* decision. Both *Scheidsgerecht Beambtenfonds* and *Broekmeulen* directly concerned the safeguarding of individual rights granted by Community law.

In *Nordsee* the safeguarding of such rights was not an issue. It was just a civil law claim where the defendant pleaded that the contract was void because of a breach of Community law. The Court's reasoning does not appear to have attached any significance to this distinction. On the contrary, the reasoning seems to be based on considerations pertaining to the protection of rights granted by Community law, even though the exercise of such rights only played an indirect role in this case and was not an issue.

---

lation of "*confié* ou laissé à des personnes privées *le soin* de faire respecter ces obligations". Compare this with "*le soin* de mettre en oeuvre de telles dispositions est *confié* à un organisme professionnel" in *Broekmeulen*. French is the working language of the Court.

It is generally accepted that one of the objectives of Article 177 is to provide a vehicle for the protection of individuals' rights, particularly in cases where they wish to exercise rights granted to them by Community law. However, it is also generally accepted that another (according to many writers the primary) objective of Article 177 is the promotion of the uniform interpretation and application of Community law.

In my view the weakness in the Court's reasoning in the *Nordsee* case is that the Court seems to close its doors to arbitrators by emphasizing the absence of elements meeting only one objective of Article 177 which by its nature applies only in certain kinds of cases (often involving the administrative authorities of a Member State in some form or another) and certainly not in this case, whereas the other objective, which is universally applicable, is only referred to obliquely in an *obiter dictum*. It is precisely this latter objective which has always been put forward as the major argument in favour of allowing arbitrators to refer preliminary questions to the Court.

In this decision the Court seems more concerned with the implementation of Community law granting rights to individuals[25] than with the administration of justice in general. In this connection, the question arises whether the Court attaches less value to the penetration of Community law into "horizontal" situations (between private parties) where no rights granted to individuals are involved than to the direct application of Community law which does grant such rights (usually against Member States). In its *obiter dicta* the Court pays some attention to the "horizontal" situations, but only in a limited manner that could perhaps best be qualified as a *"doekje voor het bloeden"* (palliative).

Before I turn to these *obiter dicta* I draw attention to one of the three elements in point 10, all of which are referred to as constituting similarities with judicial activity. The Court apparently attaches some significance to the fact that the arbitrator had to decide according to the rules of law as opposed to acting as *amiable compositeur (ex aequo et bono)*. The authority of arbitrators to decide *ex aequo et bono* has often been mentioned in the debate about the powers of arbitrators under Article 177 as an argument that such powers do not exist. I should think that this argument is incapable of being advanced in this debate, particularly in view of the pragmatic approach by the Court (see point 9), because as soon as an arbitrator refers a question under Article 177 he gives evidence that he decides according to the rules of law or at least according to Community law, which is the only relevant law in this connection.

In addition, there seems to be a trend in all Member States [26] to restrict the freedom of arbitrators to decide *ex aequo et bono* by requiring arbitrators to comply with the rules of public policy. There is uncertainty as to the extent to which Community law is public policy. I propose to come back to this question.

25. "Individuals" should be understood to include enterprises and other private parties.

26. *See Yearbook Commercial Arbitration* (YB), II (all Roman numerals refer to Volumes of the Yearbook), p. 107 for the *United Kingdom* – although Eagle Star *v.* Yuval Insurance [1978] 1 Ll. Rep. 357 has cast some doubt on the traditional view; IV, p. 73 for *Germany;* V, p. 18 for *Belgium* (where arbitrators are bound by any provision of mandatory law as well

However, for the purposes of the present argument it would seem sufficient to refer to point 14 of the *Nordsee* decision where the Court says, in so many words, that parties to a contract are not free to derogate from Community law. In this context these words must be taken to mean that the Court is of the opinion that arbitrators must always comply with Community law. It follows that, as far as the Court is concerned, the question whether arbitrators have been given the power to decide *ex aequo et bono* is irrelevant to their powers, if any, under Article 177.

4.3 The Obiter Dicta

We now turn to point 14 proper. The first observation one makes is that, despite its remark in point 9 that its jurisdiction depends on the characteristics of this specific case, in point 14 the Court demonstrates that it realizes that this decision has consequences for the whole field of "arbitration resorted to by agreement".

The second observation is that point 14 contains a number of statements which give rise to the question whether the Court in adding these *obiter dicta* has applied its usual accuracy. The first reason for this question lies in the reference to the *Broekmeulen* decision. As indicated above, the statement in point 14 goes well beyond what the Court said in the *Broekmeulen* case. In fact, it is rather different. In point 16 of *Broekmeulen* the Court referred to the obligation *of the Member States* to take the necessary steps to ensure the full implementation within their own territory of the provisions adopted by the Community institutions. This is exactly the obligation laid down in Articles 5 and 169 to 171 EEC Treaty, to which Articles reference is made in point 12 of the *Nordsee* decision. In point 14 of *Nordsee*, however, the Court refers to an obligation incumbent *on any party* to any contract within the EC to observe Community law.

Apart from being different from what the Court said in the *Broekmeulen* case, this statement is a rather sweeping one which may give a shock to many a reader. It seems to mean that the Court is of the opinion that the entire body of Community law, whether laid down in the provisions of the Treaty or in Regulations, Directives and Decisions, is of a mandatory nature so that parties to a contract may not depart from it. By now, we are used to the effect of Article 85 on contracts. We had also learned to accept that in certain circumstances private parties may not contract out of certain basic rights granted by the Treaty itself[27]. However, in these cases the Court always emphasized the mandatory nature of the Treaty provision concerned. In spite of the clear language in the *Dansk Supermarked* v. *Imerco* case [28],

---

as by *"ordre public")*; V, p. 36 for *Denmark* (not entirely clear); V, p. 73 for *Greece*; VI, p. 17 and VII, p. 12 for *France* (domestic and international arbitration respectively; in domestic arbitration arbitrators are bound by all mandatory law); V, p. 47 for *Italy;* V, p. 75 for *The Netherlands* (there is some difference of opinion as to whether arbitrators are also bound by mandatory law); note that the *Irish* Arbitration Act, 1954 is rather similar to the English Arbitration Act 1950 (see YB II, p. 10).

27. See the Court's decisions in cases 36/74, Walrave and Koch, [1974] ECR, 1405, 13/76, Donà *v.* Mantero, [1976] ECR, 1333 and 43/75, the famous Defrenne II case, [1976] ECR, 455, in particular item 39, and subsequent cases concerning Article 119 EEC Treaty.

28. Decision of 22-1-81 in case 58/80, [1981] ECR, 181, see point 17: "It must furthermore be remarked that it is impossible in any circumstances for agreements between individuals

serious doubts have been expressed until very recently [29] as to whether Articles 30 and 34 EEC Treaty could also be applicable to relations between private parties.

Now the Court has declared the whole body of Community law to be of a mandatory nature. This is new, but the scope of this ruling should not be overestimated. In view of its largely administrative nature, the bulk of Community law does not lend itself to being dealt with in contracts between private parties. Also, this ruling is obviously limited to such provisions of Community law as have direct effect on individuals[30]. The number of such provisions is relatively limited[31]. On the other hand, one wonders why in the past the Court has emphasized the mandatory or even "fundamental" nature of some of the Treaty's provisions.

The fact that the Court's reasoning in point 14 is limited to provisions with direct effect seems to support my earlier suggestion that in this decision the Court appears to focus all its attention on the implementation of Community law, even where it addresses the subject-matter of arbitration in general. It seems to lose sight of uniform interpretation of Community law which after all is also of great importance for the proper functioning of Community law, certainly if one considers the many existing or proposed harmonisation Directives. Although some provisions of some Directives have direct effect (so far this has only been recognized in the relationship between individuals and Member States), the great majority do not. This is accentuated by a very recent decision[32] in which the Court, after interpreting a provision of Directive 69/335 concerning tax on the raising of capital, declined to say that this provision had direct effect. Instead, it said that in all cases where a Directive is correctly implemented its effects reach the individuals by means of the implementing measures taken by the Member State concerned. Consequently, such a measure must be interpreted in accordance with the Directive since it was the wish of the legislator to transpose the Directive into his domestic law. Obviously, the Court will often be ready to assume that the legislator wished to transpose the provisions of a Directive into his domestic law[33] and may not find it too difficult

---

to derogate from the mandatory provisions of the Treaty on the free movement of goods". However, in view of the specific circumstances of this case the sentence quoted does not seem to have been viewed as a general rule.

29. See J.P.H. Donner in the Dutch report for the FIDE Congress Dublin 1982 on Articles 30-36 EEC in general in *Sociaal-Economische Wetgeving* 5 (1982) p. 371, and the General Report by W. van Gerven and F. Gotzen for the same Congress, *The Elimination of Non Tariff Barriers with Particular Reference to Industrial Property Rights Including Copyright, Dublin 1982*, p. 1.12.

30. Parties to a contract cannot derogate from provisions which by definition are not binding on them. For the concept of direct effect, see M. Maresceau, *De directe werking van het Europese Gemeenschapsrecht* (Kluwer 1978), in particular p. 44-61, and H.G. Schermers, *Judicial Protection in the European Communities*, 2nd ed., p. 98-109 and in the special issue of *NILR* for Prof. Tammes, 1977, p. 260-273.

31. See Schermers, *Judicial Protection*, at p. 105-106, where only a few Treaty provisions are enumerated. Of course there are also provisions in secondary Community law.

32. Dated 15th July 1982 in case 270/81, Felicitas Rickmers-Linie KG & Co *v.* Finanzamt für Verkehrsteuern Hamburg, a preliminary ruling at the request of the *Finanzgericht* Hamburg, not yet published.

33. Unless the legislator has not (yet) done so at all, in which case the Court may recognize direct effect in favour of individuals in their relationships to Member States.

to "interpret away" any (minor) defect in the implementation. Thus the diameter of the aperture through which the Court views arbitration seems to be reduced even further.

4.3.1. Involvement of Ordinary Courts

"In the context" of its statement that parties to a contract are not free to derogate from Community law, the Court observes that the ordinary courts may be called upon to examine questions of Community law arising in an arbitral procedure. The word "pourraient" in the French version seems to demonstrate the Court's awareness that there may be situations where the ordinary courts do not get an opportunity to examine questions of Community law arising in arbitration. The question, then, is whether the term *"doekje voor het bloeden"* is appropriate for these *obiter dicta* or whether they had better be qualified as "cold comfort".

The Court mentions two categories of events in which the ordinary courts could become involved:

1. either in the context of the assistance they give to arbitrators,
   a) for certain procedural matters, or
   b) in order to interpret the applicable law;
2. or in the context of a review of the arbitral award[34].

I propose to examine these categories in some detail.

4.3.1.1. *Category 1. Assistance*

4.3.1.1.a. Assistance for Certain Procedural Matters

A comparative study of the arbitration laws of all the Member States[35] shows that in all States the ordinary courts may assist in the appointment (and in some cases replacement) of arbitrators, in most States in the hearing of witnesses, and in some in deciding on the authenticity of documents. Apart from some provisions of a similar nature in a single Member State, the assistance of the ordinary courts is limited to these matters. One fails to understand how questions of Community law

34. In this connection, the Court specifies three different kinds of review, but these have different meanings in the various Member States and some of them exist only in some Member States and not in others (e.g.,appeal to ordinary courts does exist in a number of countries but not in Germany). This may be the reason why one finds *"appel"* in the French (the working language of the Court, in which the decision was drafted) version but not in the German one. The latter version mentions *"Aufhebungsklage"*, but the French equivalent (Article 1484 of the new Code of Civil Procedure) is not referred to (or could it be that the Court looked at the abolished Article 1028 which provided for *"opposition"* which is mentioned?).

35. Except for Luxemburg whose arbitration law was the same as that of Belgium until 1975 (which in turn was based on the old French *Code de Procédure Civile).* As stated by Ernest and David Arendt in *Arbitration Law in Europe* (ICC, 1981) at p. 247 "there is a definite reluctance among the public and the judges to have recourse to this type of justice" (arbitration). Therefore, no further reference will be made to Luxemburg law unless otherwise specified.

could ever be raised in such matters. In order to avoid any misunderstanding, I should add that in procedures on such procedural matters the question of the incompetence of any arbitrator due to nullity of the contract (e.g., as a result of a violation of Community law) cannot be raised[36].

4.3.1.1.b. Assistance to Interpret the Law Applicable

Assistance in order to interpretet the law applicable is provided for in only two Member States: the UK and Ireland. Under Section 2 of the English Arbitration Act 1979, the High Court has jurisdiction to determine any question of law arising in the course of arbitration, but only on application by a party and with the consent of the arbitrator or of all the parties to the arbitration. In addition, the High Court may not entertain the application unless it is satisfied that the determination of the application might produce substantial savings in costs to the parties and that the question of law is one in respect of which leave to appeal would be likely to be given (which is the case if the determination of the question of law could substantially affect the rights of one or more parties to the arbitration agreement). There is no doubt that under this substantially watered-down "special case procedure"[37] questions on Community law may be referred to the High Court[38]. However, it should be emphasized that the procedure can only be set in motion on the initiative of one of the parties and the parties may in a so-called "exclusion agreement" exclude the right to apply for a reference to the High Court[39].

Under Irish law the special case procedure still exists. This means that any question of law may be referred to the High Court, either on an application by one of the parties or by the arbitrator *ex officio.*

4.3.1.2. *Category 2. Review of Arbitral Awards*

As to the review of arbitral awards in the light of Community law, the situation is rather complicated. This is due to the fact that questions of Community law may arise in arbitration in a number of different ways and that these ways may

36. Perhaps with the exception of the appointment of arbitrators in French domestic arbitration where Article 1444 of the Code of Civil Procedure provides that the President of the Court shall not appoint arbitrators if the arbitral clause is *"manifestement nulle".* There is uncertainty about the separability of arbitral clauses in French domestic arbitration. The President might therefore infer the nullity of the arbitral clause from the nullity of the rest of the contract, but in practice the latter will often be difficult to qualify as *"manifestement nul".*

37. The special case procedure existed under S. 21 of the Arbitration Act 1950 which Section was repealed in 1979, see Clive M. Schmitthoff, "The United Kingdom Arbitration Act 1979" in YB V, p. 231.

38. It should be noted that the 1979 Act applies in England and Wales only; in Scotland there exists a mitigated special case procedure: the parties are permitted to contract out of it and the arbitrator may not state a case on his own initiative.

39. This can be done at any point in non-domestic arbitration, but only *after commencement* of domestic arbitration. The relative provisions of the 1979 Act are more detailed and rather complicated, especially as far as the definition of domestic and non-domestic arbitration is concerned.

vary from one Member State to another. Before going into any detail I have one preliminary remark.

Until now, the debate about the relationship between Community law and arbitration has been largely dominated by Article 85 EEC Treaty. This may be understandable but it is also regrettable. Article 85(2) provides that agreements prohibited by that Article are null and void[40]. Consequently, the debate has focussed on the maintenance of Community law rather than on its interpretation. It has been permeated with the notion of public policy or at least the concept of mandatory law. The *Nordsee* case did not concern Article 85, but the question of nullity as a result of a violation of other Community law was raised and, it would seem, for a good reason. The Regulations alleged to be violated in *Nordsee* did not explicitly prohibit pooling agreements. It is therefore doubtful whether the pooling agreement could be considered to be in violation of mandatory law. On the other hand, pooling was clearly against the spirit of the Regulations, but is this sufficient reason to say that they violated Community (and therefore German) public policy?

In any event, there are many questions of Community law which may arise in arbitration without nullity or public policy being involved at all. Suppose that a number of importers of meat join forces to claim refunds from their Government of any meat inspection charges levied from them in violation of Community law. One of the importers undertakes to file the claims for all. He fails to do so in respect of some claims and the limitation period expires. The others claim damages from him in arbitration as provided by the agreement. The question arises whether the charges for which refunds were not claimed were really levied in violation of Community law. There are many similar ways in which questions of pure interpretation of Community law may be submitted to arbitration without there being any question that the parties have violated or derogated from Community law. Such question could arise in genuine disputes between parties (see item 4.4.5. *infra*). In this connection, one could also think of many questions of interpretation of harmonisation Directives, particularly in the field of civil law (e.g., company law). It is submitted that where parties to an arbitration do not derogate from Community law public policy is not involved.

Now we return to the question of how matters of Community law arising in arbitration may come up for review by ordinary courts. In this connection, it is useful to distinguish first of all the various ways in which questions of Community law may arise before arbitrators.[41]

They could arise either in the context of the question of the arbitrators' jurisdiction or in the context of the application of law by arbitrators. As to the questions of jurisdiction, these could appear in the form of a question of arbitrability of a matter of Community law or in the form of questions on the validity of the arbitral clause in a contract alleged to be null and void as a result of a breach of Community law. Once the jurisdiction of arbitrators is established the question

40. The only Article in the Treaty which provides so expressly.

41. It should be noted that such questions need neither be brought to the attention of arbitrators nor expressly decided by them. Questions of Community law may be raised later in an ordinary court.

may arise whether they have correctly applied Community law. Thus we have the following topics:

a. Questions of jurisdiction
   i) arbitrability
   ii) validity of the arbitral clause
b. Questions of application of Community law.

I propose to examine in each case if and how the courts in each Member State may be called upon to examine questions of Community law which may arise. In doing so, I draw to a great extent upon the various National Reports in *Yearbook Commercial Arbitration (YB)* which contain exact and authoritative answers to many of the questions discussed here.

4.3.1.2.a.(i). Arbitrability

Arbitrability of a certain subject-matter is its capacity to be validly submitted to arbitration. The nature of the subject-matter is decisive. If a subject-matter is non-arbitrable the arbitrators have no jurisdiction. At this point in our examination, the only pertinent question relating to arbitrability is: to what extent may issues of Community law be relevant to the question of arbitrability? The answer to this question is to be found primarily in the internal law of the Member States, and may therefore be different from one State to the other.

It is generally accepted in all Member States that the test whether an issue is arbitrable or not is whether it is permissible to compromise in respect of it[42]. It is also generally accepted that no compromise can be made on an issue like divorce. However, there are differences of view where the issue concerns or affects public policy (*"ordre public"*, *"öffentliche Ordnung"*, etc. [43]) or mandatory law. It is precisely these concepts which are usually mentioned in connection with Community law. I do not know of any cases in national courts where the question was raised whether provisions of Community law should be classified as mandatory or as matters of public policy, except in relation to Article 85[44]. However, we now have the Court's ruling in point 14 of the *Nordsee* decision where it is held that parties may not derogate from any of the provisions of Community law (at least to the extent such provisions have direct effect, see 4.3 *supra*). What does this ruling mean in respect of arbitrability of issues concerning Community law? Because this ruling was very recently given and it will be some time before national courts take it into account in their decisions, I propose to answer this question only after I have examined the current state of the problem of arbitrability of *public policy* issues under the laws of the Member States.

42. See also Article 1 of the *Uniform Law on Arbitration* of 1966 which has only been ratified by Belgium.

43. The subtle differences between these concepts, and indeed the meaning of these concepts in each Member State, are beyond the scope of this contribution.

44. See *Bundesgerichtshof* 27-2-69 in SpA Massalombarda *v.* Fruchttrink GmbH & Co KG (*Entscheidungssamlung Wirtschaft und Wettbewerb BGH 1000)* where the provisions of Article 85 were held to form part of the German *öffentliche Ordnung, "soweit sie die Grundlagen des Gemeinsamen Marktes betreffen und nicht aus blossen Zweckerwägungen getroffen sind"*.

Views on the role of public policy in arbitration differ widely not only from one Member State to another, but even within some Member States. To begin with there is the "classic" view, according to which an issue is non-arbitrable as soon as it touches upon (and therefore implies the application or interpretation of) a subject-matter of public policy, e.g., anti-trust. This view was held by French courts until the early Sixties.

The "classic" view has given way to what I would call the "subject of the claim" view. This newer view makes a distinction between the *subject* of the claim and the *rules of law* which may have to be applied in the adjudication of the claim[45]. This view was clearly expressed in a 1966 arbitral award made under the Rules of the International Chamber of Commerce[46]:

> "Attendu certes qu'un litige portant essentiellement sur la validité ou sur la nullité d'un contrat au regard de l'article 85 du traité de Rome serait en dehors de la compétence d'un arbitre et qu'aucune clause compromissoire ne pourrait avoir pour effet de substituer un juge privé à un juge public pour trancher un litige intéressant *in se* et *per se* l'ordre public;
>
> Attendu en revanche que, dans un litige de droit privé, si une partie invoque comme moyen de défense que la convention dont se réclame l'autre partie est nulle pour un motif d'ordre public et singulièrement pour violation de l'article 85 du traité de Rome, l'arbitre a le devoir d'examiner si se rencontrent dans la convention les conditions matérielles et juridiques dont la réunion entraînerait l'application du dit article."

In fact, questions of Community law often arise in an indirect manner. Therefore, according to the view quoted above, arbitrators will usually have jurisdiction.

In my opinion, the distinction set out above is not clear and therefore not satisfactory. Besides, once a dispute has arisen, fortuitous circumstances (or even circumstances manipulated by one of the parties) may dictate whether the subject of a claim directly concerns public policy. I see no material difference between a claim for specific performance of a contract in breach of Article 85 [47] on the one hand and a request that arbitrators declare a contract null and void due to a breach of Article 85 on the other, whether such a request is made by way of defence or as an independent claim. In both cases the arbitrators will have to apply Article 85. The only thing that matters is whether they apply it correctly or not.

A third view, that arbitrators have jurisdiction to decide any question which directly or indirectly concerns public policy, is found in Germany[48], The

45. It would seem that this view is held in a number of Member States: YB V, p. 5 for *Belgium;* YB VI, p. 5 for *France* (domestic arbitration); YB VI, p. 33 for *Italy* (although not clearly); YB V, p. 62 for *Greece* (also not quite clear); and YB II, p. 96 for *England and Wales* (again not quite clear).

46. Published in *Journal du droit international* 1974, p. 879, without reference to names of the parties.

47. Or, for that matter, a claim for damages for breach of such a contract, see *Bundesgerichtshof* in the *Massalombarda* decision, item III, 4 (see note 44).

48. YB IV, p. 65. See also *Bundesgerichtshof* 25-10-66 in the well-known *Schweissbolzen* case *(Entscheidungen des BGH* Z46, p. 368).

Netherlands[49] and possibly Denmark[50].

In the UK, and in Ireland (I assume), a somewhat different view is held. No limitation is placed upon the powers of a validly appointed arbitrator to decide issues of law merely due to the nature of such law. However, there may be such a limitation arising from the consequences of his decision, i.e., if a decision on a point of law would imply that the agreement was void, the arbitrator cannot decide upon it (unless he is specifically so empowered) and the matter must be resolved by the court. In this regard, reference is made to item 4.3.1.1.b supra.

Let us now return to the question of what the Court's ruling in point 14 of the *Nordsee* case means for the arbitrability of issues of Community law. One should note that the Court did not say that Community law may not be dealt with by parties in their contract. It only said they may not derogate from it. In view of the second sentence of point 14 I take this ruling to mean also that arbitrators may not derogate from Community law. Thus the Court's ruling would seem to fit very well in the third view mentioned above, but it is also compatible with the "subject of the claim" view and the UK view.

My conclusion is that to some extent issues of Community law may be submitted to arbitration in all Member States. Insofar as the "subject of the claim" view is upheld there will be some scope for disputes about the arbitrability of Community law issues. Such scope will be almost non-existent where the third view prevails.

The next question is whether and to what extent questions of arbitrability (and therefore of Community law) may be brought before the ordinary courts. Since this is a matter of jurisdiction, I propose to deal with this question after having discussed the other matter of jurisdiction, the validity of the arbitral clause.

4.3.1.2.a.(ii). Validity of the arbitral clause

Here the discussion is concerned with the arbitral clause only and not with the submission of an existing dispute to arbitration because in practice such a submission will rarely be null and void, and even more rarely due to violation of Community law[51]. Unlike the question of arbitrability, the question of validity of the arbitral clause has nothing to do with the subject-matter of the arbitration,

49. *Hoge Raad* 27-12-35, NJ'36, 442 and 26-6-42, NJ' 42, 578. These decisions have been severely criticised by various authors. The main objection is the practical one that, in addition to accepting arbitrability of issues of public policy, the *Hoge Raad* refused to review arbitral awards in which public policy was violated (see 4.3.1.2.b. *infra*). It should be noted that in its 1935 decision the *Hoge Raad* added the proviso that an arbitration agreement could be null and void due to violation of public policy, for example where by concluding such an agreement the parties endeavoured to give effect to an agreement which they knew to be null and void. See also *Hoge Raad* 10-6-55, NJ '55, 570 and 6-12-63, NJ '64, 43. These two decisions, as well as the 1942 one, concerned mandatory law which was not expressed to involve public policy. However, under Dutch law the difference between the concepts of mandatory law and public policy is not clear.

50. YB V, p. 30.

51. If a submission were null and void for such a reason it would probably be because the issue of Community law agreed to be submitted is non-arbitrable. In that event reference is made to 4.3.1.2.a.(i) *supra*.

but deals only with the validity of that part of the contract which is the arbitral clause.

The main problem in this connection is whether the invalidity of the main contract due to violation of Community law also causes the arbitral clause to be void. There is double protection for the arbitral clause. The protection is provided by two different types of "separability". The first is severability – the possibility of separating one or more clauses which offend Community law from the rest of the contract. This possibility has been explicitly recognized by the Court [52] ; the nullity provided for in Article 85(2) applies only to the individual elements of the contract which fall within the prohibition of Article 85(1), provided that those elements are severable from the contract as a whole. In order to determine which provisions are severable and on what conditions, reference must be made to the applicable domestic law. It would seem that in most Member States the whole contract is only null and void if it is likely that without the invalid elements the parties would not have entered into it (or a similar test). There is no reason to think that the same rules would not apply to nullity resulting from provisions of Community law other than Article 85.

Only if the whole contract is void will the second type of separability arise – does the nullity of the contract also entail the nullity of the arbitral clause? This is purely a matter of the internal law of the Member States and the same rule applies: would the parties have entered into the contract without the invalid elements? In this case the matter would seem rather simple. Why should parties wish to enter into an agreement to submit their disputes to arbitration if there is no valid contract about which to have a dispute? However, the dispute could concern the very question of the validity or invalidity of the contract. This has been recognized in most Member States. Accordingly, the separability of the arbitral clause is accepted[53] , albeit with some slight differences, in Belgium[54] , France[55] , Germany[56] , Greece[57], Italy[58] , and The Netherlands[59] ; There is uncertainty in Denmark[60] and the only Member States where separability is not accepted are the United Kingdom[61] and Ireland.

This means that in at least six Member States questions of validity of the contract containing the arbitral clause (and therefore issues of Community law) are

52. Decisions dated 30-6-66 in case 56-65, Société Technique Minière *v.* Maschinenbau Ulm GmbH [1966] ECR, 391 and 13-7-66 in cases 56 and 58-64 Consten and Grundig *v.* Commission, [1966] ECR, 449.

53. See also Article 18(2) of the Uniform Law on Arbitration of 1966 and P. Sanders, "L'autonomie de la clause compromissoire", in *Hommage à Frédéric Eisemann* (ICC Services sàrl 1978), p. 31

54. Article 1697 (2) *Code Judiciaire*

55. Certainly as far as international arbitration is concerned; there is some uncertainty regarding domestic arbitration, see YB VI, p. 7.

56. YB IV, p. 65; see also *Bundesgerichtshof* in the case referred to in note 44.

57. YB V, p. 63.

58. YB, VI, p. 34.

59. YB VI, p. 65, van Rossem-Cleveringa, *Burgerlijke Rechtsvordering,* II, 4th ed., p. 1330.

60. YB V, p. 30.

61. YB II, p. 96.

largely irrelevant to the jurisdiction of arbitrators. Of course, this does not mean that in those Member States questions of validity of the contract containing an arbitral clause will never arise. However, except in the UK, Ireland, and possibly in Denmark and France (domestic arbitration), such questions will not normally arise in connection with the arbitrator's jurisdiction. They may arise in the context of arbitrators' decisions on the merits of the case submitted, but then this is a matter of application of Community law and will be discussed later.

First, however, we shall examine whether and to what extent questions of jurisdiction of arbitrators may be brought before the ordinary courts. There is no Member State where arbitrators have the authority to give a final decision as to their own jurisdiction. However, in all Member States except the UK and Ireland arbitrators may at least give a provisional ruling on their own jurisdiction. This is the famous question of *"Kompetenz-Kompetenz"*. The arbitrators' decision, whether explicit or implied, is always subject to review by the ordinary courts, but the conditions on which such review may occur differ widely from one Member State to another.

In Belgium and France (domestic arbitration) the lack of jurisdiction may be cured by the parties appearing voluntarily and without objection. In Germany the parties are deemed to have waived their right to invoke the lack of jurisdiction in court if they have not done so during the arbitration. To some extent this is also the case in Belgium[62].

There are substantial differences as to the time when the question of jurisdiction may be submitted to the court. This is of considerable practical importance since, if the matter cannot be brought before the court until the arbitral procedure has come to an end (as is the case in Belgium [63], Denmark [64], France, Germany and Greece), high costs may have been incurred and the losing party may not be very keen on continuing the legal battle. In Italy, Article 819 of the *Codice di Procedura Civile* provides for a suspension of the arbitral procedure to enable the parties to submit an issue to the ordinary court, but this applies only if a question of non-arbitrability arises and not if the question concerns the validity of the contract. In the UK, if an arbitrator proceeds with the arbitration notwithstanding his lack of jurisdiction, any party may seek an injunction from the court to restrain the arbitration or apply for a declaration from the court that the contract is invalid[65]. In addition, revocation of the authority of the arbitrator (or his removal) could be sought on the ground of excess of jurisdiction. In The Netherlands, any party may at any time request the court to declare that no valid agreement to arbitrate exists or that the issue is non-arbitrable, but in practice this is not done until the award has been made. As to the stage after the award has been made, lack of jurisdiction of the arbitrators is a ground for setting aside the award in all Member States. An exception is The Netherlands where lack of juris-

62. See YB V, p. 23.
63. Unless the arbitrators have decided they have *no* jurisdiction.
64. Unless there are "serious reasons" justifying an earlier intervention, see YB V, p. 35.
65. Apart from initiating a reference to the High Court as set out *infra* (provided all conditions are met).

diction is a ground for declaring the award null and void. Such actions for setting aside will be dealt with briefly below (item 4.3.1.2.b).

Before I leave the subject-matter of arbitrators' jurisdiction, I should give some attention to international commercial arbitration as defined in the *European Convention on International Commercial Arbitration*[66], to which five Member States are parties: Belgium, Denmark, France, Germany and Italy. The Convention applies to arbitration agreements concluded for the purpose of settling disputes arising from international trade between persons having their habitual place of residence or their corporate seat in different Contracting States.[67] The provision relevant to our examination is Article V.

Article V(3) provides that, subject to any subsequent judicial control provided for under the *lex fori,* the arbitrator whose jurisdiction is questioned shall nonetheless be entitled to proceed with the arbitration, to rule on his own jurisdiction, and to decide upon the existence or validity of the arbitration agreement or of the contract of which the agreement forms part.

The subsequent judicial control is to some extent limited by Article IX. In practice the question of jurisdiction is rarely brought before the ordinary courts.

4.3.1.2.a.(iii). Conclusions as to jurisdiction

My conclusions regarding the problem of the extent to which issues of Community law may come up for review by ordinary courts in the context of the jurisdiction of arbitrators are as follows:

a) There is little scope for disputes about the arbitrability of Community law issues.
b) In at least six Member States issues of Community law are largely irrelevant to the question of validity of the contract as a condition for the existence of jurisdiction of arbitrators.
c) In all Member States except the UK and Ireland arbitrators may at least give a provisional ruling on their own jurisdiction. The conditions under which such a ruling may be reviewed by the ordinary courts differ widely from one Member State to the other.

4.3.1.2.b. Questions of application of Community law.

Issues of Community law may not only arise before arbitrators in the context of questions about their jurisdiction, but also where there is a decision on the merits of the case which includes interpretation and application of the law. There is no longer any doubt that arbitrators may interpret and apply Community law[68]. When they do so they may make mistakes. The question that matters in this context is whether and to what extent their decisions on issues of Community law may come up for review by the courts. In order to answer this question, one should examine

66. Geneva 1961, *United Nations Treaty Series,* vol. 484, p. 364 No. 7041 (1963-1964).
67. It also applies to the arbitral procedures and awards based on such agreements.
68. See item 4.3.1.2.a.(i) Arbitrability.

the remedies against an arbitral award which are available in the various Member States, with particular reference to

a) the grounds on which an arbitral award may be set aside or avoided and
b) any restrictions to the use of such remedies, such as time limits.

For the purposes of this study, only grounds relating to the interpretation or application of Community law need to be taken into account. If we accept the Court's ruling that all Community law is mandatory law, then we should examine to what extent violation, or incorrect application or interpretation, of mandatory law could be a ground for setting aside or avoiding an arbitral award. The Court's ruling may imply, and in any event does not exclude, that all or some provisions of Community law are of a public policy nature. As set out above, the concept of public policy is determined by the laws of the Member States and therefore differs from one Member State to the other[69]. It is by no means certain that the entire body of Community law is considered in each Member State to be of a public policy nature. Insofar as it is so considered, we shall examine to what extent an arbitral award which is contrary to public policy may be set aside or avoided.

As to mandatory law, there are very great differences among the Member States. In some countries, such as Greece[70] and Germany[71], violation or misinterpretation of any rule of substantive law is not a ground for setting aside or avoiding the arbitral award, unless there is a violation of public policy. On the other hand, in England and Wales appeal lies on any point of law if the determination thereof could substantially affect the rights of one or more of the parties to the arbitration agreement[72]. This condition is likely to be met in almost all cases where Community law is involved. It should be noted, though, that the parties may, subject to certain restrictions[73], forego their right to appeal an arbitral award. In Ireland there are even fewer obstacles to a challenge of an award on the ground of violation or misinterpretaion of any point of law. In a number of other Member States it is generally felt that arbitrators are bound by mandatory law, but it is not clear what sanctions apply when they violate or misinterpret such law.

As to public policy, there is unanimity among the Member States that a violation of public policy is not accepted. However, there are great differences here also. In Belgium, if an award is contrary to public policy, the President of the Court must refuse leave to enforce *(exequatur)*[74].

In Germany, the other party must be heard on a request for leave to enforce and this may lead to a full trial of the issue of whether recognition of the award

69. It is very difficult to say to what extent the concepts of public policy and mandatory law overlap. Public policy is often regarded as even more fundamental and imperative than "ordinary" mandatory law.

70. See YB V, p. 78.

71. See YB IV, p. 73 and 77

72. Traditionally, the English courts have held that arbitrators must decide according to the rules of law (see YB II, p. 107), but in Eagle Star *v.* Yuval Insurance [1978] 1 Ll. Rep. 357 the traditional view was doubted and a clause providing (in effect) for a decision *ex aequo et bono* was upheld. However, questions remain.

73. See note 39.

74. But his examination is merely cursory, see YB V, p. 21.

would be contrary to public policy. The situation in the UK and Ireland is similar. In four Member States[75] questions of public policy could not arise on the occasion of granting the *exequatur* because the procedure is *ex parte,* and in these States (excluding The Netherlands) no appeal lies from the decision to grant the *exequatur.* In Denmark, no leave of enforcement is required, but in the course of enforcement proceedings objections on the ground of invalidity of the award may be raised with the bailiff (a judicial authority) and his decision may be appealed to the Superior Court.

Violation of public policy is a ground for setting aside an award in all Member States but in Italy and The Netherlands the situation is somewhat complicated. In Italy awards are not likely to be in violation of public policy because Article 819 of the *Codice di Procedura Civile* (see item 4.3.1.2.a.(ii) *supra*) must be applied where an issue involving public policy is raised during the arbitration proceedings. In cases where arbitrators fail to apply Article 819 and their award violates public policy it would seem that the award may be challenged [76], generally on the ground that the agreement was null and void (lack of jurisdiction).

In the Netherlands, all authors agree that violation of public policy is a ground to declare the award null and void for lack of jurisdiction. The action to declare an award null and void should be distinguished from the action for annulment under Article 649 of the Code of Civil Procedure. There is some doubt, however, that an award would be declared null and void for violation of public policy, because of two decisions given by the Dutch Supreme Court in the Thirties[77]. This will soon cease to be an issue since a draft Bill[78] to amend the law on arbitration provides for a single remedy against awards on grounds which include violation of public policy.

The conditions which must be met in order successfully to institute an action to set aside an award differ widely from one Member State to the other. In Germany there is a one-month limitation period, whereas Denmark and Belgium (in principle) have no time-limit at all. The various remedies against arbitral awards are so different that I shall not even attempt to describe them.

My conclusions as to the extent to which issues of Community law may come up for review by ordinary courts in the context of a review on the merits of the case are as follows:

a) There is a bewildering variety of remedies against arbitral awards – at least two in each Member State.

b) To the extent that Community law is mandatory law, its violation or misinterpretation may not be sufficient ground for setting aside or avoiding an award in some Member States, but is in others.

75. In France, Greece, Italy and The Netherlands.

76. See M.R. Mok and H. Johannes, Schiedsgerichtbarkeit und EWG-Vertrag in *Aussenwirtschaftsdienst des Betriebsberaters* 1966, p. 125, note 28. The reference to Article 829 no. 7 should be to Article 829 paragraph 2. The challenge could perhaps also be based on Article 829 paragraph 1 no. 4 (but see Article 817).

77. *Hoge Raad* 12-11-31, NJ '32, p. 121 and 27-12-35, NJ '36, 442. Concerning this doubt, see the article of Mok and Johannes referred to in the previous note, at note 28.

78. Published in September 1982, see Article 1044, para 1 sub (b)

c) To the extent that Community law is considered to be a matter of public policy, violation[79] will always constitute a ground for review by ordinary courts, except for the current doubt in The Netherlands.

4.3.1.2.c. Foreign Awards

So far I have only written about the review of domestic arbitral awards, but one of the main characteristics of arbitration is that it is a means of settling disputes in international situations. An attractive feature of arbitration in such situations is that it is often easier to enforce an arbitral award in the territory of a State other than the State where the award was made than a judgment of an ordinary court. This is particularly true for the more than 60 States which are parties to the *New York Convention*[80]. All the Member States except Luxemburg[81] are among the parties. As long as the *1978 EEC Convention of Accession to the Convention on Jurisdiction and Enforcement of Judgments in Civil and Commercial Matters* is not in force between all the Member States, arbitration will retain the enforcement advantage with respect to international situations within the Common Market. Even once the Convention of Accession applies, this advantage continues where most third countries are concerned because very few treaties for the enforcement of judgments exist between Member States and third countries.

Under the *New York Convention,* each Contracting State shall recognize and enforce arbitral awards made in the territory of another State[82]. The grounds for refusal of recognition and enforcement are very limited, but they do include the invalidity of the arbitration agreement, the fact that the award has been set aside or suspended in the country where it was made, and the fact that recognition or enforcement would be contrary to the public policy of the country where recognition or enforcement is sought (this ground includes non-arbitrability)[83].

The issue relevant to our examination is the extent to which the procedure for recognition and enforcement in another State offers additional opportunity to review an award in the light of Community law. Considering that separability of the arbitral clause has been widely recognized, issues of Community law are largely irrelevant to the validity of the arbitral clause[84]. Thus the only other relevant ground for refusal is the one relating to public policy. The reader will have noted that this is not the public policy of the country where the award was made. Viola-

79. It is submitted that public policy is not involved where there is just misinterpretation, and no violation, of Community law.

80. Convention on the Recognition and Enforcement of Foreign Arbitral Awards, New York 1958, *United Nations Treaty Series,* vol. 330, p. 38 No 4739 (1959).

81. However, Luxemburg is a party to the Geneva Protocol on Arbitration Clauses of 1923 and the Geneva Convention on the Execution of Foreign Arbitral Awards of 1927, which are the predecessors of the New York Convention.

82. All the Member States of the EC which have ratified the Convention (all except Italy) have declared that they will only apply it to awards made in another *Contracting* State.

83. Article V (1) sub (a) and (e) and (2) sub (a) and (b).

84. It would seem that arbitral awards from the UK and Ireland are not likely to be challengeable on the grounds of invalidity of the arbitral clause because in those countries that issue will usually be decided by the courts before an award is made.

tion of a country's public policy can only be a ground for review in the same country[85]. The ground referred to in the *New York Convention* does therefore offer an additional opportunity for review insofar as violation of Community law is contrary to the public policy referred to in Article V(2) of the Convention. In this connection, reference should be made to a recent thesis by A.J. van den Berg, *The New York Arbitration Convention of 1958*[86]. This thesis is based on an analysis of some 140 decisions of national courts where the Convention was applied, being virtually all decisions published (and commented on in *Yearbook Commercial Arbitration)* before 1st February 1981. Van den Berg[87] draws attention to the increasing acceptance in arbitration matters of the distinction between domestic and international public policy[88]. He cites a number of cases where the concept of international public policy was applied under the Convention. This concept is narrower than that of domestic public policy. It is interesting to read[89] that national courts refused to enforce an arbitration agreement or an arbitral award on account of public policy in only five of the roughly 140 decisions. Of these five, three were cases of non-arbitrability. None involved Community law.

4.3.2 Conclusions as to Review of Arbitral Awards (Category 2)

My conclusions about the review by ordinary courts of Community law questions arising in arbitration are as follows:

a) There are great differences among the Member States as to the extent to which questions of Community law arising in arbitration may reach the ordinary courts.

b) The chances of Community law coming up for review in ordinary courts depend to a great extent on whether or not the particular issue is considered to be a matter of public policy. I submit that public policy is not involved where the issue is merely one of interpretation rather than violation of Community law. In some Member States, particularly Germany, not all issues of Community law are considered to be matters of public policy. The same may apply under the *New York Convention.*

c) Where such issues are considered matters of public policy there will always be a possibility to reach the ordinary courts, except for the current doubt in The Netherlands.

d) Insofar as Community law is considered mandatory law only (and not public policy), violation or misinterpretation does not open the door to ordinary courts in Germany and Greece, but may do so in other Member States, albeit with certain restrictions.

85. The setting aside or suspension of the award on this ground is not a reason for refusal of recognition or enforcement in a State which is also a party to the European Convention on International Commercial Arbitration, (see Article IX (2) of that Convention).

86. Published by Asser/Kluwer – The Hague/Deventer, 1981.

87. P. 360.

88. See also Article 1502 (5°) of the French New Code of Civil Procedure which refers to *"l'ordre public international"* in international arbitration.

89. P. 366.

e) There is, therefore, no certainty that questions of Community law arising in arbitration may always be reviewed by ordinary courts, but in most cases the possibility exists.
f) In the majority of Member States, the ordinary courts cannot be, or in practice are not, called upon to examine questions of Community law "in the context of their collaboration with arbitration tribunals". If this occurs at all, the courts will do so when they review the arbitral award.
g) The possibilities for the courts to examine questions of Community law arising in arbitration are clearly much greater in Ireland and the UK than in the other Member States.
h) In practice the *New York Convention* does not appear to offer a significant additional opportunity for review of an arbitral award in the light of Community law.

With these conclusions in mind it would be interesting to know the number of cases where ordinary courts have actually examined questions of Community law which had previously been raised in an arbitration. I have searched the case-law of some Member States and inquired among lawyers in most Member States, but the yield was very meagre indeed. I found only three such cases; two decided by the German *Bundesgerichtshof* and one by a Belgian court[90]. In all three cases the questions of Community (competition) law were examined in the course of a review of an arbitral award.

The final conclusion is, therefore, that even though in most cases questions of Community law arising in arbitration may theoretically come up for review in ordinary courts, this happens very rarely in practice. Consequently, to the extent the Court's *obiter dicta* are correct[91], they offer three possible conclusions:
a) questions of Community law have only very rarely come up in arbitration, or
b) in the cases where Community law has arisen in arbitration it has only very rarely been incorrectly interpreted or applied by arbitrators, or
c) there have been a number of cases where Community law was incorrectly interpreted or applied, but the losing parties have chosen not to challenge the arbitral awards in the ordinary courts (except in the three cases referred to above).

It is impossible to prove or disprove the thesis sub(a) for lack of data, but there are very likely to be unreported cases. Considering the difficulty of many questions of Community law and the many mistakes made by professional Judges applying Community law, the thesis sub (b) seems hard to maintain. Consequently, the third conclusion would seem to be the one most likely to be correct. If so, the *obiter dicta* provide cold comfort to those who are anxious

90. The German cases are BGH 27-2-1969 – KZR 3/68 *("Yoga" fruit juices)*, see note 44, and BGH 31-5-1972 – KZR 43/71 *("Eiskonfekt")*, *Neue Juristische Wochenschrift* 1972, p. 2180. The Belgian case is *Tribunal Bruxelles* 15-2-75 in S.A. Preflex *v.* Lipski, *Journal des tribunaux* 1976, p. 493 with annotation by Louis Dermine.

91. It is surprising that the Court should have included these *obiter dicta* at all since the Advocate General had already convincingly refuted the substance of the *obiter dicta* in his opinion (item 1 (3) (b) (aa) (iii)).

to see Community law uniformly interpreted and correctly applied, whether by ordinary courts or in arbitration.

4.4. Some afterthoughts

4.4.1 It is respectfully submitted that the Court's method of reasoning in *Nordsee* is not entirely satisfactory. The "negative enumeration" of a number of characteristics which were present in the two previous cases tends to envelop the Court's real reasoning in a cloud of mystery. It may be true that the Court's real reason for denying arbitrators the status of a "court or tribunal of a Member State" lies in the absence of a "sufficiently close link" between this particular arbitration procedure and the German organization of *judicial* remedies. This point had been forcefully argued by the United Kingdom. In this respect, it is striking to note that in the French and German versions the relevant words in point 13 are almost identical to those used by the Court in its summary of the observations submitted by the United Kingdom[92]. Advocate General Reischl had also emphasized that in *Scheidsgerecht Beambtenfonds* and *Broekmeulen* the public authorities had influenced the institution and composition of the "tribunal", which was not the case in *Nordsee.*

However, if the absence of a "sufficiently close link" was the real reason in *Nordsee* one wonders why the Court made its "first important point to note" in paragraph 11. The fact that the parties were under no obligation, whether in law or in fact, to refer their disputes to arbitration seems to have little to do with the absence of the "sufficiently close link". In order to establish this fact the Court even resorted to an examination of "the facts of the case". Read in isolation, this paragraph would seem to indicate that the Court would be prepared to consider references for preliminary rulings from arbitrators in cases where the parties (or one party?) were in fact under an obligation to refer disputes to arbitration. This could be the case under all sorts of general conditions and other standard form contracts used in many branches of trade and industry. It often occurs that at least one of the parties has no choice but to enter into such a contract. Those contracts often contain an arbitration clause referring the parties to a permanent arbitral tribunal. In its observations submitted to the Court in this case, the Danish Government was prepared to accept as a "court or tribunal" a permanent arbitration tribunal which "as such has power to decide an unlimited number of disputes between parties who have not themselves created the tribunal". An arbitration tribunal set up by a trade association of which both parties to a dispute are members, or just one, seems to meet these conditions. The Advocate General too made an express exception for permanent arbitral tribunals in one of his main arguments (item I(3) (b) (bb) (iii)).

However, if the Court is really going to insist on the "sufficiently close link", then it will be unable to accept references from such permanent arbitral tribunals

92. "Rechtsschutzsystem des betroffenen Mitgliedstaats" and "système des voies de recours de l'Etat membre concerné"; cf. note 18.

and the meaning of point 11 of *Nordsee* would be difficult to understand. I would prefer to think the Court has not made its statement in point 11 without a good reason, and therefore see some chance for permanent arbitral tribunals in trade and industry to get a reference accepted.

4.4.2 It is interesting to note that the United Kingdom's argument about the "close link" was based on a literal interpretation of Article 177. The United Kingdom emphasized the word "of" in "court or tribunal of a Member State" to argue that this word implied the existence of a close link between the adjudicatory body in question and the system of legal remedies in the Member State concerned. The Advocate General in his opinion (item I(3) (a)) said that the text of Article 177 did not provide a safe basis for a solution of the problem[93]. The Court does not explicitly say that its reasoning is based on the text of Article 177, but it does quote the relevant words in the crucial point 13 as well as in point 10.

Although it is therefore possible that the Court's decision is based on the wording of Article 177, there could well be some unstated reasons which weighed more heavily. Perhaps some of these reasons could be found in the excellent opinion of the Advocate General. His opinion contains a comprehensive review of the most important arguments on both sides.

4.4.3. In the last part of the section of his opinion dealing with the applicability of Article 177, the Advocate General mentions a number of practical problems which would arise if arbitrators were authorized to refer questions to the Court. One of the problems mentioned is that if arbitrators were to have authority to refer questions to the Court there would also be an obligation to do so in most cases. I do not know if this argument impressed the Court, but my conclusions in item 4.3.2. *supra* seem to indicate that in most cases it is possible to review arbitral awards where points of Community law are concerned. To the extent that Community law is a matter of public policy such review is always possible. Thus in most cases it would be difficult to maintain that no appeal lies from the arbitrators' decisions. A reference is only mandatory under Article 177 (3) where no appeal lies from a decision.

4.4.4. Another problem mentioned by the Advocate General[94] is that serious complications could arise in cases of international arbitration, particularly *ad hoc* arbitration. In such cases it could be difficult to connect the arbitral tribunal with a specific Member State, as the word "of" in "court or tribunal of a Member State" requires. What if the arbitral tribunal were to hold sittings in a number of countries, including non-Member States? What "connecting factor" should apply if the seat is not, or cannot be, taken into account? The procedural law applicable or the

93. This also seems to be the opinion of almost all authors who have written about the problem. As the Advocate General pointed out, it could well be argued that the authors of the Treaty meant to exclude courts of non-Member States, international courts, the parties to a case before a court, as well as the Member States and their non-judicial authorities.
94. Also mentioned by the United Kingdom.

substantive law? The Court may have disliked the idea that it might one day have to answer such questions.

4.4.5. The Advocate General (and the UK) mentioned another problem which may have had quite some impact on the Judges. There is the risk that the Article 177 procedure be misused for referring questions to the Court which do not stem from a real dispute. On this point the Court has shown itself particularly sensitive, as is borne out by its two decisions in *Foglia* v. *Novello.*

In *Foglia,* two Italian parties tried to obtain a ruling in proceedings in an Italian court that the French tax system (requiring importers of Italian liqueur wine to pay tax on imports) was inconsistent with Community law. In these proceedings the individuals were in agreement as to the result to be obtained, and had inserted a clause in their contract in order to induce the Italian court to give a ruling on the point. The Italian court referred the question of Community law to the Court of Justice, which ruled that it had no jurisdiction in this case[95]. The Italian *Pretore* did not give up and referred five further questions to the Court. The Court did not give in and ruled once again that it had no jurisdiction to answer the question of substantive Community law, but it did give extensive reasons for deciding why it had no jurisdiction.[96]

In point 18 of the second decision it held:

> "It must in fact be emphasized that the duty assigned to the Court by Article 177 is not that of delivering advisory opinions on general or hypothetical questions but of assisting in the administration of justice in the Member States. It accordingly does not have jurisdiction to reply to questions of interpretation which are submitted to it within the framework of procedural devices arranged by the parties in order to induce the Court to give its views on certain problems of Community law which do not correspond to an objective requirement inherent in the solution of a dispute."

It is submitted that there are no facts to support the presumption that questions referred by arbitrators would stem from less genuine disputes than questions referred by an ordinary court. It is often just as easy (and perhaps even cheaper) to induce an ordinary court to refer "general or hypothetical questions" to the Court than to cause arbitrators to do so. Cases like *Foglia* v. *Novello* are highly exceptional, but this case did occur before an ordinary court. Nevertheless, one may expect professional judges to look at arbitrators with some reservation . This may particularly be so where the judges are thinking mainly in terms of safeguarding individual rights derived from such an august source as the EEC Treaty.

95. Decision of 11-3-80 in Case 104/79, P. Foglia *v.* M. Novello at the request of the *Pretore* in Bra, Italy, [1980] ECR, 745.

96. Decision of 16-12-81 in Case 244/80, P. Foglia *v.* M. Novello, [1981] ECR, 3045.

5. CONCLUDING REMARKS

5.1 In the foregoing I have not concealed that I find the reasoning of the Court in the *Nordsee* decision unsatisfactory. Apart from criticizing the reasons stated by the Court one could also think of reasons the Court could have stated to arrive at the opposite decision. Particularly, one could think of a reasoning based on the "jurisdictional" view on arbitration. This view is gaining ground in many countries. The special relationship between arbitration and the judiciary in the UK and Ireland indicates strong support for this view there.

However, I am not dissatisfied with the result, which I consider to be a ruling that says that in principle the Court has no jurisdiction to give preliminary rulings at the request of arbitrators. My opinion is based on considerations of a purely practical nature.

5.2 I formed my opinion by putting myself in the place of an arbitrator. A question of Community law arises in the course of the proceedings. What could I do? I would apply Community law as well as I could. What if there were serious doubts as to how one or more provisions of Community law should be interpreted? I would still interpret and apply them as well as I could. I am acting as an arbitrator by virtue of an agreement between the parties and myself. In discharging my duties as an arbitrator I am bound to have regard to the legitimate interests of the parties. In pursuit of their interests the parties have submitted their dispute to arbitration. They must have had their reasons for doing so. These are not the same in all cases, but in many cases they include speed and privacy. Often the parties also opt for arbitration because its finality makes it cheaper. That is to say that even though the arbitrators and the lawyers may charge high fees, these one-time costs are expected to be less than the cost of proceedings at two or three levels in ordinary courts.

If I were to refer a question to the Court that would surely be ignoring all the aforementioned reasons. The preliminary ruling would take about 12 months and it would be published in full detail. One could well imagine that both the parties to the *Nordsee* case and the German Federal Ministry of Food, Agriculture and Forestry were rather embarrassed when they became aware that as a result of Judge Richter's reference an illegal contract and an attempt to cover it up were exposed. An official of the Ministry and a manager of one the parties had even made fraudulent statements to the Commission, thus committing crimes. Did the *Nordsee* arbitrator's (implied) agreement with the parties allow him to bring a crime of one of them to the attention of the public prosecutor by referring questions to the Court? Would it not have been wiser to dismiss Nordsee's claim on the ground that the contract was void and leave it to Nordsee to decide whether or not to challenge the award in the ordinary courts?

Of course, the situation in *Nordsee* is likely to be rather exceptional, but privacy may often be required for perfectly honourable business reasons. If I were an arbitrator, keeping in mind the reasons for resorting to arbitration already mentioned, I would be extremely reluctant to refer a question to the Court.

Of course there will be cases where speed and privacy play no greater role than in ordinary court litigation. If one considers the wide-spread use of (institutionalized) arbitration in, e.g., commodity trading, shipping, construction, shipbuilding, it would probably be safe to say that in the (vast) majority of cases privacy and even time do not play a dominant role, although cost does. The specific expertise of the arbitrators is then often more important. However, in such cases the disputed issue will very rarely give rise to questions of Community law (as it stands today). Such issues are more likely to arise in *ad hoc* arbitration. Of the 7 arbitral awards dealing with issues of Community law I know of, 6 [97] resulted from *ad hoc* arbitration[98]. It is in this type of arbitration that privacy in particular may play a more important role.

5.3 Amidst the uncertainty about the actual number of arbitrations dealing with issues of Community law one fact stands out: during the 25-year existence of the EEC Treaty only one arbitrator has referred questions to the Court. The higher this actual number the better evidence this single reference offers for the submission that in practice arbitrators must have felt the reluctance referred to above. If there have only been a few arbitrations dealing with Community law, then the conclusion must be that the whole issue of the interpretation and application of Community law by arbitrators is insignificant. In either case the question of references by arbitrators under Article 177 is hardly of any practical consequence.

It is interesting to recall that even if there have been a number of cases where arbitrators interpreted or applied Community law incorrectly, there have been only three cases (as far as I know) where the awards have been challenged before the ordinary courts. Apparently the parties themselves are rather reluctant to step out of the confines of the arbitration. However, they may do so and if they do the ordinary courts may (or must) refer the question of Community law to the Court wherever that question involves public policy.

5.4 I would make one proviso to my opinon about the result of the *Nordsee* decision. Harmonisation of civil and commercial law is making progress. In the not too distant future we may expect a major part of company law and the law on agency contracts, bankruptcy, misleading advertising, consumer credit and possibly even product liability to be covered by EEC Directives or conventions under Article 220 EEC Treaty and thus turned into Community law. By the time this point is reached there may be a genuine need for references by arbitrators for interpretation of some of those Directives and conventions, which interpretation will have direct bearing on municipal law. I would still recommend that arbitrators care-

97. These are: three awards referred to in the court decisions mentioned in item 4.3.2 (note 90); two from the ICC, one as in note 46 *supra,* and another dated 16-3-64, published in *Revue de l'Arbitrage* 1964, p. 131 and in AR 1965, p. 80; and two Dutch awards, one dated 22-7-64, published in AR 1964, p. 240 (also in *Revue de l'Arbitrage* 1965, p. 28), and the other dated 11-3-68, published in AR 1969, p. 123.

98. The odd one out was the Dutch award of 1968 where issues of Community law had been raised by way of a not too serious defence.

fully balance the interests of the parties (privacy, speed, costs) against the consequences of a possible incorrect application or interpretation of Community law.

5.5 . As long as the Court refuses to accept references from arbitrators the considerations in item 5.5.4. offer a good case for urging that legislators of the Member States create possibilities for the judiciary to submit questions of Community law arising in arbitration to the Court of Justice. Such a possibility exists already in the UK and Ireland, but in England and Wales it was substantially restricted in 1979 (see item 4.3.1.1.b. *supra* and the notes thereto). It would seem that a similar possibility exists under Danish law on domestic arbitration. Article 3 of the Danish Arbitration Act of 1972 provides[99] : "Upon request the courts shall render assistance in the carrying out of an arbitration case. Assistance shall, *inter alia,* be rendered in the following situations: (procedural matters)". The words *"inter alia"* open the possibility of arbitrators requesting the ordinary courts to give a ruling on a question of Community law. Such a court *may* in turn, if it considers that its ruling depends on a preliminary decision on this question, request the Court to give such a decision under Article 177 paragraph 2. It may be hoped that a provision to that effect be included in the draft Bill for new rules on arbitration which is now under discussion in The Netherlands.

For the time being, however, I do not see serious objections to deferring to the Court's ruling, which might be summarized as:

Was dem Richter freisteht, steht Herrn Richter nicht frei.

99. In the English translation published in *Nordisk Tidsskrift for International Ret* p. 362.

DR. ERADES, CHAIRMAN OF TWO INTERNATIONAL ARBITRAL TRIBUNALS

by A.M. Stuyt *

Dr. Erades was chairman of two international arbitral tribunals in quick succession. The first, entitled the "Lake Ontario Claims Tribunal, United States and Canada", ended with a final decision in 1968; the second, the "Sudan-Turriff Construction (Sudan) Ltd.", ended in 1970. Both cases were described in detail in this journal by Dr. Erades; it would therefore be superfluous to repeat the facts and procedures here. We prefer a discussion of the main issues in the two cases. After a brief factual introduction on the character of the two cases, the first paragraph will deal with the organization, competence and the procedure of the tribunals. Paragraph 2 will pay attention to the meaning of the two legal solutions.

1. THE CASES

1.1 Some facts

For the first case (hereafter referred to as "Gut Dam"), refer to Dr. Erades' article in the 1969 edition of this journal,[1] and for the second case (hereafter referred to as "Sudan"), refer to the article in the 1970 edition.[2] The difference in the number of pages devoted to the two cases alone indicates that the Gut Dam case had a lengthy preliminary history, while the Sudan case had a short one. The two cases had in common the fact that the construction of a dam in Lake Ontario and the Nile respectively, gave rise to an international conflict. In this respect some other international conflicts of a more technical nature have been submitted to an international tribunal before, e.g. the Trail Smelter Question,

* Emeritus Professor of Public International Law, University of Nijmegen; Member of the Board of Editors.

1. "The Gut Dam Arbitration", NILR 1969 pp. 161-206. Dr. Erades published a shorter article on this case, entitled "Erosion and inundation damages led to an international arbitration" in Festschrift für Pan. J. Zepos, vol. II, pp. 99-115, Athens 1973. See also Ernest L. Kerby and Carl F. Goodman, "The Gut Dam Claims – A lump sum settlement disposes of an arbitrated dispute", *Virginia Journal of International Law* X (1970) pp. 300-327; Richard B. Lillich, "The Gut Dam Agreement with Canada", AJIL 1965 pp. 892-898; Report of the Agent of the US in ILM 1969, pp. 118-143.

2. "The Sudan Arbitration", NILR 1970 pp. 200-222. See also Prof.Dr. P.H. Kooijmans, "Staten en ondernemingen; enige opmerkingen naar aanleiding van de Soedan-arbitrage", in, *Uit het Recht,* Rechtsgeleerde Opstellen aangeboden aan Mr. P.J. Verdam, Deventer 1971, pp. 43-51.

which was also between the neighbouring countries of the USA and Canada.[3] Nevertheless, the cases in question differ considerably, both regarding the subject of the dispute and the nature of the claim.

The subject of the Gut Dam dispute is described in the first two paragraphs of the preamble to the Agreement between the Government of the United States of America and the Government of Canada concerning the establishment of an international arbitral tribunal to deal with United States claims relating to Gut Dam, signed at Ottawa on 25 March 1965:

"Considering that claims have been made by nationals of the United States of America against the Government of Canada alleging that their property in the United States has suffered damage or detriment as a result of high water levels in Lake Ontario or the St. Lawrence River;
Considering that these claimants have alleged further that the damage or detriment was attributable in whole or in part to the construction and maintenance of a dam in the international section of the St. Lawrence River known as and hereinafter referred to as 'Gut Dam' and have claimed compensation for such damage or detriment from the Government of Canada."[4]

The subject of the Sudan dispute – unfortunately neither the two submissions nor the award of this arbitration was published – was described by Dr. Erades as, 'disputes arising out of or in connection with a contract entered into by the (Sudanese) Government and Turriff on 16 October 1962 under which Turriff was to carry out a housing scheme in the Irrigation Area of the Khashm-el-Girba Dam subject to the contract documents attached to the said contract'.[5]

The nature of the claims of nationals of the United States, including juridical persons, concerned any legal liability to pay compensation for any damage or detriment caused by the construction and maintenance of Gut Dam to the property that was the subject of such claims.

The nature of the claim of Turriff concerned the enforcement of the 1962 contract, although the Sudan considered this to be void or voidable soon after it was drawn up.

1.2 Organisation of the Tribunals

The organisation of the Gut Dam Tribunal was described in Article I, §§ 2-5 of the Agreement.[6] The American Member was Dr. Alwyn V. Freeman, Professor of International Law at Johns Hopkins University in Washington; the Hon. Wilfrid D. Roach, retired Justice of the Court of Appeal of Ontario was appointed as the

3. A.M. Stuyt, Survey of International Arbitrations 1794-1970, Leiden/New York 1972, No. 403. Cf. the judgment of the Permanent Court of International Justice of 28 June 1937 in the case concerning diversion of water in the Meuse between the Netherlands and Belgium, the arbitral award of 16 November 1957, in the case of Lake Lanoux between France and Spain. Survey quoted above No. 425 and the follow-up in UNTS 796 p. 217.

4. UNTS 607 p. 142 and ILM 1965 p. 468.

5. NILR 1970 p. 202.

6. The Agreement was ratified on 11 October 1966 and entered into force on that date.

Canadian Member, and Dr. Erades was chosen by the two Governments together as the third Member to preside over the Tribunal as Chairman.

The organisation of the Sudan Tribunal was more complicated. Following Dr. Erades' article, the initial Submission was signed on 21 October 1966 at the International Bureau of the Permanent Court of Arbitration, the Peace Palace in The Hague. The Arbitral Tribunal at that time consisted of the Hon. Charles Cameron (Ottawa), Sayed Mohammed Yussif Mudawi of the Judiciary (Khartoum), and Roger J. Parker Q.C. (London). On 25 July 1967 a Supplemental Submission was signed at the Peace Palace. The President of the Tribunal, the Hon. Charles A. Cameron, resigned before the date fixed for the hearings (5 June 1968). Dr. Erades was appointed President by mutual agreement between the parties on 11 December 1968. In July 1969, Judge Mudawi was not in court to hear the pleadings. The Sudanese Government did not fill the vacancy within the sixty days stipulated in clause 2(1) of the Submission. Thereupon, on 6 September 1969, the solicitors of Turriff requested the President of the International Court of Justice in The Hague to fill the vacancy in accordance with clause 2(6) of the Submission. On 2 October 1969, the President appointed Professor Kwamena Bentsi-Enchill, Dean of the Law School of the University of Zambia, as a Member of the Tribunal.

1.3 Competence

Questions of competence of the Gut Dam Tribunal were thoroughly dealt with in Article II of the Agreement. Paragraph 1 begins as follows:

"The Tribunal shall have jurisdiction to hear and decide in a final fashion each claim presented to it in accordance with the terms of this Agreement. Each decision of the Tribunal shall be based on its determination of any one or more of the following questions on the basis of the legal principles set forth in this Article:

(a) Was the construction and maintenance of Gut Dam the proximate cause of damage or detriment to the property that is the subject of such claim?

(b) If the construction and maintenance of Gut Dam was the proximate cause of damage or detriment to such property, what was the nature and extent of damage caused?

(c) Does there exist any legal liability to pay compensation for any damage or detriment caused by the construction and maintenance of Gut Dam to such property?

(d) If there exist a legal liability to pay compensation for any damage or detriment caused by the construction and maintenance of Gut Dam to such property, what is the nature and extent of such damage and what amount of compensation in terms of United States dollars should be paid therefor and by whom? "

As regards the law to be applied, the following distinctions were made in paragraph 2 of that Article:

"(a) The Tribunal shall apply the substantive law in force in Canada and in the United States of America (exclusive, however, of any laws limiting the time within which any legal suit with respect to any claim is required to be instituted) to all the facts and circumstances surrounding the construction and maintenance of Gut Dam including all the documents passing between Governments concerning the construction of the dam and other relevant documents.

(b) In this Article the law in force in Canada and the United States of America respectively includes international law.

(c) No claim shall be disallowed or rejected by the Tribunal through the application of the general principle of international law that legal remedies must be exhausted as a condition precedent to the validity or allowance of any claim."

Regarding the competence of the Sudan Tribunal Dr. Erades wrote:

"The Submission conferred on the Tribunal wide powers which included, inter alia, power

(a) to interpret the Submission and to judge its own competence to decide any matter in dispute referred to it as provided in the Submission (Clause 4(1));

(b) notwithstanding any failure of one of the parties to attend any session of the Tribunal (without having previously shown to the Tribunal what the Tribunal should consider to be good and sufficient cause for absence) to proceed with the hearing of the Arbitration in the absence of that party and to make any such order or award as it should think fit (Clause 4(7))."[7]

The Supplemental Submission of 25 July 1967 contained further provisions, reproduced on page 204 of Dr. Erades' article quoted above. As regards the law to be applied, it was provided "that the Parties should by their counsel be at liberty to make submissions as to both Sudanese law and English law and that neither Sudanese law nor English law should be proved as matters of fact." (p. 205). In the absence of any text it seems that up to that time international law was not included.

1.4 Procedure

The Gut Dam Agreement contained a set of rules of procedure in Articles III to XV. According to these, each Government should appoint a Secretary of the Tribunal, who should act as Joint Secretaries of the Tribunal and should be subject to its instructions (Article IV, par. 1). In addition, the Tribunal should, with the agreement of the two Governments, adopt such rules for its proceedings as might be deemed expedient and necessary. At its meeting of 24 January 1967, the Tribunal did in fact adopt eighteen articles constituting its Rules of Procedure. According to Article VII of the Agreement, 230 US claims were filed on 9 January 1967 to a total amount of US \$ 3.842.631.

The procedure in the Sudan case was very complicated. Dr. Erades wrote that:

"(t)he International Bureau of the Permanent Court of Arbitration agreed to, and did from the time of the Submission, place its premises and organisation at the Peace Palace at the disposal of the parties for the purposes of the Arbitration in accordance with Article 47 of the Convention for the Pacific Settlement of International Disputes of 18th October 1907 to which Convention the Republic of the Sudan adhered."[8]

7. NILR 1970, p. 202.
8. NILR 1970, p. 202.

However, the said Article 47 concerns contracting and non-contracting 'Powers'.[9] As only the Sudan was such a 'Power' (French text 'Puissance') and Turriff was not, it may be asked why, in this case, the 'Rules of arbitration and conciliation for settlement of international disputes between two parties of which only one is a State', elaborated by the above mentioned Bureau in February 1962, were not taken into consideration.[10] This question is all the more pertinent, because unlike the general rule concerning the filling of a vacancy of a member of the Tribunal in Article 59 of the Hague Convention, the Rules of 1962 contain three detailed articles on that point.[11] Moreover, the question of counter-claims is not dealt with in the Hague Convention, though it is dealt with in the Rules.[12] The same can be said about non-appearance in court.[13]

Another example that may be quoted is § e of the Order of the Tribunal of 25 July 1967, which was made pursuant to the Submission and Supplemental Submission:[14]

"(The Tribunal) giving, pending further order, power to Mr. Parker [15] to hear any application on any procedural matter which might arise before the hearing and to make orders thereon and providing that any and all applications on procedural matters should be made to him."[16]

Finally, we refer from the numerous procedural intricacies described by Dr. Erades to the letter of 8 May 1969, by which the Sudanese government withdrew from the arbitration and revoked Judge Mudawi's appointment as arbitrator. Dr. Erades wrote: "In the judgment of the Tribunal, Judge Mudawi did not become incapable by reason merely of the said Order, for the Government had no power to revoke his appointment. This point is, however, immaterial."[17] Whatever the Tribunal's grounds for this statement, one may ask whether the eventual award was not a decision *ex parte,* with all the attendant consequences.

2. LEGAL CONCLUSIONS

However, it is rather tricky to draw (comparative) conclusions from the results of two international arbitrations when the text of one of the two has not been published. The text of the thorough report of the Chairman of the

9. English translation of the Hague Convention for the pacific settlement of international disputes in B. Scott, *The Hague Peace Conferences,* vol. II, p. 309; also in *International Organisation and Integration,* ed. by H.F. van Panhuys et al, Leiden 1968 p. 6.
10. French text in this Review 1962 p. 272.
11. Articles 12, 13 and 14.
12. Article 11.
13. Article 16.
14. Dr. Erades wrote that both Submissions had been signed as a form of acceptance by all members of the Tribunal. This seems to be a rather unusual procedure in international arbitration.
15. British member of the Tribunal.
16. Pp. 204-205.
17. Pp. 2-5.

two Tribunals is therefore all the more important. Bearing in mind this reservation, the results can be approached in two different ways, viz., on the one hand, from the point of view of interpretation, and on the other hand, from the point of view of discussion.

2.1 **Interpretation**

Two aspects can be distinguished: the meaning of, and the domain and consequences of the decisions

2.1.1. Sense or meaning of the final decisions

2.1.1.1. *Gut Dam Case*

A number of papers have suggested that there were actually three decisions.[18] If the first "general decision" of 15 January 1968 was published in full,[19] this unanimous opinion more closely resembles an interlocutory decision which occurs frequently in internal law. The same could be said of the second "general unanimous decision" of 13 February 1968. In this decision the Tribunal concluded,

"that the only issues which remain for its consideration are the questions of whether Gut Dam caused the damage for which claims have been filed and the *quantum* of such damages. Argument on these issues will be scheduled after consultation with the agents of both Governments."[20]

The third decision of 27 September 1968 was not a "decision" but a "final statement",[21] which bears some similarity as regards the wording (the "whereas" construction) to an Order of the International Court of Justice concerning the removal of the case from the list. The Tribunal recognized that, taking into account the joint communication of the Agents, "this agreement constitutes a compromise settlement of the matter, considered (as) a solution equitable and just to all interests concerned."[22] Thereafter, the two Parties exchanged notes signed at Ottawa on 18 November 1968, for the final disposal of the dispute, which runs as follows (not mentioned by Dr. Erades):

"(a) The Government of Canada will make, and makes herewith, a lump sum payment to the Government of the United States of U.S. $ 350,000 in full and final satisfaction of all claims of the United States for damage allegedly caused by Gut Dam.

(b) The Government of the United States for its part will not further prosecute the claims before the Tribunal and will recognize such lump sum payment of $ 350,000 as constituting full and final settlement of all claims, past, present, or future, of nationals of the United States, whether natural or juridical persons,

18. Prof. Charles Rousseau in RGDIP 1970 p. 129.
19. Six lines on p. 203.
20. Pp. 204-205.
21. Pp. 205-206.
22. P. 206. The last five words are identical to those of Article II, § 3, of the Agreement.

against the Government of Canada on account of damage or detriment attributable in whole or in part to the construction and maintenance of Gut Dam; and

(c) The settlement is made without prejudice to the legal and factual positions maintained by the parties and without precedential effect."[23]

2.1.1.2. *Sudan Case*

The award was given on 23 April 1970 at the Peace Palace, The Hague. However, it was not an award of the Permanent Court of Arbitration, but was only attained with the collaboration of its International Bureau.[24] It is very exceptional for a State, which is a party in an international arbitration, to retire during the procedure. In any case, the award was pronounced in the absence of Sudan and whereas this retirement happened before the end of the procedures, the award could be considered to be a decision *ex parte*. It so happened that Sudan, present at the beginning of the procedure, presented counter-claims. The Tribunal rejected these counterclaims, as Dr. Erades wrote:

"As the Government withdrew from the Arbitration and did not seek to establish its counter-claim, there could, in any event, be no award on the counter-claim. However, the main matters alleged by the Government in its pleadings by way of defence to Turriff's claim also formed the basis of its counter-claim and, in rejecting them as defences, the Tribunal in effect dispose also of the counter-claim. The Tribunal's grounds are not reproduced here since they are merely concerned with Sudanese (i.e., English) municipal law."[25]

2.1.2. Domain and consequences

In both cases, natural and legal persons were the claimants: the Gut Dam case concerned private claims espoused by the American Government; the Sudan case concerned claims of a legal person: the British Turriff Ltd. In the Gut Dam case the parties were two States; in the Sudan case the arbitration was between a State and a non-State. The question of sovereign immunity played only a limited role before the beginnings of the arbitral procedure, rather than during the procedure itself, namely when Canada was sued in American Courts[26] in the Gut Dam case, though it played no rule in the Sudan case.[27] The competence of the international judge is not the same as the competence of the national judge.

In the Gut Dam case, the accorded lump sum represented only 50% of the original total claims (US $ 350,000 instead of US $ 653,247.27).[28] In the Sudan case, the absent Government "was ordered to pay with regard to the contract to Turriff a total amount of £ 6.186.070, interest included, and for Turriff's own

23. UNTS 714 p. 320; TIAS 6624.
24. See the Reports of the Administrative Council of the Permanent Court of Arbitration for the years 1966 to 1970 (p. 5).
25. NILR 1970 p. 222.
26. NILR 1969 p. 188, 190.
27. Prof. Kooijmans (note 2) discusses this question in the Turriff case.
28. NILR 1969 p. 200 and 203.

costs and the costs, fees and expenses of the Tribunal, the Secretariat and the Administrative Assistant of the Tribunal, a total of £ 191.334,-."[29]

2.2 **Discussion of values**

2.2.1. The value of international law in these two cases is very small

In the Gut Dam case the only reference is the phrase in Article II § 2(a) and (b) of the Arbitral Agreement: "The Tribunal shall apply the substantive law in force in Canada and in the United States of America . . ." which "includes international law." In the Sudan award, the South African Issue was of no interest to international law.[30] In the second issue, the Repudiation Issue, Sudanese/English law was the main law applied by the Tribunal.[31] As regards the final amounts awarded to Turriff, this did "not involve any point of international law."[32]

2.2.2. The Gut Dam case could be of interest with regard to lump sum adjudication, especially since the Second World War.[33]

In the Sudan case many points of Sudanese and English law were discussed, and decided upon, before an international tribunal, by lawyers who were experts in internal law.

2.2.3. Both cases are examples of international adjudication

Article 95 of the Charter of the United Nations, Chapter XIV on the International Court of Justice, says: "Nothing in the present Charter shall prevent Members of the United Nations from entrusting the *solution* (author's italics) of their differences to other tribunals by virtue of agreements already in existence or which may be concluded in the future." In the annex to the Charter, the Statute of the Court, Article 38 does not repeat the words "the solution of differences", but states: "The Court, whose function is to *decide* (author's italics) in accordance with international law such disputes as are submitted to it, . . ." In the case concerning the Northern Cameroons (preliminary objections, judgment of 2 December 1963), the Court decided: "The function of the Court is to *state the law* . . ." (authors's italics, French text: 'dire le droit').[34] In one of the first judgments of the Court it appeared that the *solution* of a dispute was not the same thing as

29. NILR 1970 p. 222.
30. Ibidem p. 220.
31. Ibidem p. 221.
32. Ibidem p. 222.
33. Cf. George T. Yates, III, "Postwar Belgian International Claims: their settlement by lump sum agreements", *Virginia Journal of International Law,* vol. 13:4, pp. 554-618. and the bibliography cited in that publication.
34. ICJ Reports 1963 p. 33.

the *statement of the law* in that case.[35] A great deal depends on the question(s) submitted by the parties to the Court. Nowadays it seems that there is a certain tendency in present international adjudication on the one hand, to ask the tribunal to state the law and on the other hand to leave the solution of the dispute to the parties themselves.[36] Thus, in the Gut Dam case, it was not the Tribunal which resolved the dispute, but the United States of America and Canada in the bilateral Agreement of 1968. Likewise, in the Sudan case, it was not the arbitral award *ex parte* which ended the conflict, but the parties themselves: at a later date they came to a solution at a much lower level – as in the Gut Dam case – regarding the question of damages and costs. Could it be, that sovereign States do not like to be the 'losing party' in the eyes of the international community? However, the statement of the law nevertheless remains a necessary and important task for the international judge or arbitrator.

35. Corfu Channel Case, judgment of 9 April 1949, Reports ICJ p. 26.

36. Cf. Article 1 of the Special Agreement between the Governments of the Netherlands and the Federal Republic of Germany, dated 2 February 1967, in the North Sea Continental Shelf Case before the ICJ: "(1) The International Court of Justice is requested to decide the following question: What principles and rules of international law are applicable to the delimitation as between the Parties of the areas of the continental shelf in the North Sea which appertain to each of them beyond the partial boundary determined by the above-mentioned Convention of 1 December 1964? (2) The Governments of the Federal Republic of Germany and of the Kingdom of the Netherlands shall delimit the continental shelf of the North Sea as between their countries by agreement in pursuance of the decision requested from the International Court of Justice." After the judgment of the Court of 20 February 1969, both States signed in Copenhagen on 28 January 1971 a 'Treaty on the delimitation of the continental shelf under the North Sea' (Trb. 1971 No. 53 and Trb. 1972 No. 137; AJIL 1971 p. 909; ILM 1971 p. 607; UNTS 857 p. 131). A similar case was pending before the same Court: the Continental Shelf Case between Tunisia and Libyan Arab Jamahiriya. Article 1 of the Special Agreement, signed in Tunis, 10 June 1977, notified to the Court on 1 December 1978 (ILM 1979 p. 49) reads as follows: "The Court is requested to render its judgment in the following matter: What principles and rules of international law may be applied for the delimitation of the area of the continental shelf appertaining to the Socialist People's Libyan Arab Jamahiriya and to the area of the continental shelf appertaining to the Republic of Tunisia, and the Court shall take its decision according to equitable principles, and the relevant circumstances which characterize the area, as well as the new accepted trends in the Third Conference on the Law of the Sea. Also, the Court is further requested to clarify the practical method for the application of these principles and rules in this specific situation, so as to enable the experts of the two countries to delimit these areas without any difficulties." Thus in this case too there was a statement of the law by the Court, and a solution of the difference by the two countries and their experts. (Judgment 24 February 1982). Finally, one example of an international arbitral award *ex parte:* the dispute between Texaco Overseas Petroleum Company/California Asiatic Oil Company and the Government of the Libyan Arab Republic concerning compensation for nationalized property. (English translation of the award dated 19 January 1977 in ILM 1978 pp.1-37). "Approximately eight months after the Award on the Merits was rendered, Libya and the Companies reached a settlement of their disputes . . ." (ibidem p. 2).

SOFT LAW

by A.J.P. Tammes*

"Soft law" is an expression that has recently been adopted to cover a growing category of normative phenomena in those areas between law and non-binding directives. Similar phenomena, for which no satisfactory place could be found in the system of international law, already existed; the "gentlemen's agreement" and some historical cases of declarations [1] could be cited as examples. As the number of such hybrids grew, the need for an all-embracing term was felt, as well as an analysis of its legal significance. Lord McNair is said to have coined the term, and since then it has been the subject of several legal studies.[2]

From an examination of the basis of the practice it appears, on the one hand, that the term is intended to indicate phenomena that have the characteristics of "law" in their directive effect to influence the will and restrict the liberty of those to whom the "soft law" is addressed. On the other hand, it should be pointed out when referring to the term, that something is missing in the legal or binding nature of law as we know it from daily life, and even international life. What is it that can be lacking to prevent an international obligation from coming into existence, yet still leaves room for a "soft" obligation?

The existence of international obligations depends on three kinds of element: a) a convincing reason for the addressee to be bound through his consent; b) a substantive obligation of the addressee such that his future freedom of decision on a certain matter, or disposal of a certain thing, is actually restricted; c) certain means of exhortation of the addressee to follow the directives embodied in his obligation.

When considering convincing reasons for an addressee to be bound, we may consider, apart from individual situations, the kind of collective or diplomatic situations that arise at international conferences. If a binding result cannot be reached according to the rules, it is often decided to revert to an old practice of making weak but important directives. This originated at the congresses and conferences of the mid-nineteenth century, from the need to prevent the results of

* Emeritus Professor of Public International Law and International Relations, University of Amsterdam.

1. Oppenheim-Lauterpacht, *International Law* I, 8th Ed. I, para. 487. The Atlantic Charter is a recent example.

2. R.J. Dupuy, Declaratory Law and Programmatory Law: from Revolutionary Custom to "Soft Law", in *Declarations on Principles,* Sijthoff 1977, p. 247 et seq.
Seidl-Hohenveldern, International Economic "Soft Law", Hague Recueil vol. 163, p. 169 et seq., 1979. Arangio-Ruiz, Colloquium Hague Academy, 1973, p. 540.
On this subject, though the term is not used specifically: Schachter, The twilight existence of non-binding international agreements AJIL 1977, p. 296 et seq.

the deliberations from being lost, while, on the other hand, lacking the means of presenting texts destined to become binding. When this practice became an established technique of international organization, a tendency developed to attach a quasi-legal significance to it beyond the obligation, sometimes spelt out in international constitutions, of the addressee to bring the recommendation before the competent national authority for further action.[3] It is here that the idea of soft law originated.

1. THE CONCEPT OF CONSENT AND SOME OF ITS DEFICIENCIES

We will now deal with the first and principal condition on which the generation of an obligation depends, i.e., the consent of a person.[4] There has long existed in modern society a widespread preference for being bound by the proposed rules of conduct suggested by other persons or authorities, only with one's own consent. It was the basis of the Old Testament concept of the free covenant between God and His people.[5] It has returned as the "social contract" and the phrase "government with the consent of the governed" and reflects the need for a construction, whether fictitious or not, to explain and justify the social phenomenon that heteronymous conduct models are in fact imposed on the members of the group.

In international law particularly, the concept of sovereignty (when it is not used for territorial jurisdiction) similarly means that another State does not have a higher directive authority unless this is recognized as such. The current rule that a treaty does not in itself create either obligations or rights for a third State [6] is another expression of the same idea. It is in keeping with this concept of mutual independence that "the rules of law binding upon States . . . emanate from the States' own free will . . . Restrictions upon the independence of States cannot therefore be presumed to take place."[7]

There is no consent if none of the conventional methods of binding a state are employed. Therefore they may not have been a direct assumption of an obligation, either unilaterally (in the form of a promise), or by any of the other means summarised in Article 11 of the Vienna Convention on the Law of Treaties, resulting from the conclusion of bilateral or multilateral negotiations. (Consent by example is mentioned separately below.) There is no consent either, if there has been no indirect consent through the medium of a recognised authority, such

3. For a historical survey, A.J.P. Tammes, Decisions of international organs as a source of international law, Hague Recueil 1958 II, 261-364 (292 et seq.).
ILO Constitution, Art. 19, para 6(b). And see in general, Judge Hersch Lauterpacht's separate opinion in South-West Africa Voting Procedure, Advisory Opinion, ICJ Reports 1955, 90-123 (120).

4. In this paper the term "person" will be used in the very general sense of any entity on which an international obligation can rest.

5. Deut. 26, 16-18. Dias, *Jurisprudence*, 4th ed. 1976, p. 75 et seq.

6. Vienna Convention on the Law of Treaties, article 34.

7. The Lotus, PCIJ Series A, No. 10, p. 18 (1927).

as the organ of an international organization of which the subject is a member. Another possibility might be that the person does not happen to be "born into" an existing community, and is therefore not assumed to be automatically subject to the law of that community. This may be compared to the situation of the State as a natural member of the international community, as it was considered in the past, though its political existence depends on international recognition followed by the acceptance into the corpus of general international law. However, there appears to be a grey area between the certainty of a person feeling positively bound through the various modes of consent, and the state of hesitation which remains concerning the strictness of his obligation. This area will be dealt with below.

2. SOFT LAW AS SEEN BY A PARTY TO AN INTERNATIONAL INSTRUMENT

1) Sometimes subjects are given a great deal of latitude with regard to complying with the contents of a directive.

– Only the attainment of a certain result is required, regardless of the ways and means employed.[8] This gives the subject an opportunity to postpone the definite establishment of an obligation to comply and enables him to correct conduct which might lead to non-compliance while the opportunity remains.

– The result of the directive is of secondary importance; the main issue is the requirement of an attitude of constant and sincere endeavour to co-operate, to reach a peaceful solution, or to reach an agreement. In the latter case of a *pactum de contrahendo* – often made for the completion, implementation or revision of an already existing agreement – the latitude of judging one's own attitude is sometimes inhibited by additional external instructions to the negotiating parties.[9] Nevertheless, so much may be left to the goodwill of the parties that international jurisprudence has found a contradiction between an obligation to agree and the nature of an agreement as a free act.[10] The requirement of good faith or a similar commendable state of mind is sometimes used to reinforce the prescriptive weakness of the *pactum de contrahendo.* In such a case, the only connecting factor between a party and the agreement is a soft liability.

8. In this paper the term "directive" (hard or soft) is used in a very general sense. This is obviously not the sense of art. 189 of the EEC Treaty, as a norm binding only with regard to the result, while leaving domestic agencies the competence to decide on the forms and means used to achieve this result.

9. In the *pactum* to agree on the boundary of the continental shelf between two opposite States (article 6 of the 1958 Convention), the median line may be regarded as the instruction, whereas in the North Sea Continental Shelf Cases, ICJ Reports 1969, p. 3, further directives were obtained from the Court. Successful negotiations followed.

10. "An "agreement" implies consent of the parties concerned." International status of South-West Africa, Advisory Opinion: ICJ Reports 1950, p. 139, in answer to the question whether the Charter imposes upon the Union of South Africa an obligation to place the territory under the Trusteeship System by means of a Trusteeship Agreement. Also see the Tacna-Arica Arbitration (Chile v. Peru, 1922, AA II, p. 929 et seq.) where it deals with the failure of the parties to agree on the manner in which a plebiscite was to be carried out.

2) Implied consent occurs in cases where consent is assumed to be given while no explicit terms of acceptance have been used and the party which is assumed to have consented retains the feeling that if he bears any obligation at all, it is only a soft obligation. It is possible to distinguish two types of case.

First, it is possible that the expression of consent does not contain a reference to any future conduct, but only to an obligation which logically implies the acceptance of conduct which is not explicitly described. It is possible that the agent might be virtually unaware of his consent, or that he might deny it. However, the logical conclusion that he is bound is inescapable. The vote in favour of admitting an entity as a member of an organization, constitutionally composed only of States, implies the recognition of that entity as a State, along with the consequences of this recognition outside the range of action of the organization. When a Member State accepts the treaty-making power of an international organization, this implies the acceptance of the treaties made as a consequence of this power.[11] Consent to arbitration implies, inter alia, the obligation to co-operate in establishing a tribunal, even though such co-operation is not explicitly prescribed.[12]

A second group of cases of "implied consent" where no terms of acceptance are used, can be found in passages from the case law of international courts, and particularly tribunals in disputes on the competence of international organizations. In this connection the question arises whether a Member State, by accepting the constitution of the organizaton, (either because of "necessary intention" as laid down in the constitution [13]), or "implied" in it,[14] or "because it is implied as being essential to the performance" of the duties or the organization [15], accepts the unstipulated competence of the organization to realize its purposes or objectives. One constitution has clearly expressed this doctrine of "implied powers" by authorising the organization "generally to take all necessary action to attain the objective of the organization",[16] if not to go beyond the powers granted by the constitution.

It is important to indicate the different aspects of "necessary implication". It could be that the implication is of an empirical nature, as in the case to which the above quotations refer. There is then room for a difference of opinion on what is "necessary to attain the objectives of the organization". Some authorities may see no alternative ways and means: others, including the "implied consenter", may think differently. The latter may consider that he has been compulsorily put under an obligation, though it can only be felt to be a weak one.

3) *Consensus* is the current term for a procedure borrowed from an historical precedent *(acclamatio)* of avoiding the sovereign principle of consent and thus expediting the slow pace of international decision-making. Although the general introduction, since the League of Nations, of the majority rule in international organizations amounted to a giant step in diplomatic parliamentary practice,

11. For a positive rule to this effect, see EEC Treaty, article 228, para. 2.
12. Advisory opinion concerning the Interpretation of Peace Treaties, ICJ Rep., 1950, p. 65.
13. ICJ Rep., 1954, p. 57. (UN Administrative Tribunal).
14. ICJ Rep., 1949, p. 180 (Reparation Case).
15. Ibid., p. 82.
16. WHO, art. 2(V). Also see Rama-Montaldo, International legal personality and implied powers of international organizations, BYIL 1970, p. 111 et seq.

recently it has been felt that the urgency and abundance of problems of international peace necessitated a short cut through the complicated voting procedure. Further progress was made by the idea of allowing individual votes to speak for a community, instead of inventing the fiction of a majority only representing the true unanimity which should be followed. As Gierke has noted, the postglossators, in order to make majority rule more than a fiction of unanimity, distinguished between *omnes ut universi* and *omnes ut singuli;* only in the first case, when the law equated a collective multitude with a collective whole, i.e., a *universitas,* could the majority be assimilated into the whole. Similarly, in international gatherings, the majority can more easily abandon the camouflage of unanimity or quasi-unanimity, if a universitas under the flag of consensus is supposed to exist by international law.[17]

Similarly, the notion of consensus has been revived in recent parliamentary diplomacy as a fiction of universitas capable of ignoring the conflict of opposing groups by upholding a decision taken despite existing rules of procedure, and, if possible, through moral or diplomatic pressure capable of persuading dissenters to acquiesce to what they must feel is no more than a soft obligation. A number of suggestions have been put forward to prove the exigent nature of consensus: the force of opinio iuris as manifested by the spirit of discussion; the analogy with the rules on reservations in the law of treaties, i.e., that reservations which are incompatible with the basic objectives of a general multilateral agreement do not have any effect;[18] and finally, the false rule that silence means consent (though this is not actually an agreed procedural rule).[19] This applies particularly to those persons, who for reasons of their own, have not protested. Vattel has already warned against the admissibility of silence and other inactivity as sufficient proof of acquiesence, if attention is not simultaneously paid to the presence of factors such as weakness in the face of imposition of authority by a State, or the primary concern of good relations. There may be just reasons for silence, like the impossibility of speaking, or a well-founded fear or lack of means of defence "contre des princes, dont les forces redoutables avaient longtemps réduit au silence les faibles victimes de leurs usurpations." [20] [21]

17. The author's lecture in The Hague, Recueil vol. 94, p. 296 (1958).

18. Art. 16 (c) of the Vienna Convention on the Law of Treaties, see also the points mentioned earlier by Suy, in Festschrift Röling, p. 270 (1977).

19. Jessup in Studi in Onore di G. Morelli, p. 401, "Procedure by consensus; silence means consent." p. 401 et seq. (1975).

20. Book II, ch. 11, para. 144.

In his dissenting opinion appended to the International Court's decision in the Temple Case (ICJ Rep. 1962, p. 128) Judge Spender paid attention to the fact that in the early part of this century Siam was aprehensive about the aspirations of France. This was given as the reason why the Thai Government did not protest about the presence at the Temple of a French officer in full military uniform. This lack of protest was among the facts which, in the view of the Court, amounted to "tacit recognition" by Siam of the sovereignty of Cambodia (under French Protectorate) over the Temple area (loc.cit., pp. 30, 31). Also see the dissenting opinion of Judge Altamira in The Lotus, Series A, No. 10, p. 98.

21. At the Third UN Conference on the Law of the Sea a Declaration Incorporating a "Gentlemen's Agreement" was made by the President and endorsed by the Conference on 27 June 1974, which refers to the desirability of adopting a Convention on the Law of the Sea

In the course of the above discussion we came across various kinds of soft international law. They may be categorised as follows:

– Soft law which comes from an authority recognised as such by the person; for instance, the organization of which he is a member. The soft law may be intended to be a kind of admonition, guide or advice. The addressee can do with it what he thinks is best for himself and with regard to others.

– Soft law which comes from an authority whose original intentions were somewhat stronger, but who, for procedural reasons or lack of sufficient support from its membership, could not succeed in producing a clear formulation for the directive, however weak or soft. Many recommendations of international organs may thus be considered second best.

– Soft law produced by an authority which has the constitutional competence to impose an obligation if the correct procedures are used, but where the addressee is able to free himself from the obligation. We have seen this in cases where decision-making by consensus was arranged without strict procedural rules in the case of individual silence or dissent, either on the creation of any decision, or on the individual commitment of the silent or dissenting partner (see above, 3, under "consensus").

– Implied consent as an interpretation by a competent authority may be considered by the person as subject to his own judgment, if instead of being a logical commitment, it has an empirical nature which can be considered subject to his personal opinion of the conditions of the case, unless juridically bound to the judgment of an authority. We have seen this in cases where it was decided by a higher authority that a particular action of the person was "essential" to the performance of the organization, as opposed to being a logical consequence of earlier conduct (see above, 2). The judgment is only an opinion of a technical nature, with which the addressee may disagree and by which he may feel bound against his will, as opposed to his understanding of the imperative nature of a logical implication of which examples are given above.

– Soft law that is interpreted as such by a party to an agreement because he does not consider the contents of his obligation to be a substantive burden on his freedom of decision or disposal. We saw above that the *pactum de contrahendo* was applied in cases where the obligation to negotiate formally is so weakly prescribed that only a strong interpretation by the party of his own good faith could lead to a conviction that he is bound (see above, 1; the *pactum de contrahendo).*

---

which will secure the widest possible acceptance, and reads further, "The Conference should make every effort to reach agreement on substantive matters by way of consensus and there should be no voting on such matters until all efforts at consensus have been exhausted." An elaborate code of rules on decision-making was based on this "gentlemen's agreement", approved by resolution of the General Assembly, which is soft law per se.

4. REINFORCING SOFT LAW

In conclusion, it can be stated that the term "soft law" refers to two situations:

a) when there is no assumption of a real burden;

b) when none of the conditions which make the conduct model [22] a binding obligation are fulfilled.

Examples of soft law may be used for internal purposes as follows: a state may order the courts or other organs to declare that it is a matter of public policy not to deviate from the soft law; it may sanction its observance, as far as private persons under its jurisdiction are concerned, by the various measures that are available to the State, such as refusal of permission, credits etc. No involvement of courts or other institutions that belong to the official legal set-up will elevate soft law to the level of the juridical order. However, an entire "code of conduct" can be incorporated in the national law.

Apart from any internal normative use a state may make of the conduct model that is offered to it as a product of international relations, it may also expect to benefit from attempts to reinforce it externally and so elevate it to the level of valid international law. Additional agreements may be made, as has happened in the sphere of human rights where general moral statements were incorporated in conventions which were widely ratified. Nor is it necessary that current means of the peaceful settlement of disputes, courts, fact-finding, sanctions etc. should be solely the concern of hard international law. The judicial function of interpretation would not essentially change if it were applied to soft law.

5. THE SETTING OF PRECEDENTS

At the beginning of this paper attention was paid to consent as a condition of changing an available conduct model into an obligation. Deficiencies in consent were summarised in order to present, from a negative point of view, a picture of cases where the conduct model is left as a random pattern of choice. It was not necessary at that point to present a complete survey of the various modalities of consent. However, one such form remains, which can be termed "consent by conduct". No communication of will has taken place in accordance with the current forms of promise, statement of intent, acceptance, recognition etc., but it is a person's sheer action alone – which may be verbal, but does not necessarily have to contain any communicative intention – which seems to prove to the outside world that he does not object to the action concerned. The original action might be considered as the implied recognition of its just nature. We will follow here the note of the International Law Commission [23] – applying the principle *allegans contraria non audiendus est* to the loss of the right of contestation after acquiescent

22. We use "conduct model" as a more neutral term than "directive", a term used in other places.

23. YILC 1966 II, p. 239, a commentary on what became of art. 45 of the Vienna Convention. However, see PCIJ, Series A, Nos. 20/21, p. 39 (Serbian Loans).

conduct (Article 45 of the Vienna Convention on the Law of Treaties) – that the reference here to such terms as "estoppel" in municipal law has features which are not necessarily appropriate for application in international law. Thus whilst avoiding false analogies, it is possible to make a more general statement.

Setting a precedent by conduct or a statement entails an obligation for a person not to oppose any other person's conduct that is in all relevant aspects comparable with the precedent. An interpretation of a treaty cannot be opposed by anyone who "has set an example in the past" of endorsing it. A State cannot oppose an expansion of jurisdiction which, in word and action, it has itself recognized as being lawful. It was not doubt this method of recognition by example that started the chain of imitative action and consequent setting of examples which led to the rapid universalization of the new concept of the continental shelf. In more general terms, it may be stated that participation in a practice amounts simultaneously to consent by conformative conduct and the setting of a precedent. This is another example of an obligation disguised as a proposition of conduct. The only peculiar thing here is that the proposed conduct does not take place in accordance with the conventional rules of the "promise game".[24]

It is submitted that these conclusions certainly apply to those cases where many States have actively participated in normative undertakings, either by drawing up a code of human rights or by making environmental rules, or a code of conduct in the field of economic co-operation, or by creating an instrument like the Helsinki Final Act on Security and Co-operation in Europe. Instruments like this cannot *a priori* be termed treaties. This is particularly true of the Helsinki Act. Great efforts have been made – even in the choice of the title – to prove that it was not binding in any sense, nor subject to any international or national procedure such as registraton with the Secretary General of the United Nations (Article 102 of the Charter), or subject to the approval of a constitutional organ, i.e., that it was "soft law" though that term was not used. However, for a participating State there is no way of denying the validity of rules which it has supported in an important public gathering. Other participants may well have done the same and the reciprocal effect would be that any action taken in accordance with the common standpoint of the conference could not be considered as unlawful or improper, even though it might not be officially recognized by any act of ratification.

6. SOFT LAW AND MORAL LAW

As various aspects of soft law have now been discussed, it might be useful to clarify a few misunderstandings which might easily arise in connection with this subject.

Soft law should not be compared with customary law since it is not generated by a succession of acts of acceptance as law: soft law is accepted per se. Even the repetition of soft law by authorities of high standing cannot generate customary law.

24. See R.M. Hare, The promise game, in *The "is"/"ought" question,* 1969, p. 143.

It is not strictly correct to describe soft law as "unsanctioned": certain measures with which we are familiar for supporting the observance of general international law, are suitable for sustaining soft law without detracting from its "softness". Mention ought to be made of agreed ways of checking its observance by fact-finding methods: consultation, reporting and inquiry. Furthermore, means of settlement of disputes of interpretation may be agreed upon. Measures of "retorsion", formerly always referred to as a mild counterpart of retaliation by reciprocating an unfriendly or noxious act with a similar unfriendly or noxious act, has gradually receded into the background as a consequence of the fact that so many once unfriendly acts, thanks to codification activities, have gradually fallen under the scope of positive international law where retaliation would be the adequate measure. A glance at the historical examples of "unfriendly acts" shows them to be soft law "avant la lettre". However, termination and suspension might still be adequate measures of sanctioning the original soft arrangement. *(Non adimplendi non est adimplendum.)*

These days, moral obligations cannot be considered to be soft, even when they are imposed without consent. Some moral obligations have become entirely positive under the influence of modern jurisprudence, the progressive codification and the application of equity and justice in the light of human rights in peace and war, and the activities of international development. This is not confined to the prevention and invalidation of the international law which is charged with serious moral deficiencies, as in the case of conflict of treaties with peremptory norms of general international law.[25] However, the existence of a general obligation can also be distinguished by the duty actively to support the removal of existing inequitable law and situations. In fact "moral law" is not soft at all,[26] but has taken highest precedence in the hierarchy of sources of international law.

25. A norm of general international law accepted and recognized "by the international community of States as a whole as a norm from which no derogation is permitted and which can be modified only by a subsequent norm of general international law having the same character" (art. 43 of the Vienna Convention on the Law of Treaties).

26. As used by the ICJ for the crime of genocide (ICJ Rep. 1960, p. 23).

THE FORUM ACTORIS AND INTERNATIONAL LAW

by J.P. Verheul*

Quis judex non subditum cogat ad id, quod extremum est in Jurisdictione?

Van Bynkershoek

The judgment of 8 January 1979 [1] of the District Court of Rotterdam contained some reflections on adjudicatory jurisdiction which, because they seem at first sight to be superfluous, have provoked a number of questions. It was the second interlocutory judgment in the Rhine pollution case, brought by Dutch nursery gardens and the *Stichting Reinwater* against the French company *Mines de Potasse d'Alsace S.A.* In the first interlocutory judgment, the District Court had declined jurisdiction, but this decision had been reversed by the Court of Appeal of The Hague after a preliminary decision of the Court of Justice of the European Communities. The Court of Appeal of The Hague expressly stated that "the District Court of Rotterdam had jurisdiction to hear the case", and remitted the case to that Court for a decision on the merits. Thus, the issue of jurisdiction seemed to be definitely settled in the proper manner. Nevertheless, the District Court tackled the issue again in the following words:

> "The question arises – though this point was not raised by the parties in the present proceedings – whether inhabitants of The Netherlands can ask a Dutch court to deliver judgment on the lawfulness of a French legal person discharging waste salts in France into an international river – the Rhine – and whether the Dutch court, if it considers such discharges unlawful, can order the French legal person to pay compensation for damage sustained by those inhabitants as a result of the discharges".

The District Court then answered the question affirmatively, with reference to international legal writings and cases on transnational pollution (see NYIL 1980 p. 329)

This approach suggests that the Court *might* have answered the question negatively on the strength of rules of customary international law, if the Court had found that such rules exist.

* Professor of Private International Law, University of Leiden; Member of the Board of Editors.

1. NJ 1979 113, NYIL 1980 326, NILR 1981 63 note Duintjer Tebbens. The judges were: Erades, Fransen and Van der Weij. See the references in NILR 1981 p. 63 n. 1. The Court of

Two possible underlying policies can be distinguished: a certain aversion to the forum actoris in general (jurisdiction of the court of the plaintiff's domicile or nationality) on the one hand, and an awareness of the public aspect of this specific case, on the other.

1. THE FORUM ACTORIS

The Court was perhaps particularly on its guard, because it was the court of the plaintiffs' domicile, whereas the defendant was a company established abroad. In this case, as in most pollution cases, the plaintiffs' domicile was at the same time the place where the damage occurred. The judgment leaves the impression that, if the domicile of the plaintiffs had been the *only* connecting factor, the Court might have been tempted to decline jurisdiction.

This impression is reinforced by two other decisions. The first was rendered by the President of the same Court[2]. He refused to intervene in the behaviour abroad of foreign companies established abroad.

> A Dutch company sued an English company, two Japanese companies, and a German company before the President of the District Court of Rotterdam in *kort geding* (summary proceedings). The action was based on a solus tie agreement and sought injunctions against the defendants, restraining them from importing into or selling in the Netherlands, or to a Dutch inhabitant other than the plaintiff, certain products in the field of industrial sewing-machines. In addition, a mandatory injunction was sought against the first defendant enjoining him to perform the plaintiff's orders regularly. The President held, of his own motion, that he had no jurisdiction, considering that the injunctions sought pertained to behaviour which was to take place outside the Netherlands and would only have any effect afterwards within the Netherlands, and that Dutch courts, subject to international conventions to the contrary, had no jurisdiction to direct injunctions which have to be performed abroad against foreign natural or legal persons established outside Dutch territory.

Justice of the EC interpreted in Article 5(3) of the EEC Convention on Jurisdiction and Judgments ("A person domiciled in a Contracting State may, in another Contracting State, be sued: in matters relating to tort, delict or quasi-delict, in the courts for the place where the harmful event occurred") the expression "harmful event" as referring to the tort as well as to the damage.

2. Pres. DC Rotterdam (Vice Pres. Erades) 3 Dec. 1974, NYIL 1975 365. The President of the D.C. did not specify whether he applied the "rule which sets aside municipal law in conflict with either written or unwritten international law", or "displayed adroitness in reading conflicts out of existence" by interpreting national law in the desired direction (Erades & Gould, *The relation between international law and municipal law,* Leyden 1961, p. 351). The judgment was reversed by the CA of The Hague 28 Feb. 1975, WPNR 1981 789. The Court of Appeal considered that the plaintiff was a Dutch company established in the Netherlands and that, moreover, the mandatory and prohibitory injunctions sought did pertain partly to behaviour within Dutch territory, thus leaving undecided whether the former consideration (domicile of the plaintiff; Article 126(3) of the CCPr) would alone be sufficient to oblige the court to assume jurisdiction. Neither the President nor the CA referred to Article 18 of the EEC Convention on Jurisdiction and Judgments which, in my opinion, barred the *ex officio* use of the forum non conveniens doctrine. The parties had declared at the trial that they had agreed to submit the case to the President of the District Court of Rotterdam.

In the second case[3], the District Court stated in so many words that "the forum actoris is not appropriate in international relationships", and refused to recognize a judgment of a French court which had based its jurisdiction on Article 14 of the French Civil Code (i.e., on the nationality of the plaintiff). The court not only refused recognition, which is quite normal, but also criticized the French legislature for having adopted Article 14 CC contrary to international law, under which "a State's jurisdiction is confined to its own territory".

This case concerned a direct action instituted before the District Court of Marseilles by a French company against Dutch insurers for damages in relation to a carriage by sea. The Dutch defendants had been unsuccessful when submitting the plea of no jurisdiction in the French proceedings. The plaintiff started an "action on the foreign judgment" in Rotterdam, invoking the *res judicata* effect of the French judgment (rendered before the entry into force of the EEC Convention on Jurisdiction and Judgments).

From these decisions, taken in combination, it may be inferred that the Court assumes the existence of a rule of customary international law set against the forum actoris.

2. TRADITION AGAINST FORUM ACTORIS

The idea is not new. In earlier times it was directly inferred from the principle of sovereignty. Van Bynkershoek[4] asserted that judicial jurisdiction, being a function of the sovereign, can only be exercised over persons (or property) within his power, i.e., persons domiciled in the forum country. How could a judge force a person not subjected to him to obey the decision, whose execution is the ultimate purpose of any judgment? A second rule, which is the main subject of Van Bynkershoek's work, maintains that an ambassador is not subjected to the jurisdiction of the country where he is accredited. This second rule was logically reconciled with

3. DC of Rotterdam (Erades, Van Benthem, Van Deth) 28 June 1976, WPNR 1979 635, NYIL 1978 321.

4. *De foro legatorum*, 1721, chap. II. French translation by Jean Barbeyrac, *Traité du juge competent des ambassadeurs*, La Haye, 1723, from which I quote the relevant passage: "Toute *Jurisdiction, & Civile, & Criminelle,* appartient au *Souverain* seul, qui peut l'exercer ou par lui-même, ou par autrui. Mais de quelque maniére qu'il en dispose, elle ne sauroit jamais s'étendre plus loin, que sur les Personnes, ou les Biens, qui dépendent de sa domination [Latin: Imperio ejus subditas]: car comme, selon la maxime du Droit Civil, *on peut impunément refuser d'obéir à un Juge qui veut connoître de ce qui est hors de son ressort;* c'est aussi une régle inviolable du Droit des Gens, *Qu'on ne doit commander, qu'à ses Sujets* [Latin: ita Juris Gentium vox, impera, sed in subditos]. Tout dépend donc ici de la *Sujettion,* sans laquelle la *Jurisdiction* n'a aucune force, non plus que l'*Assignation en Justice,* qui la précéde. Si une personne étant appellée en Justice, n'y va point, elle encourt, selon le Droit Romain, la peine d'une amende: or peut-on condamner à une amende, quelcun qui ne dépend point de nous? . . . Un Juge peut-il contraindre quelcun, qui ne dépend point de lui, à faire ou souffrir ce que porte la Sentence, dont l'exécution est le but & la fin de tout Jugement? . . . Le Juge compétent d'une *Personne,* est celui du lieu de son domicile, parce que chacun dépend du Magistrat établi dans l'endroit où il demeure, à moins qu'il n'ait quelque privilége particulier qui l'en exemte."

the first one by the fiction, borrowed from Grotius, that the ambassador is "considered" not to be present in that country. The second rule was, as it still is, undoubtedly a rule of international law; bearing in mind the logical relationship between the two rules[5], it is not surprising that the first rule was also ascribed to international law. Van Bynkershoek, it must be granted, expresses himself with great caution: "As, according to the civil law maxim, a court administering justice outside its territory can be disobeyed with impunity, it is also a rule of the Law of Nations that one can only command one's own subjects".

Other sources roundly declared that the forum actoris was "openly contrary to the Law of Nations"[6], i.e., contrary to the *actor sequitur forum rei* (the plaintiff follows the forum of the defendant).

3. THE RATIONALE BEHIND THE FORUM REI RULE

The "sovereignty" argument, as the rationale behind the forum rei rule, is rather weak and inconsistent. It presumes that the defendant will lose the case and will be ordered to pay or to do something. This can only be ordered, the theory maintains, by the court of his domicile. But in situations where the plaintiff loses the case and is ordered to pay the costs, or in the case of a counter claim, the reasoning is apparently abandoned. The same is true of situations where the defendant is not domiciled within the jurisdiction of the court, but submits voluntarily to it.[7]

In fact, the relationship between a sovereign and his subjects does not decide anything, when the parties belong to different jurisdictions. It offers no logically compelling reason to prefer the defendant's forum to the plaintiff's[8].

There is a parallel with the way in which the question of choice of law was solved when everybody was said to have a right to be judged under his personal law. This maxim did not suffice in civil cases between two persons living under different laws. Therefore the supplementary rule was adopted that nobody can *lose* or

5. The "power" reasoning is interwoven with another, more social contract type reasoning. The inhabitants are presumed to have voluntarily submitted to the jurisdiction, whereas ambassadors cannot be supposed to have done so (Ch. VIII § III). Here, too, there is a narrow relationship between the first and the second rule.

6. Conclusion of the *Substitut du Procureur du Roi* in the case *Rangoni*, judged by the *Parlement de Provence* in 1779, cited by J. Hudault, "Sens et portée de la compétence du juge naturel dans l'ancien droit français", Rev. Crit. 1972 p. 258. See also French case law and authors mentioned in this. In Holland, Pieter Vromans, *De Foro Competenti*, 1736 5, p. 13, described the forum actoris as "forbidden, improper" (our translation from Dutch).

7. Prorogation is as a rule permitted, according to Van Bynkershoek, because the parties can ignore what has been established in their behalf Ch. XXIII § V).

8. In France, the expression "natural judge" has also been used for the plaintiff's forum. See Hudault, loc. cit., p. 35 et seq. D. Holleaux, *Compétence du juge étranger et reconnaisance des jugements*, 1970, p. 235, even goes so far as to state that "la doctrine classique du juge naturel ignore donc la règle *actor sequitur forum rei*". Vromans, loc. cit. p. 82, says that "it behoves to no judge to administer justice on questions and disputes arising between various persons ["verscheyde Personen"] outside his jurisdiction", a formula which does not seem to distinguish between plaintiff and defendant. However, in the following text he stresses that jurisdiction implies the possibiliy of enforcement (referring to Aristotle), and then continues with the rule that a case must be brought before the "competent judge of the *reus*".

transfer a right except according to his personal law. This accounts for the application of the law of the seller to a contract of sale, of the law of the defendant in legal proceedings, and of the law of the injured person (later, on the contrary, of the law of the *laedens*, as being obliged to pay compensation)[9]. These elaborations show the arbitrary nature of the supplementary rule.

The forum rei rule[10] has to a certain extent a similar arbitrary nature. Historically, the rule can be explained. In criminal cases the rule was practicable because there was only one party who could claim to be judged by his own court. In civil cases, a choice had to be made, but the temptation to assimilate *the defendant* with the accused must have been so strong that there was hardly any choice. In old Germanic law no distinction was made between civil and criminal matters. In various legal systems the service of a summons sometimes took the form of simply dragging the defendant/accused before the court by physical force [11], which obviously required his presence within the territory of the sovereign in whose name this happened. Huber [12] still required presence in case of prorogation, since "service of a summons is an act of jurisdiction".

However, at the time Huber and Van Bynkershoek were writing, the possibility of serving a summons on a defendant not present in the territory had already been introduced for quite a long time, I mean the service according to the *clausula edicti*, i.e.,by public proclamation of the summons by the town crier in the frontier municipality nearest to the defendant's foreign domicile, combined with notification by post.[13] The justification of the forum rei rule as the general rule therefore probably shifted from the necessity of personal service to the more remote necessity of executing penalties inflicted upon the defendant for not appearing, and eventually to the necessity of executing the final judgment. Traces of all these stages in the reasoning can be found in the quotation from Van Bynkershoek (note 4).

What remains is that the forum rei has an advantage of effectiveness, if the court decides in favour of the plaintiff. A judgment against a defendant domiciled in the forum country, and consequently having his property there, is more likely to be

9. E.M. Meijers, "L'histoire des principes fondamentaux du d.i.p. à partir du Moyen Age", *Recueil des Cours* 1934 III pp. 555, 557, 572.

10. Historically related to the application of the law of the defendant, see Meijers, ibid. pp. 572, 573, 593.

11. A. Engelmann et al., *A history of continental civil procedure*, 1928, p. 8, 118, 345.

12. Huber, *Heedensdaegse Rechtsgeleertheyt*, 1742 4 p. 587. Along the same lines, Philips Wielant, *Practijcke ende maniere van procederen in materie civile*, 1622 3, I. XIX. 2 et seq., mentions that the *forum contractus* and the *forum delicti commissi* only applied if the defendant was "found" on the spot. In the same sense Gerardi à Wassenaer, *Praxis Iudiciaria*, 1669, p. 2 (also in case of prorogation, p. 4), and Vromans, op. cit. p. 14, 15 and 101.

13. Huber, op. cit. p. 702. Van Bynkershoek ch. IV, 3. The translator explains in note 2: "la personne absente doit être citée, au son de la Cloche, dans le lieu du ressort du Juge qui a donné le Mandement, lequel lieu est le plus proche du domicile de celui qu'on cite, & à qui on envoie en même tems les Lettres de Citation". See also Willem de Groot, *Inleyding tot de Practyck van den Hove van Holland*, 1667 2, 29, who adds that "all this being done, it is assumed to be equivalent to the defendant being personally served". On the *citatio edictalis*, see Engelmann, op. cit., p. 891 n. 3.

executed than a judgment against a foreign defendant. However, this has nothing to do with sovereignty and allegiance, only with the convenience of the parties, or rather *of the plaintiff.* More important, this practical advantage disappears with the appearance of international conventions which provide for reciprocal enforcement. It is curious that these conventions maintain as a matter of course the forum rei rule, while at the same time they take away its only justification.

New rationales have been proposed to support the obstinately persisting forum rei rule. These propositions, however, consist of mere words, e.g., the expression "natural judge". Properly speaking this is just a neutral shorthand for the judge who administers justice in the name of the sovereign in whose territory one lives.[14] Nevertheless the expression is used in a normative sense [15] and is associated with "natural law" [16]. Those who abandon the expression "natural judge", continue to consider the forum actoris to be contrary to reason [17] or to "natural justice" and "due process" [18]. In my view, the forum rei rule cannot be justified by its intrinsic value. In proceedings between parties domiciled in different countries, there is no reason whatsoever to favour the defendant. The plaintiff may be in the right; in roughly 50% of the cases he is. Why should he, rather than the defendant, be required to travel abroad? The rule *actori incumbit probatio* has nothing to do with jurisdiction [19].

However, these remarks are irrelevant. If the forum rei rule cannot be justified by referring to its contents, it can be justified by referring to its mere existence. It operates as a traffic regulation: it avoids collisions and furthers a well-balanced apportionment of litigations among the national judiciaries. Nobody would contend that keeping to the right on a road is in itself better than keeping to the left, or would try to justify the keeping right rule by the fact that most people are right-handed. However, there must be a rule, no matter what its contents are. Keeping to the left is not "excessive" as such, but it becomes so where the rule is contrary to this. Changing an already existing rule is pointless, unless it is done in order to join the majority of countries.

The forum rei rule is such a rule. Its arbitrary content, or in other words, its purely organizational character (not based on any consideration of equity) does not prevent it from being generally accepted. So let us now turn to the question, which

14. The French word *naturel* also means "indigenous". Cf. *lettres de naturalité,* naturalisation. In this sense the *substitut* in the *Rangoni* case speaks of proceedings between a *"natural français"* and a foreigner (cited by Hudault, loc. cit. p. 257).

15. E.g. by J.D. Meijer, *Esprit, origine et progrès des institutions judiciaires des principaux pays de l'Europe,* IV, 1820, p. 386.

16. As early as 1565 by Ayrault, see Hudault, loc. cit. p. 54.

17. D.J. Jitta, *Internationaal Privaatrecht,* 1916, p. 164, 591.

18. A.T. Von Mehren, "Recognition and enforcement of foreign judgments", *Recueil des Cours* 1980 II p. 99/100. See also K.H. Nadelmann, "Jurisdictionally improper fora in treaties of recognition of judgments", 67 Col. L. Rev. (1967) p. 1001 and *passim.* Asser Instituut, *Erkenning en tenuitvoerlegging van vreemde vonnissen in vermogensrechtelijke zaken* 1969, p. 35.

19. On the maxim *actor sequitur forum rei,* see C.C.A. Voskuil, *De internationale bevoegdheid van de Nederlandse rechter,* 1962, p. 78 et seq., and especially the succint analysis by J. Schröder, *Internationale Zuständigkeit,* 1971, p. 229 et seq., with references.

is still open, whether the forum actoris violates international law. The answer to this empirical question should be sought in contemporary national legislation, international conventions, and writings of legal scholars.

4. INTERNATIONAL LAW VERSUS FORUM ACTORIS

The forum rei rule, being the most constant and generally adopted of all jurisdiction rules [20], may certainly be said to be a principle recognized by civilized nations. However, no practical inferences can be drawn from that statement, since the forum rei is not exclusive. Throughout history and in all places there have been additional fora such as the *forum contractus*. Consequently, the forum rei rule is in any case not a positive rule of international law in the sense that *any* deviation from it would violate international law. It might be a permissive rule in the sense that a forum rei, provided for in national legislation, never violates international law, but this is an obvious and practically useless statement. The important question is, *to what extent* national legislatures are free to deviate from the rule, and more especially, whether the *forum actoris* does or does not violate international law. (The same question may be put as regards other "exorbitant" fora, but these are left out of consideration here.)

The forum actoris is not generally accepted (apart from particular matters such as maintenance). It exists in France and Luxembourg as the forum of the plaintiff's nationality [21], and in the Netherlands as the forum of the plaintiff's domicile [22]. A weaker form exists in Portugal [23], Italy [24], and Belgium [25].

Article 14 of the French CC has provoked retaliatory statutory provisions in Portugal, Italy, Belgium and Austria, which make the forum actoris available against nationals of a state that itself has that forum [26].

20. J.D. Meijer, op. cit. p. 374. In the Netherlands too, it is the general rule (Article 126(1) CCPr). The forum actoris only plays a role if the defendant has no known domicile or residence in the Kingdom (Article 126(3) CCPr). In France it is the general rule between foreigners: Batiffol/Lagarde, 1976 6, II, Nr. 673. For the EEC Countries in general: F. Pocar (see note 29) p. 91.

21. Article 14 CC, somewhat rashly introduced, see H. Gaudemet-Tallon, *Recherches sur les origines de l'article 14 du CC,* 1964.

22. Article 126(3) CCPr.

23. Article 65(1) (a) of the Portuguese CCPr bases the jurisdiction, *inter alia,* on the circumstance that "the action has to be brought in Portugal according to the Portuguese rules of territorial competence (venue)", whereas these latter rules indicate as competent, if the defendant is neither resident nor present within Portuguese territory, the forum of the plaintiff's domicile or, if the plaintiff is domiciled abroad, the court of Lisbon (Article 85). These provisions apparently only apply in cases in which the defendant has Portuguese nationality. Article 65(1) (c) provides that if the defendant is a foreigner and the plaintiff Portuguese, the Portuguese courts have jurisdiction if in the reverse situation the Portuguese could be sued before the courts of the State of which the other party is a national.

24. Articles 18(2) and 4(4) CCPr have the same tenor as the Portuguese Articles 85 and 65(1) (c) respectively.

25. *Idem,* Articles 638 and 636 (in a negative formula with the same effect) of the Code judiciaire.

26. Articles 65(1) (c) of the Portuguese CCPr. 4(4) of the Italian CCPr. 636 of the Belgian Code judiciaire. See the preceding notes. Para. 101 of the Austrian Jurisdiktionsnorm. In the Netherlands too, Article 127 CCPr (a translation of Article 14 French CC) was introduced

As far as enforcement treaties are concerned, they usually provide for the recognition and enforcement only of those judgments that are rendered by a court which has jurisdiction. In order to indicate which courts are considered to have jurisdiction, each treaty contains a list of accepted fora. These lists never include the forum actoris. It can therefore be argued that this forum is disapproved of to a certain extent, i.e., as a rule of jurisdiction of foreign courts. It is considered suitable for internal use only, not for exportation to the other contracting State(s). In so-called *traités doubles,* the jurisdiction is directly regulated, apart from the question of recognition and enforcement. Here the forum actoris is banished in a more radical fashion. It is also disapproved of for internal use, i.e., as a rule of jurisdiction of domestic courts. However, even here it is maintained in certain situations, i.e., where the defendant is not domiciled in a contracting State, or (in earlier treaties) where the defendant is not a national of or not domiciled in the other contracting State [27].

From this state of affairs one can conclude that the forum actoris is unusual and unpopular, but it would certainly be going too far to say that it violates international law. Its existence may have provoked some retaliatory statutory provisions, but it has not provoked diplomatic action of any relevance and frequency. On the contrary, the States which are Parties to the EEC Convention on Jurisdiction and Judgments [28] included it as part, although only a marginal part, of the system.

Legal scholars often flatly declare that customary international law does not impose any restrictions on the jurisdiction of courts in civil cases [29]. If they think it does, they speak of "extreme limits" [30], or mention, e.g., actions in rem concer-

---

because otherwise" "Dutchmen would be deprived of a privilege which others can use against them". Article 126(3) of the Dutch CCPr was originally meant as a supplementary venue provision. Later case law has ruled out Article 127, and Article 126(3) became the *sedes materiae* of the forum actoris, now based not on the nationality, but on the domicile of the plaintiff. See Joan van den Honert, *Handboek voor de burgerlijke rechtsvordering,* 1839, ad Article 127. C.C.A. Voskuil, op. cit., p. 68 et seq.

27. Article 4 of the EEC Convention of 1968. Articles 9, 10 and 3(2) of the Dutch-Belgian Treaty of 1925. Article 10 of the French-Belgian Treaty of 1899. Article 1(2) of the French-Swiss Treaty of 1869.

28. This convention may be classed as a "particular international convention" in the sense of Article 38(1) (a) of the Statute of the International Court of Justice. The permissive attitude was reciprocal, since the other Contracting States had their own exorbitant fora (patrimonii, arresti) accepted in the same way. Nadelmann speaks of an "odd alliance of nations with jurisdictionally improper bases".

29. A. Miaja de la Muela, "Les principes directeurs des règles de compétence territoriale des tribunaux internes en matière de litiges comportant un élément international", *Recueil des Cours* 1972 I p. 33 et seq., with references. *Adde* J. Schröder, *Internationale Zuständigkeit,* 1971, 234, 766. A.A. Ehrenzweig/E. Jayme, *Private International Law,* II, 1973, p. 7. M. Akehurst, *A modern introduction to international law,* 1977 3, 104. F. Pocar, in: Inst. Univ. Int. Luxembourg, *L'influence des Communautés européennes sur le d.i.p. des Etats membres,* 1981, p. 81.

30. W. Wengler, *Völkerrecht,* 1964, p. 947 n. 4: "äusserste völkerrechtliche Grenzen". He mentions as an example that no state may assume jurisdiction in matrimonial cases on the sole basis of the presence of assets belonging to the plaintiff. Cf., W. Jellinek, *Die zweiseitigen Staatsverträge über Anerkennung ausländischer Urteile,* 1953, p. 18. Brownlie, *Principles of public int. law,* 1979 3, p. 299.

ning foreign immovables [31], and disputes on execution taking place abroad [32]. The opinion that the forum actoris is contrary to international law is hardly ever voiced. Mulder raises the question in relation to Article 126(3) of the Dutch CCPr but does not answer it. He does think that Article 127 CCPr (= Art. 14 French CC) is "probably" contrary to international law but this is only because it discriminates against foreigners [33].

5. EXTRA-TERRITORIAL EFFECT OF FORUM ACTORIS JUDGMENTS

There is more to be said in favour of the proposition that international law forbids the exportation of a judgment rendered by a forum actoris.

The rule, that a foreign judgment originating from a forum actoris is not recognized or enforced, is fairly generally accepted in p.i.l., even in France and the Netherlands [34]. As regards treaty law, the *traités simples* have also adopted the rule, since they never include the forum actoris in their jurisdictional list.

It is true that the *traités doubles* do provide for reciprocal recognition and enforcement of such judgments if the defendant is not an inhabitant (national) of a contracting State. But this exception is a contingency rather than a wilful infringement of the rule. It is caused by the combination of an incomplete regulation of jurisdiction (for the protection of inhabitants or nationals only) on the one hand, and an overall regulation of reciprocal enforcement, on the other hand. The real point is that *within* the scope for which both topics have been thoroughly regulated, recognition and enforcement are made conditional upon a jurisdictional test, [34a]

31. Kosters-Dubbink, *Algemeen deel van het Nederlandse internationaal privaatrecht,* 1962, p. 729.

32. Cf. Cass. 12-5-1931 Sirey 1932.1.137 and the note by Niboyet, both referring to the principle of independence and sovereignty of States.

33. A.C.J. Mulder, *Internationaal privaatrecht,* 1947 2, p. 48. The authors mentioned in note 39 come closest to the opinion that the forum actoris violates international law. Compare also the protest of the US Department of State against the service of a summons for a Greek Court by the Greek consul in New Orleans on a US citizen resident in Louisiana. The summons related to action arising out of an automobile accident which occured in Louisiana involving a US citizen and a Greek national. According to the US Department of State, this exercise of jurisdiction was "not generally accepted under international law'. *(Digest of US Practice in International Law,* 1975, 339, referred to by Wengler, *Internationales Privatrecht,* 1981, p. 754 n. 5). I do not know on which Greek jurisdiction provision the case was based.

34. Holleaux, op. cit., p. 332, mentions the frequent use of the *actor sequitur* in checking the jurisdiction of foreign courts. Niboyet, *Cours de d.i.p.,* 1946, p. 655: "Aucun pays étranger n'acceptera la valeur d'un jugement rendu contrairement aux règles normales de la compétence". Batiffol/Lagarde p. 479 (at least "si le domicile du défendeur est en France"). For Dutch law, see: Asser Instituut, *Erkenning en tenuitvoerlegging van vreemde vonnissen in vermogensrechtelijke zaken,* 1969, 35. French version in: D. Kokkini-Iatridou et J.P. Verheul, *Les effets des jugements et sentences étrangers aux Pays-Bas,* 1970, p. 11, also in: *Neth. Reports to the VIIIth int. congress of comp. law,* Pescara 1970, Deventer 1970, p. 139. *Adde:* DC of Rotterdam 16 jan. 1976, WPNR 1979 p. 635. For Belgium, expressly, Art. 570(2) (3) Code judiciaire as regards the forum of the plaintiff's nationality.

34 a. As far as the EEC Convention on Jurisdiction and Judgments is concerned, this is only true in a broad sense. The judge, granting the order for enforcement, does not usually check the jurisdiction of the first court (Article 28). However, the drafters of the Convention considered that the first court should, and normally will, conform to the jurisdiction rules of Title II.

in which there is no room for the forum actoris. In addition, this marginal exception to the rule, through which the effective radius of the exorbitant fora is extended, was the target of strong protests [35] which were raised to the diplomatic level, in a manner of speaking, when the Hague Conference drafted the Supplementary Protocol to the Hague Convention on the Recognition and Enforcement of Foreign Judgments in Civil and Commercial Matters, of 1971. Article 2 of this Protocol provides:

> "Recognition and enforcement of a decision . . . *shall be refused* . . . where the decision was based, and in the circumstances could have been based, only on one or more of the grounds of jurisdiction specified in article 4" (italics added).

Article 4 sums up the *fora non grata,* which include the forum actoris.

The Convention and Protocol have so far only been ratified by the Netherlands and Cyprus, but at the Conference there was no objection to the tenor of Article 4 (b) and (c), which condemned the forum of the plaintiff's nationality and domicile, respectively. These provisions were unanimously accepted [36].

In the EEC Convention on Jurisdiction and Judgments, Article 59 was inserted so as to enable the Six to join the Hague Convention. The EEC Convention, including Article 59, has been in force since 1 February 1973.

The European Convention on State Immunity, of 16 May 1972, which has already entered into force between a few States,[37] is particularly interesting in this respect. This Convention deals mainly with immunity, but it also contains rules on jurisdiction and foreign judgments for situations in which the defendant State cannot claim immunity. To that extent this Convention falls under the category of international conventions which deal with jurisdiction and/or foreign judgments, such as the EEC Convention and the above-mentioned Hague Convention. The difference is that the Convention on State Immunity is concerned only with proceedings in which the defendant is a foreign State. Apart from this difference, however, there is a great deal of similarity. The Convention on State Immunity is acccompanied by an Annex, which adopts an almost identical black list of excessive fora to that of the Protocol to the Hague Convention. The complicated provisions of Articles 20(3)(a) and 25(3)(b) of the Convention on State Immunity imply that (in the matters concerned) a Contracting State is not obliged to give effect to a judgment rendered by one of these excessive fora mentioned in the Annex [38]. Thus, this Convention is another example of the opinion, already accepted in the various national p.i.l. systems and in other international conventions, that a judg-

35. Nadelmann, loc. cit. Von Mehren, loc. cit.

36. *Actes & Documents,* 1966 p. 490. When the final text of the Protocol as a whole was put to the vote, France and Germany abstained for some other reason (p. 491).

37. 11 ILM 470(1972). Tractatenblad 1973 No. 43. This Convention was ratified by Austria, Belgium and Cyprus (in force 11 June 1976) and afterwards by the U.K. (in force 4 October 1979). Among the signatory States are The Netherlands, Luxembourg and Portugal.

38. W.G. Belinfante, "Het Europese verdrag inzake de immuniteit van Staten", *Med. NVIR,* No. 67, May 1973, pp. 24, 26.

ment of a forum actoris (or other excessive fora) is as a rule not liable to recognition and enforcement in other countries.

Bearing in mind the above, it could be argued that the following rule is on the verge of becoming, or has already become, a rule of customary international law:

> A judgment rendered by a forum actoris shall not be granted extra-territorial effect, subject to international conventions to the contrary applicable to the case.

6. JUS GENTIUM CONSTITUENDUM. A MISSING LINK

If we suppose this rule to be a rule of customary international law, there is a striking inconsistency between it and the acceptance of the forum actoris as far as the jurisdiction of domestic courts is concerned. If the products of the forum actoris are not considered good enough for exportation, there can be no other reason than that there is something wrong with the forum actoris itself. The next logical step would be to prohibit the forum actoris in the national rules on international jurisdiction of domestic courts. By virtue of its inconsistency, international law itself suggests this step. To claim for oneself a wider jurisdiction than that which one recognizes to be possessed by a foreign court "is a claim which conflicts with the general principles of comity between civilized nations"[39].

There are already some indications that international law is making attempts to smooth out the above-mentioned inconsistency. At the Hague Conference the UK and USA delegations tried to link together the jurisdiction of foreign courts and the jurisdiction of domestic courts, and proposed that the exorbitant jurisdiction-rules *"shall cease to be applicable"* between the Contracting States.[40] This part of the proposal had to be dropped because some delegations were afraid to exceed their mandate. The drafters of the European Convention on State Immunity had more success in linking together the two topics. Article 24(2) provides that the courts of a State *shall not be entitled to entertain proceedings* against another Contracting State, as described in paragraph 1 of that Article, "if their jurisdiction could have been based solely on one or more of the grounds mentioned in the Annex". This is a direct jurisdictional rule like those contained in Title II of the EEC Convention on Jurisdiction and Judgments.

Drafters of international conventions are not the only creators of international law. National courts, inter alia, also have a task in this field. A single national court cannot change international law but it can at least contribute to its development in the desired direction. The two judgments of the District Court of Rotterdam mentioned in notes 2 and 3 may be intended to be modest contributions of this type towards a consistent condemnation of the forum actoris, i.e., not only from the point of view of the recognition of foreign judgments, but also in the context of the rules of international jurisdiction of domestic courts.

39. Mackender v. Feldia (1967) 2 WLR 119, CA., *per* Diplock. See also F.A. Mann, "The doctrine of jurisdiction in international law", *Recueil des Cours* 1964 I p. 75. L.I. de Winter, "Excessive jurisdiction in p.i.l.", ICLQ, 1968, 806.

40. *Actes & Documents*, 1966, p. 288.

These two judgments cannot be said to apply international law as it stands now, but they are attempting to develop it. Since international law, like any other field of law, is not static and its development is unavoidable, the *jus constituendum* cannot be dispensed with as a guideline in judicial practice[41]. In the field of tension between *jus constitutum* and *jus constituendum,* whether one wants to be the first sheep to leap over the ditch, or rather stay behind with the "timorous souls", is ultimately a matter of preference and character.

Of the above-mentioned two judgments, one refers expressly to international law, the other does not. This difference is fairly immaterial. Akehurst [42] has rightly warned that those writers and courts who spoke or speak in this context of a rule belonging to the "Law of Nations", often mean none other than *jus gentium* in the original Latin sense, as the law common to all people.[43] In this sense it is just a comparative observation, perhaps mixed with a feeling that it is *desirable* to conform to such a rule, but not implying that conforming is *obligatory.* However, the reverse may also be true. Courts may consciously *not* refer to public international law, especially when it does not seem to conform with their national law. In order to avoid an open conflict between the two, they sometimes prefer to manipulate the possibilities existing within their national legal system, e.g., by using public policy or the doctrine of *forum non conveniens* [44]. To a court it is not very relevant whether it is developing public international law or (national) private international law, as long as it can contribute to the desired universal uniformity. Unless one is overestimating the verbal aspects, one must admit that such decisions, irrespective of the construction used, may play a part in the process by which a rule shifts from the domain of mere comity to that of public international law [45].

7. THE PUBLIC ASPECT OF THE RHINE POLLUTION CASE

In the Rhine pollution case, however, the District Court had no leeway whatsoever to decline jurisdiction, either under international law or under Dutch law.

41. Cf., G. van Hecke, "Principes et méthodes en d.i.p.", *Recueil des Cours,* 1969 I, 419. As regards the part (to be) played by national courts in the formation of international law, see Erades & Gould, op. cit. p. 223 et seq., and Erades, "International Law and the Netherlands Legal Order", in: *International law in the Netherlands,* III, 1980, 375.

42. Akehurst, "Jurisdiction in International law", BYIL 1972-73, 145, at p. 212.

43. Hence formerly also called "natural law", and sometimes identified with Roman law. Dutch authors described the *forum arresti* as contrary to "written law" or to Roman law, but nonetheless considered it to be valid law in force in Holland (Vromans, op. cit., p. 121, Pieter Bort, *Alle de wercken,* 1731 3, p. 466. J. van der Linden, *Verhandeling over de judicieele practijck,* 1794, p. 269). The traditional supplementary idea was that "particular" laws deviating from the "common" law were permitted but had only local validity. Compare the conclusion in the judgment mentioned in note 3, that the French judgment was "valid only within French territory".

44. Cf., District Court of Alkmaar 1 Dec. 1977, NILR 1981 210, profiting from an uncertainty in the law in order to decline jurisdiction based on garnishment for situations in which a recognizable judgment can be obtained from the foreign forum rei. In Mackender *v.* Feldia, the Court was also exercising a discretion (see note 39).

45. G. van Hecke, loc. cit., p. 418.

Even if customary international law contains civil jurisdiction rules, they are certainly not *jus cogens* and must give way to international conventions to which the forum State is a party. The EEC Convention on Jurisdiction and Judgments, as interpreted by the European Court of Justice, prevailed.

Furthermore, a court is bound by the rules of the game of the legal system from which it received its mandate, even in its interpretation and application of rules of international law [46]. This statement, whatever its consequences may be in other respects, obviously entailed in this case that the District Court was simply obliged to obey the Court of Appeal's decision that the Disctrict Court did have jurisdiction. The *forum non conveniens* doctrine could not be used. Even the formula "True, I have jurisdiction, but I do not see fit to exercise it", would have amounted to evasion and disobedience after all that had happened [47].

In my opinion, the District Court did not dream of declining jurisdiction, and its dicta on this point were inspired by a practical motive. (In this context aversion to the forum actoris may have played a secondary part.) A practical lawyer does not like to enter into expensive and time consuming proceedings merely for an academic purpose. The final judgment must be executed. In the present case, if the Court decides in favour of the plaintiffs, execution in France will have to proceed on the basis of the EEC Convention on Jurisdiction and Judgments. Under this Convention, the French judge, asked to grant the order for enforcement, may refuse it if enforcement would be contrary to French public policy (Articles 27(1) and 34). This escape clause might be utilized by the French judge, reasoning as follows: The term "public policy" includes the public interests, or the social and economic policies of the French State. The issue of the Rhine pollution is far more important than the private interests of the litigating parties. It has been the subject of laborious negotiations between the riparian States, and of social unrest in the Alsace where an alternative solution was sought for the dumping of waste salts. Closing down the *Mines de Potasse* would increase unemployment. The decisions to be made by the French Government require a careful weighing up of opposing interests. In other words, the issue is a "political question" in which even a French court would perhaps hesitate to interfere. Thus, a decision of a foreign court, which is moreover the forum of the plaintiffs and which has applied their own law, is contrary to French public policy. In my opinion such reasoning would be incorrect because it extends the concept of public policy beyond its natural limits and amounts to a disguised review of the merits, forbidden by Article 29 of the Convention. But it cannot be denied that the case is not an ordinary private case.

The District Court recognizes the public character of the controversy, but adds another twist. The issue "is primarily a question for international adjudication". It would be best if litigation between the two States were to take place before the

46. H.F. Van Panhuys, "Relations and interactions between international and national scenes of law", *Recueil des Cours,* 1964 II, p. 48.

47. Let alone the fact that the controversy revealed real contacts with the forum country.

International Court of Justice.[48] Now that the District Court is obliged to deal with it, the Court makes the best of it and stresses that the way in which the case is handled is *in conformity* with public international law, as regards jurisdiction as well as the substance. The Court thus reduces a possible suspicion of partiality[49], and ensures that the future final decision will approximate as closely as possible to the solution which an international court would have reached. Since the applied Dutch law "includes the unwritten rules of international law" which are also valid in France, it will be difficult to declare the solution contrary to French public policy. And since the court's jurisdiction may also be justified from the viewpoint of customary public international law, it may be considered as a substitute organ of the international community of which France is a part.

In this context the forum actoris problem only arises in the consideration that public international law does not object to the forum actoris in pollution cases, where it is also the *forum damni.* However, in addition there is a slight possibility that the Court's scruples on the point of jurisdiction are partly the result of the fact that the real defendant was the French State. The doctrine of State immunity, although not applicable in the present case, might have the side effect of creating the feeling that it is uncourteous to sue a State before the court of another State, when that court is a forum actoris or other exorbitant forum.[50]

However this may be, the Court's main motive must have been Van Bynkershoek's practical wisdom that the ultimate purpose of any judgment is its execution.

48. I reserve commenting on the question of exhaustion of local remedies, not mentioned by the Court. An interesting question is, whether the application in France for an order for enforcement of a Dutch judgment could count as a local remedy in this sense.

49. J.G. Lammers, "New international legal developments concerning the pollution of the Rhine", NILR 1980, 190.

50. Cf. article 24(2) of the European Convention on State Immunity. In the District Court of Alkmaar 1 Dec. 1977 (note 44) the defendant was the Republic of Malta, and the Court a *forum arresti.*

ON "GIVING A HAND" IN SWEDISH LAW OF CIVIL PROCEDURE: Recent developments in the law on handräckning.

by C.C.A. Voskuil*

1. INTRODUCTION[1]

In 1960 the Swedish Government decided to entrust to the law commission *(Lagberedningen)* the preparation of a comprehensive reform of the law on execution in matters of private law.

The law commission has since worked out a range of proposals with regard to the various sections of this area of the law. As usual, an elaborate process of consultations followed. It all led in the end to the drafting of a new Code of execution, named *Utsökningsbalk,* by which to replace the then existing rules on execution in civil matters, as contained, mainly, in the now abolished *Utsökningslag* (Act on execution) of 1877 (1877:31)[2].

The Bill introducing the *Utsökningsbalk* was passed in 1981. The new Code came into force on 1 January 1982 along with a number of affiliated statutes.[3]

> In Sweden, the legislative process is very much an exercise in democracy. The commission to which the preparation of a reform of the law has been entrusted will do the initial spade-work as well as the preliminary drafting. It will then submit its findings and proposals to a great variety of institutions in the community for advice. Such consultations are by no means a mere formality. In as far as the preparatory work for the *Utsökningsbalk* is concerned, one is struck by the impact that interventions on the part of a considerable number of "consulted institutions" *(remissinstanser)* have made on proposals in respect of the law reform submitted by *Lagberedningen.*[4]

* Director, T.M.C. Asser Institute for International Law, The Hague; Member of the Board of Editors.

1. The present article was written in the course of a research visit to the University of Uppsala, Sweden, which was made possible by the European Science Foundation, Strasbourg, as part of a research scheme initiated by that Foundation and aimed at conducting a comparative study of summary adjudication in a number of European countries. The author wishes to express his sincere gratitude to the European Science Foundation for the invaluable support received, and to the Faculty of Law in Uppsala University for the hospitality and assistance enjoyed throughout the period of his stay in Uppsala.

2. For the publication of Swedish statutes, references are made to *Svensk Författningssamling (SFS).*

3. The word *balk,* as in *Utsökningsbalk,* is an ancient notion in Swedish law, which may best be defined as "section" of the comprehensive collections of statutes, or as "section" of the entire Code of Law. In this essay we shall use the term "code". For a survey of the "affiliated statutes", see *Utsökningsbalken,* a commentary by Gösta Walin, Torkel Gregow and Peter Löfmark (all actively engaged in the present reform of execution law in Sweden), Stockholm 1982, pp. 605 et seq. References to this commentary will further be made by mention of the first author, Chairman of the Law Commission charged with preparing the present law reform, G. Walin.

4. For a brief survey of the work of the Law Commission, see G. Walin, *op. cit.,* pp. 5-7 *(Förord).*

The law reform that has led to the introduction of the *Utsökningsbalk* brought about some important changes in respect of the institutions of summary judicial intervention, collectively known by the ancient notion of *handräckning:* summary judicial "assistance" *(handräckning)* for the purpose of providing instant relief[5]. First of all there was a rather radical reorganization of the machinery of execution which resulted in the office of the chief execution authority being abolished. Under the former *Utsökningslag* the chief execution authority *(överexekutor)* had played a major part both in matters of execution proper and in, *inter alia, handräckning*-proceedings.

Secondly, the reform in the field of execution coincided at some stage with, if not entailed, a revision of the law of summary adjudication for the collection of money debts *(lagsökning* and *betalningsföreläggande).*

At the outset, the plans to reorganize the machinery of execution did not only include the abolition of the office of the *överexekutor.* A reorganization of the office of the lower execution authority *(kronofogde)* was envisaged as well. The idea was that the number of *kronofogde*-districts should be restricted. At the same time it was proposed that the (remaining) districts be reinforced and that the lower execution authorities be granted wider powers in the field of summary adjudication. Apart from taking over the functions of the *överexekutor* in *handräckning*-proceedings, the proposed lower execution authorities were meant to become the intervening authorities in matters of *lagsökning* and *betalningsföreläggande.*[6] In fact, the planned reorganization of the office of the *kronofogde* constituted a prime motive for a reform of the latter proceedings to be taken up.

As the preparatory work proceeded both as regards the law of execution and the law on *handräckning* as well as on *lagsökning* and *betalningsföreläggande,* the plans to reorganize the office of the lower execution authorities so as to restrict the number of *kronofogde*-districts and simultanously to upgrade them to some extent, were dropped.[7] Consequently, a major reason for the law on *lagsökning* and *betalningsföreläggande* to be reformed, had disappeared.

However, the original scheme did not fail to have an impact on the reform that was yet to be carried out – the reform of the institution of summary adjudication that had hitherto been among the tasks of the *överexekutor:* summary judicial assistance *(handräckning)* under Paragraphs 191 and 192 of the *Utsökningslag.* Since the reform of the law of execution did go ahead and the office of the *överexekutor* was to be abolished, something had to be done in any event about the law on *handräckning.* What was done in the end bears the hallmarks of the original scheme according to which the new *handräckning* proceedings were to be modelled after – and indeed merged with – the proceedings in *lagsökning* and *betallningsföreläggande.*

5. For a survey in English of the various *handräckning*-proceedings, see Ruth B. Ginsburg and Anders Bruzalins, *Civil Procedure in Sweden* (Columbia University School of Law Project on International Procedure) (The Hague 1965), pp. 216 et seq.
The work was published well before the present law reform resulted in the changes discussed in this essay. For a brief but excellent survey in Swedish see, Publication of the Ministry of Justice, Ds Ju 1977: 5: *Summarisk Process.* Further, Lars Heuman, *Specialprocess Utsökning och Konkurs* (Lund 1981) pp. 43 et seq; Per Olof Ekelöf, *Rattegång* III, 4th ed. (Stockholm/ Lund 1980) pp. 7 et seq; Åke Hasseler, *Specialprocess* (Stockholm 1972) pp. 81 et seq.

6. For a discussion of proceedings in *lagsökning* and *betalningsföreläggande* see, *infra* section 5.

7. For the consequences of this change of policy see, in particular, *infra* section 4.

As a result of these developments we cannot possibly limit ourselves to a discussion of just the new rules on *handräckning,* as contained in the recently introduced *Handräckningslag.*[8] We shall have to pay some attention to the Swedish law of summary adjudication in general as well as to summary debt-collecting proceedings in particular.

After the present introductory chapter we shall first have a look at the now abolished office of the chief execution authority *(överexekutor)* and particularly at the judicial functions that were entrusted to the *överexekutor* under the *Utsökningslag* of 1877.

A third chapter will be reserved for a general survey of summary adjudication, if only for the purpose of introducing a scheme for the discussion of the various institutions of summary judicial intervention provided for in the Swedish law of civil procedure.

Following this general discussion of summary proceedings, we shall take a closer look at the law reform efforts which led to the introduction of the *Handräckningslag.*

Next we shall focus our attention on the reform which has been undertaken in respect of summary proceedings in matters of debt collecting, but which have been extended so as fundamentally to affect the reform of *handräckning*-proceedings.

Once we have reached this stage, we shall be adequately equipped for an assessment of the *Handräckningslag* and of what it reflects: a comprehensive reform of summary adjudication in Sweden.

As we proceed we shall include references to Dutch law and compare Swedish procedural institutions with their counterparts in The Netherlands. The emphasis will be very much on Swedish law, however, and on the contents of the *Handräckningslag,* the text of which will be partly included in the final chapter.

2. THE OFFICE OF THE CHIEF EXECUTION AUTHORITY

As the notion of *överexekutor* suggests, the chief execution authority had its primary responsibilities in the field of execution. According to the now abolished *Utsökningslag* (para. 1), proceedings for the enforcement of judicial decisions and other executory titles[9] "are to be taken up and handled (by the *överexekutor)* unless otherwise provided". The deviations from the general rule were many and in matters of execution proper much of the work was actually carried out by the common execution authority, the office of the *utmättningsman,* known by the name of *kronofogde.*

Apart from being charged with duties in the field of execution, where he had a role to play but where, at the same time, he would supervise the office of the *kronofogde (Utsökningslag,* para. 2), the chief execution officer was also entrusted

8. *Handräckningslag* of 25 June 1981, in force 1 January 1982 (1981:847).

9. Titles for execution, listed in para. 1, Ch. 3 *Utsökningsbalken.* See for commentary, G. Walin, *op. cit.*, pp. 66 et seq.

with a number of judicial functions. His offices could be engaged by any creditor who wished his claim against a reluctant debtor to be secured through measures such as provisional attachment *(kvarstad),* an injunction by which to prevent interference with the debtor's assets *(skingringsförbud)* or a travel restraint *(reseförbud).*[10] It was, moreover, the *överexekutor* whose intervention was required whenever enforcement was sought of judicial decisions issued in any of the other Scandinavian countries, or of arbitral awards issued in Sweden.

In spite of the judicial nature of these and other functions of the *överexekutor* the organization of the execution authorities to which he belonged *(exekutiva myndigheter)* is in no way formally linked to the Judiciary. In practice, however, the functions of the *överexekutor* could well be entrusted to members of the Judiciary.
The dividing line between, on the one hand, judicial functions and, on the other, offices of the Executive, has been tested before in Swedish law of procedure when the *kronofogde* was the authority to whom to apply in matters of *lagsökning* and *betalningsföreläggande,* – a situation that was changed by the *Lägsökningslag* (1937) which provided for intervention in these matters by a common first instance court.[11]

Among the judicial functions of the *överexekutor* was that of summary adjudication in *handräckning*-proceedings. This form of summary judicial intervention had its statutory basis in the now abolished *Utsökningslag,* which in paragraphs 191 and 192 provided for two closely related kinds of *handräckning.*[12] We have already seen, that the provisions of paragraphs 191 and 192 of the *Utsökningslag* have not been replaced by corresponding provisions in the new Code of Execution, but by a separate statute: the *Handräckningslag,* of 25 June 1981 (1981:847), which came into force, along with the *Utsökningsbalk,* on 1 January 1982.

Later on we shall have a closer look at the now abolished provisions of paragraphs 191 et seq. of the *Utsökningslag.* Before this, and before dealing with the question of how the gap was filled which was left by the departure of the *överexekutor,* we shall examine some aspects of summary adjudication and outline a scheme for the discussion of the Swedish law reform from which the *Handräckningslag* resulted.

3. SUMMARY JUDICIAL INTERVENTION
some general observations

One of the early attempts at drafting a comprehensive and systematic Code of Law was made in the name of Frederick the Great of Prussia. This eighteenth century monarch, known for his enlightened style, his musical talents, his perception

10. For a brief discussion of security measures see, *infra* section 3.
11. See, P.H. Lindblom, *Lagsökning de lege ferenda,* note 9, pp. 412/3 and p. 402, *sub* 4.3: *Handläggande myndighet.*
12. For a discussion of these provisions see, *infra,* section 6.1

of military matters and for so much more, deserves to be remembered too for a most remarkable legislative endeavour, incomplete and defective as it may have been: his attempt at preparing and introducing a Code of Law, *"based on Reason and on the constitutions of the lands".* A true monument to the Age of Reason. The introductory part contains the Plan of the King in which it is explained why a Code was needed and what purpose it was to serve. One of the aims to which particular attention is given is the repression of the then current practices in the legal trade which were considered the cause of lengthy, time-absorbing proceedings. These practices are exposed in pretty tough language. Delays are, it is maintained, very much to the benefit of the profession but constitute a harmful and unneccessary disadvantage to those who seek justice. No trial, it is argued in the Introduction that follows upon the *"Plan du Roi"*, should be allowed to last for more than one year.

The desire to repress the negative effects of the often frustrating time factor in civil proceedings is hard to satisfy. The process of finding the law that is to be established between the parties in litigation does inevitably take time. Even in our days in which the procedural machinery is so much more sophisticated and better equipped than in Frederick's eighteenth century Europe, we do not seem to be able in general to meet the requirements set out by the Prussian prince.

Efforts to reduce delays and to minimize the disadvantages they may cause have led, *inter alia,* to the introduction of all kinds of summary proceedings.

There is, indeed, a rich variety of institutions of summary adjudication in both systems of civil procedure under survey, ranging from merely shortened versions of the ordinary full proceedings on the merits, to special forms of procedure, summary and on the merits, designed for specific classes of claims. To this we may add the institutions of provisional judicial intervention which, particularly in The Netherlands, have nowadays come to play such a significant role in civil procedure. Moreover, security measures may help to avert disadvantages which could result from lengthy procedural delays.

Three categories of procedural institutions which reflect the everlasting struggle with time appear from this brief survey:

(1) First the summary proceedings which lead, as the case may be, to final judicial decisions on the merits. They may be more or less general in scope such as, in the Netherlands the "brief delay proceedings" *(civiele procedure op verkorte termijn)*[13], and, in Sweden, the "proceedings involving limited values" *(mål om mindre värden)*[14]. They may, on the other hand, be of a more restricted nature such as in both countries the proceedings, summary and on the merits, for the collection of money debts. In The Netherlands these special proceedings are limited

13. Art. 145 Dutch Code of Civil Procedure *(Wetboek van Burgerlijke Rechtsvordering,* hereafter: Rv.).

14. Act of 4 January 1974 (1974:8), *om rättegången i tvistemål om mindre värden (Småmålslagen).* This Act plays an essential part in the recent plans for revising the Swedish Code of Procedure, as is explained in Section 4 hereafter.

in scope: they may only be instituted for the collection of small money debts[15]. The Swedish counterpart is of a more liberal nature. It includes two separate procedural institutions: *lagsökning* (a documentary process for the collection of debts) and *betalningsföreläggande* (a procedural means to put pressure upon the reluctant debtor in cases in which the claim cannot be supported by a written instrument). Either process may only be instituted for the collecting of a definite sum of money. Both proceedings have been provided for in a separate statute: the *Lag om lagsökning och betalningsföreläggande*[16].

Many more examples could be taken from either system of procedural law of summary proceedings restricted to special classes of claims. The proceedings for the collection of money debts have been singled out because of the particular significance of the Swedish institution of *lagsökning* in the law reform operation which had a direct bearing upon the *Handräckningslag,* introduced January 1982.

(2) The second category which appeared from the brief survey above consists of summary proceedings leading, as the case may be, to provisional judicial decisions.

In civil procedure the term "provisional" is a rather complex notion. It is used in connection with two very different situations:
On the one hand it is applied to judicial intervention as such so as to indicate that a particular judicial decision is not strictly based on a determination of the legal rights and obligations of the parties concerned, but rather on an appreciation of the – legally relevant – interests involved in the case. If so conceived, the judicial decision may provide a title for execution but it will not be final. The provisional judicial decision is enforceable – often provisionally so[17]; its authority, however, is not supported by the *res iudicata* effect as regards (main) proceedings that may be subsequently instituted.[18]
In respect of execution or enforcement, on the other hand, the notion of "provisional" is used to indicate that enforcement is or may be carried out in spite of the fact that ordinary remedies are still available to the defendant. Under Dutch law of civil procedure, for instance, the enforcement of a judgment will normally be barred if appeal has been lodged. (Comp. Article 350 of the Dutch Code of civil procedure.) A first instance court may, however, in certain circumstances order "provisional enforceability" *(uitvoerbaarheid bij voorraad)* of a judgment, so as to enable the plaintiff to have the judgment enforced without delay. (Comp. in Swedish law: Ch. 17, para. 14, *Rättegångsbalken.)*
Security measures, necessarily provisional and temporary, are enforceable under similar conditions: they are taken in anticipation of the outcome of proceedings on the merits.

15. Rv. 125 k et seq. Claims for the collection of small money debts are handled by the lower first instance courts *(Kantongerechten).*

16. For a discussion of this Act see, *infra* section 5.

17. "Provisionally" in terms of execution; see next paragraph.

18. Comp. W. van Rossem, R.P. Cleveringa, *Burgerlijke Rechtsvordering,* Note 6 to Art. 289, pp. 766-7.

In Dutch law of civil procedure the proceedings conducted *in kort geding* (literally: in summary process, an institution which is akin to the *référé*-proceedings in French law of civil procedure) are the obvious example to refer to. They are conducted before the President of a first instance court *(Arrondissements-Rechtbank)* in cases where judicial intervention is required "without delay". The President if acting as *référé*-judge is not supposed to speak out on the rights and obligations of the parties in litigation. He will base his decision on an appreciation of the legally relevant interests involved in the case.[19] There is no real counterpart in Swedish procedural law. Summary adjudication as provided for in paragraphs 191 et seq. of the now ablished *Utsökningslag* did contain elements of provisionality but, as we have seen, these provisions have been replaced by the *Handräckningslag* of 1981 which leaves very little room for the taking of decisions that are of a merely provisional nature.[20]

One of the striking features of the Swedish law reform in the field of procedure and execution is the trend towards establishing a sharp division between, on the one hand, adjudication, full or summary but in any case on the merits and final, and, on the other, the taking of provisional measures, either in the course of proceedings or separately but in any case strictly linked to proceedings on the merits. There is no middle road; no room, it seems, for the kind of provisional summary adjudication provided for in the Dutch law on the *référé*-proceedings; no provisional adjudication to be carried out independently from any pending or subsequent litigation on the merits. We shall come back to this when in the following section we take a closer look at Swedish law of civil procedure, particularly at the rules on summary adjudication and at the changing landscape in the fringe area between adjudication proper and execution.

The granting of provisional orders in *référé*-proceedings shows certain similarities to the taking of security measures. In practice the dividing line may be very vague indeed, particularly so if the comparison is between provisional – possibly even temporary – prohibition orders issued in *référé*-proceedings, and security measures – necessarily provisional and temporary – taken with a view to prohibiting conduct that would be apt to interfere with or impede future performance or execution. There is therefore every reason to include security measures in the present scheme even though the *Handräckningslag* which we have set out to discuss does not provide for security measures but for summary adjudication on the merits.

(3) In that brief survey which marks the beginning of the present chapter on summary judicial intervention in general, security measures were mentioned as a third category in the scheme of procedural institutions devised for the purpose of reducing procedural delays or averting the harmful effects that delays may cause.

19. Statutory basis of *référé*-proceedings in the Netherlands; Rv. 289 et seq.
20. For a discussion of paras. 191 and 192 *Utsökningslag* and of the *Handräckningslag* which replaced these provisions see, *infra* section 6.

Intervention by a court or some other authority – like, in Sweden, previously the *överexekutor* – for the taking of security measures is not commonly put on a par with summary adjudication. Yet, depending on the kind of security measures available under a given system of procedural law, the two may come very close and, under circumstances, even overlap in practice. Swedish law in respect of security measures contains all the ingredients by which to demonstrate this.

We have come across some of the Swedish security-measures *(säkerhetsåtgärder)* when we discussed the various functions of the *överexekutor* under the former *Utsökningslag.* Their proper habitat is in Chapter 15 of the Swedish Code of Procedure *(Rättegångsbalken),* which contains rules on both civil and criminal procedure . The provisions contained in this chapter have been revised as part of the law reform that led to the introduction of the *Utsökningsbalk* on 1 January 1982. The revision resulted, *inter alia,* in the merger of the institutions of *kvarstad* (provisional attachment) and *skingringsförbud* (injunction by which to prevent interference with the debtor's assets), as well as in the abolition – at least as a measure in civil procedure – of the *reseförbud* (travel restraint), which was considered a measure which unduly affected the freedom of the individual.

Chapter 15 of the *Rättegångsbalk* contains yet another provision on the taking of security measures: the provision of paragraph 3, which has also been revised as part of the reform of execution law.

Before its revision, paragraph 3 of Chapter 15, *Rättegångsbalken* read as follows:
"If a party to a pending action has shown good ground to support his claim and it can be reasonably expected that the adverse party, by carrying on a certain activity, or performing or refraining from performing a certain act, or by any other conduct, will prevent or render difficult execution of an anticipated judgment, or diminish substantially its value for the claimant, the court may direct the adverse party, on penalty of a fine, to perform or refrain from performing an act, or may appoint a custodian to administer the property, or impose any other sanction necessary to secure the claimant's legal right. Such orders may also issue in other cases in which provisional relief is of special importance to the claimant and is not substantially detrimental to the adverse party."[21]

Measures as provided for in paragraph 3 – and indeed in the paragraphs on the other security measures, like *kvarstad* – could be ordered by the *överexekutor* as well, either pending court proceedings or in anticipation of proceedings on the merits. (See in connection with para. 3: para. 187a of the former *Utsökninglag.)*
Under the revised rules of Chapter 15 *Rättegångsbalken,* the powers formerly entrusted to the chief execution authority are now with the courts of first instance. At the request of a litigant the courts may take security measures either by way of interim decisions or outside court proceedings. In the latter case, however, subsequent litigation on the merits is a condition: the measures will lose effect if within thirty days after they have been ordered, proceedings on

21. The Swedish Code of Judicial procedure, transl. and introd. by Ginsburg and Bruzelius, The American Series of foreign penal codes, N. 15, Stb. Hackensack/London, 1968, p. 68.

the merits are not instituted – before a court, before arbitrators or before any other competent judicial authority (para. 7).
In their brief commentary to paragraph 3 of the revised Chapter 15, *Rättegångsbalken* the authors of the textbook on the *Utsökningsbalk* and affiliated statutes[22] make the following observation:
"A provisional arrangement of the legal relationship between the parties, before the case has been handled by a court or by another (judicial) authority, should not be made without firm reason. The conflicting interests of the parties must be balanced against each other."

It is all apt to remind us strongly of the *référé*-proceedings under Dutch law of civil procedure: the kind of injunctions to which paragraph 3 pertains, the summary nature of the court's intervention, the threat of fine which may be included so as to support the decision, the fact that the decision will be based on an appreciation of the interests rather than on a determination of the rights and obligations of the parties concerned – these are all elements which perfectly fit the *référé*-proceedings.

Yet, there is an essential difference between the two institutions. The measures to which paragraph 3 of Chapter 15 *Rättegångsbalken* relates are security measures, closely linked with pending or subsequent litigation on the merits and as such of a strictly temporary nature.

The rules on *référé*-adjudication in Dutch law of civil procedure do not impose any such restriction on the decision of the Court's President. The latter may well include restrictions in his provisional judgment. He may introduce a time-limit or even make his judgment conditional on subsequent institution of proceedings on the merits. But, normally, it will be entirely up to the parties whether to accept the provisional interest-orientated decision as virtually final and leave it at that, or to fight on to have their legal relationship conclusively defined by a judicial authority in the form of a final judgment on the merits.

The remarkable thing is that parties more often than not refrain from instituting proceedings on the merits once a provisional judgment has been obtained from the President of a first instance court, or, on appeal, from a court of appeal acting in *référé*-adjudication.

It may be so that in many cases people are more interested in having their disputes settled by an independent authority than in obtaining the final word in justice.

In Sweden, rules on the basis of which summary adjudication of the kind known as *référé*-proceedings might have been developed, were contained in paragraphs 191 et seq. of the former *Utsökningslag.* As was mentioned before, however, the *Handräckningslag* which replaced those provisions, leaves little room for truly provisional adjudication of the kind provided by the law regarding *référé*-proceedings.

22. G. Walin, *op. cit.* p. 662.

4. THE LAW REFORM: LANDSCAPING IN THE FIELD OF CIVIL PROCEDURE

When in Sweden the new rules on execution, presently enacted in the *Utsökningsbalk* were being drafted and it was decided that the *överexekutor* should be removed from the legal scene, the obvious question was: what to do with his legacy? What authority had to be charged with his functions in the field of execution? Who was going to take over his judicial duties?

Initially there appears to have been a strong feeling in the drafting commission that, quite generally, a somewhat upgraded office of the *kronofogde* (the ordinary execution authority) should replace the chief execution authority in its various functions, whether purely executionary or judicial in character.[23]

This approach coincided and indeed fitted in with plans of the Ministry of Justice to prepare a reform of the law on summary proceedings for the collection of money debts, presently enacted as we have seen, in the *Lag om lagsökning och betalningsföreläggande.* The idea was to revise the debt collecting procedures so as to make them a more – or even more – efficient device.[24] A merger of the two institutions of *lagsökning* and *betalningsföreläggande* was contemplated and made part of a new design.

As has been explained before, this new design had a decisive impact on the revision of the *handräckning*-proceedings, which resulted in the present *handräckningslag.* It has, in the meantime, become very doubtful whether the design will be carried out completely. With regard to the revision of the law of civil proceedings as a whole, fresh initiatives have been developed which may well lead to an entirely new approach to the reshaping of the law on summary adjudication in Sweden. The legislative strategy which is likely to replace the plans for a merger of *handräckning,* and *lagsökning*-proceedings[25], has clearly been inspired by an article, published in 1977 in the *Tidskrift för Sveriges Advokatsamfund* (TSA) by Per Henrik Lindblom, Professor of Procedural Law in Uppsala University.[26] In this article Lindblom thoroughly and critically discusses the original design as laid down in an official publication of the Ministry of Justice in Sweden *(Departements-promemoria* Ds Ju 1977-5, published under the title: *Summarisk Process).* Even though the *Handräckningslag* which we have set out to discuss was not really affected by the new developments in legislation with regard to procedure, we cannot just ignore these developments; they have become part of the landscape to which the *Handräckningslag* belongs.

In 1977 the Swedish Ministry of Justice published the proposals for a reform of, inter alia, the law on *lagsökning* and *betalningsföreläggande* in the *promemoria* entitled *Summarisk Process* (Ds Ju 1977-5). The publication contained a draft

23. *Summarisk Process,* Ds Ju 1977: 5, pp. 12 et seq. (Publication of Ministery of Justice).

24. *Rationellare summarisk betaliningsprocess,* Ds Ju 1981: 11 (Publication of Ministry of Justice). This publication contains statistical information, as well as information on the reform plans as regards summary proceedings for the collection of money debts.

25. Ds Ju 1977-5, *Summarisk Process.*

26. Per Henrik Lindblom, *Lagsökning de lege ferenda, Tidskrift för Sveriges Advokatsamfund,*

for a new *Lagsökningslag,* which covered both the proceedings for the recovery of money debts *(lagsökning* and *betalningsfördläggande)* and the *handräckning*-proceedings as provided by paragraphs 191 et seq. of the *Utsökningslag,* which at the time was still in force: a merger of two – or rather three – important institutions of summary adjudication.

In as far as *handräckning* was concerned, a reform was necessary as a result of the planned reform of the law on execution and, more particularly, of the envisaged abolition of the office of the *överexekutor.* We discussed this earlier. It was similarly explained that the plans to reform the *lagsökning*-proceedings lacked that same compelling ground. The reform of execution law did not really affect the latter proceedings and since the plans to reorganize the office of the lower execution authorities *(kronofogde)* had been dropped, the main consideration for reforming the law on *lagsökning* and *betalningsföreläggande* had vanished.

Lindblom opens his article in TSA with a survey of the various reform plans that preceeded the proposals contained in Ds Ju 1977-5. He then lists the changes that the latest plan is to bring about before engaging upon a detailed discussion of that plan. He does not challenge that there is a case for law reform in the area under discussion, not only as regards the *handräckning*-proceedings which are directly affected by the reform of the law of execution, but also as regards summary adjudication in a wider sense. However, he rejects the policy of conducting a fragmentary reform as proposed in the *promemoria* arguing that this reform is based on grounds which do not appear compelling at all.

Under the heading *Perspektivet* (the perspective) the author introduces ideas that may well be regarded as basic in the approach to a future reform policy in the field of civil procedure. Here again he rejects the piecemeal reform policy that is reflected in the departemental draft for a new *Lagsökningslag* and points out that if a comprehensive reform of the law on summary adjudication were to be undertaken, the law on proceedings involving minor values *(Småmålslagen),* might well be deemed the more suitable procedural institution from which to start.[27] *Smålmålslagen* provides for an efficient, rather informal and summary means of conducting proceedings in cases involving only minor values. These proceedings deviate in many respects from the common procedural pattern under *Rättegångsbalken* (the Swedish Code of – both civil and criminal – Procedure), far more so than *lagsökning,* which, like proceedings under *Småmålslagen* is summary in character but which largely fits the traditional scheme of civil litigation.[28] Whilst referring to the modern law on proceedings involving minor values as the suitable law upon which to model in future the law on summary adjudication in Sweden, the author points out that there is good reason to make a comprehensive reform of summary adjudication in Sweden part of the revision of *Rättegångsbalken,* a revision which had been initiated in that same year in which Ds Ju 1977-5 *(Summarisk Process)* was published.

This very idea of integrating a comprehensive reform of summary adjudication in Sweden in the revision of *Rättegångsbalken* and of making *Smålmålslagen* the

43 (1977) 9, pp. 397 et seq.

27. *Småmålslagen,* Act of 4 January 1974 (1974:8) *om rättegången i tvistemål om mindre värden. Småmålslagen* is proposed by Lindblom as a model from which to start in reforming the law on summary adjudication because of the advantages of its basic structure. In the approach of the author it is certainly not implied, that *Småmålslagen* is a perfect model which in itself would not call for some improvements.

28. See, *infra* section 5.

starting point in this operation, forms the overriding theme in Lindblom's discussion of Ds Ju 1977-5.
The law committee for the revision of *Rättegångsbalken* has recently completed a first stage of its task. In the summer of 1982 it published a report on the revision of proceedings – both civil and criminal – before the first instance courts *(Tingsrätt)*. The title of this publication, which has appeared in two volumes, reflects the mandate of the committee: *Översyn av Rättegångsbalken.*[29]
The proposals of the committe with regard to civil litigation remind us very much of the ideas put forward by Lindblom – who as an expert took part in the work of the committee – in his article in TSA, *Lagsökning de lege ferenda.* Summary adjudication, including *lagsökning, betalningsföreläggande,* and *handräckning* (as formerly provided in paragraphs 191 et seq. *Utsökningslag* and as presently enacted in the *Handräckningslag),* is comprehensively dealt with and made an integrated part of the main pattern of civil litigation before the courts of first instance. The summary proceedings involving minor values, as presently provided for by *Småmålslagen,* are taken by the committee as the starting point in their proposals for a reform of summary adjudication.
As has been pointed out earlier, this most recent product of the Swedish legislative studios had no direct bearing upon the *Handräckningslag* which came into force on the first of January 1982 and which we have set out to discuss. Yet, it does change significantly the perspective in which to place the latter. The *Handräckningslag* which came into being as a by-product of the reform of execution law and – at the same time – as a somewhat premature result of the initial effort to merge *lagsökning-* and *handräckning*-proceedings in one statute (cf. Ds Ju 1977-5, *Summarisk Process),* may no longer be regarded as just an overture to such a statutory integration of *handräckning* and *lagsökning*-proceedings.

The original plan to integrate *lagsökning,* and *handräckning*-proceedings – a plan reflected in the present *Handräckningslag* which is modelled on a *lagsökning*-formula – constitutes a reform strategy of farreaching consequences. Under the original design *lagsökning* is – and is to remain – an institution of summary adjudication on the merits. Decisions taken in *lagsökning*-proceedings are, of course, liable to be challenged.[30] They are, however, potentially final and will be conceived as such: that is to say, that the *lagsökning*-decisions will be based upon a determination of rights and obligations rather than on a necessarily provisional appreciation of legally relevant interests.

Earlier, I pointed out that a striking feature of the reform exercise is the tendency to establish a sharp division between adjudication: final and on the merits, on the one hand, and the taking of security measures, provisional and temporary, on the other. No middle road, I said, no provisional adjudication which is neither temporary nor on the merits. No room for a *référé* type of civil proceedings.

Here, in this chapter on the landscaping operation which is currently being carried out in Swedish law of civil procedure and execution, we have hit upon plans which support that stringent strategy. Since the *handräckning*-proceedings of the now abolished paragraphs 191 et seq. of the *Utsökningslag* have been brought

29. *Översyn av Rättegångsbalken,* I, Volumes A and B – *Processen i Tingsrätt* (Litigation in the first instance courts), – *delbetänkande av rättegångsutredningen* (Stockholm 1982).
30. For a more extensive discussion, see, Åke Hassler, *op. cit., supra* n. 5, pp. 81 et seq.

into line with *lagsökning,* there is no room left for truly provisional judicial intervention other than for the purpose of ordering temporary security measures.

We have seen that in the meantime the reform plans that are contained in Ds Ju 1977-5, *Summarisk Process,* and particularly the envisaged merger of *lagsökning* and *handräckning*-proceedings, may well be pushed into the background by the reform plans of the committee entrusted with the revision of *Rättegangsbalken.* If this is to happen, – which seems far from unlikely – no room will be left either for a *référé* type of judicial intervention to develop under Swedish law of civil procedure. According to the proposals of the revision committee, summary adjudication, to be comprehensively regulated as an integrated part of full litigation before the common courts of justice, will be basically aimed at procuring final decisions on the merits. No room will be left, indeed, for provisional judicial intervention which is not bound up with pending or subsequent litigation and which is interest-adjudication rather than adjudication through which to establish the legal position of the litigant parties.

The new *Handräckningslag* fully reflects the reform plans that have been developed with regard to *lagsökning* and *betalningsföreläggande.* We cannot, therefore, avoid pursuing another sideline, however briefly, before engaging upon a discussion of the new *Handräckningslag.* We shall have to take a closer look at the law pertaining to the proceedings for debt collecting as presently contained in the *Lag om lagsökning och betalningsföreläggande.*

5. SUMMARY DEBT COLLECTING PROCEEDINGS IN SWEDEN *lagsökning and betalningsföreläggande*

Civil litigation in Sweden follows a pattern which is very different from that in the Netherlands. The Dutch pattern is basically that of a dialogue in writing. As a first step by which to initiate proceedings on the merits, the defendant will be summoned by the plaintiff through the intermediary of the execution officer *(deurwaarder)* to appear before a first instance court. The case will be entered in the court's record of cases (the *rol)* and allowing for exceptions, which one particularly finds in the area of summary proceedings, an exchange of written pleadings will normally follow. Oral pleadings may round off the exchange of written pleadings if so requested by one of the parties, and various incidents may interrupt the normal course of litigation. Interim decisions as well as the final judgment will be in writing even though they will be communicated to the parties – normally their representatives in litigation *(procureurs)* – in sessions that are regularly held in accordance with the *rol.* Essentially, the civil proceedings are one-stage affairs; there is no division between the pre-trial stage and the actual trial.

In Sweden, civil litigation follows basically a two-stage pattern: the trial is preceded by pre-trial discovery. The summoning process is in writing. The plaintiff will first enter a written request to the court of first instance *(tingsrätt)* whose intervention he seeks. The court will examine its competence[31] and decide whether

31. In matters of venue the court will take a more passive stand when engaged in full

the plaintiff should be given leave to pursue his action. If so, the court will act as the intermediary in summoning the defendant. Normally the proceedings are conducted orally at both stages.

The summary process of *lagsökning*[32] has been designed so as to fit in with this general pattern. It is summary in that the case will be decided upon early in the discovery stage on the basis of the written request and the documents entered by the plaintiff and, as the case may be, on the written reply submitted by the defendant.

The request which is to be entered by the plaintiff is to include information on he parties concerned, the actual claim, the interest that is demanded and the facts that may further determine the competence of the court. Documents by which to support the claim are to be added.
The court will *ex officio* decide on its competence. For this it will go by the factual information furnished by the plaintiff as long as there is no apparent reason to assume that the information is defective or wrong.
If the claim is insufficiently supported by the documents entered by the plaintiff or if there is any other obstacle for the court to render its offices, the request will be dismissed.
If the action is admitted, the court will see to the defendant being summoned. The defendant will have to reply in writing within a short period of time, normally a week. Depending on the contents of the reply the court will either decide that the case be referred for litigation in full proceedings or that the case will be adjudicated in a summary fashion.
Once judgment has been given for the plaintiff, the defendant, irrespective of whether or not he replied to the initial claim, may challenge the court's decision by lodging "opposition" *(återvinning)*, a remedy normally reserved for challenging judgments rendered in default *(treskodom)*.
The term for opposition is one month as of the day on which the defendant is notified of the *lagsökning*-decision. Opposition will lead to a reopening of the proceedings before the court originally engaged. The proceedings will not be conducted in a summary fashion if they have been reopened as a result of opposition against a decision in *lagsökning*.
Judgments *(utslag)* obtained in *lagsökning*-proceedings provide a title for execution. The fact that they may be challenged in opposition does not make them provisional. They are conceived as final judicial decisions on the merits. After the time for opposition has elapsed, they stand and their authority is supported by the rule of *res iudicata*.

Langsökning is among the institutions of summary adjudication that belong to the first of the three categories indicated and explained earlier. It is to remain an institution of summary and (potentially) final adjudication on the merits, whether cast in the form envisaged by the drafters of the (newly designed) *Lagsökningslag* (Departments-promemoria Ds Ju 1977-5) or in the uniform regula-

---

proceedings than when its intervention is sought in summary litigation; cf. *Översyn av Rättegångsbalken* I, Part B, (previous note), p. 70.

32. *Infra* section 5. Summary adjudication for the collection of money debts comprises two institutions: *lagsökning* and *betalningsföreläggande*. The latter is to be merged into the former as a result of the present law reform. Here we shall restrict ourselves to a discussion of *lagsökning*.

tion of summary adjudication as proposed by the Committee charged with the revision of proceedings, both civil and criminal before the courts. The *Handräckningslag* reflects the legislative policy behind the former.

6. *HANDRÄCKNING*

The Handräckningslag of June 1981 has been introduced so as to replace the provisions of paragraphs 191 et seq. of the *Utsökningslag,* which in turn was replaced by the *Utsökningsbalk.* One of the results of the reform operation that led to the introduction of the latter Code was the abolition of the office of the chief execution authority: the *överexekutor.* It was this authority from which *handräckning* as provided for in paragraphs 191 et seq. of the *Utsökningslag* had to be obtained. The *Handräckningslag* is to fill a gap that resulted from the abolition of the office of the *överexekutor.*

In filling this gap the Swedish legislator did not just restrict its efforts to replacing the *överexekutor* by another judicial authority: the Judiciary and more particularly the courts of first instance *(tingsrätten).* It engaged upon a thorough revision of the former rules and modelled the institutions of *handräckning,* which were to be covered by the *Handräckningslag,* after the main institution of summary adjudication for the collection of money debts: *lagsökning.*

We have discussed all this and we have seen the policy that is behind this reform operation: a reform of summary adjudication according to the pattern provided by the rules on *lagsökning.* The revision of the latter rules had not yet been completed at the time that the *Utsökningsbalk* was to be introduced and the office of the *överexekutor* was to be abolished. A temporary solution had to be found for the *handräckning*-proceedings of paragraphs 191 et seq. of the *Utsökningslag.* That temporary solution, dressed up according to what the drafters may have regarded as the coming fashion, is provided by the statute on which we shall finally focus our attention: the *Handräckningslag,* a parking place for provisions which are to be included in future legislation.

6.1 *Handräckning* following paras. 191-192 *Utsökningslag*

First a few words about the provisions that were replaced by the *Handräckningslag:* paragraph 191 and paragraph 192 of the now abolished *Utsökningslag.*

Following paragraph 191 the *överexekutor* could be requested to intervene *"without delay"* in the event that someone had *"arbitrarily appropriated something or* (had) *divested somebody else of his possession or if he* (had) *in some other way arrogated a right to himself"* (sect. 1, first part).

In the final phrase quite an opening is left for a wide application of this provision. And legal practice has made use of it.[33]

33. See, Åke Hassler, *op. cit., supra* n. 5, pp. 81 et seq.

It was up to the *överexekutor* to return *"immediately"* the possession that had been affected or to restore the afflicted situation and to answer in court the person who had committed the infringement (sect. 1, second part). The decision taken on the basis of paragraph 191 was a provisional one: *"The person against whom 'assistance' (handräckning) is granted shall not be denied the opportunity to plead his case in court"* (sect. 2). The law did not, however make *handräckning* of this kind (or of the kind to which para. 192 pertains) dependent on pending or subsequent litigation.

Both paragraph 191 and paragraph 192 were included in Chapter 17 of the *Utsökningslag,* the heading of which reads: On *kvarstad, skingringsförbud* and *reseförbud* as well as other (forms of) *handräckning* to be administered by the *överexekutor.*
Paragraph 188 in that same chapter closely linked the security measures named in the heading to pending or subsequent litigation. It was not, however, made to apply to paragraphs 191 and 192.[34] In view of the fact that paragraph 192 together with 194 required the plaintiff to give security, subsequent litigation might, however, have been hard to avoid.
This does not seem surprising at all. Technically, *handräckning* of the kind to which the latter provisions pertained, had little to do with *handräckning* by way of ordering security measures. Measures taken following paragraph 191 and paragraph 192 were not meant to secure performance claimed or about to be claimed in court proceedings or in any other kind of judicial process. In practice, they might under circumstances have that same effect, but it was certainly not their purpose. They could best be defined as "police measures" fitted into the system of civil procedure, rather than as security measures. Essentially, they were not unlike the measures taken by the executive under the law of criminal procedure and aimed at returning stolen property to the rightful owner. Rules on the taking of "police measures", fitted into the sytem of civil procedure so as to become instances of summary and provisional adjudication – that is what the provisions of paragraph 191 and 192 amounted to.
Paragraph 192 was somewhat more limited in scope than paragraph 191. The former dealt with the intervention by the överexekutor *for the eviction of tenants*[35] from property which they illegally occupied.
Apart from its having a wider scope, paragraph 191 had a special attractiveness in that the law did not make the giving of a security conditional upon the taking of measures. Paragraph 194, which requires security to be given as a condition for *handräckning,* did apply to *kvarstad, skingringsförbud* and *reseförbud,* as well as to *handräckning* following paragraph 192. It did not, however, apply to *handräckning* as provided in paragraph 191.
The *överexekutor* could strengthen his intervention following paragraphs 191 and 192 by threat of fine *(vite).*

The decision *(utslag)* taken by the *överexekutor* in *handräckning*-proceedings of the kind discussed here was not final in the sense that it would have prevented

34. In view of the fact that para. 194 required the plaintiff to give a security for *handräckning ex* para. 192 to be obtained, subsequent litigation might not always have been easy to avoid.

35. "Tenants" in the widest sense, including persons occupying living quarters, appartments or whatever other part of a building. Para. 192 mentions *arrendator, hyresgäst* and *bostadsrättshavare.*

the parties from taking the underlying case to court for it to be adjudicated on the merits (paras. 191(2) and 192(3) *Utsökningslag).* No time-limit was provided, however, whether directly or indirectly.

The decision of the *överexekutor* could be challenged in appeal before *hovrätten* and subsequently, though subject to specific conditions, before the Surpreme Court *(Högsta Domstolen).*

Earlier, in section 3, we divided the institutions of civil procedure that are aimed at reducing procedural delays and at averting disadvantages that such delays may cause, into three categories. The second category covered the institutions of summary and provisional adjudication like that of the *référé*-proceedings under Dutch law of civil procedure.

Handräckning in the setting of paragraphs 191 and 192 of the former *Utsökningslag* belonged to that same category. That is not to say that the two institutions – *référé*-proceedings on the one hand, and *handräckning ex* paragraphs 191 and 192 on the other – were similar in design. That was certainly not the case. An essential rule in *référé*-proceedings requires the President of the first instance court to decide by balancing the interests rather than by precisely determining the rights and obligations involved in the case. A similar rule was not formally included in the law on *handräckning.* Yet, the powers of the *överexekutor* can hardly be said to have been much wider, his intervention being of a merely provisional nature.

> The provisional character of *handräckning* following paragraphs 191 and 192 *Utsökningslag* is denied by Ginsburg and Bruzelius who state[36] : "The Code of Execution now in force authorizes chief execution officials to render final rather than provisional determinations, enforceable in the same manner as judicial judgments, in claims for eviction and for the restoration of possession or custody disturbed through self-help *(självtäkt).*
> In addition, case law has extended the scope of the chief execution authorities' summary adjucatory powers to cover most situations in which, upon proper judicial hearing, a performance judgment could be entered for specific relief – relief involving something other than payment of money."
> There is no doubt that in practice the decisions taken by the *överexekutor* on the basis of the *handräckning*-provisions under survey will commonly have been final. Technically, however, they were no more than measures which provided title for execution but which did not finally settle the underlying case. Their authority was not supported by the rule of *res iudicata.*[37]

The observation made by Walin et al. in their commentary to paragraph 3, Chapter 15 *Rättegångsbalken* as to the need to balance the interests of the parties when ordering provisional measures, would also have applied to adjudication following paragraph 191 of the (former) *Utsökningslag.*

All this belongs to the past now. The *Utsökningslag* has been abolished and with it the office of the *överexekutor* and the provisions contained in paragraphs 191

36. *Op. cit., supra* n. 5, p. 226.
37. For a more extensive discussion, see, Åke Hassler, *op. cit., supra* n. 5, p. 81 et seq.

and 192 have disappeared. Let us, finally, turn to the statute that replaced these provisions: the *Handräckningslag.*

6.2 The *Handräckningslag*

After all that has been said in the previous chapters and particularly in that on *lagsökning,* the various provisions of the *Handräckningslag* will require little explanation. A few introductory observations and a brief commentary on some of the most important provisions should suffice.

6.2.1 *The organization of the statute*

The opening provision deals with the scope of the statute and with the competent authorities to which to apply for *handräckning* (para. 1).

The following four provisions cover questions of a preliminary nature: the requirements that should be met by the plaintiff in respect of the introductory request, the determination of its competence by the court *(tingsrätt),* the conditions for the granting of "leave" or "admission", and grounds for dismissal (paras. 2, 3, 4, 5).

Next the statute sets out how the *handräckning*-proceedings are to be conducted once the preliminary hurdles have been jumped, and what decisions the proceedings may lead to (paras. 6, 7 and 8).

Provisions on procedural costs are contained in paragraphs 9 and 10.

However summary the *handräckning*-proceedings may be, room is left for the taking of provisional interim measures (para. 11).

Paragraph 12 provides for the remedy of "opposition" *(återvinning).*

Paragraph 13 contains a provision which forms a truly – though rudimentary – provisional element in the statute: if the court does not give judgment *(utslag)* for the plaintiff, the latter may still initiate proceedings before a common court of justice after the period for *återvinning* has elapsed.

The conduct of proceedings in *återvinning* is regulated in paragraph 14.

Paragraph 15 deals with the composition of the court in *handräckning* - proceedings.

The final provision deals with specific forms of *handräckning* in respect of which the execution authorities used to have competence under special statutes and will remain competent due to the limited scope of the *Handräckningslag* in respect of such special statutes.

6.2.2 *The provisions of the Handräckningslag*[38]

Paragraph 1: In cases where parties would be free to settle a dispute between themselves, claims for the performance of an obligation shall be tried by *tingsrätt*

38. The translations into English of the various provisions are made by the present author and should not be regarded as in any way formally authorized.

(common first instance court) following a request for *handräckning* according to the present Act.

(1) The scope of the present statute is larger than that of paragraphs 191 and 192 of the former *Utsökningslag.* An altogether feasible extension in view of the fact, that in the present statute *handräckning* has been modelled on *lagsökning* and has so completely lost its original and exceptional character of constituting a procedural means for the taking of "police measures".
(2) The opening phrase – "where parties would be free to settle" – refers to the distinction, commonly made in regard to Swedish law of civil procedure, between *dispositiva* and *indispositiva* legal issues.
(3) The authority that is to replace the *överexekutor* is the common court of first instance. The initial idea to entrust adjudication in *handräckning* to the *kronofogde* has been dropped and *tingsrätt* has been made the competent authority, very much because adjudication in *handräckning* was considered to be a judicial activity which should preferably not be exercised by an execution authority.

Paragraph 2: The request for *handräckning* will be entered in writing. As to the court's competence, the provisions pertinent to (common) lawsuits apply. Disputes involving tenancy, rent and lodging shall, however, be taken up by the *tingsrätt* at the place where the real property is situated.

The court shall determine its competence *ex officio.* The information furnished by the plaintif as to the circumstances on which the court's competence depends, shall be accepted if it is not to be presumed false.

(1) In both sections the provision forms a fair reflection of the corresponding rules in respect of *lagsökning* (comp. section 5).
One wonders why the rule on competence of the court should be so stringent. Competence in this case is the corollary of venue, a procedural issue which is not commonly decided *ex officio* by Dutch first instance courts (with some exceptions like the competence of the lower first instance courts: the *Kantongerechten* – Article 98a Rv.) and which is very liberally treated in *référé*-proceedings.[39]

(2) The rule that the information furnished by the plaintiff in the request or in the writ of summons forms the basis for the competence of the court, is a common rule both in Swedish and in Dutch law of civil procedure. A different solution would hardly be feasible.

Paragraph 3: In his request the plaintiff shall indicate the circumstances by which his claim is supportable. He shall submit information on the factual basis on which the competence of the court depends to the extent to which such information would not result from facts that are otherwise introduced.

The request shall be accompanied by written evidence and other documents which the plaintiff wishes to invoke. Written statements made by someone in

39. W. van Rossem, R.P. Cleveringa, *op. cit., supra* n. 18, Note 1 to Art. 290, pp. 781-3.

respect of the case submitted for *handräckning* may be invoked as evidence in the lawsuit.

Paragraph. 4: If the request is so defective that it cannot be made the basis for the case to be tried, and if the plaintiff does not follow the indications given to remove the defects, the request shall be dismissed. If any other impediment appears to prevent the request from being admitted, it shall be dismissed without delay.

The initial request is submitted to the court. If the court considers the request an insufficient basis for litigation, it will not necessarily refuse to grant "leave"' The plaintiff may be given the opportunity to amend his request in accordance with indications he will receive from the court. If he fails to comply with the court's indications, dismissal will inevitably follow. If he does comply and "leave" is given by the court, the latter will see to the defendant being summoned.
In all this the position of the Swedish first instance court is very different from that of a court of first instance in the Netherlands, where the summoning process is generally a matter for the parties alone and, to some extent, for the execution authority *(deurwaarder)* through whose offices the defendant is actually summoned.
It should be pointed out in this connection, that litigation before *tingsrätten* does not require the parties to be represented by counsel generally as is the case in proceedings conducted before the Dutch counterpart: the common (as opposed to the lower[40]) first instance court. In Dutch *référé-proceedings*, mandatory representation by counsel does apply to the plaintiff.[41]

Paragraph 5: If it is obvious that the claim is unfounded, the request will be rejected without delay.

(1) The request will be rejected without notice being given to the opposing party.
(2) The notion of "obviously unfounded" *(uppenbart ogrundad)* is used in a similar way in the law on default-proceedings; see: Chapter 44, paragraph 8 *Rättegångsbalken.*

Paragraph 6: If the request is admitted, the case shall be prepared for final decision in proceedings that will be conducted in writing.

The defendant will be given notice that he is to give his opinion on the request within a certain period of time after it has been communicated to him. The period shall not, without particular reason, be fixed so as to extend beyond two weeks. When notice is given to him, the defendant will be informed that the case will be finally decided even if he has not given his opinion within such period. If necessary, the plaintiff shall be given the opportunity to comment upon what has been raised by the defendant. There will be no room for any further exchange of notes.

If the request is withdrawn the case shall be removed from the record.

40. Lower first instance courts in the Netherlands: *Kantongerechten.*
41. Rv. Art. 290.

The most remarkable provision in this paragraph is the final one: the defendant will not have the opportunity to have the case judged if the plaintiff withdraws his claim. This is a clear deviation from the common pattern of civil procedure (comp. Chapter 13, para. 5 *Rättegångsbalken).* One has to keep in mind, however, that in case the claim is not withdrawn but dismissed, the defendant would not be shielded from a subsequent lawsuit on the same issue (comp. para. 13 *Handräckningslag).*

Paragraph 7 deals with the way in which notice – as mentioned in paragraph 6, section 2 – has to be given to the defendant. The rules on summoning apply here. It will be remembered that after having admitted a request, entered by the plaintiff, the court will see to the defendant being summoned.

Paragraph 8: The plaintiff shall prove the circumstances which he invokes in support of his request. His account of the circumstances shall be made the basis of the examination to the extent to which the account has remained unopposed by the defendant and it is not obvious that it is incorrect.

If the defendant opposes the request, it should not be granted if the defendant shows probable ground for his objection or if the right of the plaintiff appears to be otherwise ambiguous.

The provision nicely fits the pattern of proceedings on the merits. In principle full proof is required. If anything, the present paragraph confirms the shift in the law on *handräckning* as previously contained in paragraphs 191 and 192 of the former *Utsökningslag.*

Paragraphs 9 and 10 deal with procedural costs. They need no discussion here.

Paragraph 11: If it is made to appear probable *(Göre de sannolikt)*; – that the case does not tolerate delay, the court may grant the measure applied for, even if the defendant has not expressed his opinion on the request. This does not apply, however, if the request pertains to an obligation pending upon a previous owner or rightful user *(nyttjanderättshavare)* to remove himself from real property, an appartment or some other room in a building.

If a measure has been granted following the first section, the court shall re-examine the decision as soon as possible.

Appeal shall be lodged separately against decisions as meant in the first and second section.

(1) The article provides for *interim*-measures. Similar instant and provisional relief may be obtained in the form of security measures under the rules of Chapter 15 *Rättegångsbalken.* However, as we have seen earlier, the security measures of Chapter 15 *Rättegångsbalken* will only be ordered if the person who applies for them gives a security. No such security is required in respect of the interim measures provided for in the present paragraph.
(2) Appeal *(besvär)* has to be lodged within two weeks as of the day on which the defendant has been given notice of the decision *(beslut).* The appeal court is *hovrätten.*

Paragraph 12: When the exchange of notes has been concluded, final decision shall be given in the case without delay. The court will give its decision in the form of *utslag*. Against *utslag* following the present Act the parties may seek *återvinning* (opposition) with the court. *Återvinning* shall be applied for, by the defendant, within one month as of the day on which notice has been given to him of the *utslag*, or on which the *utslag* has been wholly or partly enforced, and by the plaintiff within a month as of the day before the *utslag* was issued. If an application for *återvinning* has been submitted, the proceedings will be deemed to have been initiated at the time of the entering of the request for *handräckning* with the court.

If a party is dissatisfied with the court's *utslag* only in so far as the decision *(beslut)* in respect of the repayment of costs is concerned, he may as to that part complain through appeal *(besvär)* within the period of time indicated in the second section.

(1) As pointed out before, *återvinning* is the remedy commonly applied to challenge default judgments. The basic pattern of civil litigation in Sweden is that of proceedings in two stages – pre-trial discovery and the actual trial – conducted orally. Both default proceedings and *handräckning* proceedings deviate from that pattern in that litigation is concentrated in the early part of the discovery stage; in *handräckning:* an exchange of notes between the plaintiff who enters his request and supporting documents, and the defendant who will be given the opportunity to submit a written reply.
(2) *Återvinning* leads to a reopening of the proceedings, in principle before the same court that intervened in *handräckning*. The proceedings will be considered to have been introduced when *handräckning* was applied for, but they will not be conducted in a summary fashion. Rules on how *återvinning*-proceedings are to be conducted are contained in paragraph 14.
(3) Once *återvinning* has been formally initiated, the *utslag* obtained in the preceeding *handräckning*-proceedings will lose its quality of providing a title for execution.

Paragraph 13: *Utslag* by which the plaintiff's lawsuit has not been supported will not prevent the parties from instituting proceedings before the judicial authority prescribed for litigation in general after the period for *återvinning* has elapsed.

This provision has been touched upon before *(supra, ad* para. 6 and sub a).
Paragraph 14: see *supra*, sub paragraph 12.
Paragraph 15 deals with the composition of the court in matters of *handräckning:* assistance in the form of *handräckning* shall only be granted by an experienced judge – not by a layman. Under Dutch law on the organization of the Judiciary, laymen do not but very exceptionally participate in the administration of justice in civil and criminal cases. Swedish law presents an altogether different picture. That is why a provision like the one contained in the present paragraph had to be included now that the legislator wished to restrict intervention in *handräckning*-proceedings to those members of *tingsrätten* who are professionally trained judges. The second section of paragraph 15 contains a provision on the way notice is to be given of *utslag* in *handräckning*-proceedings.

Paragraph 16 comprises a reference to the parts of *Rättegångsbalken* which deal with civil litigation. (Criminal procedure is also regulated in the Swedish Code of Procedure). To the extent to which particular rules have not been included in the *Handräckningslag*, the relevant rules of civil procedure, as contained in *Rättegångsbalken*, will apply.

Paragraph 17, finally, excludes certain forms of *handräckning*, which, following special statutes, are not administered by the courts of first instance, from the provisions of the *Handräckningslag*.

7. CONCLUSION

This essay is about a Swedish Act, recently introduced and – possibly – soon to be abolished. I have named it a parking place for provisions to be included in future legislation. A parking place is not a particularly festive thing to refer to in a contribution to a *Festschrift*. It might have been more colourful to compare the *Handräckningslag* to a butterfly. Perhaps more appropriate too: short-lived and most remarkable for the stage it marks in the metamorphosis. (It is tempting at this point to refer to the section on landscaping and bring in the caterpillars.)

The metamorphosis has been very much the focal point in our discussion of the *Handräckningslag*. The law reform exercise from which it resulted would basically change the statutory law of summary adjudication in Sweden, if it were to be carried through.

Here again reference is to be made to the work of the Committee for the revision of the proceedings before the common courts, which has made it not at all likely that the *Handräckningslag* will soon die in the arms of an all-embracing law reform based on a revised *lägsökning*-model. But even so, the odds seem to be against the present *Handräckningslag*. As has been pointed out before, the revision-committee has designed its draft rules on summary adjudication so as to make them cover the entire spectrum of summary adjudication existing in Sweden under the present statutes. *Handräckning* of the kind presently provided for in the *Handräckningslag* is included, too. So, the butterfly is likely to disappear anyway.

As seen from the point of view of Dutch law of summary adjudication, the most striking feature of the new *Handräckningslag* appears to be the sharp division between summary, but final, adjudication on the merits, on the one hand, and provisional judicial intervention for the taking of security measures, on the other. As a result of the law reform as carried out so far, no room appears to be left for summary provisional adjudication which is not, as in the case of security measures, closely linked with pending or subsequent litigation.

A type of process as that is provided in Dutch law on *référé*-proceedings has never been part of Swedish law of civil litigation. We did, however, touch upon two institutions of Swedish procedural law which show some features similar to those to be found in *référé*-adjudication.

On the one hand are the prohibition orders of paragraph 3, Chapter 15 *Rättegångsbalken*. They may be issued by way of interim measures, but also outside proceedings. They are typical *handräckning*-measures in that they are aimed at providing instant relief. But as seen from the point of view of expedient, low-cost litigation, their summary character is a bit deceptive. Being security measures they can, when issued outside court proceedings, hardly be more than an opening to litigation on the merits, full or summary.

On the other hand are the former *handräckning* orders of paragraphs 191 and 192 of the now abolished *Utsökningslag.* Historically both provisions were very limited in scope. They constituted a means by which to counter infringements of possessory rights: police measures fitted into the system of civil procedure which were originally of a purely executory nature. That is why one had to apply to the chief execution officer for *handräckning* of this kind. Practice extended the scope of, particularly, paragraph 191. It never developed to become a procedural institution comparable to the *référé*-proceedings, but it had all the vital elements of the latter: the summary character; judicial intervention limited – at least potentially – to interest-balancing rather than aimed at the determination of rights and obligations; (consequently) provisional in nature, leading to a decision which provided an executory title without being final; not necessarily linked with pending or subsequent litigation and, as a result, not necessarily temporary in character.

There is no room for this collection of "*référé*-ingredients" in the *lagsökning*-model, which stands for an institution of summary proceedings, final and on the merits. Now that the rules on *handräckning* as formerly contained in paragraphs 191 and 192 *Utsökningslag* have been accommodated to that model, any further development of provisional interest-adjudication on the basis of the particular *handräckning*-proceedings under survey could be barred. The same is true if the proposals of the revision committee would be adhered to, as has been pointed out above. Provisional adjudication based on an appreciation of the interests involved in a given case, is to be and will remain confined to the area of security measures. In the reports on the discussions that preceded the introduction of the *Handräckningslag,* there is little to show that the total exclusion of (potential) summary interest-adjudication proper has been considered much of a hurdle for those engaged in the law reform operation. Much attention has been given to the judicial character of intervention in summary proceedings. We have seen that the initial plan to make the *kronofogde* the intervening authority was dropped, because it was realized that summary adjudication is a judicial activity which should be exercised by the Judiciary rather than by execution authorities.

Sound reasoning, I think, and one which has led to the proper solution. But once it has been established that judicial intervention of the kind under discussion should be entrusted to the courts, there still remains a question to be answered – a question which springs from the comparison we made between Swedish and Dutch law of summary adjudication and to some extent from what is now Swedish procedural history: should judicial intervention be necessarily aimed, in the short run or, via temporary provisional measures, in the long run, at defining the legal rights involved in a case, or should the law of civil litigation leave room for provisional interest-adjudication of the *référé* type?

Legal practice as developed under the rules on *référé*-proceedings in The Netherlands and elsewhere demonstrates that parties do not always seek judicial intervention to have their dispute settled by a final judgment on the merits. Interest-adjudication often suits them well. Interest-adjudication is provisional. It does not bar the parties from instituting proceedings on the merits. But parties may – and do quite frequently – refrain from fighting on for the final determination of their rights. The choice is with the parties. Subsequent litigation on the merits is not imposed by statute.

The *lagsökning*-formula which dominated the drafting of the *Handräckningslag,* is that of summary adjudication on the merits. Security measures, including the prohibition orders of paragraph 3, Chapter 15 *Rättegångsbalken,* may well require the balancing of interests rather than the determination of rights, but they do not bring about a settlement with which the parties may choose to comply without further litigation.

From a comparative point of view – both in relation to Dutch law of summary adjudication and in historical perspective – the exclusion of provisional interest-adjudication proper may well be considered a most significant feature of the *Handräckningslag.*

EXECUTIVE AND JUDICIARY IN FOREIGN AFFAIRS
– Recognition of Foreign Lawmaking Entities

by J.A. Wade*

The interplay of the powers and competences of the judicial and executive organs of State is in every country a complex and shifting relationship. A facet which is of particular importance and interest to international lawyers is the relationship between judiciary and executive in foreign affairs. The purpose of this paper is to examine one aspect thereof in the light of the law and practice of the United Kingdom and The Netherlands, namely, the approach of the judiciary to foreign lawmaking entities against the background of executive policy on the recognition of States and governments.

With regard to UK law and practice much has been written of late, reflecting recent developments in both political and judicial approaches to the problem of when and in what manner to accord recognition to changes in sovereign or executive power in foreign territories. The practice of the judiciary in this has been, and remains, the subject of much criticism, and evidence of a willingness to mitigate the results of the judicial policy and even, more recently, to depart from it, has been warmly received.

By contrast, in The Netherlands the debates on the issue appear to have been put firmly in the past and the position now appears to be settled and without dissent. It is of interest here to note that UK developments in judicial recognition may be moving towards a position akin to that adopted in The Netherlands. It will be interesting to see if Dutch executive practice subsequently moves towards that of the United Kingdom.

1. RECOGNITION BY THE EXECUTIVE

In April 1980 the then Foreign Secretary, Lord Carrington, somewhat unexpectedly, announced in the House of Lords that the British policy on recognition had been revised. He informed the House that Her Majesty's Government

> "have decided that we shall no longer accord recognition to Governments. The British Government recognise States in accordance with common international doctrine."[1]

* Deputy Director, T.M.C. Asser Institute for International Law, The Hague; Member of the Board of Editors.

1. *Hansard,* House of Lords, Vol. 408, col. 1121, quoted in Warbrick, "The New British Policy on Recognition of Governments" (1981) 30 ICLQ 568 at 574, which provides a valuable analysis of the manifold issues arising.

With regard to the recognition of States this simple reference to "common international doctrine" is of uncertain scope. To a great extent the recognition of States and that of governments are interdependent.[2] It may be accepted that a prerequisite of Statehood lies in the existence of an effective and independent government [3], certainly in the sense that the existence of effective government, with centralized administrative and legislative organs, is the best evidence of a stable political community and that where such community supports a legal order in a certain area [4] it may qualify for the description of State.[5]

This would certainly accord with the view of the Government of The Netherlands. The Minister for Foreign Affairs has stated in Parliament, in answer to the question what criteria are applied in determining whether a State qualifies for recognition as such, that:

"Existence as a 'State' in international law requires the presence of three elements:
a. a defined territory;
b. an established population;
c. a government exercising effective authority over that territory."[6]

Recognition of a State may take the form of recognition of a government, although non-recognition of a government is often not tantamount to denying the existence of the State allegedly represented by that government [7] and may be a reluctance on the part of the non-recognising State to enter into normal political relations.[8] The borderline between recognising States and according recognition to or withholding it from governments claiming to represent the State is often uncertain.

What also remains uncertain [9] as a result of Lord Carrington's recent announcement on British policy is whether Her Majesty's Government presently subscribe to the view that there exists a duty to recognise a State where it qualifies as such by reference to the criteria established by international law, which was clearly the position adopted previously:

2. Brownlie, *Principles of Public International Law,* 3rd ed. (1979) pp. 91, 95; François, *Handboek van het Volkenrecht,* (1949) Vol. 1 pp. 179-180.

3. *Ibid.* p. 95.

4. Crawford, *Creation of States in International Law,* (1979) pp. 27-8.

5. Brownlie, *op. cit., supra* n. 2, p. 75.

6. See, *Netherlands Yearbook of International Law* (1975) p. 252. For a useful discussion of these "classical" criteria see, Crawford, *op.cit., supra* n. 4, pp. 36-47.

7. François, *op.cit., supra* n. 2, p. 180, argued that in the case of a change of government in an existing State, such State remains recognised (given that the essential elements of people, territory and sovereignty have not been lost), even though the Government is not recognised. In his view recognition of a State goes to effective existence and not to recognition *de facto* or *de iure* which incorporate preparedness to establish diplomatic relations, of which there can be no question as long as the Government has not been recognised. For the U.K. position, e.g., towards Kampuchea, see, Warbrick (1981) 30 ICLQ 234.

8. Brownlie, *op.cit., supra* n. 2, p. 95; François, *op.cit., supra* n. 2, p. 187.

9. For discussion see, Warbrick, *loc.cit., supra* n. 1, p. 575.

"the existence of a State should not be regarded as depending upon its recognition but on whether in fact it fulfills the conditions which create a duty for recognition."[10]

The view that recognition is constitutive certainly appears to have influenced former British government policy on recognition.[11] According to the constitutivists [12] the act of recognition is a precondition of the existence of legal rights: that full international personality as a subject of international law derives from the decision of other States to recognise Statehood. To this has been coupled the view that there is a legal duty on States to accord recognition where the criteria for Statehood under international law are satisfied.[13] With respect, such views fail to be convincing. A particular difficulty would appear to be, to whom is the alleged duty to recognise owed? That it is owed to other States, i.e., the community of States being those States that by virtue of the fact of recognition are subjects of international law, is not readily conceivable, for there would appear to be no legal interest in seeing the duty fulfilled. Indeed, the 'parent' State, previously recognised and contesting the claim to Statehood, would certainly appear to have a legal interest in the non-fulfilment of such alleged duty. That a duty to recognise is owed to the entity alleged to fulfil the criteria for Statehood is perhaps more susceptible of argument as a proposition. When allied to, and indeed subject to, the proposition that Statehood derives from recognition the contention assumes a paradoxical character. It is submitted that the validity of such an approach is verifiable by reference to generally accepted propositions: that the subjects of international law are (preponderantly) States; that States enjoy full legal personality; that personality is the state of being burdened by duties and of possessing rights. The lynchpin of the constitutive theory is that an entity that

10. Quoted by Crawford, *op.cit., supra* n. 4, p. 16 n. 60. Brownlie, *op.cit., supra* n. 2, pp. 91-3, 94-5, provides an eminently sensible reflection on the doctrinaire debate between the declaratist and constitutivist schools. See also, François, *op.cit., supra* n. 2, pp. 186-87.

11. Warbrick, *loc.cit., supra* n. 1, p. 570, with particular reference to the views of Lauterpacht, who "was one of the more subtle and persuasive proponents of a form of the constitutive position": Crawford, *op.cit., supra* n. 4, p. 17.

12. A number of adherents are given in Brownlie, *op.cit., supra* n. 2, pp. 92 n. 2, 93 n. 3; Crawford, *op.cit., supra* n. 4, p. 17 n. 62.

13. Lauterpacht, *International Law: Collected Papers,* (1970) Vol. 1, pp. 308 et seq.: "Recognition . . . is declaratory in the sense that it ascertains, as a fact, the existence of the requirements of statehood and the consequent right of the new community to be treated as a normal subject of international law; it is declaratory in the sense that in the contemplation of the law the new community is entitled to it as a matter of right and that one may safely disregard the objection that, not being recognized, it cannot be 'legally entitled'; it is declaratory in the sense that, once given, its effect dates back to the commencement of the existence of the new State as an independent community; it is declaratory in the sense that the recognising State does not part with any of its rights by way of grant, concession, or act of grace. On the other hand, it is constitutive in the sense that, so long as discretion in ascertaining the existence of the conditions of statehood is exercised in good faith, it is decisive for the creation of the international personality of the new community and its rights as such . . ." (pp. 319-20). *Contra,* François, *op.cit., supra* n. 2, pp. 186-87: "How it was possible to call a State into being by a synallagmatic legal act to which that not yet exisiting State was a party, remained unclear . . . The existence of a State is dependent on the existence of factors legally determining Statehood." (Translation of the present writer.)

satisfies the legal criteria for Statehood nevertheless does not thereby possess such legal personality: recognition is required to clothe that factual situation with legal consequences. Such consequences flow from the fulfilment of the duty to recognise. The duty is allegedly imposed under international law on all States, i.e., on those persons having legal personality. It is axiomatic that rights and duties attach only to those who are recognised by law as having legal personality, as being subject to law and as being competent to be burdened by duties and to possess rights. For a duty to exist, i.e., that the law recognises that a person subject to law is so burdened, it is necessary that a corresponding right also exists, i.e., that the law recognises that a person subject to law possesses a right from which the non-fulfilment of the duty derogates. The existence and nature of any alleged duty is determined by the existence and nature of the corresponding right from which it derives. Similarly, the person to whom the duty is owed is likewise identified. Self-evidently, the alleged duty of recognition is not imposed on non-States, for they do not possess legal personality until, it is alleged, the act of recognition invests them with the status of Statehood. Equally, however, they are not competent to possess any right corresponding to the duty allegedly owed. If the right does not exist, the alleged duty from which it flows must also fail. Conversely, if it be maintained that a duty to recognise does exist, it must follow that a corresponding right also exists, which right can be possessed only by an entity having legal personality, in which case the act of recognition cannot be constitutive of legal personality. To the contention that the act of recognition, although not constitutive of Statehood, is nevertheless constitutive of the rights and duties associated with full Statehood, it may be pointed out that in this connection care must be taken to identify correctly those rights only whose creation is subject to acceptance by another of the duties to which they correspond. Certain rights are primary in the sense that their existence must be postulated without reference to the agreement of persons who have thus become burdened by corresponding duties. The loosely phrased expression 'duty of recognition' obscures this dichotomy, not least because, as has been demonstrated above, it tends to divert attention away from the more promising, but still inadequate, formulation 'right of recognition'. It cannot be contended that a non-State has a right of recognition as a State. On the other hand, it has been thought promising to advance the view that a State has a right of recognition being a primary right arising autonomously upon the State's coming into being, whereby all other States are under a duty to accord it recognition. On closer examination, however, it may be submitted that a correct analysis of a 'right of recognition' leads to the conclusion that a State has instead the right not to be denied unjustifiably its status of Statehood.[14] Thus, premature recognition may be a breach of duty to the extent that it con-

14. Compare, Brownlie, *op.cit., supra* n. 4: ". . . It is clearly established that states cannot by their independent judgment establish any competence of other states which is established by international law and does not depend on agreement or concession." (p.92). "Recognition, *as a public act of state,* is an optional and political act and there is no legal duty in this regard. However, in a deeper sense, if an entity bears the marks of statehood, other states put themselves at risk legally if they ignore the basic obligations of state relations . . . In this context

stitutes an unjustifiable denial of another State's status of Statehood. Once an emerging entity satisfies the criteria for Statehood it has the right not to be denied unjustifiably its status. Any act of recognition of its status as State would not constitute any breach of duty owed to another State because it would not be unjustified. Any refusal to recognise Statehood can be tested only by reference to the criteria for Statehood. If refusal is grounded on the decision that the entity does not in fact satisfy the legal criteria, the refusal will by definition not be unjustified and in certain cases will be no more than the fulfilment of the duty owed to another State. Where the claimant is held by the evaluating State to satisfy the criteria and recognition is nevertheless refused on other grounds, such refusal is an unjustifiable denial constituting a breach of duty owed to that State. The reference to satisfying the criteria must be understood in the light of the fact that there exists no independent tribunal competent to pronounce on the moment when the entity can be said objectively to satisfy the legal criteria for Statehood established by international law. Such question must fall to be determined by each State individually. It is not less a question of law for that. The right arises autonomously with the status of State and this is not to be gainsaid by recourse to uncertainty as to the moment of creation due to the element of subjectivity involved in effecting an evaluation of fact and criteria. What is at issue is whether the conduct of one State constitutes a breach of duty not to deny unjustifiably the acquired status of another State. In this respect, it follows that where a State declines to issue a declaration as to recognition there is no element of unjustifiable denial and no breach of duty. In the same way, if a State were to adopt the policy of not granting any declarations of recognition, no breach would be committed because no denial of status would be contained in such a policy, for the duty owed is not to deny unjustifiably, it is not the duty to affirm status.

Whatever might be the merits or otherwise of the above analysis there would appear to be much commonsense commending the view that the process subsumed under the expression recognition of States and, to the extent that they are interdependent, governments, is a complex issue of law, fact and policy, and which is not profitably reduced to the oversimplification of a doctrinal dispute.[15] A distinction should be drawn between determination of a claim to Statehood and any subsequent public declaration of recognition. The view may also be adopted that the determination by a State of a claim to Statehood by a foreign entity raises a question of law but is a process falling entirely within its own competence and against which there is no appeal to an independent tribunal competent to

of state *conduct* there is a duty to accept and apply certain fundamental rules of international law: there is a legal duty to 'recognize' for certain purposes at least, but no duty to make an express, public, and political determination of the question or to declare readiness to enter into diplomatic relations by means of recognition. This latter type of recognition remains political and discretionary." (pp. 94-5).

See also, Crawford, *op.cit., supra* n. 4, p. 23: "the proper position is that in principle the denial of recognition to an entity which otherwise qualifies as a State cannot entitle the non-recognizing States to act as if the entity in question was not a State".

15. *Ibid.*, pp. 91, 93-94. For the view that the debate has not been without benefit see, Crawford, *op.cit., supra* n. 4, pp. 23-4; Bot, *Non-recognition and Treaty Relations* (1968) p. 19.

pronounce upon the propriety or manner of exercise of such judgment.[16] It is generally accepted that premature recognition would be unlawful.[17] That a State is at liberty to decline to issue a public declaration of recognition is equally accepted [18] and this clearly must encompass both the situation where the State has reached an internal determination that the foreign entity does not qualify as a State and also the situation where an internal positive determination in favour of the existence of Statehood has been reached but, for political reasons, no declaration of recognition is to be made. The postulate that there exists a duty to recognise when the conditions for Statehood established by international law have been fulfilled would appear, as has been demonstrated above, to be incorrectly grounded but may be regarded as containing the premiss that the issue of recognition highlights the individual responsibility to effect the determination bona fide and not to recognise if the legal conditions therefore are not fulfilled. Whether to proceed to public recognition remains, however, a matter of policy.

This would appear to be the position taken by the Government of The Netherlands. The unilateral declaration of independence of the Portuguese colony of Guinea-Bissau by the principal liberation movement Partido Africano da Independência da Guiné e Cabo Verde led the then Prime Minister Den Uyl to reply to questions in Parliament:

> "The question is whether international law permits the recognition of such independence. The Government . . . feels obliged to apply the rules of international law, including those relating to the recognition of new States . . . given the facts now available recognition would not yet be expedient. The fact is that there are still doubts as to whether the authority of the liberation movement yet extends to the near totality of the population of Guinea-Bissau . . . As soon as a situation has been reached that makes recognition in international law possible, the Netherlands will not hesitate to contact politically related countries and to propose a joint recognition of Guinea-Bissau. The Dutch position will not be dependent on the attitude of these countries should The Netherlands have decided that recognition under international law is justified."[19]

The view adopted is that the determination of the legal basis for a decision whether formally to accord recognition is to be made independently of the views of other countries, thus individually, and by reference to the criteria established by international law for Statehood.[20] Only on this basis would subsequent recognition of

16. Bundu, "Recognition of Revolutionary Authorities: Law and Practice of States", (1978) 27 ICLQ 18 at 43-4. Note also the pertinent observation by Chen, *International Law of Recognition,* (1951) p. 130: "No State has ever been sued for damages for failure to recognise another's government, and recognising States constantly show that they regard recognition purely as an act of discretion and of policy."

17. See, NYIL (1979) p. 315.

18. Brownlie, *op.cit., supra* n. 2, p. 94.

19. NYIL (1975) p. 252. It is interesting to note that Guinea-Bissau had at this time already been recognised by some seventy States: Kuyper, "Recognition: Netherlands Theory and State Practice", in *International Law in The Netherlands* (1978) Vol. 1, p. 374.

20. *Tinoco Concessions Arbitration* (1923) UN, Reports of International Awards, Vol. 1, p. 369: "Such non-recognition for any reason . . . cannot outweigh the evidence disclosed . . .

the State be justified under international law. The notion that there exists a legal duty to recognise is not supported by many Dutch commentators [21] and has been denied specifically in the case of East Germany, when the Minister for Foreign Affairs stated forcefully that it is "an erroneous conception that the *de facto* existence of the German Democratic Republic must, under international law, necessarily lead to recognition."[22]

With regard to the recognition of governments, the positions adopted by the British and Dutch Governments have been not dissimilar.

Prior to 1980 the British policy was that announced by the Foreign Secretary in 1951.

"It is international law which defines the conditions under which a Government should be recognised *de iure* or *de facto* and it is a matter of judgement in each particular case whether a regime fulfils the conditions. The conditions under international law for the recognition of a new regime as the *de facto* Government of a State are that the new regime has in fact effective control over most of the State's territory and that this control seems likely to continue. The conditions for the recognition of a new regime as the *de iure* Government of a State are that the new regime should not merely have effective control over most of the State's territory, but that it should, in fact, be firmly established. His Majesty's Government considers that recognition should be accorded when the conditions specified by international law are, in fact, fulfilled and that recognition should not be given when these conditions are not fulfilled. The recognition of Government *de iure* or *de facto* should not depend on whether the character of the regime is such as to command His Majesty's Government's approval."[23]

The position of the Dutch Government was restated by the Minister for Foreign Affairs in February 1976, in the following terms:

"Recognition is, in the opinion of the Netherlands Government, an act of factual purport, a formal establishment that a particular government actually exercises, on a reasonably permanent basis, authority over a major part of the territory and population of a State. It is therefore a judgement of a factual situation which does not imply any moral judgement [24], or support the regime in question. It has nothing to do with approval, but everything to do with the situa-

---

as to the *de facto* character of Tinoco's government, according to the standard set by international law."

21. For a review see, Kuyper, *loc.cit., supra* n. 19, pp. 393-4.

22. Quoted, ibid., p. 393. See also, NYIL (1979) p. 315: "Although the decision to recognise may be made when these conditions [of a territory and a people over which effective and stable authority is exercised] are fulfilled, recognition is not obligatory . . .". Recognition of the GDR was made conditional on a satisfactory settlement between the two Germanies and its timing was later subordinated to the prior accession of both to membership of the UN: see, Kuyper, ibid., p. 376.

23. *Hansard,* House of Commons, Vol. 485, cols. 2410-11, quoted in Warbrick, *loc.cit., supra* n. 1, p. 570.

24. See the position taken by the Minister for Foreign Affairs when refusing calls to make recognition of the Provisional Revolutionary Government of South Vietnam dependent on religious freedoms being respected by that Government: "Although there is no right of recognition, I would not make the timing of recognition dependent on such conditions. But I would be willing to use the newly established relations to urge, in an appropriate manner, compliance with religious and spiritual freedoms."; NYIL (1976) p. 231.

tion as actually found . . . A recognition policy based on factual criteria is, in the Government's opinion, the only possible basis for a consistent foreign policy. With a government which does not embody the constituted authority or represent the majority of the population of a country, no agreements or arrangements can be made which are really binding on that country. Diplomatic relations would become a mockery . . . Before the Second World War recognition used to be based on approval . . . absurd situations will occur if recognition is not based on factual situations, but on approval . . ." [25]

It appears that, *inter alia,* it was the difficulty of effectively securing the politically desirable divorce between the fact of recognition and the implication of approval that persuaded the British Government to adopt a new policy on recognition in April 1980, which was stated in the following terms:

". . . we shall no longer accord recognition to Governments. The British Government recognise States in accordance with common international doctrine.

Where an unconstitutional change of regime takes place in a recognised State, Governments of other States must necessarily consider what dealings, if any, they should have with the new regime, and whether and to what extent it qualifies to be treated as the Government of the State concerned . . . We have . . . concluded that there are practical advantages in following the policy of many other countries in not according recognition to Governments. Like them, we shall continue to decide the nature of our dealings with régimes which come to power unconstitutionally in the light of our assessment of whether they are able themselves to exercise effective control of the territory of the State concerned and seem likely to do so."[26]

The consequences of this change of policy will emerge fully in due course, but it has already allowed the British Government to avoid recognising changes of government which would have fallen to be recognised under the former policy.[27] As a means of more finely tuning the degree of its relationship with another government, it clearly offers considerable advantages over the former policy, and the present Dutch policy, of being faced with the options of, on the one hand, recognising and trying to persuade other governments that recognition does not imply any degree of approval and, on the other, not recognising and persuading the incumbent government, and its friends, that no disapproval is implied.

In practical terms, it appears that the basis on which the relationship with a régime coming to power unconstitutionally is to be determined has a closer affinity with the position previously adopted in cases of determining whether to accord *de facto* recognition, than to that of *de jure* recognition. It may be accepted, however, that this is here probably a distinction without a difference. In legal terms the distinction has a limited ambit [28] and in the context of the new policy would appear to have no role to play, at least in so far as international relations are concerned. It remains to be seen what use will be made of such terms in

25. NYIL (1976) p. 231.

26. *Hansard,* House of Lords, Vol. 408, cols. 1121-22, quoted in Warbrick, *loc.cit., supra* n. 1, pp. 574-5.

27. Warbrick, *ibid.,* pp. 575-6.

28. Brownlie, *op.cit., supra* n. 2, pp. 96-7.

internal affairs and what weight will be attached thereto by the courts to such distinctions.[29] It is of particular significance for the purposes of the present paper to what extent the new policy on recognition will have an effect on the practice of British courts in matters where the recognition or not of a State or government plays a role.

2. RECOGNITION BY THE JUDICIARY

Issues of recognition arise in proceedings before municipal courts under three broad sets of circumstances: whether a foreign entity is a State and, being so, may appear as plaintiff in the proceedings; whether a foreign entity is a State and therefore entitled to immunity; whether the legislative decrees and executive acts of a foreign entity are those of a State entitled to be applied or recognised in judicial proceedings. The interplay between Executive and Judiciary arises most acutely when the Executive has not recognised the foreign entity as a State or, having recognised the State, it has not recognised or does not yet recognise the government in, or claiming to be in power in that State or, thirdly, territory has been ceded to or annexed by another State, which cession or annexation is not recognised by the Ececutive.

To speak of recognition by the judiciary in respect of countries such as the United Kingdom is not strictly accurate, as will be seen, for what is then under discussion is the response of the court to the fact of recognition or not by the Executive and how that response manifests itself in cases of which the court is seized. In regard to countries such as The Netherlands it would not appear to be abusive of the term to speak of judicial recognition. Here one is confronted with a different situation. As has been observed in another context but which is equally pertinent to the present discussion:

> "The Court that is invited to speak out on the sovereign nature of a foreign entity must judge independently whether that entity complies with the concept of state under international immunity law."[30]

By contrast, it is a characteristic consequence of the approach presently prevailing in the United Kingdom that the issue of determination, including the

29. The court recognises entitlement to exercise extra-territorial powers as vesting in the *de iure* government.

30. Voskuil, "International Law of State Immunity, as reflected in the Dutch Civil Law of Execution", NYIL (1979) p. 245 at 253. See also, Voskuil, *De Nederlandse rechtspraak betreffende de Staatsimmuniteit* (Preadvies: Nederlandse Vereniging voor Internationaal Recht) (1973) p. 18: "Recognition of a foreign State or government by the Executive is a political act which allows for the establishment of normal diplomatic relations between sovereign States. Interpretation of the concept State upon application of the immunity rule requires a legal judgement that is independent of the political approach of the Executive . . . Recognition of a foreign State by the Executive ought not to be decisive for the judgement of the court seized of the issue of immunity, although its factual importance is great." (Translation of the present writer.) For an English summary of this Report see, NILR (1973) p. 302.

question to what legal criteria the question of law involved must be referred, is rendered non-justiciable. The Executive decision to recognise carries the implication that a prior determination, presumably in accordance with the (essentially legal) criteria publicly announced by the Executive as governing such determination, has been effected. One cannot, however, infer from the fact of recognition or non-recognition that a determination in such terms has in fact been effected and deductions from public utterances as to the criteria that may actually have been employed in such cases remain at best conjectural. The court considering itself compelled to treat the decision to recognise, and in principle also the decision not to recognise, as conclusive, the matter effectively ends there, even where the Executive's professed employment of the criteria established by international law might not appear to be sustainable upon objective examination.

As a consequence thereof, the real nature of the question that falls to be determined in such cases remains unresolved. This matter comes squarely to the forefront in those countries, such as The Netherlands, where the issue, which is seen as being the concept of foreign State, can arise for determination independently of the Executive's decision whether to recognise a foreign entity as State (or its government). The Dutch position is that "the concept of state . . . is essentially a concept of international law".[31] Accordingly, the criteria established by international law are determinative and not the position taken by the Executive with regard to the issue of recognition.

As was indicated in the preceding section, both The United Kingdom and The Netherlands appear to subscribe to the proposition advanced above that the determination by a State of claims to Statehood raises a question of law to be resolved by application of the criteria established by international law. Determination by the State necessitates a determination by some organ of the State; that is, in broad terms, by the Executive and/or the Judiciary. The issue of which organ has the responsibility for effecting such a determination may be regarded as an internal matter to be resolved by reference to each State's constitutional law. In short, the view may be taken that each State establishes for itself and by reference to its own constitutional law which of its organs is or are internally competent. It may be presumed that advocates of exclusive Executive competence would derive comfort from such a view. It is clear, however, that such an analysis fails to accommodate the claim that international law is of a higher order than national law, including national constitutional law. Recent developments in the United Kingdom indicate that this and other related problems will fall to be resolved. Attempts to do so may derive some assistance from the Dutch experience.[32]

As indicated above, the positions presently adopted by the British and Dutch courts are in striking contrast. In both countries the courts are justifiably proud of their judicial independence from interference by the Executive and that independence is carefully preserved. Yet in respect of the recognition of States and

31. Voskuil, *ibid.*, p. 255.

32. For an extensive discussion of such matters in the Dutch legal order see, Erades and Gould, *The Relation between International Law and Municipal Law*, (1976).

governments the British judiciary had adopted a position far removed from the Dutch viewpoint that "even in international affairs, the independent judgement of the national courts should be maintained at the risk of 'discordant voices expressing the sovereign will of the nation'."[33] At the time when the Dutch Supreme Court *(Hoge Raad)* was prepared to hold that the judicial decisions given by the courts of an insurgent *de facto* regime, namely the Belgian rule in the Southern Netherlands, could be accepted [34], the English court had held that "sound policy requires that the Courts of the King should act in unison with the Government of the King."[35] Adherence to such a policy can lead and arguably has led to a certain confusion of thought in that separate issues may not be distinguished and by reason of the failure to perceive the distinction, the justification for subsuming the one, e.g., the legal status of a State or government, to the other, namely, the exclusivity of the power of the Crown to accord recognition to a State or government, is not examined and judicially defended. Thus, on the issue of immunity of a sovereign from the jurisdiction of the British courts, Lord Dunedin was led to say in *Duff Development Co. Ltd.* v. *Government of Kalentan:*[36]

"It seems to me that once you trace the doctrine for the freedom of a foreign sovereign from interference by the courts of other nations to comity, you necessarily concede that the home sovereign has in him the only power and right of recognition. If our sovereign recognises and expresses the recognition through the mouth of his minister that another person is a sovereign, how could it be right for the courts of our sovereign to proceed upon an examination of that person's supposed attributes to examine his claim and, refusing that claim, to deny to him the comity which their own sovereign had conceded."

This may be compared with the reasoning adopted by the Court of Appeal Amsterdam in *Weber* v. *USSR* [37], where the Court was faced with the issue of immunity at a time before The Netherlands Government in London had recognised the Soviet Government as *de iure.* The Court perceived (although not fully) a distinction between the fact of Executive recognition and the fact of Statehood:

". . . what we are here confronted with is only the non-recognition of a government, since the Russian State, notwithstanding alterations in the form of government, has retained its identity and hence its status as a recognized State; whereas the principle of immunity . . . from jurisdiction is a consequence of the recognition of and respect for the sovereignty of a foreign State and that such State sovereignty is independent of the recognition or non-recognition of the government which at that moment is in power in a recognized State."

33. Tammes, "Netherlands Courts and International Recognition", in *Symbolae Verzijl* (1958), p. 362, quoting, The Rogdai (1920) 278 Fed. 294. For recent discussion of judicial recognition, see also, Kuyper, *loc.cit., supra* n. 19, pp. 387-391; Mann, *Studies in International Law,* (1973) Chap. 11; Merrills, "Recognition and Construction" (1971) 20 ICLQ 476; Nedjati, "Acts of Unrecognised Governments" (1981) 30 ICLQ 388; Warbrick, *loc. cit., supra* n. 1, pp. 576-592. For a review of UK caselaw, see, Brownlie, *op. cit., supra* n. 2, pp. 101-108.

34. HR 22 September 1840, 28 August 1847, W. 124 & 872.

35. Taylor *v.* Barclay (1828) 2 Sim. 213, 221.

36. [1924] AC 797, 820. Cf. Roche J., *infra* n. 42.

37. Hof Amsterdam, 30 April 1942, NJ 1942, No. 757.

In *Poortensdijk* v. *Soviet Republic of Latvia* [38] the fact of Executive recognition or non-recognition of the new situation in Latvia was not explicitly considered in the judgments of the District Court or Court of Appeal Amsterdam but it is most unlikely that the Court of Appeal was not cognizant of the continued recognition by The Netherlands of Latvia.[39] On an interpretation of the Soviet Constitution the Court of Appeal concluded that the Soviet Republic of Latvia was a sovereign State within the Socialist Union, alternatively that the nationalization decrees with which the USSR must have been in agreement could not be held to be unlawful without denying the sovereign rights of that State and thus the Court gave effect to the incorporation of Latvia by the USSR.

On the issue of the applicability of the legislative decrees and acts of a non-recognised entity, the Dutch position is quite clearly that the fact

> "that the Netherlands Government has not recognised the Soviet Republic forms no obstacle to a Dutch Court viewing the juridical relations within that country in the light of the regulations enacted by the Government of the Republic."[40]

The position of the British judiciary as to this is equally clear. In *Aksionairnoye Obschestvo A.M. Luther* v. *James Sagor & Co.* [41] the plaintiffs were a company incorporated in 1898 under the law of Czarist Russia. Soviet authorities took possession of the plaintiff's factory and wood stocks, acting under a decree of confiscation of June 1918. The defendants purchased in 1920 a quantity of wood from the Soviet authorities and imported it into England, whereupon the plaintiffs claimed a declaration that the goods were their property, an injunction restraining further dealing and damages. The defendants contended that the confiscation and subsequent sale were acts of a sovereign State which had validly transferred the property in the goods to them. At first instance, Roche J. held that the validity of the Soviet legislative act *depended* "upon whether the power from which it purports to emanate is what it apparently claims to be, a sovereign power" [42] and that where

> "a foreign Government or its sovereignty is not recognised by the Government of this country, the courts of this country either cannot, or at least need not, or ought not, to take notice of or recognize such foreign Government or its sovereignty."[43]

Consequently, the conclusion was reached that at the material time the Soviet decree was ineffective to pass property in the goods to the defendants. On ap-

38. Rb. Amsterdam, 14 January 1941, NJ 1941 No. 338; Hof Amsterdam, 3 December 1942, NJ 1943 No. 340. Criticised, Voskuil, *loc.cit., supra* n. 30, p. 254, on the ground that the contitutional law of the foreign State could not afford a legal basis for recognition, although it might have a significant factual value.

39. Tammes, *loc.cit., supra* n. 33, p. 384.

40. Hof Amsterdam, 4 November 1942, NJ 1943 No. 496, Herani *v.* Wladikawkas Eisenbahngesellschaft.

41. [1921] 1 KB 456.

42. At p. 473.

43. At p. 474.

peal [44], this decision was reversed on the different ground that as the Foreign Office had subsequently stated in reply that it recognised the Soviet Government as the *de facto* Government of Russia, the confiscatory decree was rendered effective due to the retroactive effect that was to be given to the recognition to 1917.

This view of the total non-applicability of the law of non-recognised entities reached what one may only hope is its high water mark in *Carl Zeiss Stiftung* v. *Rainer & Keeler Ltd. (No. 2)* [45], which raised as an interlocutory question the issue whether the plaintiffs, who derived their authority to pursue a passing-off action from legislative and administrative acts of the German Democratic Republic, had *locus standi.* The Foreign Office certificate requested by the Court stated that Her Majesty's Government recognised the USSR as the *de iure* governing authority in respect of the territory in question and "have not recognised either *de iure* or *de facto* any other authority purporting to exercise governing authority" on that territory. In the Court of Appeal it was held that

> "The *lex loci actus,* to the consequences of which the English courts will give effect, is thus limited to laws made by or under the authority of those persons who are recognised by the Government of the United Kingdom as being the sovereign government of the place where the thing happened, and will not treat the happening as having in England any legal consequences which are claimed to result from a law made by persons who are not recognised as being the sovereign government of that place or persons authorised by that sovereign government to make laws for that place."[46]

The House of Lords reversed the Court of Appeal, accepting that the conclusion to which the Court of Appeal had been forced was "a most deplorable result in respect of any highly civilised community, with which we have substantial trading relationships I believe, which should be avoided unless our law compels that conclusion."[47] The escape route devised by their Lordships was ingenious but lacks conviction: as the Executive certificate stated that the Soviet Government was recognised as the *de iure* government and as the East German Government had been established by the Soviet Government, therefore the acts of the unrecognised German Democratic Republic were to be regarded as those of a subordinate authority acting under and with the consent of the *de iure* authority of the USSR – a patently fictitious concept of agency.[48] While the desire to escape from *Luther* v. *Sagor* is understandable, it is an unconvincing distinction to argue that executive recognition in the circumstances of that case was essential to give international validity to the acts of a revolutionary government claiming authority over an existing State (Russia), but was not necessary in the case of the German Demo-

44. [1921] 3 KB 532.
45. [1966] 2 All ER 536.
46. [1965] 1 All ER 300, 315 *per* Diplock LJ.
47. [1966] 2 All ER 536, 569 *per* Lord UpJohn.
48. Criticised, Mann (1967) 16 ICLQ 760, Merrills, *loc.cit., supra* n. 33, p. 487.

cratic Republic, which is authorised to make laws in respect of a territory where a *de iure* sovereign is recognised.[49]

This may be compared with the view taken by the District Court Amsterdam in *Exportchleb* v. *Goudeket,* where the defendant had contended that the contract had been concluded with a representative of the USSR and that as the Soviet Government had not been recognised by The Netherlands, neither the Russian Government nor the plaintiff as assignee had standing before the Court, which replied,

> "that this defence must be rejected on the ground that, though non-recognition of the actual Russian Government by the Netherlands certainly involves the absence of diplomatic intercourse between the two States, its non-recognition by no means entails the consequence that in this country the *de facto* Government of the Russian State cannot appear on behalf of that State in matters of civil law."[50]

What is then settled is that in the United Kingdom a foreign entity claiming to be a State may appear as plaintiff, may successfully claim immunity and its decrees and acts will be recognised and applied only if it is recognised by Her Majesty's Government, as to which fact the Executive Certificate is conclusive.

By contrast, in The Netherlands a State or government that has not been recognised by the Government of The Netherlands can be granted *ius standi in iudicio,* may successfully plead immunity and its decrees and acts will generally be applied and recognised because the Dutch courts consider themselves free to pronounce on and attribute legal effect to international fact-situations independently of the Executive's assessment of such situations, or lack of it.[51] As the Netherlands does not know the Executive certificate and as the Dutch judge would not apply to the Executive for its views or for information, the Dutch court seeks to establish the relevant facts and proceeds to apply the appropriate law. It does, however, take judicial notice of Executive policy relevant to the issue at hand but only to the extent that such is fact to be evaluated.[52] In *Lesser* v. *Rotterdamse Bank and Kling* [53], the Rotterdam District Court had to decide whether the succession to the estate of a resident of Kaunas, who had died in 1943, was governed by Lithuanian or by Soviet Law. In 1940 Lithuania had been occupied by Soviet troops and incorporated into the USSR, whereby the Soviet Civil Code was introduced and Soviet nationality conferred on its inhabitants. German troops re-occupied the territory in 1941. Although the District Court regarded the German occupation as no more than an *occupatio bellica* and thus without effect on the civil law of the territory, it held that the elections held there during the Soviet

49. [1966] 2 All ER 536, 580 *per* Lord Wilberforce.
50. Rb. Amsterdam, 15 February 1935, NJ 1935, p. 1058.
51. For other instances, see, Kuyper, *loc.cit., supra* n. 19, *passim;* for the practice of the Dutch courts in the application of treaties to subjects of States whose governments have not been recognised, see, Bot, *op.cit., supra* n. 15, pp. 213-17; Tammes, *loc.cit., supra* n. 33, pp. 367-372.
52. Tammes, *loc.cit., supra* n. 33 passim. Voskuil, *loc.cit., supra* n. 30, p. 253.
53. Rb. Rotterdam, 30 December 1953, NJ 1954 No. 769; *Netherlands International Law Review* (1955) pp. 420-25 note Erades.

occupation and the resulting incorporation into the USSR was a matter falling outside its competence. Given that it was confronted with two situations, each of which could be condemned as contrary to international law, it preferred to interprete in conformity with the recognition by The Netherlands of the USSR in 1942.

"Although the *de jure* recognition of the USSR by the Dutch Government in 1942, granted without any reservation regarding Lithuanian territory, is not without more decisive of the question whether the Dutch courts must consider the legislation introduced in the Soviet Republic of Lithuania in 1940 to be valid as from that date, nevertheless such recognition leads to an affirmative answer to that question. For such recognition must be deemed to imply recognition of the law previously put into effect by the USSR incorporating the Soviet Republic of Lithuania into the USSR. This entails recognition of the other legislation referred to and introduced in 1940."

At the heart of the British Courts' approach lies the Executive certificate, which is a statement generally in writing under the authority of a Secretary of State and delivered to the court or to a party to the judicial proceedings in reply to questions addressed to the Secretary of State. Alternatively, it may be presented by the Attorney-General to the court. It has now been established beyond doubt, by the courts, that the Executive certificate is conclusive as to the matters to which it addresses itself,[54]

"It is a firmly established principle that the question whether a foreign state, ruler or government is or is not sovereign is one on which our courts accept as conclusive information provided by Her Majesty's Government: no evidence is admissible to contradict that information."[55]

The odd feature of this standpoint is that the Executive certificate has been given more weight than it is necessarily entitled to. In the first place, although it is accepted that the certificate addresses itself to questions of fact, it has often been regarded as conclusive also of law, which province should be exclusively reserved to the courts.[56] Secondly, the type of fact to which it addresses itself is generally given what may permissibly be regarded as an extended meaning. Thus, when a certificate attests to whether a State is recognised, it would appear to be arguable that it is not the legal status of State to which the certificate is attesting but only to the fact that Her Majesty's Government recognise the State as having that status.[57] It may be that the absence of clear distinctions in such matters has its roots in possibly related issues of constitutional law.[58] It is clear, however,

54. Duff Development Co. Ltd. *v.* Government of Kelantan [1924] AC 797; The Arantzazu Mendi [1939] AC 256.
55. Carl Zeiss Stiftung *v.* Rainer & Keeler Ltd. (No. 2) [1966] 2 All ER 536, 544 *per* Lord Reid.
56. Mann, *op.cit., supra* n. 33, p. 405.
57. Warbrick, *loc.cit., supra* n. 1, p. 577.
58. See, R. *v.* Bottrill ex p. Kuechenmeister [1947] KB 41, 57 *per* Scott LJ: "In the British Constitution, which is binding on all British Courts, the King makes both war and peace . . . Whether international law has a different rule is irrelevant."

that statute can settle the matter beyond doubt, as has recently been done in section 21 of the State Immunity Act 1978, which states that

"A certificate by or on behalf of the Secretary of State shall be conclusive evidence on any question
(a) whether any country is a State for the purposes of Part 1 of this Act, whether any territory is a constituent territory of a federal State for those purposes or as to the person or persons to be regarded for those purposes as the head or government of a State . . ."

What this does not settle, however, is the extent to which the certificate is exclusive as to those matters to which it addresses itself, however conclusively. There would also appear to be room for development in the practice of requesting certificates. In both these respects, the new policy on recognition announced in 1980 could be of influence.

It has been stated with great authority that the courts are under an obligation to request a certificate, "that not only is this the correct procedure but it is the only procedure by which the Court can inform itself of the material fact . . ."[59]. Recently, however, in *Spinney's (1948) Ltd. & Ors* v. *Royal Insurance Co. Ltd.*,[60] the court rejected the plaintiff's argument that a certificate should be requested so as to determine whether the Lebanese conflict of 1976 amounted to a civil war. The plaintiffs owned property in Beirut looted during the disturbances in January 1976 and they claimed under insurance policies which exempted loss caused directly or indirectly by 'civil war'. Mustill J. said:

"There are, of course, well-recognised situations in which it is the practice of the Court to consult the Secretary of State, and on which his response is treated as conclusive. These are mainly, if not exclusively, cases in which the State of the United Kingdom's diplomatic relations forms an integral part of the issue in suit . . .

The present case is not in this category. The issue is not whether the events in Lebanon were recognised by the United Kingdom as amounting to a civil war in the sense . . . that this country would, if the occasion had arisen, have accorded to the participants the rights and demanded of them the duties appropriate to belligerents. The question here is whether there was a civil war within the meaning of the policy. The two questions are not the same, and a pronouncement by the Secretary of State on one will not suffice to decide the other . . . when deciding whether the expected perils apply, the ascertainment of primary facts is only one step in the process. The real problem is to interpret what was happening, in the light of the words used in the policy."[61]

This case may be grouped with others that have been termed "construction" cases [62], the more so as Mustill J. relied on the authority of *Kawasaki Kisen Kabushiki Kaisha* v. *Bantham Steamship Co. Ltd.* [63] and *Luigi Monta of Genoa*

59. The Arantzazu Mendi [1939] AC 256, 264 *per* Lord Atkin.
60. [1980] 1 Lloyd's R. 406.
61. At. p. 426.
62. Merrills, *loc.cit.*, *supra* n. 33.
63. [1939] 2 KB 544: "war".

v. *Cechofracht Co. Ltd.* [64], to which others might be added.[65] These cases are said to have established that it is for the court to construe terms used in documents by reference to the intentions of the author and that to this end evidence can be received other than that provided by the Executive certificate. The argument is a valuable one although it is with difficulty that one can fully equate the construction of terms in such admitted documents as charterparties and insurance contracts, which regulate the relations between parties to the proceedings, with the construction of terms in British statutes.[66]

The significance of Mustill J.'s decision would seem to go further than his determination that the issue was whether there was a civil war within the meaning of the policy and that such an issue was in some way an exception to the rule requiring executive certification. Rather, his Lordship appears to have regarded the rule as being instead a "practice" in those situations where the diplomatic relations of the United Kingdom constitute "an integral part of the issue in suit", in other words, that the Executive certificate should be sought in those cases concerning the conclusive establishment of facts the creation or recognition of which fall within the Crown's prerogative of conducting foreign affairs.[67] In other cases the certificate need not be sought, indeed, should not be sought:

> "It is true that the Court will, on occasion, invite the opinion of the Secretary of State on questions of fact not directly connected with formal acts of recognition by the United Kingdom . . . This would involve the Executive in expressing in public a formal opinion . . . This might very well be a source of constraint and I do not consider that the Court should ask the Executive to engage upon such a task unless satisfied that some really solid benefit would ensue."[68]

On the basis of the fact that Executive certificates in the past have frequently referred matters back to the court for determination [69] and in the light of the new policy on recognition, it may be conjectured that the Executive would welcome such a development.

64. [1956] 2 QB 555: "government". *Cf.* White, Child and Beney, Ltd. *v.* Simmons (1922) 11 Lloyd's LR 7.

65. Reel *v.* Holder [1981] 1 WLR 1226: "country".

66. As in Re Al-Fin Corporation's Patent [1969] 2 WLR 1405: "foreign state", s. 24 Patents Act 1949.

67. Advocated as early as 1945 by Mann, *op.cit., supra* n. 33, p. 403.

68. [1980] 1 Lloyd's Rep. 406, 426, a view in accord with that of Lord Greene in Kawasaki, *supra* n. 63: "I do not myself find the fear of the embarrassment of the Executive a very attractive basis upon which to build a rule of English law", at p. 552.

69. See, the replies of the Secretary of State in, e.g., Re Al-Fin Corporation's Patent, *supra* n. 66: "that, in providing the above information the Foreign Office is expressing no view as to whether there were 'hostilities between His Majesty and any foreign State' within the meaning of section 24 of the Patents Act, 1949, which is regarded as a question for determination by the court on the basis of all the relevant evidence and in the light of the true interpretation of the Statute"; Luther *v.* Sagor, *supra* n. 41: "difficult and, it may be, very special questions of law upon which it may become necessary for the courts to pronounce"; White, Child and Beney Ltd. *v.* Simmons, *supra* n. 64: "any opinion as to how far or over what area the power of the Soviet Government was effective, the questions being also questions of fact for the courts to determine on the evidence laid before them". Similarly, The Arantzazu Mendi, *supra* n. 59.

Given the conclusiveness of the Executive certificate as to the matters to which it addresses itself, there remains the question of its exclusiveness. Recently, in *Hesperides Hotels Ltd.* v. *Aegean Turkish Holidays Ltd. and Muftizade* [70], the Court of Appeal admitted substantial evidence on the situation in Cyprus following the Turkish invasion in 1974 and the establishment in the north of the island of the Turkish Federated State of Cyprus, despite an Executive Certificate stating that the United Kingdom did not recognise that State "as being the government of an independent de facto sovereign state". Lord Denning MR was prepared to challenge the rule in *Luther* v. *Sagor* and to accept that there were circumstances in which the court should take notice of the laws of an unrecognised entity and that, as a consequence, it should admit evidence to prove the state of affairs in the territory allegedly controlled by the unrecognised government.

> "The executive is concerned with the *external* consequences of recognition, vis-à-vis other states. The courts are concerned with the *internal* consequences of it, vis-à-vis private individuals . . . the courts are entitled to look at the state of affairs actually existing in a territory, to see what is the law which is in fact effective and enforced in that territory, and to give such effect to it – in its impact on individuals – as justice and common sense require: provided always that there are no considerations of public policy against it."[71]

Such an approach is in line with the view that although the court may consider itself prevented by virtue of overriding constitutional law from "recognising" the unrecognised government, it is nevertheless open to the court to apply the law operative in the governed territory.[72] There would appear to be much to commend such an approach. To the extent that the court is not empowered to grant standing or immunity to a non-recognised entity, it is so prevented under English constitutional law. It should not be overlooked, however, that in regard to matters that raise a question of recognition the court will often be faced with a preliminary issue in a case involving a reference to the forum's conflict of laws. It may not be perceived in such terms for the reason that the admission of evidence to establish fact falls to be decided, under the forum's conflict of laws rule, by reference to the *lex fori,* and that this is so whether the preliminary issue relates to the construction of a term in a statute or document, or to the status of one of the parties to the dispute or whether it involves the status of the territory indicated by the forum's conflict of laws rule as being the *lex causae.* In connection with such cases the *lex fori* contains rules of law which will be operative given a particular fact-situation and will also contain rules as to the determination of fact. Such determination may be regarded as resting with the Crown in the exercise of its prerogative.

70. [1977] 3 WLR 656.

71. Lord Denning based his decision on the issue on the ground that it "is not the province of these courts to resolve such a dispute", which echoes that of Lord Atkin in The Arantzazu Mendi, *supra* n. 59, that, "The non-belligerent state which recognizes two Governments, one *de jure* and one *de facto,* will not allow them to transfer their quarrels to the area of the jurisdiction of its municipal courts", noted by Brownlie, *op.cit., supra* n. 2, p. 105. On appeal the House of Lords expressed no opinion: [1978] 3 WLR 378.

72. Advocated by Mann, *op.cit., supra* n. 33, pp. 412-13; Greig, "The Carl Zeiss Case and the Position of an Unrecognised Government in English Law", (1967) 87 LQR 96.

For example, the rules of the *lex fori* relating to the immunity of foreign sovereigns or diplomatic personnel may be applicable only given an appropriate determination as to fact by the Executive. It is trite knowledge that rules governing procedure and evidence are apt to prejudice determination of questions of law. The view that an Executive determination as to fact is exclusive as to the procedure governing the admission of evidence has as its effect that such determination of fact is also conclusive as to the question of law raised. It is this that is questioned by the proposition that a reference to the *lex fori* is to be interpreted as a reference to municipal law as that does not derogate from international law. In regard to the issue of the applicability of the legislative decrees and acts of an alleged but unrecognised foreign lawmaker, this aspect may be regarded less emotively: the matter may properly fall to be decided by reference to the foreign *lex causae,* subject to the public policy of the forum. The English conflict of laws directs that where its rules lead to the application of a foreign law, the English judge should apply the law that the foreign judge would apply to the issue. The fact that the government whose legislative decrees and acts such foreign judge would apply has not been recognised by Her Majesty's Government would be a matter of total indifference to that judge in the application of such law. Such an approach, were it to be adopted by the English courts, would reflect the view taken by the Court of Appeal Amsterdam in *Herani* v. *Wladikawkas Eisenbahngesellschaft* [73], and to the extent that the foreign government would thereby be judicially acknowledged as having a factual existence, irrespective of the fact of its Executive non-recognition, it would come close to the functional distinction drawn some thirty years ago in The Netherlands by François.[74] The qualification as to the operation of public policy mentioned by Lord Denning reflects the decision of the District Court and Court of Appeal The Hague in *N.V. Trust Mij. "Helvetia"* v. *N.V. Assurantie Mij. "De Nederlanden van 1845"* [75] that a Soviet decree of 1918 on the expropriation of the assets of private assurance companies without compensation was contrary to Dutch public policy, irrespective of the non-recognition of the Soviet Government by The Netherlands.

Such conflict of laws approach would not in itself be an answer to the broad spectrum of issues that arise, even if it were to be adopted by the courts [76], but it can be of assistance in the search to arrive at more recognisably justifiable results, as has been achieved in the relations between the Federal Republic of Germany and the German Democratic Republic with the development of inter-

73. *Supra* n. 40.

74. François, *op.cit., supra* n. 2, p. 181 et seq., distinguished *de facto* and *de jure* recognition, which fall exclusively within the province of the Executive (p. 183), from recognition as *de facto* government ("erkenning als feitelijke regering"). The former are governed by political considerations which are of no relevance for the courts, which are concerned exclusively with those facts that determine existence (p. 184).

75. Hof The Hague, 3 June 1937, NJ 1937 No. 1168.

76. See the observation by Roskill LJ [1977] 3 WLR 656 at 672: ". . . it is clear that at some future date difficult questions may well arise as to the extent to which, notwithstanding the absence of recognition, the English courts will or may recognise and give effect to the laws or acts of a body which is in effective control of a particular area or place".

zonal law by analogy with rules of the conflict of laws. It is interesting to note that the effect of a decision of the English High Court refusing to recognize a Southern Rhodesian divorce granted by a judge appointed there after the unilateral declaration of independence in November 1965 was subsequently reversed by Order in Council, which was then replaced by a provision that domicile or residence in Southern Rhodesia may, subject to conditions, be treated in divorce petitions as domicile or residence in England.[77]

The above approaches may be furthered by two recent developments: the new Executive policy on recognition of 1980 and the decision in the *Trendtex* case.[78] As Her Majesty's Government will no longer formally accord recognition to a government, it will be left to be inferred from the nature of the dealings, if any, which are established with it whether it qualifies to be treated as a government. It would seem that increasingly the court will be in a position, with or without recourse to the Executive certificate as to such dealings, to conclude that the foreign entity is a government that has in fact been 'recognised'. It is clear that international law and practice knows of implied recognition[79], at least in limited circumstances. When certificates are requested the emphasis therein may come to lie on the fact of non-recognition of foreign entities as governments. As this would be conclusive under the present state of the law, it may be interesting to see the development of the view that the certificate is not exclusive. International law confers at least limited status on *de facto* governments.[80] Since the House of Lords established in *Trendtex Trading Corp.* v. *Central Bank of Nigeria*[81] that customary international law is directly incorporated into English law, the court ought arguably to recognise *de facto* governments by reference to international law. Should they decide to do so then they will move towards the position that has been defended in The Netherlands.

> "The Judiciary and the Executive . . . are both supposed to exercise public authority by standards derived from international law. The nature of the responsibilities carried by each state organ differs greatly, however. The Executive has a responsibility, and indeed an accountability, towards Parliament, for its administration of the state's foreign affairs. The Judiciary, on the other hand, is constitutionally charged with the administration of, *inter alia,* civil law, including international law in private matters. It cannot judge by extra-legal standards or requirements, however important or even crucial such standards or requirements may be for the State's administration of foreign affairs. Their importance is at the most of a factual, not of a normative nature."[82]

This view is based on the premiss that the rule of law underlies the strict separation of the two organs of State of Executive and Judiciary and that not only is

77. Adams *v.* Adams [1970] 3 All ER 572, reversed by S.I. 1972 No. 1718, replaced by Southern Rhodesia (Matrimonial Jurisdiction) Order 1970, S.I. 1970 No. 1540, now contained in Domicile and Matrimonial Proceedings Act 1973, s. 17(3).

78. *Infra* n. 81.

79. Brownlie, *op.cit., supra* n. 2, p. 98; Kuyper, *loc.cit., supra* n. 19, p. 397.

80. *Ibid.,* p. 82.

81. [1977] 2 WLR 356.

82. Voskuil, *loc.cit., supra* n. 30, p. 284.

the Judiciary free to take an independent stand in matters involving interests and even responsibilities of the Executive but that it is necessary that it should do so. To the question, "who ultimately is to decide in any given situation what kind of obligation rests with the State under international law", the answer is given,

> "that in a legal system based on the Rule of Law it is the Judiciary and not the Executive that ultimately decides on the meaning and scope of legal rules that affect the rights of legal subjects under civil law."[83]

The possibility that the British court might act in opposition to the Executive on the ground that it had proceeded in contravention of the State's international obligations is now possible on the basis of *Trendtex,* although unlikely. As a means of circumventing the common law rules as to *locus standi,* it would have no application and as a means of evading the conclusive force of a certificate issued under section 21 of the State Immunity Act 1978 it would possibly instigate a constitutional crisis. Under Article 65 as amended of the Dutch Constitution of 1953 legislation can be tested by reference to conformity with the treaty obligations of the State.[84] It is also possible, although the Dutch courts have not gone so far, that the recognition of a foreign government could be held to be void as contrary to an international obligation not to recognise. The judgment of the District Court Rotterdam in the Lithuanian case [85] is suggestive that executive recognition is not decisive, a view to be found also in the judgment of the Court of Appeal Amsterdam in *Weber* v. *USSR.*[86] Certainly the courts have declared that national law is "governed by generally recognised principles of international law."[87] It has been pointed out that a possible development in the United Kingdom is that a too uncritical reception of the position advocated in *Hesperides,* which is supportable to an extent in *Namibia A.O.* [88], might lead to judicial recognition of foreign entities such that the United Kingdom would fail to comply with its international obligations of non-recognition.[89] It may also be pointed out that equally the duty to ensure that rights secured under international law are not denied attaches to the State as legal subject and it would seem at best inelegant for one State organ to aver that it is not severally and jointly responsible for the proper discharge of such duty.

83. *Ibid.,* at p. 285.
84. See, generally, Erades and Gould, *op.cit., supra* n. 32, pp. 371-2, 393-419.
85. *Supra* n. 53.
86. *Supra* n. 37. *Cf.* Voskuil, *loc.cit., supra* n. 30 (Preadvies), p. 18: "The quality of State for the purposes of the immunity rule cannot, in my opinion, be denied to a defendant that is as such already recognised by the Executive." (Translation of the present writer.)
87. Hof The Hague, 5 January 1925, NJ 1925, p. 402. Also, Rb. Rotterdam, 3 April 1917, NJ 1917, p. 434, Rb. Rotterdam, 29 December 1950, NJ 1951, No. 79, discussed, Erades and Gould, *op.cit., supra* n. 32, p. 255.
88. (1971) ICJ Rep. 16: "this invalidity cannot be extended to those acts, such as, for instance, the registration of births, deaths and marriages, the effects of which can be ignored only to the detriment of the inhabitants of the territory", at p. 56.
89. A caution properly entered by Crawford, (1978) *British Yearbook of International Law,* p. 261,

3. CONCLUSION

In the case of both the United Kingdom and The Netherlands it is clearly established that under the Constitution it is the prerogative of the Crown to represent the nation in foreign affairs.[90] The content and conduct of the nation's foreign policy is dependent on the advice and competence of the Ministers responsible and it is this that leads one into the strictly speaking unconstitutional but understandably pragmatic error of referring to recognition by the Executive. The point is not, however, one merely of linguistic accuracy. It would be pedantic to insist that all references be to the Crown were it not for the fact that reference to the latter keeps in focus that the extensive power of the Court in the discharge of its task is limited at least in this respect, that it is constitutionally not empowered to challenge the Crown's proper and lawful use of its prerogative in foreign affairs, neither in legal nor in practical terms: the courts cannot make foreign policy nor do they represent the nation in foreign affairs.

This does not mean that the court is enjoined not to act when seized of a dispute some aspect of which touches upon foreign affairs or to act only in conformity with instructions given to it by the Crown, or by the Executive acting lawfully on behalf of the Crown. This would appear to be self-evident and the Dutch judiciary has long accepted this to be so and conforms to the view that, "there is no reason why in matters relating to foreign affairs, the courts should not abide by the rule that nothing they decide will amount to the making of policy and why in matters international they should not guard their independence as jealously as in matters municipal."[91]

The adoption of an analogous position by the judiciary of the United Kingdom is now increasingly advocated by commentators who express disquiet at the apparent willingness of British judges to deny their competence in matters touching upon foreign affairs and to defer to the real or imagined wishes of the Executive. Recently there have been indications that the British judiciary is beginning to accept that its own established position, that "Our State cannot speak with two voices on such a matter, the judiciary saying one thing, the executive another" [92], is no longer tenable and that a change, perhaps even a radical change, is required. The search now would seem to be for an approach that would allow the British courts the means, if not to abandon the existing position, at least to re-evaluate the division of competences so as to fulfil the task of ensuring justice between the parties according to law, including international law. In the fields of State immunity, both domestic and foreign, one has witnessed the challenge to the prerogatives of the sovereign State which denied to the individual legal remedies for the vindication of his rights against the state by asserting a privileged position in the field of

90. Article 58, Constitution of 1953; see, Erades and Gould, *op.cit., supra* n. 32, p. 197.
91. Mann, *op.cit., supra* n. 33, p. 395.
92. The Arantzazu Mendi, *supra* n. 59, *per* Lord Atkin at p. 264.

procedure.[93] In the field of recognition there is a growing acceptance that the argument of damage to the foreign relations of the State, should the judgment of the Judiciary at least rank with that of the Executive, is no longer decisive in a period in which the securing of the rights of the legal subject has become a matter of particular concern.

The matter, naturally, is not without theoretical difficulty involving as it does diverse issues of procedural and evidential law, constitutional law and conflict of laws, international law and the relationship of this to national law, the whole reflecting, at times distortingly so, not clearly articulated political considerations. Nevertheless, the significance of the practical consequences residual to this *mélange* prompts a re-evaluation of the central issue of what law is to govern the preliminary question whether an entity possesses personality sufficient to invoke the existence and operation of legal rules.

The experience of the Dutch in this area is instructive but is unlikely to be determinative of the means whereby a solution is to be found for analogous problems arising in the United Kingdom. Differing histories and patterns of constitutional development militate against embracing uncritically the Dutch approach. Although the results arrived at may be admired, nevertheless the two legal systems are sufficiently dissimilar to make it desirable that individual routes to a solution be followed.

93. Lauterpacht, "The Problem of Jurisdictional Immunities of Foreign States", BYIL (1951) p. 220.

1937
"Interrcgionaal echtscheidingsrecht", *Nederlands Juristenblad,* 1937, 299.

1938
De invloed van oorlog op de geldigheid van verdragen, Doctoral dissertation, Leiden, Amsterdam 1938.

1942
"Naar aanleiding van een volkenrechtelijke beslissing van den Hoogen Raad, *Nederlands Juristenblad,* 1942, 75.

1946
"Art. 3 Wet A.B. en het volkenrecht", *Nederlands Juristenblad,* 1946, 457.
"Verkenning van de volkenrechtelijke positie van de Nederlandse Regering te Londen", *Nederlands Juristenblad,* 1946, 629, 649.

1949
Waar volkenrecht en Nederlands staatsrecht elkaar raken, Haarlem 1949.
"Volkenrechtelijke aspecten van het Neurenbergse vonnis", *Rechtsgeleerd Magazijn Themis,* 1949, 249.

1950
"De verhouding tussen volkenrecht en nationaal recht in Nederland", *Nederlands Juristenblad,* 1950, 217, 246.

1951
"De onafhankelijkheid van de rechter en het volkenrecht", *Nederlands Juristenblad,* 1951, 380.
"Toetsing van wet aan tractaat", *Nederlands Juristenblad,* 1951, 663.

1952
"De voorstellen tot herziening der Grondwetsbepalingen betreffende het buitenlandse beleid", *Rechtsgeleerd Magazijn Themis,* 1952, 170.

1953/54
"Het rechtseffect van nationalisatie-maatregelen genomen door vreemde staten", *Mededelingen Nederlandse Vereniging voor Internationaal Recht,* 1954, 1.

Reviews of Judicial Decisions:
HR 23 June 1953, NJ 1953, No. 668; HR 15 December 1953, NJ 1954, No. 69; Rb Rotterdam, 9 April 1954; 1 NILR 1953-4, 328, 329, 430.

"Editorial Notice", 1 NILR 1953/4, 27.
"In memoriam" E.M. Meijers, ibid., 233.

Reviews of:
J.W. van der Zanden, Verdrag gaat voor wet, ook in nationale rechtsbetrekkingen, Zwolle 1952, ibid., 81.
B. Landheer, J.L.F. van Essen, Fundamentals of Public International Law, Leyden 1953, ibid., 207.

Catalogue des sources de documentation juridique, Unesco Paris 1953, ibid., 424.
B. Landheer, J.L.F. van Essen, Recognition in international law, Leyden 1954, ibid., 425.

1955

Reviews of Judicial Decisions:
Rb Rotterdam, 21 May 1953, HR 4 May 1954, NJ 1954, No. 382; Rb Amsterdam, 8 April 1954, NJ 1954, NJ 1954, No. 639; Rb Rotterdam, 30 December 1953, NJ 1954, No. 769; 2 NILR 1955, 92, 296, 420.

"In memoriam" B.M. Telders (1903-1945) 2 NILR 1955, 123.

Reviews of:
Jahrbuch für internationales Recht, 3. Band – 4. Band, Göttingen 1954, 2 NILR 1955, 203.
Eelco N. van Kleffens, The place of law in international relations, Rede gehouden op 29 november 1954 in de Princeton Universiteit: Jhr. Mr. C.M.O. van Nispen tot Sevenaer en Prof. Mr. A.J.P. Tammes, De gerechtigheid in de internationale verhoudingen en de weerstand, die zij daar ondervindt, Zwolle 1954, ibid., 204.
J.P.A. François, Grondlijnen van het Volkenrecht, Zwolle 1954, ibid., 290.

Reviews of:
Europäisches Recht, Textsammlung übernationalen und internationalen Rechts, Herausgegeben von Helmut Coing, Hermann Mosler und Hans-Jürgen Schlochauer, Frankfurt a.M., 2 NILR. 1955, 293.
Osteuropa-Recht, Gegenwartsfragen aus dem Sowjetischen Rechtskreis, Stuttgart 1955, ibid., 293.
A Bibliography of the Charter of the United Nations, New York 1955, ibid., 416.
Yearbook on Human Rights for 1952, New York 1955, ibid., 416.

1956

"De invloed, die de Nederlandse rechtspraak met betrekking tot verdragen aan de oorlog toekende", 3 *Netherlands International Law Review* 1956, 105.

Reviews of Judicial Decisions:
Rb Roermond, 17 February 1955, NJ 1955, No. 716; HR 13 January 1956, NJ 1956, No. 141; 3 NILR 1956, 167, 397.

Reviews of:
W. Riphagen, De juridische structuur der Europese Gemeenschap voor Kolen en Staal, Leiden 1955, 3 NILR 1956, 77.
Repertory of Practice of United Nations Organs, Volumes I, II and III, New York 1955, ibid., 79.
Tauno Suontausta, La souveraineté des Etats, Helsinki 1955, ibid., 162.
Jahrbuch für Internationales Recht, 5. Band, Hefte 1, 2/3, Göttingen 1955, ibid., 163.

1957

"Een regel van volkenrecht als twistappel van cassatierechters", *Volkenrechtelijke Opstellen* ter Ere van de Hoogleraren B.M. Telders, F.M. Baron von Asbeck en J.H.W. Verzijl, Zwolle 1957, 69.

Reviews of Judicial Decisions:
HR 10 December 1954, NJ 1956, No. 240; Raad van het Rechtsherstel, 29 June

1956, *Rechtsherstel* 1956, 1345, NJ 1956, No. 471; Rb Rotterdam, 13 April 1956, NJ 1956, No. 545; 4 NILR 1957, 85, 211.

Reviews of:
M.E. Bathurst and J.L. Simpson, Germany and the North Atlantic Community, A legal survey, Londen 1956, 4 NILR 1957, 82.
Reports of International Arbitral Awards – Vol. VI, New York 1956, ibid., 83.
P. Adriaanse, Confiscation in private international law, The Hague 1956, ibid., 424.
Jurisprudentie van het Hof van Justitie, Deel I en II, Luxemburg z.j., ibid., 426.
Yearbook of the International Law Commission 1956, Vols. I and II, New York 1957, ibid., 426.

1958
Reviews of:
International Law Opinions, selected and annotated by Lord Mc Nair, Cambridge 1956, 5 NILR 1958, 83.
J.P.A. François, Grondlijnen van het Volkenrecht, 2nd ed. Zwolle 1957, ibid., 84.
Symbolae Verzijl, The Hague 1958, ibid., 321.

1959
"Promulgation and Publication of International Agreements and their internally Binding Force in the Netherlands", *Varia Juris Gentium,* Liber Amicorum J.P.A. François, Leiden 1959, 93.

Dutch report on the theme, "I tribunali internazionali e sopranzionali nei loro caratteri en nei loro scopi fonamentali quali risultano dai tratti e dalle convenzioni vigenti, e quali appaiono dal loro funzionamento en dal loro anelito verso l'avvenire", voor het Eerste internationale congres van de rechterlijke macht te Rome 1958, Milaan 1959, deel II, p. 835.

Reviews of Judicial Decisions:
Hof The Hague, 15 June 1956, HR 1 June 1956, NJ 1958, No. 424; 6 NILR 1959, 399.

Review of:
Sparsa Collecta – Een aantal der verspreide geschriften van Jonkheer Mr. W. J.M. van Eysinga, Leyden 1958, 6 NILR 1959, 193.

1960
"Recht en rechter in Nederland en in de Europese Gemeenschappen", 7 *Netherlands International Law Review* 1960, 334.

Reviews of:
Fontes Iuris Gentium, Series A, Secto II, Tomus 2, Entscheidungen des deutschen Reichsgerichts in völkerrechtlichen Fragen, Cologne-Berlin 1960, 7 NILR 1960, 166.
Karl Strupp, Wörterbuch des Völkerrechts, Vol. I, 2nd rev. ed., Berlin 1960, ibid., 395.
John G. Hadwen & Johan Kaufmann, How United Nations Decisions are made, Leyden 1960, ibid., 395.
Sciences Humanitaires et Intégration Européenne, Leyden 1960, ibid., 396.

L.C. Green, International Law Through the Cases, 2nd ed., London 1959, ibid., 397.
Europäisches Recht, Frankfort, 1959, ibid., 398.

1961

The Relation between International Law and Municipal Law in the Netherlands and in the United States; in cooperation with Wesley L. Gould, Leiden-New York, 1961.

Reviews of Judicial Decisions:
Rb Maastricht, 25 June 1959, NJ 1960, No. 290; Krijgsraad Oost, 22 January 1959, Hoog Militair Gerechtshof, 12 April 1960; Hof The Hague, 4 February 1959, NJ 1960, No. 339; HR, 13 May 1960, NJ 1960, No. 494; Hof The Hague, 24 June 1959, NJ 1960, No. 527; HR, 26 August 1960, NJ 1960, No. 556; Kantonrechter Leiden, 7 December 1959, Rb The Hague, 6 May 1960, NJ 1961, No. 149; 8 NILR 1961 190, 194, 291, 294, 380, 383.

Reviews of:
Hof van Justitie van de Europese Gemeenschappen, Vol. V, Luxembourg 1960, 8 NILR 1961, 178.
Milton Katz & Kingman Brewster Jr, International Transactions and Relations, London 1960, ibid., 181.
Georg Schwarzenberger, A Manual of International Law, 2 vols., 4th ed., London-New York 1960, ibid., 182.
European Commission of Human Rights, The Hague 1959 – Yearbook of the European Convention on Human Rights, The Hague 1960, ibid., 188.
Dr. J.P.B. Tissot van Patot en Mr. Th. E. Rueb, De navolging van de Amerikaanse vervoerspolitiek en van de Interstate Commerce Commission in de Europese Gemeenschappen, Rotterdam 1961, ibid., 279.
Hof van Justitie van de Europese Gemeenschappen, Vol. VI, part 1, Vol. VI, part 2, issue 1, Luxembourg 1961, ibid., 280.
Méir Ydit, Internationalised Territories – From the "Free City of Cracow", to the "Free City of Berlin", Leyden 1961, ibid., 281.
Edvard Hambro, The Case Law of the International Court, Vol. II, Leyden 1960 – Fontes Iuris Gentium, Series A, Sectio I, Tomus 5, Cologne-Berlin-Munich-Bonn 1961, ibid., 281.
Charles de Visscher, Théories et réalités en droit international public, 3rd ed., Paris 1960, ibid., 282.
Herdenking van Professor Jhr. Mr. W.J.M. van Eysinga door de Faculteit der Rechtsgeleerdheid van de Rijksuniversiteit te Leiden, Leyden 1961, ibid., 282.
Mr. Th. W. Vogelaar, Het eigendomsrecht van Euratom over bijzondere splijtstoffen, Leyden-Assen 1961, ibid., 283.
Documents on the St. Laurence Seaway, London-New York 1960, ibid., 283.
Legal Problems of the EEC and the Efta, London 1961, ibid., 284.
A. Mast, Verdragen, Bruges 1961, ibid., 360.
Karl Strupp, Wörterbuch des Völkerrechts, Vol. II, Berlin 1961, ibid., 360.
Prof. Mr. B.V.A. Röling, De wetenschap van oorlog en vrede, Groningen 1961, ibid., 361.
Sydney D. Bailey, The General Assembly of the United Nations, London 1960, ibid., 361.
R.P. Cleveringa Jzn., Zeerecht, 4th ed., Zwolle 1961, ibid., 375.

1962

"Application of Private International Law by the International Court of Justice", *De conflictu legum,* Feestbundel Kollewijn-Offerhaus, Leiden 1962, p. 145.

"The Internal Effects of International Agreements", Contributions néerlandaises au 6me. Congrès international de droit comparé, Hambourg 1962.

"Enige vragen betreffende de artt. 65 en 66 van de Grondwet", *Nederlands Juristenblad* 1962, 356.

Reviews of Judicial Decisions:

Hof The Hague, 7 April 1961, NJ 1961, No. 204; HR, 18 April 1961, NJ 1961 No. 733; HR, 19 January 1962, NJ 1962, No. 107; 9 NILR 1962, 198, 315, 317.

Reviews of:

Lord Mc Nair, The Law of Treaties, Oxford 1961, 9 NILR 1962, 187.

Arthur Larson, When Nations Disagree, Louisiana State University Press, 1961, ibid., 192.

Grenville Clark en Louis B. Sohn, Wereldvrede door Wereldrecht, Haarlem 1961, ibid., 193.

American Enterprise in the European Common Market, Ann Arbor 1960, ibid., 194.

J.W. Schneider S.J., Treaty-making power of international organizations, Geneva 1959, ibid., 195.

Badr Kasme, La capacité de l'Organisation des Nations Unies de conclure des traités, Paris 1960, ibid., 195.

Erich Kaufmann, Der Staat in der Rechtsgemeinschaft der Völker, Göttingen 1960, ibid., 306.

Conférence de La Haye de Droit International Privé, 3 vols., The Hague 1961, ibid., 307.

1963

"Poging tot ontwarring van de "self-executing" knoop", *Nederlands Juristenblad,* 1963, 845.

Review of Judicial Decisions:

HR 6 March 1959, NJ 1962, No. 2; 10 NILR 1963, 82.

Reviews of:

Karl Strupp, Wörterbuch des Völkerrechts, deel III, tweede druk herzien onder redactie van Hans-Jürgen Schlochauer, Berlijn 1962, 10 NILR 1963, 66.

Amos J. Peaslee, International Governmental Organizations – Constitutional Documents, The Hague 1961, ibid., 80.

ΣΥΜΜΙΚΤΑ ΣΕΦΕΡΙΑΔΟΥ, Mélanges Sefériadès, Athene 1961, ibid., 300.

Jean Leca, Les techniques de révision des conventions internationales, Paris 1961, ibid., 300.

Hans-Joachim Hallier, Internationale Gerichte und Schiedsgerichte, Cologne, Berlin, Munich, Bonn 1961, ibid., 301.

Charles van Reepinghen et Paul Orianne, La procédure devant la Cour de justice des Communautés, Brussels-Paris 1961, ibid., 301.

A.H. Robertson, The Law of International Instructions in Europe, Manchester-New York 1961, ibid., 302.

Quincy Wright, The Role of International Law in the Elimination of War, Manchester-New York 1961, ibid., 302.

Wereldpolitiek en ABC'wapens, Universitaire Pers, Leiden 1961, ibid., 303.

Zs. Szirmai, Sowjetrecht en rechtsvergelijking, Leiden 1961; A.M. Stuyt, Gespleten volkenrecht? 's-Gravenhage, ibid., 303.

Johanna K. Oudendijk, De beoefening van volkenrechtsgeschiedenis, Leiden 1962, ibid., 304.
H. van den Heuvel, Prejudiciële vragen en bevoegdheidsproblemen in het Europees recht, Deventer-Antwerpen 1962, ibid., 304.
Hof van Justitie van de Europese Gemeenschappen, Jurisprudentie deel VI, band 2 aflevering 2 (1960) t/m deel VIII, afl. 1 t/m 4 (1962), ibid., 305.
Volkenrechtelijke Opstellen aangeboden aan Prof. Dr. Gesina H.J. van der Molen, Kampen 1962, ibid., 305.
Shabtai Rosenne, The World Court, What it is and how it works, Leyden-New York 1962, ibid., 306.
Studies in Polish Law, Leyden 1962, ibid., 307.
H.G. Schermers, De studie van het internationale institutionele recht, 1963, ibid., 307.
Common Market Law Review, London, Leiden, South Hackensack, N.J. ibid., 368.

1964

"De verhouding van de rechtspraak van het Hof der Europese Gemeenschappen tot die van de nationale rechters in de Lid Staten", *Mededelingen Nederlandse Vereniging voor Internationaal Recht,* 1964, 3.
"Le problème des dispositions directement applicables (self-executing) des traités internationaux et son application aux traités instituant une Communauté européenne", *Revue hellénique de droit international,* 1964, 221.
"Het recht van de Europese Gemeenschappen in de opmars", *Nederlands Juristenblad,* 1964, 1105.

Reviews of Judicial Decisions:
Kantonrechter Roermond, 11 January 1961, VR 1961, No. 49; HR 11 April 1961, NJ 1962, No. 71; VR 1961, No. 48; HR 28 November 1961, NJ 1962, No. 90; 11 NILR 1964, 81, 82.

Reviews of:
Karl-Hartmann Necker, Der räumliche Geltungsbereich der Haager Regeln, Berlin 1962, 11 NILR 1964, 67.
International Legal Materials, Current Documents I, Nrs. 1 & 2, Washington 1962, ibid., 193.
Alexandre-Charles Kiss, Répertoire de la pratique française en matière de droit international, tomes I et V, Paris 1962, ibid., 194.
Yearbook on the European Convention on Human Rights, Vols. 3 & 4, The Hague 1961 and 1962, ibid., 195.
Publications de la Cour Européenne des Droits de l'Homme, Série B: Mémoires, plaidoiries et documents 1962–Affaire "De Becker", Strasbourg 1963, ibid., 196.
H.J. Roethof, De norm in het volkenrecht, The Hague 1962, ibid., 196.
Talks on American Law, edited by H.J. Bergman, New York 1961, ibid., 283.
Hans-Joachim Hallier, Völkerrechtliche Schiedsinstanzen für Einzelpersonen und ihr Verhältnis zur innerstaatlichen Gerichtsbarkeit, Cologne-Berlin 1962, ibid. 283.
Jean Aimé Stoll, L'application et l'interprétation du droit interne par les juridictions internationales, Brussels 1962; ibid., 285.
Antonio Cassese, Il diritto interno nel processo internazionale, Padua 1962, ibid., 285.
R.-L. Perret, De la faute et du devoir en droit international, fondement de la responsabilité, Zürich 1962, ibid., 286.

Sydney D. Bailey, The Secretariat of the United Nations, New York-London 1962, ibid., 288.
The British Yearbook of International Law, Vol. 1961, London-New York-Toronto 1962, ibid., 292.
C. Wilfred Jenks, The Proper Law of International Organizations, London-Dobbs Ferry, N.Y. 1962, ibid., 295.
Georg Schwarzenberger, The Frontiers of International Law, London 1962, ibid., 298.

1965

Reviews of Judicial Decisions:
HR 18 May 1962; NJ 1965, No. 115; HR 10 April 1964, NJ 1964, No. 439; Rb Maastricht, 28 May 1964, SEW 1964, 657; Rb Assen, 25 July 1964, SEW 1964, 658; 12 NILR 1965, 318, 401.

Reviews of:
Belgian Review of International Law, Belgisch Tijdschrift voor Internationaal Recht, Revue Belge de Droit International, Brussels 1965, 12 NILR 1965, 65.
George Schwarzenberger, The Frontiers of International Law, London 1962, ibid., 70.
Gerhard Bebr, Judicial Control of the European Communities, London 1962, ibid., 71.
F.A.M. Alting von Geusau, European Organisation and Foreign Relations of States, A Comparative Analysis of Decision Making, Leiden 1962, ibid., 72.
J.J.A. Ellis and H. van den Heuvel, Europees mededingings- en kartelrecht, Deventer-Alphen a.d.Rijn 1962, ibid., 73.
Laurens, J. Brinkhorst and Geoffry M. Wittenberg, The Rules of Procedure of the Court of Justice of the European Communities, Leiden 1962, ibid., 73.
J.J.G. Syatauw, Decisions of the International Court of Justice, A Digest, Leiden 1962, ibid., 164.
W. de Valk, La signification de l'intégration européeenne pour le développement du droit international moderne, Leiden 1962, ibid., 165.
Georges Langrod, The International Civil Service, Leiden-Dobbs Ferry, N.Y. 1963, ibid., 165.
Edvard Hambro, The Case Law of the International Court of Justice, Individual and Dissenting Opinions, vols. III A and B, Leiden 1963 *and* Fontes Iuris Gentium, Series A, Sectio I, Tomus 4, Handbuch des ständigen internationalen Gerichtshofs 1934-1940, Cologne-Berlin 1964, ibid., 166.
Canada-United States Treaty Relations, ed. by David R. Deener, Durham, N.C.-London 1963, ibid., 166.
The Canadian Yearbook of International Law–Annuaire Canadien de Droit International, Vol. I (1963), Vancouver, B.C. 1963, ibid., 167.
British International Law Cases, Vol. I, London-New York 1964, ibid., 168.
Lawrence F. Ebb, Regulation and Practice of International Business, St. Paul, Minn. 1964, ibid., 163.
Hof van Justitie van de Europese Gemeenschappen, Jurisprudentie, Deel IX, 1963, afl. 1, 2 en 3, Luxemburg 1963 *and* Organisatie, Bevoegdheden en Procesregels van het Hof, Luxemburg 1963, ibid., 169.
The British Yearbook of International Law 1962, London–New York-Toronto 1964, ibid., 169.
Mélanges Offerts à Henri Rolin, Problèmes de droit des gens, Paris 1964, ibid., 170.
Charles de Visscher, Problèmes d'interprétation judiciaire en droit international public, Paris 1963; Rudolf Bernhardt, Die Auslegung völkerrechtlicher

Verträge, Cologne-Berlin 1963; V.D. Degan, L'interprétation des accords en droit international, The Hague 1963 *and* Alan H. Schechter, Interpretation of Ambiguous Documents by International Administrative Tribunals, London 1964, ibid., 311.
A.H. Robertson, Human Rights in Europe, Manchester-Dobbs Ferry, N.Y. 1963 *and* Conseil de l'Europe. Convention européenne des droits de l'homme, Manuel, Strasbourg 1963, ibid., 314.
Yearbook of the European Convention on Human Rights, Vol. V (1962), The Hague 1963, ibid., 314.
Publications de la Cour Européenne des Droits de l'Homme, Série B: Mémoires, plaidoiries et documents 1960-1961, Affaire Lawless, Strasbourg?, ibid., 315.
The Canadian Yearbook of International Law–Annuaire Canadien de Droit International, Vol. II (1964), Vancouver, B.C. 1964, ibid., 315.
Lord McNair, The Expansion of International Law, Jerusalem-London 1962, ibid., 316.
Richard A. Falk, The Role of Domestic Courts in the International Legal Order, Syracuse N.Y. 1964, ibid., 397.

1966

"International Law, European Community Law and Municipal Law of Member States", *International and Comparative Law Quarterly,* 1966, 117.
"Het inéêngrijpen van bovenstaats en nationaal recht", *Nederlands Juristenblad,* 1966, 313.
"De Proeve 1966 en de artt. 60-67 Grw.", *Nederlands Juristenblad,* 1966, 603.

Review of Judicial Decisions:
HR 17 April 1964, NJ 1965, No. 22; 13 NILR 1966, 58.

Reviews of:
Yearbook of the European Convention on Human Rights, The European Commission and European Court of Human Rights, deel VI 1963, The Hague 1965, 13 NILR 1966, 50.
Alexandre-Charles Kiss, Répertoire de la pratique française en matière de droit international, Deel III, Paris 1965, ibid., 51.
Rapport Généraux au VIe Congrès International de Droit Comparè, Hamburg 1962, Brussels 1964, ibid., 52.
Arthur Taylor von Mehren and Donald Theodore Trautman, The Law of Multistate Problems, Boston–Toronto 1965, ibid., 52.
The British Yearbook of International Law, 1963, 39th year, Oxford–London –New York–Toronto 1965, ibid., 54.
Staatsrechtelijke Beslissingen, ed. by F.J.F.M. Duynstee, ibid., 55.
D.G. Valentine, the Court of Justice of the European Communities, Vol. I Jurisdiction and Procedure, Vol. II Judgments and Documents 1954-1960, London – South Hackensack 1965, ibid., 55.
Wilhelm Wengler, Völkerrecht, Berlin–Göttingen–Heidelberg 1964, ibid., 186.
Alan Campbellen, Restrictive Trading Agreements in the Common Market, London – South Hackensack, N.J. 1964-1965 *and* David Kent Waer, Common Market Antitrust, a guide to the law, procedure and literature, The Hague 1965, ibid., 188.
L.J. Brinkhorst, De jurist en de Europese Economische Gemeenschap, The Hague–Leyden, ibid., 197.
C. Wilfred Jenks, the Prospects of International Adjudication, London – Dobbs Ferry N.Y. 1964, ibid., 197.
Hof van Justitie van de Europese Gemeenschappen, Jurisprudentie van het Hof van Justitie, deel X, Luxemburg 1964-1965, ibid., 199.

P. van Goethem – E. Suy, Beknopt Handboek van het Volkenrecht, Antwerp – Amsterdam, ibid., 199.
Ernst Reibstein, Völkerrecht – Eine Geschichte seiner Ideen in Lehre und Praxis, Freiburg – Munich 1958 (Deel I) and 1963 (Deel II), ibid., 200.

1967

Review of Judicial Decisions:
Rb Arnhem, 4 February 1965, NJ 1966, No. 418; HR 21 June 1966, NJ 1966, No. 416; 14 NILR 1967, 107.

Reviews of:
J.H.W. Verzijl, The Jurisprudence of the World Court. Leyden 1965-1966, 14 NILR 1967, 75.
L'intégration européenne. Genève 1964., ibid., 99.
Paul-F. Smets, L'assentiment des Chambres législatives aux traités internationaux et l'article 68 al. 2 de la Constitution belge. Brussels 1964, ibid., 99.
Vooruitzichten van de Rechtswetenschap. Ed. by J.M. Polak, Deventer-Antwerp 1964, ibid., 177.
Die Anwendung des völkerrechts im innerstaatlichen Recht; Ueberprüfung der Transformationslehre. Bericht von Karl Joseph Partsch. Berichte der deutschen Gesellschaft für Völkerrecht, Teil 6. Karlsruhe 1964, ibid., 178.
Law, State and International Legal Order. Essays in honor of Hans Kelsen. Ed. by S. Engel and R.A. Métall. Knoxville 1964, ibid., 179.
Hof van Justitie van de Europese Gemeenschappen, Jurisprudentie van het Hof van Justitie, deel XI, Luxemburg 1965, ibid., 181.
Zehn Jahre Rechtsprechung des Gerichtshofs der Europäischen Gemeinschaften; Dix Ans de Jurisprudence de la Cour de Justices des Communautés Européens. Cologne-Berlin-Bonn-Munich 1965, ibid., 181.
Europäische Rechtsprechung 1953-1962. Cologne-Berlin-Bonn-Munich 1965, *and* Répertoire de la Jurisprudence relative aux traités instituant les communautés européennes 1953-1962. Cologne-Berlin-Bonn-Munich 1965, ibid., 182.
Idem 1963 1964. Cologne-Berlin-Bonn-Munich 1965, ibid., 182.
The Yearbook of World Affairs 1965. London 1965, ibid., 183.
F.A.M. Alting von Geusau, Vreedzame verandering en internationale organisaties. Leyden 1965, ibid., 183.
J.J. Lador-Lederer, International Non-Governmental Organisations and Economic Entities – A Study in Autonomous Organisations and Ius Gentium. Leyden 1963. ibid., 290.
Amos J. Peaslee, Constitutions of Nations. Volume 1, Africa, 3rd revised edition. The Hague 1965, ibid., 291.
J.E.S. Fawcett, The British Commonwealth in International Law. London 1964, ibid., 291.
Nations Unies, Annuaire juridique 1963. New York 1965, ibid., 411.
British International Law Cases (Volume III). London-Dobbs Ferry N.Y. 1965, ibid., 411.
Shabtai Rosenne, The Law and Practice of the International Court. Leyden 1965, ibid., 426.
Edvard Hambro, The Case Law of the International Court (1959-1963). Deel IV A en IV B. Leyden 1966; *and* J. Douma, Bibliography on the International Court of Justice Including the Permanent Court (1928-1964). Leyden 1966, ibid., 427.

1968

Reviews of:
The Canadian Yearbook of International Law – Annuaire Canadien de Droit

International. Vol. III (1965). Vancouver B.C. 1965, 15 NILR 1968, 68.
D.P. O'Connell, International Law. London-Dobbs Ferry N.Y. 1965, ibid., 68.
J.G. Gastel, International Law Chiefly as Interpreted and Applied in Canada. Toronto 1965, ibid., 69.
Annuaire de l'A.A.A. – Yearbook of the A.A.A. Vol. 34 (1964) and 35 (1965). The Hague 1965 resp. 1966, ibid., 70.
Jürgen Schilling, Völkerrecht und staatliches Recht in Frankreich, Hamburg 1964, ibid., 70.
Hans Aufricht, The International Monetary Fund, London 1964, ibid., 70.
Les Conséquences d'orore interne de la participation de la Belgique aux organisations internationales. Institut royal des relations internationales. Brussel-Den Haag 1964, ibid., 71.
L'Adaptation de la Constitution Belge aux réalités internationales. Brussel 1966, ibid., 71.
Christian Tomuschat, Die gerichtliche Vorabentscheidung nach den Verträgen über die europaïschen Gemeinschaften. Keulen-Berlijn 1964, ibid., ibid., 71.
British International Law Cases. London-Dobbs Ferry, N.Y. 1966, ibid., 199.
Amos J. Peaslee, Constitutions of Nations. Vol. II, Asia, Australia and Oceania. Rev. 3rd edition. The Hague 1966, ibid., 417.
Klaus König, Die Anerkennung ausländischer Verwaltungsakte. Cologne-Berlin-Bonn-Munich 1965, ibid., 418.
Gerhard O.W. Mueller-Edward M. Wise, International Criminal Law. South Hackensack, N.Y.-London 1965, ibid., 418.
Ignaz Seidl-Hohenveldern, Völkerrecht. Cologne-Berlin-Bonn-Munich 1965, ibid., 419.
Georg Schwarzenberger, The Inductive Approach to International Law. London-Dobbs Ferry, N.Y. 1965, ibid., 420.
G. Leibholz-H.J. Rinck, Grundgesetz für die Bundesrepublik Deutschland. Keulen-Marienburg 1966, ibid., 421.

1969

"The Gut Dam Arbitration", 16 NILR 1969, 161.

Reviews of Judicial Decisions:
HR 8 November 1968, NJ 1969, No. 10; HR 17 March 1967, NJ 1967, No. 237; Rb Leeuwarden, 30 November 1967, NJ 1968, No. 244; 16 NILR 1969, 97, 321.

Reviews of:
Paul Guggenheim, Traité de Droit international public, avec la collaboration de Dietrich Kappeler. Geneva 1967, 16 NILR 1969, 94.
The British Yearbook of International Law 1964. London-New York-Toronto 1966, ibid., 96.
Pierre Lardy, La force obligatoire du droit international en droit interne. Paris 1966, ibid., 207.
Ingrid Detter, Law Making by International Organizations. Stockholm 1965, ibid., 290.
Yearbook of the European Convention on Human Rights – The European Commission and European Court of Human Rights. The Hague 1966, ibid., 290.
Holle Kuschel, Die NYUGAT – ein umstrittener Seekriegsfall. Hamburg 1965, ibid., 291.
Clive Parry, The Sources and Evidences of International Law. Manchester-Dobbs Ferry N.Y. 1965, ibid., 292.

D.H.M. Meuwissen, De Europese Conventie en het Nederlandse Recht, Leyden 1968, ibid., 405.

1970

"The Sudan Arbitration", 17 NILR 1979, 200.

Reviews of:

Stuart A. Scheingold, The Rule of Law in European Integration – The Path of the Schuman Plan. New Haven-London 1965, 17 NILR 1970, 68.

Europees Kartelrecht. Deventer 1965. Europees Kartelrecht in ontwikkeling. Deventer 1968, ibid., 68.

Heinz Wagner, Grundbegriffe des Beschlussrechts der Europäischen Gemeinschaften. Cologne-Berlin-Bonn-Munich 1965, ibid., 69.

Encyclopédie Dalloz, Répertoire de droit international. Paris 1968, ibid., 70.

Ernst Steindorff, la sauvegarde des droits privés et la procédure dans le droit des Communautés européennes. Brussels 1965, ibid., 70.

Cambridge Essays in International Law. London-Dobbs Ferry N.Y. 1965, ibid., 71.

International Co-operation in Litigation. The Hague 1965, ibid., 72.

La fusion des Communautés européennes. Liege-The Hague 1965, ibid. 72.

Vrijheid van vestiging en dienstverlening in de EEG. Deventer 1965, ibid., 72.

Zur Integration Europas. Karlsruhe 1965, ibid., 73.

Arthur Larson, C. Wilfred Jenks and others, Sovereignty within the Law. Dobbs Ferry N.Y.-London 1965, ibid., 73.

Walter Wiese, Der Kampf um das Bricker-Amendment. Hamburg 1965, ibid., 74.

The Yearbook of World Affairs - 1966. London 1966. The Yearbook of World Affairs 1967. London 1967, ibid., 74.

The British Yearbook of International Law - 1965 - 1966. London-New York-Toronto 1968, ibid., 75.

The Canadian Yearbook of International Law 1966 and 1967. Vancouver BC, ibid., 75.

Gedächtnisschrift Hans Peters. Berlin-Heidelberg-New York 1967, ibid., 76.

British International Law Cases. Londen-Dobbs Ferry N.Y. 1967, ibid., 76.

Manual of Public International Law, ed. Max Sørensen, London-New York 1968, ibid., 77.

En hommage à Paul Guggenheim, Geneva 1968, ibid., 78.

Gerhard Boehmer, Der völkerrechtliche Vertrag im deutschen Recht. Cologne-Berlin 1965, ibid., 78.

J.H.W. Verzijl, International Law in Historical Perspective. Part I: General Subjects. Part II: International Persons. Part III: State Territory. Leyden resp. 1968, 1969 and 1970, ibid., 175.

Lord MacNair/A.D. Watts, The Legal Effects of War, Cambridge 1966, ibid., 176.

Legal Advisers and International Organizations, edited by H.C.L. Merillat, Dobbs Ferry N.Y. 1966, ibid., 176.

W. Paul Gormley, The Procedural Status of the Individual before International and Supranational Tribunals. The Hague 1966, ibid., 189.

Sir Francis Vallat, International Law and the Practitioner. Manchester-Dobbs Ferry N.Y. 1966, ibid., 190.

Achim André, Beweisführung und Beweislast im Verfahren vor dem Europäischen Gerichtshof. Cologne-Bonn-Berlin-Munich 1966, ibid., 190.

Alexandre-Charles Kiss, Répertoire de la pratique française en matière de droit international public. Parts II and VI. Paris 1966 and 1969, ibid., 190.

Ian Brownlie, Principles of Public International Law. Oxford 1966, ibid., 190.
Nederlands recht in kort bestek. Deventer 1968, ibid., 191.
B.A. Wortley, Jurisprudence. Manchester-Dobbs Ferry N.Y. 1967, ibid., 191.
J.S. Schultsz, Arresten over internationaal privaatrecht. Haarlem 1967, ibid., 191.
Les Cours d'eau internationaux. Centre européen de la dotation Carnegie pour la paix internationale, Geneva 1967, ibid., 192.
Gerhard Hans Reichel, Die auswärtige Gewalt nach dem Grundgesetz für die Bundesrepublik Deutschland vom 23. Mai 1949. Berlin 1967, ibid., 192.
Kaye Holloway, Modern Trends in Treaty Law, London - Dobbs Ferry N.Y. 1967, ibid., 192.
Georg Schwarzenberger, A Manual of International Law, London 1967, ibid., 193.
William Gorham Rice, A Tale of Two Courts. Maditson-Milwaukee-London 1967, ibid., 193.
W. Friedmann, Legal Theory. London 1967, ibid., 193.
Berichte der Deutschen Gesellschaft für Völkerrecht. Issues 7, 8 and 9, Karlsruhe resp. 1967, 1968 and 1969, ibid., 193.
Walter Rudolf, Völkerrecht und deutsches Recht. Tübingen 1967, ibid., 194.

1971

Reviews of:

D.P.O'Connell, State Succession in Municipal and International Law, Cambridge, 1967, 18 NILR 1971, 116.
Eleventh Conference of the International Bar Association, Den Haag, 1966, ibid., 116.
Report of a Study Group on the Peaceful Settlement of International Disputes, Londen, 1966, ibid., 117.
C.F. Ameransinghe, State Responsibility for Injuries to Aliens, Oxford, 1967, ibid., 117.
Ingrid Detter, Essays on the Law of Treaties, Stockholm-Londen, 1967, ibid., 117.
Verdrag tot oprichting van de Europese Economische Gemeenschap – Verdrag tot oprichting van de Europese Gemeenschap voor Kolen en Staal – Verdrag tot oprichting van de Europese Gemeenschap voor Atoomenergie, Zwolle, 1967, ibid., 118.
Répertoire des décisions et des documents de la procédure écrite et orale de la Cour permanente de justice internationale et de la Cour internationale de justice, Genève, 1967, ibid., 118.
David M. Sassoon, CIF and FOB Contracts, Londen, 1968 en Nagendra Singh & Raoul Colinvaux, Shipowners, Londen, 1967, ibid., 118.
Publications de la Cour européenne des Droits de l'Homme, Straatsburg, 1967, ibid., 119.
Hof van Justitie van de Europese Gemeenschappen, Luxemburg, 1967, ibid. 119.
A. Gündüz Okçün, Trans-Municipal Law, Ankara, 1968, ibid., 119.
J.P. Verheul, Aspekten van Nederlands Internationaal Beslagrecht, Deventer, 1968, ibid., 120.
L'adhésion de la Grande Bretagne aux Communautés, Brussel, 1968, ibid., 120.
Dr. Herbert Günther, Zur Entstehung von Völkergewohnheitsrecht, Berlijn, 1970, ibid., 120.
Georg Schwarzenberger, International Law as applied by International Courts and Tribunals, Londen, 1968, ibid., 121.
Rudolf Alàdar Métall, Hans Kelsen – Leben und Werk, Wenen, 1969, ibid., 121.
Amos J. Peaslee, Constitutions of Nations, Den Haag, 1968, ibid., 122.

Edvard Hambro, Arthur W. Rovine, The Case Law of the International Court (1964-1966), Leiden 1968, ibid., 122.
The Work of the International Law Commission, New York, ibid., 122.
Revue roumaine d'études internationales, Bucarest, 1967, ibid., 123.
Jan Ramberg, Unsafe Ports and Berths, Oslo, 1967, ibid., 123.
Eenvormige Wet betreffende het Internationaal Privaatrecht, Amsterdam, 1968, ibid., 123.
The Relevance of International Law (A Festschrift for Professor Leo Gross), Cambridge, 1968, ibid., 123.
Dr. J.R. Thorbecke, Staatsinrigting en Staatsbestuur, Arnhem, 1968, ibid., 124.
J.E.S. Fawcett, The Law of Nations, New York, 1969, ibid., 124.
The Canadian Yearbook of International Law, Vancouver, (Vol. VI 1968, Vol. VII 1969), ibid., 124.
Les Nouvelles Conventions de la Haye: leur application par les juges nationaux. Receuil des décisions et bibliographie, Den Haag, 1970, ibid., 139.
American International Law Cases, New York, 1971, ibid., 247.
Ioan Voïcu, De l'interprétation authentique des traités internationaux, Parijs, 1968, ibid., 248.
A.E. Gotlieb, Canadian Treaty-Making, Toronto, 1968, ibid., 248.
J.E.S. Fawcett, The Application of the European Convention of Human Rights, Oxford, 1969, ibid., 249.
British International Law Cases, Londen, 1969, ibid., 249.
Hersch Lauterpacht, International Law, Cambridge, 1970, ibid., 365.
Fontes Juris Gentium, Series A, Sectie II, Tome 4, Keulen-Berlijn 1970, ibid., 365.
H.U. Jessurun d'Oliveira, De antikiesregel, Deventer, 1971, ibid., 373.

1972

"In memoriam M. de Winter, Member of the Board," 19 NILR 1972, 99.

Review of:
Michel Waelbroeck, Traités internationaux et juridictions internes dans les pays du Marché commun, Brussel en Parijs 1969, ibid., 203.

1973

"Erosion and Innundation led to an International Arbitration", Festschrift für Pan. J. Zepos, Athene-Freiburg i.B., Cologne 1973, p. 99.
"Is *stare decisis* an Impediment to the Enforcement of International Law by British Courts?", 4 NYIL 1973, 105.

Reviews of:
Brinkhorst, L.J. & Schermers, H.G., Judicial Remedies in the European Communities, A Case Book, Deventer/London/South Hackensack NJ 1969, 20 NILR 1973, 63.
Schermers, Henry G., International Institutional Law, Vol. I: Structure, Leiden 1972, ibid., 63.
Zweigert, K. & Kropholler, J., Sources of International Uniform Law, vol. II: Transport Law, Leiden 1972, ibid., 63.
Canadian Yearbook of International Law – Annuaire canadien de droit international, Vol. III 1970, Vol. IX 1971, Vancouver 1970 – 1972, ibid., 64.
Grotian Society Papers 1968 – Studies in the History of the Law of Nations, Edited by C.H. Alexandrowicz, Den Haag 1970, ibid., 64.
Deener, David R., (Ed.), De lege pactorum – Essays in honor of Robert Renbert Wilson, Durham N.C. 1970, ibid., 65.

Waart, Paul J.I.M. de, Het onderhandelingselement in de vreedzame regeling van geschillen tussen Staten (academisch proefschrift), Amsterdam 1971, ibid., 65.
Herczegh, Geza, General Principles of Law and International Legal Order, Boedapest 1969, ibid., 66.
Investissements étrangers et arbitrage entre états et personnes privées – La Convention B.I.R.D. du 18 mars 1965, Parijs 1969, ibid., 66.
Zuleeg, Manfred, Das Recht der europäischen Gemeinschaften im innerstaatlichen Bereich, Keulen 1969, ibid., 66.
Eisemann, P.M., Coussirat-Coustere, V. & Hur, P., Petit manuel de la jurisprudence de la Cour internationale de Justice, Parijs, 1972, ibid., 67.
Syatauw, J.J.G., Decisions of the International Court of Justice – A Digest, Leiden 1969, ibid., 67.
Tammes, A.J.P., Het universele rechtsstelsel beschreven aan de hand van een classificatie, Amsterdam 1969, ibid., 67.
Alder, Claudius, Koordination und Integration als Rechtsprinzipien, Brugge 1969, ibid., 68.
Jurisprudentie van het Hof van Justitie, Delen XV 1969, XVI 1970 en XVII 1971, Hof van Justitie van de Europese Gemeenschappen, Luxemburg, ibid., 68.
Buergenthal, Thomas, Law Making in the International Civil Aviation Organization, Syracuse N.Y. 1969, ibid., 69.
Fisher, Roger, International Conflict for Beginners, New York/Evanston/London 1969, ibid., 69.
Constantinesco, Léontin-Jean, Die unmittelbare Anwendbarkeit von Gemeinschaftsnormen und der Rechtsschutz von Einzelpersonen im Recht der EWG, Baden-Baden 1969, ibid., 70.
Schweizerisches Jahrbuch für internationales Recht – Annuaire Suisse de droit international, vol. XXVII, 1971 Zürich 1972, ibid., 70.
Convention européenne des Droits de l'Homme – Receuil des décisions de tribunaux nationaux se reférant à la Convention, Raad van Europa, Straatsburg 1969, ibid., 71.
Lauwaars, R.H., Lawfulness and Legal Force of Community Decisions, Leiden 1973, ibid., 199.
Lauwaars, R.H., Rechtmatigheid en rechtskracht van gemeenschapsbesluiten, Leiden 1970, ibid., 199.
Louis, Jean Victor, Les règlements de la Communauté économique européenne, Brussel 1969, ibid., 199.
Smith, S.A. de, Constitutional and Administrative Law, Harmondsworth, Middlesex 1971, ibid., 199.
American International Law Cases 1783 - 1963, Collected and Edited by Francis Deak, Vols. II, III and IV, Dobbs Ferry N.Y. 1971 en 1972, ibid., 200.
O'Connell, D.P., International Law, London 1970, ibid., 200.
Brownlie, Ian, Principles of Public International Law, Oxford 1973, ibid., 201.
Verzijl, J.H.W., International Law in Historical Perspective, Vols. IV and V, Leiden 1971 en 1972, ibid., 201.
Miscellanea W.J. Ganshof van der Meersch – Studia ab discipulis amicisque in honorem egregii professoris edita, Brussel/Parijs 1972, ibid., 202.

1974

Review of:

Déak, Francis (ed.), American International Law Cases, 1783-1968, vols. V-VIII, 21 NILR 1974, 352.

1975

Reviews of:

Heijnsbergen, mr. P. van, Compendium van het Volkenrecht, 22 NILR 1975, 104.

Mertens, Pierre, Le droit de recours effectif devant les instances nationales en cas de violation d'un droit de l'homme, ibid., 104.
Suy, Prof. Dr. E., Leerboek van het volkenrecht, vols. I-II, ibid., 104.
Annales d'études internationales/Annals of International Studies, ibid., 105.
Bleckmann, Prof. Dr. Dr. Albert, Probleme der Anwendung multilateraler Verträge, ibid., 105.
Académie de droit international de La Haye/The Hague Academy of International Law, Livre Jubilaire/Jubilee Book, ibid., 106.
McNair, Lord, Selected Papers and Bibliography, ibid., 106.
Parry, Clive and J.A. Hopkins (eds.), Commonwealth International Law Cases, vols. 1 & 2, ibid., 107.
Rodière, René, Traité général de droit maritime – Evénements de mer, ibid., 108.
Stuyt, A.M., Survey of International Arbitrations 1794-1970, ibid., 108.
British Year Book of International Law 1971, The, ibid., 109.
Parry, Clive and J.A. Hopkins (eds.), British International Law Cases, vol. 9, ibid., 109.
Verzijl, J.H.W., International Law in Historical Perspective, vols. VI (Juridical Facts as Sources of International Rights and Obligations) & VII (State Succession), ibid., 109.
Institut de droit international, Annuaire, vol. 55, Session du Centenaire, ibid., 111.

1979

"The Editor-in-Chief looks back some twenty-five years", 26 NILR 1979, 1.

1980

"International Law and the Netherlands Legal Order", *International Law in the Netherlands,* Alphen aan den Rijn-Dobbs Ferry N.Y. 1980, vol. III, p. 375.
"General Maritime Law", *Recht door Zee,* Liber amicorum H. Schadee, Zwolle 1980, p. 67.
"Limitation of Non-contractual Liability resulting from Collisions at Sea", Hague-Zagreb Essays, 3 (1980) p. 83.

1981

"Volkenrechtelijke aspecten van strafbare feiten, gepleegd in ambassades of consulaten", *Ad personam,* Feestbundel Prof. Mr. Ch.J. Enschede, Zwolle 1981, p. 47.

1982

Review of:
J.A.L.M. Loeff, Vervoer ter zee, deel I, Zwolle 1981, *Rechtsgeleerd Magazijn Themis* 1982, 55.

Annotated judicial decisions involving questions of international law in which Judge Erades participated.

International

Lake Ontario Claims Tribunal United States and Canada 1967-1968;
Turiff Construction (Sudan) Ltd. v. *Government of the Republic of the Sudan:* Arbitral Tribunal in the Permanent Court of Arbitration 1968-1970;

National

– *as Acting Advocate General to the Supreme Court of the Netherlands*
Conclusion, HR 7 November 1975, RvdW 1975, no. 91; NJ 1976, no. 274; 7 NYIL (1976), 349.
Conclusion, HR 25 November 1977, RvdW 1977, no. 112; NJ 1978, no. 186; 9 NYIL (1978), 317.

– *as Judge at the Arrondissements-Rechtbank, Rotterdam*
7 October 1949, NJ 1950, no. 509; 16 AD (1949), no. 110.
29 December 1950, NJ 1951, no. 79; 17 ILR (1950), no. 112.
18 January 1952, NJ 1952, no. 327; 19 LLR (1952), no. 13.
16 May 1952, NJ 1953, no. 427; 1 NILR (1953/4), 87; 19 ILR (1952), no. 29.
17 December 1952, 19 ILR (1952), nos. 35 and 108.
17 April 1953, 1 NILR (1953/4), 89; 20 ILR (1953), 164.
21 May 1953, NJ 1954, no. 382; 2 NILR (1955), 94, 21 ILR (1954), 3.
29 May 1953, NJ 1955, no. 80; 3 NILR (1955), 83; 20 ILR (1953), 665.
14 January 1954, NJ 1954, no. 768; 1 NILR (1953/4), 331; 21 ILR (1954), 276;
9 April 1954, NJ 1955, no. 44; 1 NILR (1953/4), 430, 21 ILR (1954), 300.
24 June 1955, NJ 1955, no. 713; 2 NILR (1955), 425; 22 ILR (1955), 634.
6 April 1956, 3 NILR (1956), 408; 24 ILR (1957), 938.
13 April 1956, NJ 1956, no. 545; 4 NILR (1957), 211; 24 ILR (1957), 172.
2 January 1957, S & S 1957, no. 35; 5 NILR (1957), 393; 24 ILR (1957), 97.
27 September 1957, NJ 1968, no. 223; 6 NILR (1958), 393; 24 ILR (1957), 99.
18 June 1963, NJ 1964, no. 328; 10 NILR (1963), 309.
8 December 1964, NJ 1965, no. 435; 12 NILR (1965), 91; 4 ILM (1965), 257.
30 May 1967, 1 NYIL (1970), 225.
3 December 1968, SEW 1969, 379; CDE 1970, 191.
16 March 1971, 3 NYIL (1972), 301.
27 April 1971, S & S 1971, no. 73; 3 NYIL (1972), 289.
19 December 1972, S & S 1973, no. 34; 5 NYIL (1974), 326.
13 November 1973, S & S 1974, no. 14; 6 NYIL (1975), 341.
3 December 1974, AK no. 935; 6 NYIL (1975), 365.
12 May 1975, 22 NILR (1975), 203; 7 NYIL (1976), 344.
19 January 1976, S & S 1976, no. 42; 8 NYIL (1977), 284.
28 June 1976, AK no. 1161; 9 NYIL (1978), 323.
17 January 1977, S & S 1977, no. 60; 9 NYIL (1978), 323.
6 June 1977, S & S 1977, no. 84; 10 NYIL (1979), 500.
20 November 1978, 10 NYIL (1979), 504.
8 January 1979, NJ 1979, no. 113; 11 NYIL (1980), 326.

GPSR Compliance

The European Union's (EU) General Product Safety Regulation (GPSR) is a set of rules that requires consumer products to be safe and our obligations to ensure this.

If you have any concerns about our products, you can contact us on ProductSafety@springernature.com

In case Publisher is established outside the EU, the EU authorized representative is:

Springer Nature Customer Service Center GmbH
Europaplatz 3
69115 Heidelberg, Germany

Batch number: 10830937

Printed by Printforce, the Netherlands